W9-AQE-240

The Justice Cascade

The Justice Cascade

HOW HUMAN RIGHTS PROSECUTIONS
ARE CHANGING WORLD POLITICS

Kathryn Sikkink

W. W. Norton & Company
New York • London

For information about permission to reproduce selections from this book,
write to Permissions, W. W. Norton & Company, Inc.,
500 Fifth Avenue, New York, NY 10110

For information about special discounts for bulk purchases, please contact
W. W. Norton Special Sales at specialsales@wwnorton.com or 800-233-4830

Manufacturing by RR Donnelley, Harrisonburg
Book design by Chris Welch Design
Production manager: Julia Druskin

Library of Congress Cataloging-in-Publication Data

Sikkink, Kathryn, 1955–
The justice cascade : how human rights prosecutions are
changing world politics / Kathryn Sikkink.—1st ed.
p. cm.
Includes bibliographical references and index.
ISBN 978-0-393-07993-7 (hardcover)
1. Crimes against humanity. 2. Criminal liability (International law) 3. Prosecution—
International cooperation. 4. Criminal justice, Administration of—International cooperation.
5. International criminal courts. 6. World politics—1989– I. Title.
KZ7145.S55 2011
345'.0235—dc23

2011018827

W. W. Norton & Company, Inc.
500 Fifth Avenue, New York, N.Y. 10110
www.wwnorton.com

W. W. Norton & Company Ltd.
Castle House, 75/76 Wells Street, London W1T 3QT

1 2 3 4 5 6 7 8 9 0

In memory of Ellen Lutz (1955–2010), friend, coauthor, human rights advocate, from whom I learned so much about law, justice, and friendship.

CONTENTS

Contents

Part IV
CONCLUSIONS

The Justice Cascade

1

Introduction

I don't remember when I first heard it would be possible to hold state officials criminally accountable for human rights violations. No one mentioned it in 1976 when I lived in Montevideo, Uruguay, as a university exchange student. In 1973, the elected president of Uruguay, Juan María Bordaberry, and the Uruguayan military had overthrown the democratic government, closed down the Congress and the Supreme Court, and started imprisoning and torturing their opponents. Bordaberry continued to serve as president, and his participation gave a veneer of legitimacy to the new authoritarian regime. Once known as the Switzerland of Latin America for its small size, long democratic tradition, and mature social welfare policies, Uruguay quickly gained notoriety as "the torture chamber of Latin America."

I talked with people in Uruguay who had been imprisoned and tortured. It was hard for them to foresee an end to the dictatorship, and no one imagined that someday it would be possible to judge those responsible for human rights violations and send them to prison. At no time was such foresight more difficult than in 1976, when the country saw its darkest moments. In May of that year, Uruguayans were terrified to learn of the murders of two of the most revered Uruguayan opposition politicians living in exile. If even they could be murdered, no one was safe.

These assassinations took place in Argentina, where several leading opponents to Bordaberry's coup had sought refuge following the closure of the Uruguayan Congress. These opponents included Senator Wilson Ferreira Aldunate, the former presidential candidate for the main opposition

Blanco Party; Congressman Héctor Gutiérrez Ruiz, the Speaker of the House; and Senator Zelmar Michelini, one of the most eloquent spokesmen of the leftist opposition coalition, the Broad Front (*Frente Amplio*). The exiles' situation took a grim turn with the Argentine military coup in March 1976. Their relative safety evaporated, and they started to receive death threats. Michelini planned a trip to the United States, where he intended to meet with members of the U.S. Congress and staff from Amnesty International to brief them on what was happening in Uruguay. The plane ticket was reserved, and the U.S. government had already granted him a visa. But the Uruguayan foreign minister, Juan Carlos Blanco, gave explicit instructions to deny the renewal of Michelini's passport, so he was unable to travel. Without current documentation, his situation in Argentina was even more precarious. He wrote to a friend in the United States: "Since I don't have legal status in Argentina, I am now practically a man without a country, a prisoner in this land. . . . You can't imagine my anger, my grief, my impotence. . . ."[1]

On May 18, 1976, groups of armed men kidnapped Gutiérrez Ruiz and Michelini from their apartments in Buenos Aires. Three days later, both men were found murdered, with signs of torture on their bodies. When the kidnappers bungled a similar attempt to capture Wilson Ferreira, he fled to London. He left an open letter to the new military president of Argentina, General Jorge Videla, describing at length the kidnapping and murders of Gutiérrez Ruiz and Michelini. Ferreira understood that the kidnappings had been an action coordinated between the Uruguayan and Argentine military governments. The letter ended: "When the hour arrives of your own exile, which will arrive, have no doubt, General Videla, if you seek refuge in Uruguay, a Uruguay whose destiny will be once again in the hands of its own people, we will receive you without cordiality and affection, but we will grant you the protection that you did not give to those whose deaths we are today grieving."[2]

Wilson Ferreira, in his hour of greatest despair, could envision a distant future of democracy in his country and in Argentina when General Videla would be forced into exile and Uruguay would be again in the hands of its people. But, at that time, he could *not* imagine accountability for the human rights violations he had just witnessed. He did not say that he awaited a time when Videla would be extradited or tried for his crimes. Ferreira assumed that in the future, as in the past, leaders responsible for human rights violations would go into exile abroad, where they would be given protection, if not affection. This had long been the political tradition in Latin America, where military coups were a commonplace instrument of politics. Even the very viciousness of the crimes he had just witnessed did not change Ferreira's perception that leaders would not, or could not, be judged for their crimes. But Ferreira was not alone in being unable to imagine criminal prosecutions of state officials. No one I spoke with in Uruguay mentioned the possibility of prosecuting Bordaberry or the Uruguayan military. In a series of interviews and conversations since that time, I've asked friends and colleagues in Uruguay when they first thought it was viable to hold human rights prosecutions. They point to different dates, but never before 1983, when Argentine human rights movements started publicly demanding trials for past violations in Argentina.

President Bordaberry also believed he could not be judged for his actions. In a speech in December 1974, he said of the military and the June 1973 coup: "the armed forces must enjoy supreme tranquility, knowing that their stance of having accompanied and supported the government in the historic events of June 1973 cannot be judged by the citizenry. . . . It would be like assuming you could judge a man who broke the formal law to defend his mother, in this case, his motherland. And this stance cannot be the object of a judgment."[3]

Thirty-two years after this speech, Bordaberry found that he could in fact be the object of judgment. In 2006, a Uruguayan judge indicted Bordaberry and his minster of foreign affairs, Juan Carlos Blanco, ordering them into preventive prison to await trial for the murders of Gutiérrez Ruiz and Michelini. In 2010, the eighty-one-year-old Bordaberry was convicted and sentenced to thirty years in prison. Other top officials of the dictatorial government, including Blanco, and Gregorio Alvarez, the military president after Bordaberry, shared his fate, having since been convicted and sentenced to prison terms of twenty to twenty-five years.

The story of Jorge Bordaberry is just one of many stories of state officials for whom the unimaginable had occurred: criminal accountability for violations of human rights. A watershed moment for such accountability came in October 1998, when General Augusto Pinochet of Chile was arrested in London by British police executing a Spanish extradition request. The Spanish court wanted Pinochet to stand trial in Spain for crimes committed in Chile during his military dictatorship. No one predicted this arrest, certainly not in London, where Pinochet had just weeks before taken tea with his old friend Margaret Thatcher. The Law Lords (the British Supreme Court) decided that Pinochet could be extradited to Spain.[4]

As soon as it became conceivable to hold perpetrators criminally account-able, some observers began to make dire predictions about the effects of such trials. After Pinochet was brought into custody, many argued that it would lead to the demise of democracy in Chile because his supporters would carry out another coup. Ultimately, the British government allowed Pinochet to return to Chile because of his poor health. When he died there in 2006, facing domestic prosecutions both for human rights violations and for corruption, democracy was alive and well in Chile.

Some analysts offered similarly dire predictions in 1999, when Presi-dent Slobodan Milošević of Yugoslavia became the first *sitting* head of state to be indicted for war crimes. Critics argued that actions taken by the International Criminal Tribunal for the Former Yugoslavia (ICTY) in The Hague would lead Milošević to entrench himself in power and prolong the agony in the Balkans. But Serbians began to realize that Milošević was a liability, and they voted him out of office less than a year and a half after his indictment. Facing intense pressure from the United States and the European Union, the new Federal Republic of Yugoslavia government eventually extradited Milošević to The Hague to stand trial, where he died before he could be convicted for his crimes. In March 2003, a second sitting president was charged for war crimes, when the Special Court for Sierra Leone indicted Charles Taylor, the warlord president of Liberia. Taylor went into exile in Nigeria in August 2003 after his forces were defeated by a rebel group. In 2006, he was turned over to the Special Court, where he is currently on trial for human rights violations and war crimes. In 2009, the International Criminal Court (ICC) indicted a third sitting president, Omar al-Bashir, for war crimes and crimes against humanity in the Darfur region of Sudan.

I group the prosecutions that I have just mentioned, along with others that are currently underway across the globe, into three basic types. Some are *international*, like the trial of Milošević in The Hague. International tri-als happen when states, typically acting on behalf of the United Nations, set up tribunals such as the ICTY and the ICC. In this category, I also include so-called "hybrid" criminal tribunals, such as the Special Court for Sierra

Leone that is prosecuting Charles Taylor, which combine international and national legal processes. Other prosecutions are *foreign*, meaning that a state decides to use its domestic courts to try an official from another state, sometimes using a procedure known as "universal jurisdiction." An example is the case of Pinochet, which included legal action in courts in both the United Kingdom and Spain. The third and most common type is a *domestic* prosecution, like that of Bordaberry in Uruguay, when courts within the country where the human rights violations occurred assume the task of trying human rights criminals.

Together, these three kinds of prosecutions comprise an interrelated, dramatic new trend in world politics toward holding individual state officials, including heads of state, criminally accountable for human rights violations.[5] In this book, I call this trend the "justice cascade." Originally, this term served as the title of an article that I wrote with my friend and colleague Ellen Lutz, an attorney with extensive experience as a human rights activist, scholar, and mediator.[6] By justice cascade, I *do not mean* that perfect justice has been done or will be done, or that most perpetrators of human rights violations will be held criminally accountable. Rather, justice cascade means that there has been a shift in the *legitimacy of the norm* of individual criminal accountability for human rights violations and an increase in criminal prosecutions on behalf of that norm. The term captures how the idea started as a small stream, but later caught on suddenly, sweeping along many actors in its wake.[7]

In retrospect, the justice cascade may seem an inevitable reaction to the unprecedented violence of the twentieth century. But this wave of prosecutions was by no means preordained. The seeds of the justice cascade have been present for decades—the legal underpinnings were outlined in the Nuremberg Tribunals from 1945 to 1949. The Nuremberg and Tokyo trials after World War II were in many ways both the beginning of the trend and the exception that proved the rule: only in cases of complete defeat in war was it possible to hold state perpetrators criminally accountable for human rights violations. The Nuremberg precedents then lay dormant for decades. It was not until the mid-1970s, around the time when Michelini and Gutiérrez Ruiz were murdered in Buenos Aires, that the newly democratic government in Greece resurrected the idea of individual criminal accountability for past human rights violations when it put its past state officials on trial for torture and murder. The puzzle is why

Greece and other states chose to hold state officials accountable and how the practice spread.

In this book, I explain why this new trend has emerged and evaluate its impact. I have organized this analysis into three parts around three big questions. Part I uses a historical approach to answer the question of *emergence*: what are the origins or sources of new ideas and practices concerning individual criminal accountability for human rights? In Chapters 2 and 3, these origins are traced by looking at the first three cases of domestic trials in Greece, Portugal, and Argentina. In Part II, I try to answer how and why these ideas *spread or diffused* across regions and, ultimately, across the globe. Chapter 4 examines the diffusion of prosecutions, first in domestic courts, and later in foreign courts and international tribunals. Part III tackles questions about effects: what is the *impact* of these trials? Can human rights prosecutions actually help prevent future human rights violations? Chapters 5 and 6 present work I have done demonstrating that these trials are not dangerous, as some worry, and that they can actually improve protection for human rights. But a skeptic will ask: "If this is really a global trend, what difference does it make for powerful countries like the United States or China?" To begin to answer this question, Chapter 7 focuses on U.S. practices during the so-called "war on terror."

Throughout these chapters, several kinds of evidence are employed. I draw on years of travel and interview-based field research conducted mainly in Argentina and Uruguay, but also in Guatemala, Chile, Greece, Portugal, Italy, Belgium, Spain, the Netherlands, and Brazil. To answer the first question about why human rights prosecutions first emerged, I compare Greece and Portugal, the countries that first used prosecutions, to Spain, a country in the same region that chose not to pursue human rights prosecutions. Similarly, Argentina, an early adopter of prosecutions, can be compared to Brazil and Uruguay, countries in the same region with political transitions around the same time that adopted different approaches to justice. To answer the second question about why practices and ideas about accountability spread from one country to another, I compare why there was much greater diffusion of the Argentine prosecutions than of prosecutions in Portugal and Greece. To answer the third question, about the effects of prosecutions, in addition to field research I use statistical analyses. These analyses are based on a database of human rights prosecutions compiled with the help of colleagues. The point of the statistical research is to systematically test some arguments that have emerged from the work of journalists and scholars who have also observed the spread of trials. My goal is to address the questions and puzzles above and to communicate to both academic and non-academic audiences.

This book is a story not only about changes in the world but also about my own personal and scholarly journey. In some ways, I came upon the unfolding processes of justice by accident. But this discovery has shaped my outlook on the world and its possibilities, leaving me at times both frustrated and inspired. I hope this work will offer insights about crafting accountability for past human rights violations, including for Americans, as we grapple with whether and how to hold individuals accountable for torture and cruel and degrading treatment during the administration of George W. Bush.

Part I: Creating Individual Accountability

To answer the first question about the origins of ideas and practices of individual criminal accountability, I had to go back and explore a period through which I had lived personally. After returning to the United States from Uruguay in 1977, I finished my undergraduate degree, then applied for and was awarded an international human rights internship by the Ford Foundation. The program placed me as a long-term paid intern with the Washington Office on Latin America (WOLA), a small human rights organization based in Washington, D.C. I arrived at WOLA in December 1979, and was assigned to work on Argentina and Uruguay. Over the next two years, part of my job was to receive human rights leaders and members of the opposition who arrived from Argentina or Uruguay, or from exile, and help them make contact with policy makers in Washington to explain their histories and their concerns. I set up interviews with congressional staff (sometimes with members of Congress, when we were very fortunate), meetings in the State Department, interviews with the press, and receptions for civil society leaders. I accompanied our visitors to their meetings, translated for them, and sometimes put them up in my small apartment. I also worked with Argentines and Uruguayans living in Washington, D.C., who had set up small human rights or solidarity committees.

The unofficial head of the Argentine committee, a political exile named Juan Méndez, helped teach me about Argentina and guide my work in that early difficult time in Washington. As a member of the Peronist Youth, the left wing of the Peronist Party in Argentina in the early 1970s, Méndez had been a labor lawyer, defending workers, including labor activists who had been imprisoned for political activity. Because of his work the police arrested Méndez in August 26, 1975, nine months before the military coup in 1976. In prison, he was tortured and repeatedly interrogated, in his words, "about my clients, about my contacts, about the relatives of my clients, about the ways in which lawyers like me were able to file petitions for habeas corpus after someone had been arrested by the security forces."[8]

Méndez believes that if he had been arrested after the coup, he probably would not be alive today. Of the group of lawyers working with him, seven were arrested after the coup, and they were among the thousands of "disappeared" people whom the military kidnapped and killed. In 1976, Amnesty International adopted Juan Méndez as a prisoner of conscience. The members of the first Amnesty International mission to Argentina in 1976 asked specifically about Méndez's case when they met with Argentina's minister of interior. Less than three months later, Méndez was released from prison into exile in the United States. Clearly, external pressure was important for his release. Méndez also speculated that the government thought that "I wasn't that important. It was easy enough to get Amnesty International out of their hair."

If the Argentine government had realized what a thorn in their side Juan Méndez in exile would be, they might have reconsidered their decision. He recalls thinking upon his arrival in the United States, "I had to work on behalf of all these people who were staying behind. It was almost an obsession." The prisoners called the cell block where Juan spent the last weeks of his imprisonment "death row." The military arbitrarily took some inmates, including four of Méndez's close friends, out of the prison and killed them. Before leaving, he memorized the names of all the people in his cell block because he had the sense that "all would be killed unless I did something."[9] When he arrived in the United States in 1977, Méndez gained asylum, began the arduous task of studying U.S. law, and passed the bar exam. He helped organize the Argentine exile community in Washington, D.C., into a coherent human rights group. Méndez and the Argentine group became my mentors, prodders, and accomplices in our work to keep the case of human rights violations in Argentina in the minds of U.S. policy makers.

During my first year at WOLA, President Jimmy Carter was still in office. The Carter administration State Department had made Argentina and Uruguay two of its three priority countries for applying its new human rights policy, so official Washington was relatively receptive to talking to human rights leaders from these countries. Some of the top people from Argentina and Uruguay visited us in Washington. In my first week on the job, I set up a reception for Wilson Ferreira, who arrived from exile in London. The head of the Mothers of the Plaza de Mayo, an imposing woman named Hebe de Bonafini, arrived with other Mothers to lobby Congress to pressure the Argentine government to stop disappearances. Bonafini and the Mothers were fearless advocates for their cause, and I was a little intimidated by her, mostly because I felt I could never meet her expectations. As far as Hebe was concerned, any time I wasn't devoting to helping the Mothers was not well spent. At the same time, Juan Raul Ferreira, an ardent D.C.-based advocate for Uruguay and the son of Wilson Ferreira, thought I should instead be devoting all my time to advancing human rights in Uruguay. It was also around this time that I met Emilio Mignone, who set up the most important legal human rights organization in Argentina, the Center for Legal and Social Studies (*Centro de Estudios Legales y Sociales*, or CELS).

During my internship year in Washington in 1980, Ronald Reagan defeated Jimmy Carter in the presidential elections. Reagan had criticized the Carter human rights policy and promised to renew support for anti-Communist allies around the world, including the authoritarian regimes in Latin America. To signal this new policy after his inauguration in 1981, Reagan invited the military "president-designate" of Argentina, General Roberto Viola, to be the first Latin American leader to make an official visit to Washington. In a speech given while in the United States, Viola underscored his ideas about justice. He argued: "A victorious army is not investigated. If the Reich's troops had won the last World War, the Tribunal would have been held not in Nuremberg but in Virginia." In some ways, Viola was only expressing a worldview held by many contemporary realists in international relations—that international law is the tool of the powerful, who use it against their enemies. But the comments did not play well in Washington, since they equated U.S. behavior during the war with Nazi war crimes. Even the censored press of Buenos Aires criticized Viola's remarks. "Viola is supposed to be a moderate, and if moderates think the only thing the Nazis did wrong is lose, the normal mind will find it hard to imagine what the view of the hardliners must be," editorialized the *Buenos Aires Herald*.[10] Yet Viola's comments suggest that he was at least subliminally worried about accountability. Despite some embarrassment, the Reagan administration pressed ahead on its proposal to improve relations with authoritarian allies like Viola.

Just four years later, in 1985, General Viola was prosecuted in Buenos Aires in what was an unprecedented trial of top military leaders for human rights violations. True to Viola's predictions, by the time of the prosecutions, the Argentine military had lost a war in the Malvinas/Falkands Islands. Yet the trials were not for what they did during the war they lost, but for crimes committed during the struggle they claimed to have won against a leftist insurgency, and for human rights violations during the military government. By the time of the trials, I was living in Argentina, conducting the research for my doctoral dissertation (on the completely different topic of economic policy making). The trial of the Juntas in Argentina transfixed the Argentine public—and me, of course—during the entire year of 1985. They were open to the public, and I was able to visit one day and watch the proceedings from the visitors' gallery. Just weeks before I left Argentina, the tribunal handed down its sentence, convicting Generals Videla and Viola to life in prison—the first time that a court in Latin America had ever convicted heads of state for human rights violations.

Over the next twenty-five years, Viola and Videla were joined by other authoritarian leaders in the region. Ex-President Alberto Fujimori of Peru was sentenced in 2009 to twenty-five years in prison for human rights violations; the former authoritarian presidents of Uruguay, Alvarez and Bordaberry, were convicted; and ex-President General Ríos Montt of Guatemala is the subject of ongoing trials in Spain and Guatemala. So, what happened between Viola's triumphant speech in Washington and these trials that started to change the way we think about accountability? Contrary to Viola's predictions, all these governments had defeated leftist insurgencies in their countries, and yet they were being held accountable for massive human rights violations during their authoritarian regimes.

When I first started the research for this book, I wracked my brains for a memory of the first time one of the activists from Argentina or Uruguay mentioned the possibility of prosecuting state officials for human rights violations, and I could not pinpoint the moment. Surely Emilio Mignone or Juan Méndez, each immersed in the human rights legal culture of the time, was already talking about prosecutions in 1981? Emilio Mignone died in 1998, and I can no longer rely on his impeccable memory. Juan Méndez can't pinpoint the moment, either. This book then is partly about the frailties of human memory. For almost two years I was part of a network that later became a main advocate for individual criminal prosecution, and yet I cannot identify the instant when the idea first appeared and started to flourish. So, my research began as a kind of detective work to locate the sources of the ideas and practices that I would later call the "justice cascade."

The justice cascade began as a new norm. Social scientists think of a norm as a standard of "appropriate behavior." A norm is not just any old rule about what to do; it is a special type of rule that has a quality of "oughtness." It is seen as the appropriate thing to do. So, for example, not smoking in public places is now an accepted norm in most of the United States. It is not just a rule like "Don't smoke so you won't get cancer"—but it takes the form of a widely held belief that "Good people don't smoke in public places." Norms are "intersubjective," that is, they are held by groups of people. But norms start as ideas held by a handful of individuals. These individuals try to turn their favored ideas into norms, which is why we call them "norm entrepreneurs." Most norm entrepreneurs fail, but some succeed. This book follows the contributions of norm entrepreneurs like Juan Méndez, and many others, who started with some ideas about the need for individual criminal accountability and, by campaigning and agitating, helped make this norm global in scope.

When these norm entrepreneurs succeed, norms spread rapidly, leading to a norms cascade. Social life is full of cascades, involving issues from the most trivial to the most serious. Smoking in public in the United States, for example, was subject to a norm cascade. In a relatively short time, smoking went from being a widely accepted practice in every American bar and workplace to being banned in most public spaces. Initially, people had to work hard to persuade every legislator or City Council member that a ban would drastically reduce health risks to their constituents. But at a certain point, prohibiting smoking in public places reached a "tipping point," and cities everywhere began to outlaw smoking. Eventually, strong norms can become internalized: they become taken for granted. So, for instance, an international norm like that prohibiting slavery is internalized; no one debates it anymore, it is simply accepted. But the norm of individual criminal accountability of state officials for human rights violations is not anywhere near becoming internalized or taken for granted. It is the topic of heated debate, which makes it more interesting to study.

Cascade phenomena have been studied by scientists and popularized in books such as *The Tipping Point* by Malcolm Gladwell.[11] The tipping point is the moment in the cascade where a critical mass of actors has adopted a norm or practice, creating a strong momentum for change. Cascades with tipping points occur in disparate phenomena from crime fighting to fashion; Gladwell's book includes a long discussion of the rise in popularity and sales of Hush Puppies in the mid-1990s. Here, I'm only interested in a subset of cascade phenomena involving norms, which have that quality of "oughtness" that mere fashion fads do not.

The norm of individual criminal accountability is powerful because it relates to broader ideas about justice. "Justice" means many things to many people. It can mean fairness, political and economic equality of both opportunity and outcome, and accountability. An immense body of philosophical and theoretical writings is devoted to this theme.[12] Here, I refer to only one of many meanings of justice: legal accountability for crimes. This is a common way to talk about justice in domestic judicial systems. What is new is to demand justice for previously immune state officials and to envisage the possibility of international prosecutions in addition to domestic prosecutions.

Today, as in the past, if an ordinary individual kills someone, there is an expectation that an official apparatus will try him (or her) for murder, and possibly convict and imprison him. But in the past, if a head of state like General Videla gave orders for thousands of people to be killed, the expectation was that nothing would happen either domestically or internationally. When their regimes ended, ex-dictators like Idi Amin of Uganda, Jean-Claude ("Baby Doc") Duvalier of Haiti, or Alfredo Stroessner of Paraguay traditionally lived a comfortable exile, free from fear that they would face criminal trials for launching campaigns of premeditated kidnapping and murder. When I speak of the "justice cascade," I certainly don't mean that all state officials who have committed crimes will be sent to prison. I simply mean that the norm that state officials should be held accountable for human rights violations has gained new strength and legitimacy.

Three key ideas underpin the justice norm: the first is the idea that the most basic violations of human rights—summary execution, torture, and disappearance—cannot be legitimate acts of state and thus must be seen as crimes committed by individuals. A second, related idea is that the individuals who commit these crimes can be, and should be, prosecuted. These seem like simple, even obvious ideas. But they run counter to centuries of beliefs about the state. It took a major movement to move such new ideas forward, embed them in law, and put them into practice. The third idea is that the accused are also bearers of rights, and deserve to have those rights protected in a fair trial.[13]

It is this third set of practices about protecting the rights of the accused that most clearly differentiates a human rights trial from political trials or kangaroo trials. As Judith Shklar has pointed out: "Political trials scorn the principle of legality."[14] Legality means to have a fair trial with due process, including protections for the rights of the accused. Trials without due process are not human rights trials. For example, after the fall of the Communist regime led by Nicolae Ceaușescu in Romania, the leader and his wife and political partner Elena were put on trial for their crimes. The trial was about human rights violations, and the individuals were being held criminally accountable, but we would not consider it a human rights prosecution because the accused were not given even a minimally fair trial. On the morning of December 25, 1989, the Ceaușescus appeared before an ad hoc military tribunal. Before the prosecution began, the panel of judges knew that it was a foregone conclusion that the Ceaușescus would be executed that afternoon. After a two-hour trial in which little hard evidence was presented and the defendants were not allowed a strong defense—as even their defense lawyer accused them of crimes—they were given a death sentence and executed "commando-style" in the same room where the "trial" occurred.[15] This is not a human rights prosecution but a political trial of the kind that has long been common during and after violent regime changes.

The emergence of this new justice norm follows decades of efforts to ensure greater accountability for past human rights violations. By "accountability" I mean practices where some actors hold other actors to a set of standards and impose sanctions if these standards are not met.[16] States have used three different "models" of accountability for past human rights violations: (1) the immunity, or "impunity" model; (2) the state accountability model; and (3) the individual criminal accountability model. By far the most common has been the impunity model, where no one is held accountable for human rights violations. Under a state accountability model, the state is held accountable, and it provides remedies and pays damages. Under a criminal model, individuals are prosecuted, and if convicted, they go to prison.[17]

Prior to World War II, the "reigning orthodoxy" was the impunity model, dictating that neither states nor state officials should be held accountable for past human rights violations.[18] The impunity model relied on the doctrine wherein the state itself and officials of the state should remain indefinitely immune from prosecution in domestic courts and particularly in foreign courts. Intellectual histories of the doctrine of sovereign immunity trace it to various sources. Some say it stems from the ancient English principle that the monarch can do no wrong; others from the inherent power of the state to prevent prosecution. Others claim that governments need to be protected from lawsuits so that they can concentrate on governing and not be distracted from the tasks of office. Whatever the explanation, before World War II it was taken for granted that state officials were safe from prosecution for human rights violations, both in their own domestic courts and in foreign courts or international tribunals.[19]

The immunity model began to erode shortly after the war. The Holocaust was the shock that revealed the deep moral and political flaws of the reigning orthodoxy. States and non-state actors alike realized that there was a complete lack of international standards and accountability for massive human rights violations. The Allies initiated the Nuremberg and Tokyo tribunals after World War II to provide individual criminal accountability for war crimes and aggressive warfare. They also took action through the newly formed United Nations, first by drafting a set of standards in the Universal Declaration of Human Rights in 1948, and later by creating a series of more detailed human rights treaties. In these treaties, states proposed a new model of accountability in which the state as a whole was held accountable for human rights violations and was expected to take action to remedy the situation. But the state accountability model went hand-in-hand with the idea that state officials themselves were still immune from prosecution for human rights violations. For example, when a state violated rights under the Covenant on Civil and Political Rights, in some cases individuals could bring petitions before the UN Human Rights

Committee. But these petitions were against the state itself, not a particular state official. States adopted this accountability model because it was the standard applied in other issue areas covered by international law. Yet there was an uneasy fit between the state accountability model and human rights that would be exposed in the coming years.

The state accountability model began to be the "new orthodoxy" for accountability. It continues to be the model used by virtually the entire human rights apparatus in the United Nations, including almost all of the treaty bodies. Most human rights treaties had weak enforcement mechanisms: there were lots of rules, but they didn't have teeth. There were few consequences for states and no consequences for individuals who violated human rights. Many scholars and policy makers have long argued that human rights treaties would have little impact because of this lack of enforcement.

Under the state accountability model, if the state refused to take action to change its policies or to provide remedies to victims, there were few forms of recourse available. Using the so-called "name and shame strategy," Amnesty International, the United Nations, or a foreign government would issue a report documenting human rights violations, and call on the country to improve its record. Sometimes states would also cut military or economic aid or bring other pressures to bear on recalcitrant human rights violators. In some cases, such pressures succeeded in bringing about important modifications in human rights practices.[20] But the actual individuals who carried out violations were beyond reach.

During the 1980s and 1990s, after decades of drafting and ratifying human rights treaties, it began to appear that human rights violations were getting worse, not better. In this context, some activists argued that as long as individuals were not held personally responsible, there would be no strong incentives for changing behavior. They suggested that holding individual state officials criminally accountable could help to supplement state accountability and provide a new way to enforce human rights law. Human rights prosecutions give teeth to the law because they can put formerly powerful people behind bars. If human rights law didn't work because it lacked strength, this new form of enforcement should help improve compliance.

The other accountability models didn't disappear. Instead, all three models—immunity, state accountability, *and* individual criminal accountability—continued to exist side by side. Immunity is still common and victims still have relatively few avenues for recourse, but the rise of institutions for individual criminal accountability adds new options that weren't available before. If a state refuses to respond to pressures for state accountability, victims can bring cases against state officials in their domestic courts. If the domestic courts refuse to respond, victims can bring cases against individuals forward in foreign courts.

This new individual criminal accountability model does not apply to the whole range of civil and political rights but, rather, to a small subset of rights sometimes referred to as *physical integrity rights,* the "rights of the person," or, when violated, "core crimes." These include prohibitions on torture, summary execution, and genocide, as well as on war crimes and crimes against humanity.[21] This model involves an important convergence of international law (human rights law, humanitarian law or the laws of war, and international criminal law) and domestic criminal law.[22] A blurring of the distinction between international law and domestic law is not unique to this area but characterizes many areas of global governance.[23]

The justice norm is "nested" in some larger global movements. First, it is part of the "human rights revolution," involving the acceptance of global standards and the expansion of human and civil rights litigation in courts around the world.[24] And like the broader rights revolution, the justice cascade is a result of "deliberate, strategic organizing by rights advocates."[25] Second, it is part of a bigger movement for accountability for past human rights violations. Trials are not the only or even the most important way that countries grapple with their past human rights violations. Today, states are also using truth commissions, like the Truth and Reconciliation Commission (TRC) that the South Africans set up to deal with crimes during the apartheid regime. After emerging from years of Soviet rule, many Eastern European countries passed "lustration" laws to make sure that former officials who had collaborated with the secret police could not hold political office in the new democratic regimes. Around the world, states and non-state actors set up "memory sites," as well as archives and oral history projects.[26] These include memory museums, such as the Tuol Sleng Genocide Museum in Cambodia, on the site of the notorious prison where the Khmer Rouge government imprisoned, tortured, and killed an estimated 17,000 people. Finally, many states have provided reparations for victims of past human rights violations, to compensate them or their families for imprisonment or death. It is now common to refer to these various efforts to address past human rights crimes as "transitional justice," because they are mainly adopted after countries have made a transition from authoritarian rule to more democratic governments.[27] The pervasiveness of such measures led one scholar to write in 2004 that "one of the most dramatic transformations of global politics in recent years is the emergence of a new field known as 'transitional justice.'"[28]

Of all of these transitional justice mechanisms, it is perhaps most difficult to explain why states adopted human rights prosecutions, because they challenged two interrelated doctrines at the core of world politics: sovereignty and sovereign immunity. One key element of sovereignty is the idea that it is nobody's business how a state leader treats his own citizens, while the doctrine of sovereign immunity protects a sovereign state or state official from being prosecuted. Why would states and their leaders undermine the very doctrines designed to protect them from prosecution? Why wouldn't they use their power to prevent this trend? Activists didn't just pull the individual criminal model out of the air. They drew on their domestic judicial systems. Scholars of international politics did not believe that the practices and rules used in domestic criminal law could be used to confront the power of states and their leaders.[29] How could law challenge the long-held practice that powerful leaders could treat their citizens as they wished and still anticipate a secure retirement at home or abroad? Powerful leaders also believed that they could not be held criminally accountable. General Pinochet thought he could travel to the United Kingdom without worrying about being arrested. Even after he had been indicted by the International Tribunal for the Former Yugoslavia, Slobodan Milošević initiated a campaign of terror against the people of Kosovo, convinced the Tribunal could not touch him. And George W. Bush, Dick Cheney, and Donald Rumsfeld were not dissuaded by the possibility of accountability when they ordered the use of kidnapping, indefinite detention without trial, and torture against terrorism suspects after 9/11. Pinochet and Milošević discovered that human rights law was not as weak as they had believed, and both died facing prosecution with a high likelihood of conviction. As for the engineers of the U.S. torture policy, the response is not as obvious, as we shall see in Chapter 7.

The emergence of the individual criminal accountability model for basic human rights violations means that the huge disjuncture between the treatment of crime in the domestic and the international realms has started to narrow. Because we are in the midst of change, it is sometimes difficult to stand back and see the process unfolding. Most previous discussions of these issues have only looked at pieces of the overall trend, for example, examining only international trials, specific international tribunals, a chosen few foreign trials, or domestic trials in certain countries.[30] I argue that we need to zoom out and look at all of the pieces together in order to see the global trend unfolding. It is a *global* trend because, though it is not equally distributed across regions, it has reached all areas of the world.

I believe that what is emerging is a decentralized but interactive system of accountability for violations of core political rights with fragmented enforcement, which is primarily undertaken by domestic courts. Let me unpack that claim. A system of accountability is starting to emerge because many domestic and international courts are now drawing on a body of domestic and international law that permits individual criminal accountability for core crimes. It is decentralized because there is no single international court or agency deciding who should be prosecuted, yet it is interactive because decisions made at one level have effects at other levels. Even the International Criminal Court (ICC) is only doing a small part of the work of enforcement. Decisions about who to prosecute are made in hundreds of different courts around the world, most of them domestic courts. As such, enforcement is often fragmented and haphazard; whether a state official is prosecuted for human rights violations depends mainly on whether determined and empowered domestic litigants are pressing for accountability.

To understand how this new model of accountability now functions at the global level, we need to look at a picture of the entire international system, including the new International Criminal Court. The Rome Statute of the ICC embodies this new model of individual criminal accountability, but because of the importance of domestic courts, the ICC is *not* the main institution through which the new model is enforced. The ICC Statute makes clear that the Court functions under a doctrine of "complementarity." What this means is that domestic courts have priority, and that the ICC can only exercise jurisdiction if domestic courts are "unwilling" or "unable" to prosecute.[31] The doctrine of complementarity in the ICC can be seen as a broader expression of the new model in which the primary institutions for enforcement are domestic criminal courts, and the

ICC and foreign courts are the backup institutions or "last resort" when the main model of domestic enforcement fails.[32] Such backup institutions, however, are necessary to create a fully functioning international model. If the model depended only on domestic courts, perpetrators could always escape either by blackmail or veto in domestic polities (take, for example, the rattling of sabers and coup attempts that former military leaders in Argentina and Chile tried each time they faced the possibility of domestic prosecution), or by retirement abroad in a friendly third country. The backup provided by foreign and international prosecutions makes such options less likely than before. When enforcement was only achieved through domestic courts, it was more subject to "capture" by domestic repressors, while the move to create a more transnational system of accountability reduced the control that perpetrators in any single country had in preventing prosecution.

Many critics of the ICC or the specialized courts have not understood their role as backup institutions in a global system of accountability. One observer argues that international tribunals "have squandered billions of dollars" and that domestic solutions would be more cost-effective.[33] Whether or not international tribunals are cost-effective depends on the alternatives. Human rights tribunals, for example, may be very cost-effective compared to military intervention to promote human rights. It would indeed be costly if the ICC or international tribunals were designed to provide comprehensive criminal justice by themselves, but that is not how the decentralized system is currently operating. The use of international tribunals or foreign courts as a backup is the exception, not the rule, in the new model. For the most part, the newly decentralized system of enforcement depends primarily on human rights prosecution in domestic courts. Because the system is decentralized, the quality of the enforcement varies with the quality of criminal justice systems in different countries.

Big differences continue to exist between the areas of national and international criminal justice. In national systems, more or less effective police forces arrest suspects and bring them in for questioning or prosecution. In the international arena, no such international police force exists. As the world learned in the case of the former Yugoslavia, even when NATO forces were on the ground keeping the peace, they were hesitant to expand their mandate to include arresting indicted war criminal suspects to turn over to the international tribunal, the ICTY.

Despite these differences, important change is occurring, and for the most part, it has been neither anticipated nor explained by social scientists. International relations theory has been notoriously weak when it comes to explaining change. For example, most theorists failed to anticipate the end of the Cold War, much less explain it satisfactorily.[34] In this book, I will grapple with this important and puzzling change in the world, and I will explore what it tells us about the nature and process of change in world politics.

These new practices of accountability would not have emerged without the combination of new human rights movements, new human rights law, and regional institutions to implement the law. The "third wave of democracy," beginning in the 1970s, gave human rights activists the opportunity to press for human rights prosecutions. Because the idea of accountability was so new, activists were initially more likely to succeed where previous authoritarian leaders had been delegitimized, usually by losing a war. In all three of the first cases of accountability I discuss—Greece, Portugal, and Argentina—authoritarian leaders had lost wars or been displaced by a revolution.

But once it became possible to imagine accountability for individual leaders, the model chosen was often an extension of the criminal legal system already in place for common crime in domestic courts. For hundreds of years, most societies have prosecuted crimes like murder or kidnapping with domestic trials charging individuals under existing criminal law. One key explanation for both the initial adoption and the spread of the criminal accountability model was that it was familiar and obvious to people from their experience with it domestically.

Part II: Spreading Ideas About Individual Accountability

For years, scholars were unaware of the magnitude of the move toward individual accountability because there was no data on human rights prosecutions in the world. Without data, it was difficult to detect the presence of a new norm. To respond, I worked with some of my graduate students to create a small database of domestic, foreign, and international judicial proceedings for individual criminal responsibility for past human rights violations. The justice norm involves the belief that it is appropriate to hold state officials individually criminally accountable for past violations. It is notoriously hard to measure beliefs, so we tried to gauge the strength of the justice norm by documenting the increasing use of criminal prosecutions at the domestic and international level. Eventually, we included information on human rights prosecutions for *all* transitional countries—that is, countries moving from an undemocratic to a more democratic regime. More than five years later, the project that I thought wouldn't be especially time-consuming has blossomed into a major research initiative.

The graph below summarizes a striking trend in the world that would have been impossible to see without a comprehensive dataset. When one counts by country the number of years that prosecutions were held and then adds these figures together over time, what is revealed is an unprecedented spike in worldwide efforts to address past human rights abuses by focusing on individual criminal responsibility.[35]

Figure 1.1 visually depicts the global norm cascade that is the centerpiece of this book. Looking at the graph, one can see that until the mid-1980s, an increase in prosecutions is hardly noticeable. By the early 1990s, the number of such events began a steep increase. It is striking that the rapid diffusion of the idea follows almost immediately after the end of the Cold War and the fall of the Soviet Union in 1989–91.

There is significant variation in the frequency of prosecutions in different regions of the world. As the pie chart in Figure 1.2 indicates, the trend toward domestic human rights prosecutions has been most pronounced

Figure 1.1. **The Justice Cascade**

(Stacked Area Chart of Cumulated Prosecution Years by Type)

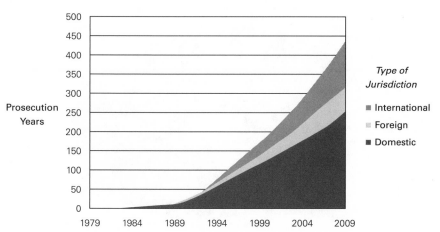

in Latin America and in Central and Eastern Europe. Prosecutions are underway in Asia, Africa, and the Middle East, but to a lesser extent than in Europe and the Americas. International and foreign prosecutions are also unevenly distributed across different regions in ways that don't simply reflect where the worst human rights violations in the world have occurred. Figure 1.3 records the regions of the countries whose nationals have been subject to outside efforts to achieve justice, not the countries where the prosecution occurred. Europe is heavily represented, in large part because of the prosecutions of the International Criminal Tribunal for the Former Yugoslavia of individuals from what are now six different European states. There is a common perception that international and foreign prosecutions are used by countries in the global North to try individuals from the global South. In fact, currently the bulk of international prosecutions are held in Europe for violations committed in Europe.

So, why did the justice norm begin to spread (unevenly) around the globe? A growing number of studies show that many international policies and actions diffuse: they are rapidly adopted by many different countries for reasons that appear to have less to do with their domestic politics or internal pressures, and more to do with imitating policies other countries are adopting. Increasingly, the best explanation for the spread of democracy to a country is how many other countries in the region are democratic,

Figure 1.2. **Regional Distribution of Domestic Prosecutions, 1979–2009**

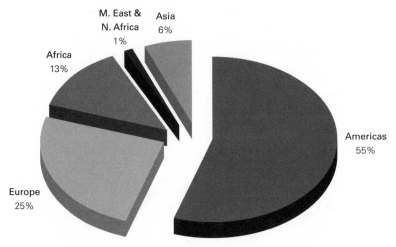

not factors long associated with democracy like the wealth of the country or its level of education. There are similar explanations for the spread of policy innovations like neoliberal economic institutionalization and pension reform.[36] It would seem that states, like people, care about what other states are doing, both as a source of new ideas and as information about how to fit in with global trends.

Diffusion occurs when actions and choices in one country are "systematically conditioned by prior policy choices" made elsewhere in the world.[37] Some scholars even talk about "contagion" models of diffusion, where one state "catches" a new policy or government just like people catch a cold.[38] What policy makers choose to do about human rights trials is indeed systematically conditioned by prior policy choices made elsewhere, but "diffuse" is far too passive a verb to convey the activity and struggle through which ideas about justice have moved around the globe. One problem with the academic diffusion literature is that real people are often absent from its stories.[39] At a tipping point, disembodied ideas may travel rapidly, but at the beginning of any norm cascade, specific people work hard to propose new ideas and policies, and they share their ideas with others, who carry them to new settings. The early adopters of new human rights norms don't

Figure 1.3. **Regional Distribution of Foreign and International Prosecutions, 1979–2009**

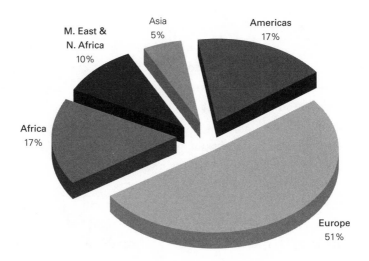

contract the ideas through the air like a virus, but always through struggle, innovations, and often just plain luck.

The justice cascade was not spontaneous, nor was it the result of the natural evolution of law or global culture in the countries where the prosecutions occurred. These changes in ideas were fueled by the human rights movement. The cascade started as a result of the concerted efforts of small groups of public interest lawyers, jurists, and activists, who pioneered strategies, developed legal arguments, recruited plaintiffs and witnesses, marshaled evidence, and persevered throughout years of legal challenges. The work of these norm entrepreneurs was facilitated by two broader structural changes in the world: the third wave of democracy and the end of the Cold War. The first multiplied the number of transitional countries open to the trends described here, and the second opened space for countries to consider a wider range of policy options. This book tells the full story of human rights prosecutions from their beginnings with advocates in Athens and Buenos Aires to the rapid spread of ideas and practices of individual criminal accountability in the early twenty-first century.

Part III: Do Human Rights Prosecutions Make a Difference?

Once scholars and policy makers were convinced that human rights prosecutions were on the increase, lively debates started about their desirability and impact. Some people oppose more prosecutions because they think domestic judicial systems already place too much emphasis on retribution and punishment. Many victims believe, on the other hand, that too few perpetrators of human rights crimes have been held accountable. Most important, though, an intensifying debate centers on the effects of these prosecutions. What difference do they make? Can these efforts at accountability actually contribute to improving human rights? Or do prosecutions actually undermine democracy and threaten peace talks during civil wars? In the final part of the book, I turn to these crucial questions.

This debate has important policy implications since governments, international organizations, and non-governmental organizations (NGOs) are engaged in continual decision making about whether they should advocate or carry out prosecutions and, if so, what type and level of trials are suitable. Many scholars and practitioners like Juan Méndez believe that such prosecutions are both legally and ethically desirable and practically useful in preventing future violations.[40] Others are far more skeptical about the impact of trials. In the mid-1980s, scholars of transitions to democracy generally concluded that trials for past human rights violations were politically untenable and likely to undermine new democracies.[41] Even many actors directly involved in transitions were equally pessimistic. José Zalaquett, a respected Chilean human rights lawyer whom I met in the offices of WOLA in the 1980s, and who later served on the Chilean Truth Commission, argued that it was possible and desirable to seek the truth, but that human rights prosecutions were more difficult when dealing "with perpetrators who still wield considerable power." He was clearly thinking of General Pinochet, who at the time was still commander in chief of the Chilean armed forces.[42]

I wasn't surprised that an activist like Zalaquett, writing in the late 1980s or the early 1990s, might be concerned about the impact of human rights trials. But today, skepticism about the negative impact of such trials is as pronounced as it was in the 1980s. Skeptics contend that the threat of prosecution could cause powerful dictators or insurgents to entrench themselves in power rather than negotiate a transition from authoritarian regimes or civil war.[43] Political commentators have echoed such sentiments in high-profile publications to make a political argument against the International Criminal Court and other international tribunals.

One of the most striking characteristics of the transitional justice scene is how heated and contested the debate has been. In particular, advocates of prosecutions have often clashed with those who prefer "restorative justice," truth-seeking, or no accountability at all. While we can understand why perpetrators and victims might feel strongly about transitional justice, why have scholars and practitioners also been so passionate, even vituperative, in their positions?

One reason may be that these debates invoke our ideals and expectations for justice. The justice cascade has resonated and spread around the globe exactly because so many actors hold powerful ideas about justice. Yet the very magnetism of the ideals that gave impetus to the cascade also sets it up for failure, when measured against those ideals. Justice—like democracy—is one of those powerful concepts that in practice always falls short of our ideals. Victims, among the most ardent of the advocates of transitional justice, are ultimately disillusioned with institutions that can neither heal their broken bodies and minds nor return their loved ones.

Perpetrators find them biased at all times, even when courts lean over backwards to provide due process. State sponsors find justice slow, expensive, and uncertain. Scholars point to the disconnect between the glowing words used to justify international justice and the always glum reality. Because people believe so firmly in justice, they are not only discontented but often feel betrayed. In 2001, former Army of Republic Srpska General Radislav Krstić, an old man, was convicted of genocide and sentenced to an unprecedented forty-six-year prison term by the ICTY. Hearing the news, Munira Subašić, leader of the Mothers of the Enclaves of Srebrenica and Žepa in Bosnia, issued the following statement: "We, survivors of the Srebrenica massacre, don't think that justice has been served. . . . He should have been sentenced to life."[44]

Thus, to put it mildly, there is still little agreement about the impact of human rights trials. In such a situation, how can we talk about the effects of the justice cascade? Although the institutions of justice must always be judged against our ideals, as a social scientist, I advocate the use of empirical comparison, including both qualitative and quantitative analysis, to systematically evaluate claims about the impact of human rights prosecutions. In this book, I do not intend to compare reality to my ideals about justice. Instead, I wish to show the contrast between outcomes for countries that have used prosecutions and other countries that have not used prosecutions. The focus is on whether prosecutions lead to improvements in human rights, democracy, and levels of conflicts compared to the same country before it used prosecutions or to other countries that have not used prosecutions.

Chapter 5 examines the ways in which prosecutions can have an impact on human rights practices, democracy, and conflict in specific countries in Latin America. I focus on Latin America because it has had more prosecutions than any other region, and because many Latin American countries were early innovators of human rights trials so that the passage of time makes it possible to evaluate their impact. Here again my research shows that holding prosecutions has not weakened democracy nor led to an increase in violations or conflict in the region. Twenty-five years after the first trials, not a single Latin American democracy has been undermined because of the choice to use trials.

The results of a quantitative analysis, presented in Chapter 6, show that transitional countries in which human rights prosecutions have taken place are less repressive than countries without prosecutions. Contrary to the arguments made by trial skeptics, transitional prosecutions have not tended to exacerbate violations. The quantitative study shows that countries with more accumulated years of prosecutions after transition are less repressive than countries with fewer accumulated years of prosecutions. In addition, countries surrounded by more neighbors with transitional prosecutions are less repressive, which may suggest a deterrence impact of prosecutions across borders. These findings refute the arguments made by the skeptics that human rights trials lead to more repression, and demonstrate instead that prosecutions and truth commissions can have a positive effect on human rights practices.

While it is possible that Latin America is exceptional, equally possible is that the trial skeptics have based their arguments on a few powerful but as yet unresolved cases. Just as the frightening but ultimately unsuccessful coup attempts in Argentina drove the pessimism in early reflections on political transition, the failure of international justice to dampen nationalism in Serbia or to help end conflicts in Uganda or Sudan may fuel the current skepticism. And just as the literature was too hasty in its judgments about the impossibility and undesirability of trials in Latin America, current skeptics might be well advised to monitor the situations in the former Yugoslavia, Uganda, and Sudan longer before jumping to conclusions about the pernicious effects of trials.

The research findings that human rights prosecutions and truth commissions can contribute to lessening repression also have important lessons for policy makers. Human rights research to date has not been very helpful about giving ideas for how to lessen repression. In the past, major studies concluded that violations were caused by factors over which governments had little short-term control, including poverty, authoritarianism, civil war, and population size.[45] I continue to see the impact of these factors, but my study also suggests that more microlevel policy responses such as prosecutions and truth commissions also can have an impact on practices, thus providing policy makers with more viable short-term options. Some of my colleagues reach different conclusions. I spend quite a bit of time in this book discussing these debates with colleagues because I believe they have important policy implications. If the skeptics are correct and prosecutions are associated with worsening human rights practices, then we should question the decision to use them. We need the best possible social science research from which to draw coherent recommendations.

Trials are one factor that can contribute to cultural change and the internalization of human rights norms among state officials; but not all state officials internalize norms to the same extent, as we saw in the revival of debates about the legitimacy of torture in the United States after 9/11. Chapter 7 looks at U.S. noncompliance with the prohibition on torture in order to probe the most difficult question in the literature on social norms. If a law or norm truly has some teeth, we would expect that, after a period of time, it would be able to have an effect on even the most powerful state—in this case, the United States. The U.S. decision to use torture even after the Pinochet litigation had established the legitimacy of universal jurisdiction over torture is an indication that some state officials still believed only a short time ago that they were above the law. American officials simply did not see that the Pinochet precedent applied to them, even though the United States committed torture after ratifying the International Convention Against Torture and implementing it in domestic law. Yet Chapter 7 shows that there is some indication that even U.S. state officials are not completely immune from the possibilities of future prosecution. Finally, Chapter 8 provides an overview of how human rights prosecutions are changing world politics, together with some ethical reflections and policy recommendations distilled from the experiences of the countries discussed in this work.

The most striking theme in this book is the persistence of the demand for justice: human rights prosecutions will not go away. Such prosecutions are not a panacea for all the ills of society, and they will inevitably disappoint as they fall short of our ideals. They represent an advance, however, over the complete lack of accountability of the past, and they have the potential to prevent human rights violations in the future.

Part I

CREATING INDIVIDUAL ACCOUNTABILITY

2

Navigating Without a Map

HUMAN RIGHTS TRIALS IN SOUTHERN EUROPE

My database on worldwide human rights prosecutions indicates that the Greeks and the Portuguese were the first in the post–World War II era to hold their own state officials criminally accountable for past human rights violations.[1] As the earliest adopters of trials, it seemed likely that Greece and Portugal would offer crucial clues about why citizens of a country would come to believe it was possible to hold their former leaders accountable. I pored over the small literature on the trials in Greece, but couldn't find a satisfactory explanation. On the Portuguese case, there was virtually nothing written, in either English or Portuguese, about the prosecutions. So, in the summer of 2008, I packed my bags and headed off to Southern Europe to interview former political prisoners, lawyers, and academics, among others, about their experiences with trials. One of my students, Filipa Raimundo, had written a master's thesis on the prosecutions in Portugal, the first study of its kind in English or Portuguese.[2] Not only was Filipa's thesis an invaluable resource for me, but she helped me arrange interviews with some of the people who had been most informative for her research. In Greece, my friend Maria Piniou-Kalli, a former political prisoner during the dictatorship, and the founder and director of a treatment center for victims of torture in Athens, shared her insights with me and arranged for me to speak with some of the people who had testified at the trials. My colleague at the University of Minnesota, Theo Stavrou, who teaches modern Greek history, put me in contact with key scholars of the period. Meanwhile, my friends and family were incredulous. "Let's get this straight—you're going to Greece and

Portugal this summer to do *research*?" No amount of discussion could persuade them that I wasn't going for my own enjoyment, evidence perhaps of how much images of Greece and Portugal have transformed since the dark days of the dictatorships.

The prosecutions in Greece and Portugal are particularly puzzling when set against the case of their neighbor, Spain, which also experienced a transition around the same time, but did not hold any trials for past human rights violations—even though the scale of repression in Spain during the Civil War was greater than that during the authoritarian regimes in either Greece or Portugal. Why did the Greeks and Portuguese hold their state officials accountable for past violations while the Spanish, experiencing transition at the same time and in the same region, chose not to do so? Why did such a novel move seem possible and desirable in some countries but not in others? And why did these trials take such different forms in these countries?

Here the scholarly literature on transitions to democracy offers some insights. The longtime Spanish dictator General Francisco Franco was still in power when he died in his bed in 1975. His regime did not collapse, but rather experienced a negotiated transition to democracy. None of the main political actors could impose a solution, so they negotiated agreements about how the transition would proceed. Scholars call this a "pacted" transition, recognizing that the power holders from the previous regime retain much more power to determine the policies of the new government.

The transitions in Portugal and Greece during the 1970s were quite different. On April 25, 1974, middle-rank rebel military officers in Portugal carried out a coup against the forty-eight-year-old dictatorship and initiated a transition to democracy. People flooded the streets to join the soldiers, putting carnations in their gun barrels, in what became known as the "Carnation Revolution." One of the most hated symbols of the dictatorship had been the political police, the PIDE/DGS (*Polícia Internacional de Defeša do Estado/Direcção Geral de Segurança*), because they carried out intelligence on and repression of the opposition through imprisonment, torture, and surveillance. During the revolution, PIDE officers holed up in their headquarters, and when a crowd spontaneously gathered shouting "Death to PIDE!" some officers fired on them from inside the building, causing the few deaths of the entire revolution. Most people know the story of the Carnation Revolution in Portugal. But very few remember that as part of this transition, hundreds of members of the PIDE police and their informants were arrested, detained, and ultimately tried for their participation in repression under the Portuguese dictatorship.

Just two months after the Portuguese revolution, on July 23, 1974, the Greek authoritarian government was overthrown. The Greek and Portuguese transitions were similar in that they were both "ruptured" transitions, where the outgoing authoritarian regime could not negotiate the conditions of its exit from power. In both cases, perceived military failure was one reason for the transition. In Portugal, the rebel officers argued for a political rather than a military solution to the disastrous colonial wars in Africa; in Greece, the policy of the military Junta had led to the Turkish invasion of Cyprus and brought Greece to the brink of a war with Turkey that it could not win. Greeks were outraged about the military debacle, and when the Junta fell, celebrations spilled over into the streets of Athens, where people chanted their support for democracy and the constitution. They also shouted, "All the guilty to Goudi!" meaning that the Junta leaders should be tried and sent to the barracks in the Goudi neighborhood of Athens where executions were traditionally held. In 1975, Greece held unprecedented trials of military personnel for crimes during the previous regime and imposed heavy punishments on a significant number of individuals, including the top leaders of the Junta.[3] Some saw these as the Greek equivalent of the Nuremberg and Tokyo trials, but they were actually quite different. At Nuremberg, the Allied powers used an international tribunal to judge the leaders of defeated Germany, while in Greece and Portugal, citizens judged their own state officials—in their own domestic courts— for the rights violations of the authoritarian regimes.

Neither "Death to PIDE!" nor "All the guilty to Goudi!" is a human rights slogan. They hearken back to ancient cries of "Death to the King!" which were not about legal accountability, but about some kind of ritual cleansing of the body politic through the sacrifice of the leader. The people in the streets were calling for old-style political trials, not for a juridical process that would observe the rights of both perpetrators and survivors of violent repression. In both countries, however, the governments and citizens transformed anger in the streets into public support for what would become the first domestic human rights prosecutions since World War II. In this sense, the initial demand reflected a more primal urge for punishment or revenge, but it was transmuted into the process of individual criminal accountability.

Since there were so few precedents for these kinds of trials, the new Greek and Portuguese governments were inventing procedures as they went along. Many of the young army officers who carried out the Portuguese revolution, known as the "Captains of April," were only in their thirties. When I met him in the summer of 2008, one of these captains, Vasco Lourenço, explained that they were "navigating without a map," so they had to *navegar a vista* (navigate by sight), as sailors do when they don't know the route and must watch the coast to avoid obstacles. This is an apt metaphor in a country like Portugal with a long and proud tradition of seafaring. The more idiomatic translation into English might be "flying by the seat of your pants."

The trials in Greece and Portugal took place against the backdrop of changing international and regional attitudes about authoritarianism and human rights. Powerful leftist movements emerged in Europe, the United States, and elsewhere in the late sixties and early seventies, motivated in part by opposition to the U.S. war in Vietnam. These movements questioned the American policies of unwavering support for authoritarian anti-Communist regimes like those in Greece, Spain, and Portugal. In 1973, after the United States withdrew its final troops from Vietnam, President Nixon traveled to China, initiating the period of détente, or relaxation, in the tense Cold War atmosphere between East and West. The rise of movements on the left and the period of détente both opened more space for an emerging human rights consciousness in Europe and around the world, even though a legalistic approach was quite different from the revolutionary approach favored by some.

The regional context was a crucial factor that facilitated the early use of human rights prosecutions, especially in Greece. In Europe, an awareness of human rights was initiated in the wake of the crimes of the Holocaust and World War II. Many Europeans believed that abuses were linked to the causes of the war, and that protecting human rights could also lead to increased security. Human rights issues were present in the earliest discussions of the postwar European order. Non-governmental organizations promoting European unity focused on these issues.[4] Their call for a European human rights charter and court was later taken up by the newly created Council of Europe, and the Statute of the Council of Europe made respect for human rights and the rule of law conditions of membership in the council. Greece, then under a democratic government, joined the Council of Europe in 1949, just after it was founded. Spain and Portugal, both under dictators at the time, were excluded until after their transition to democracy.

From 1948 until 1953, the Europeans moved quickly and consciously to build a regional human rights system. First, states drafted the European Convention for the Protection of Human Rights and Fundamental Freedoms. The convention focused on civil and political rights, and imposed specific legal obligations to protect human rights on any state that ratified the treaty. It does not mention a duty to punish perpetrators of human rights violations, but it calls upon states to "ensure rights," and says that victims have a right to an "effective remedy," even if a violation was committed by "persons acting in their official capacity." While this article creates some basis for human rights prosecutions, the convention does not clarify at all that an effective remedy need take the form of prosecutions for individual criminal accountability.

The convention created two new regional human rights institutions, the first of their kind: the European Commission of Human Rights and the European Court of Human Rights. Greece ratified the convention in March 1953 and, with that, became one of the early movers helping to bring it into effect by September of that year. The European Commission could investigate and monitor human rights situations, and the European Court made the final decisions in the cases the commission referred to it. Both institutions got off to a slow start in the 1950s and 1960s. But in 1956 and 1957, Greece submitted the first two interstate cases ever filed with the European Commission of Human Rights. Both were filed against the United Kingdom and were related to the situation in Cyprus, when the island was a British colony. In these cases, Greece alleged that the British had permitted practices of torture and ill-treatment. When a political settlement was reached over the status of Cyprus, both Greece and the United Kingdom requested that the commission terminate the proceedings.[5] The Cyprus cases demonstrated the possibility of using the convention to investigate allegations of torture and ill-treatment. And since Greece had been an early and active user of the commission and the convention, this made it more difficult for Greece to repudiate the commission when other European countries later filed their case against the Greek government for human rights violations under the military regime.

Portugal and Spain, both under authoritarian regimes, were sidelined from building the new Europe. However, Portugal inadvertently had its influence on the emerging human rights network. A British lawyer, Peter Benenson, founded Amnesty International in 1961 after reading how two students in a Portuguese café had been imprisoned for raising their glasses "to liberty." He published a front-page appeal in the *Observer* for the "forgotten prisoners" and coined the term "prisoner of conscience." The outpouring of support from the appeal gave birth to Amnesty International.

Thus, by the early 1960s, the basic institutions of the regional human rights system were in place in Europe, and NGOs were beginning to operate and create more public awareness about human rights. For the first time ever in history, binding human rights law, combined with authoritative human rights institutions empowered to implement that law, and NGOs like Amnesty International capable of bringing cases of abuse to public attention, were all in place and poised to act in the region. The 1967 coup in Greece was the first major rights-related event that occurred after the regional human rights regime was firmly in place. In this sense, we can think of it as a test of whether human rights law could respond adequately and help improve a grave situation. No one knew what might happen. The Europeans were indeed navigating without a map.

Greece

In its early years, Amnesty International was a small organization, mostly dependent on the volunteer work of individuals. As a young Swedish member, Thomas Hammarberg went to Athens soon after the coup in 1967 to collect evidence about torture. Hammarberg was struck by the widespread fear in the Greek community. "To testify to a foreign human rights organization involved a serious risk," he recalls. Hammarberg later became the secretary general of Amnesty International (1980–86), and he invoked the Greek case as "a defining lesson for human rights policies in Europe."

He commented that "The coup in the early morning of 21 April, 1967, was a shock for democrats all over Europe: how was it possible that a simple group of colonels could wipe out democracy in one of the oldest member states of the Council of Europe? The shock deepened when it became known that the Greek parliament was closed and the political parties dissolved; that strict media censorship was introduced; that about 6,000 politicians, journalists, and others were taken prisoner; and that many of them were tortured during interrogation."[6]

Amnesty's work on Greece was sustained by information it received on prisoners from contacts within the country. One of Amnesty's contacts used a different public telephone each time to speak to a staff person in London, who then compiled the information for use by Amnesty's Urgent Action network and its local groups working on prisoner of conscience cases. The chain of information led from the prisoner networks inside Greek prisons to Greek opposition contacts, who fed it to reliable foreigners in Greece, who then passed it on to Amnesty International and to journalists at organizations like the BBC.[7]

In January 1968, Amnesty issued a small report entitled "Torture in Greece," based on an investigative trip to Greece by two volunteer lawyers. The lawyers met with the minister of the interior of Greece, General Stylianos Pattakos, and informed him that there was evidence that prisoners in Greek prisons had been tortured. Mr. Pattakos denied all the charges, saying they were trumped up by Communists. When the Amnesty lawyers intimated that the use of torture could lead to Greece's expulsion from the Council of Europe, Pattakos responded: "Let them throw us out . . . the Greek Government has to protect itself against the communist enemies. A communist is not a Greek. We must put our own security first."[8] At the time, Amnesty International stressed the sanction of expulsion from the Council of Europe, but did not mention the possibility of prosecuting individuals for human rights crimes. What happened between Amnesty's meeting with Pattakos in 1967 and the transition to democracy in 1975 that made human rights trials imaginable?

As Pattakos's comments make clear, new human rights norms weren't entering into an ideological vacuum, but, as new norms always do, were emerging in a densely populated ideological space. Cold War anti-Communist ideology was pervasive in all three of the authoritarian countries considered here, as well as in the Latin American countries discussed in the next chapter. One variant of Cold War thinking was "national security ideology," which saw internal leftist and Communist groups as posing a major security threat to the nation, and justified authoritarianism and repression as legitimate, indeed necessary, to confront subversion. Portugal and Greece were NATO members, and all three countries—Spain, Portugal, and Greece—received substantial military and economic aid from the United States, which treated them as bulwarks against the expansion of the Soviet bloc. Greece and Spain in turn provided valuable military bases to the United States.

In the context of the Vietnam War, and in the wake of the student movements of 1968, many young people in Europe became particularly concerned about human rights.[9] In Greece, Portugal, and Spain, the left—including the Communists—formed an important part of clandestine opposition to the authoritarian governments. These governments singled out Communist Party members for repression, and the Party, as a transnational institution, organized global solidarity in protest. Communist and Socialist ideas were a powerful part of the ideological debate of the times. In the case of the Portuguese revolution, in particular, the left was a central force in the new political order. Amnesty International, however, stressed that human rights violations happened in all types of political systems, so it instructed its adoption groups to work on cases in the Communist world as well as in right-wing authoritarian countries.

In 1968, Norway, the Netherlands, Denmark, and Sweden filed a joint suit with the European Commission of Human Rights against the military government of Greece for the violation of a number of human rights provisions in the European Convention. It was the Amnesty January 1968 report on torture in Greece that later prompted the Scandinavian governments to add charges of torture to their original suit against Greece before the European Commission.[10]

According to a Dutch foreign policy official at the time, the impetus for Dutch involvement in the Greek case didn't come from the Foreign Ministry itself, but was done "for public relations, or at least to make Parliament and public opinion happy. But there was not much of conviction behind it in the ministry."[11] International human rights issues began to galvanize activism, and activists put more pressure on their governments to live up to their human rights commitments. The coup had led to a large exodus of liberal and leftist Greeks to other parts of the world, where they organized committees pressuring for human rights and a return to democracy in Greece. These exiles and their associations in turn brought the attention of the Council of Europe, the European Commission, and member governments to the problems of imprisonment and torture within the country. So, for example, the Hellenic Alliance for the Rights of Man and the Rights of Citizens, a group affiliated with the Paris-based International Federation for Human Rights, presented reports to the Council of Europe. In the Netherlands, there was a committee on Greece with very prominent people, who kept pressure on Parliament to do something about human rights violations in Greece.[12] Amnesty International also had a particularly strong presence in the Netherlands. Jan Herman Burgers, a Dutch government official who would later work tirelessly in the drafting and passage of the UN Convention Against Torture, became a member of Amnesty in the early 1970s. "You couldn't miss it," he recalls. "At that time, when I subscribed to Amnesty, it was very, very prominent, at least here in Holland."[13]

In the United States as well, human rights violations in Greece motivated policy makers to pay more attention to such problems. Some policy makers and members of the public began to criticize U.S. support of the military regime in Greece, advocating cutoffs of U.S. military aid. The father of U.S. human rights policy, Democratic congressman Donald Fraser of Minnesota, recalled that the military coup in Greece was one of the events that brought human rights issues to the fore. Greeks in his Minnesota district made clear their opposition to the military takeover in Greece, and urged Fraser to try to do something about it.[14]

But concern about violations in Greece did not translate directly into demand for prosecutions for individual accountability there. While exile groups and NGOs like Amnesty International pressured foreign governments to condemn such violations, they did not make a clear demand for holding Junta members individually accountable. For example, *The Hellenic Review*, a prominent Greek exile magazine printed in the United Kingdom throughout 1968, was full of references to human rights violations and institutions, but contained no demand for trials for Greek state officials.

In response to the complaint filed by the Dutch and the Scandinavians, the European Commission of Human Rights conducted a thorough investigation of the situation in Greece, including hearings in Athens. In its final report, the commission concluded that the Greek military government had indeed violated a number of the articles of the European Convention on Human Rights. The large second volume of the commission's report deals entirely with torture and inhumane and degrading treatment. The commission said that it had established "beyond doubt" that since April

1967, the Athens Security Police had inflicted torture or ill-treatment on political prisoners. The commission concluded that the Greek authorities, although they had received many complaints of these acts, had failed "to take any effective steps to investigate them or to ensure remedies for any such complaints or allegations found to be true."[15] The possibility or desirability of individual criminal prosecutions was not specifically mentioned. The emphasis on the Greek government's failure to "ensure remedies" does suggest that the commission members were perhaps thinking of accountability, but it gives no additional details about how the state was to pursue it. This report led Greece to withdraw from the Council of Europe to avoid expulsion.[16]

After the European Commission's seminal report on Greece, and before the Greek transition to democracy, Amnesty International launched its first worldwide campaign, the "Campaign for the Abolition of Torture," in December 1972. As the centerpiece of the campaign, Amnesty published a long report on the use of torture around the world, including the cases of Greece and Portugal, and recommended international tribunals to investigate torture. Amnesty did not focus on domestic criminal prosecutions, but mentioned the need for "international tribunals independent of governments."[17] It could be that Amnesty, just like most of the other observers at this period, simply could not yet imagine a time when the dictatorships would be over, and courts within abusive states would be willing and able to hold their own officials accountable. Amnesty stressed that such an international tribunal had to provide safeguards for the accused, one of the three defining characteristics of a human rights trial. This is the first example of a high-level demand for human rights prosecutions for torture.

Eight months after Amnesty launched its campaign against torture, the Chilean military carried out a brutal military coup against the elected Socialist government of Salvador Allende, including an aerial bombing of the presidential palace, and ending in the death of Allende himself. When the Chilean military's widespread use of torture was publicized, the outrage it provoked added more fuel to Amnesty's campaign against torture. The situation in Chile drew far more world attention than the related coup in Uruguay earlier that same year. Events in Chile and Uruguay were worlds apart from the situation in Greece, but there were striking similarities not lost on some outside observers. Chile and Uruguay were among the oldest democracies in Latin America. The regimes set up in both countries seemed to echo the pattern in Greece, where democracies were replaced by repressive U.S.-supported military governments. Just as the case of Greece had captured the attention of the public and policy makers in Europe and in the United States, so too did the case of Chile. Membership in Amnesty International in Europe and the United States rose dramatically in this period, and other new human rights organizations were created. The U.S. section of Amnesty, for example, expanded from 3,000 to 50,000 members between 1974 and 1976.[18]

By 1973, the military government in Greece was weakening. Through inept and repressive rule, the colonels had alienated almost all of their supporters. The government's bloody repression of the student uprising at the Athens Polytechnic university on November 17, 1973, further undermined the regime. The government eventually sent a tank to crash through the gates of the University, and ordered troops to fire on civilians, killing dozens and injuring hundreds.[19] But it was the military debacle in Cyprus that was the final blow to the regime. The Greek military government instigated a crisis in Cyprus that provoked a Turkish invasion of the island, which the Greek regime was then militarily incapable of confronting. This defeat led the Greek military itself, in the summer of 1974, to overthrow the seven-and-a-half-year military regime and turn over power to the civilian ex-prime minster, Constantine Karamanlis.

Karamanlis was not new to politics in Greece when he was called back from exile in France to serve as prime minister after the fall of the military Junta. He had served in many positions in almost all the postwar governments, including as minister of defense, before three terms as prime minister from 1955 to 1963, when he formed and led a party of the right. His prior experience in politics would color his new administration.

When he took over in 1974, Karamanlis was sixty-seven years old, almost deaf, and with a faint bald spot. He was six feet tall, with a strong face, "dominated by lush eyebrows that made him look a bit like some giant bird."[20] As prime minister in the 1950s and early 1960s Karamanlis was favored by King Paul and by the U.S. government, but he left office in 1963 over a dispute with the Greek royal family. Karamanlis went into eleven years of self-imposed exile in France, leaving Greece well before the colonels' coup. During the Junta, he refused any collaboration with the colonels, but there is little evidence that Karamanlis had any special human rights connections or concerns, so his personal history didn't fore-shadow why he would permit the first human rights prosecutions.

Karamanlis was still prime minister when one of the most dramatic political crimes of the postwar period occurred in Greece—the murder in 1963 of Gregoris Lambrakis, an MP and anti-Fascist resistance icon. Lambrakis was "a doctor who had run a free clinic for the poor, a leader in the Greek peace movement, which opposed Vietnam and called for an end to the Cold War, and a member of the United Democratic left party."[21] Shortly after he gave a keynote speech at an anti-war rally in Thessaloniki, two right-wing extremists ran down Lambrakis with a truck. The murder so shocked the population that it led to the fall of Karamanlis and his party, and the formation of a new youth movement, the Lambrakis Youth.

Lambrakis's murderers were convicted in a trial that exposed links between corrupt police, army officers, and right-wing paramilitary extremists. Although no evidence was ever presented that directly linked Karamanlis to the crime, Georgios Papandreou, the leader of the main opposition party, said that the prime minister was "morally responsible for [Lambrakis's] death" because he had tolerated the existence of violent right-wing extremist groups, some of which had links to the state.

The Lambrakis murder was immortalized in the political novel *Z* by Vassilis Vassilikos, and later brought to a larger public in a 1969 movie directed by Costa-Gavras, starring Yves Montand as Lambrakis. Mikis Theodorakis, of *Zorba the Greek* fame, wrote the music while in Greece during the dictatorship. He later smuggled the tapes out of the country. *Z* was a great artistic and political success, and gained iconic status among the left in the late sixties and early seventies.

Karamanlis was living in exile in Paris when the film first opened there. The portrayal of the Greek regime is so grim that most observers later associated it with the military regime in power when the film was released, not with the semi-democratic period that preceded it. One of the histori-ans of the period recalls that Karamanlis believed the Lambrakis murder had damaged his prestige and was a "black spot" on his reputation.[22] One reason he may have permitted trials is that he wanted to break with the past and erase this stain from his record.

Although his first weeks in office in 1974 were uncertain, Karaman-lis firmly took the reins of government and worked quickly to reestablish civilian control. But whatever action Karamanlis took, to the left in Greece he would always be a man of the right. The bulk of the victims of the dictatorship were people of the left, many of them members of the Communist Party, which had faced persecution in Greece ever since the Greek Civil War in 1946–49. To his detractors, Karamanlis would always be "too conservative, too authoritarian for the times."[23]

On the first day after the overthrow of the dictatorship, July 24, 1974, the Greek people took to the streets of Athens to celebrate their new-found freedom. My friend Maria Piniou-Kalli told me how she was there with her two-year-old son sitting on her shoulders to watch the crowds. Maria had been a young medical student in Thessaloniki working in the same hospital where Lambrakis died. She joined the Lambrakis Youth, which she described as "a vibrant and open sixties youth movement," and rose to become a student leader. For her political activity, the dictatorship imprisoned Maria in the notorious prison camp on Yaros Island, where 6,000 people from all over Greece were held. The prisoners lived in wards built by previous prisoners, including Maria's father, who had been imprisoned on Yaros after the Civil War. While she was at Yaros, Maria was adopted as a prisoner of conscience by Amnesty International, and was eventually released after falling gravely ill. After her release Maria avoided politics, but she could not resist joining the crowds in the streets to celebrate the downfall of the Junta, spontaneously chanting slogans in favor of democracy and the constitution. She recalls as well the chants to send the guilty members of the military government to the Goudi barracks to be executed.[24]

During the first weeks of the transition, in late July and early August, everyone was too fearful for the stability of the government to speak of trials for the military. It was rumored that President Karamanlis himself slept in a different place every night, or on a yacht in the harbor guarded by the more loyal navy, in order to protect himself against a military coup by a still potentially mutinous army. After seven years of harsh military rule, people wanted democracy, and no one wished to upset the fragile new government. So the initial reaction of the government was not to imprison anyone, or send them into exile, or even mention prosecutions. Leaders of the military regime lived in freedom and walked the streets of Athens.

An amnesty decreed just two days after the civilian government of Karamanlis took over was worded ambiguously. One of the primary demands of the opposition was to see political prisoners, especially those on Yaros

Island, released immediately. An important type of amnesty concerned political prisoners of authoritarian regimes. These prisoners had been accused of crimes, such as sedition, and needed to be pardoned in order to be released from prison. Amnesty International chose the word "amnesty" for its name because it supported this kind of clemency for political prisoners. But it is hard to write an amnesty for political prisoners without also inadvertently extending it to members of the authoritarian regime. The wording of the Greek amnesty decree, designed to exonerate all the jailed opponents of the military regime, remained unclear as to whether it also exonerated the members of the military regime itself.[25]

After over a month of stability, demands for accountability started to emerge. Newspaper reports from this period record "a growing public demand for retribution against the former dictators."[26] A resistance organization, Democratic Defense, made the first public calls on record for prosecuting those responsible for the authoritarian regime. In late August 1974, an opposition leader, Andreas Papandreou, son of the former Socialist prime minister Georgios Papandreou, published a carefully worded call for a trial of perpetrators in a major Greek newspaper.[27]

The first concrete legal step toward trials was a criminal case filed by an individual lawyer, Alexandros Lykourezos, against the leaders of the military government, for high treason. Lykourezos, scion of a well-known family of lawyer/politicians associated with a centrist party, had gone into exile during the military regime after his father had been imprisoned for a time. While in London, he formed part of the active exile community campaigning for a return to democracy in Greece, but no one in London at the time was yet talking about the possibility of trials. Only when he returned to Athens after the transition did Lykourezos begin to ask himself what could be done legally to hold the Junta leaders accountable: "When I came back to Greece after the return of Karamanlis, I realized that all the colonels and all those responsible for the Junta were living around us free, and I thought that was an insult to our democratic sensibility. . . . Someone has to take the initiative. The article of the criminal code says high treason includes 'one who attempts by force or by threat of force to change the form of government of the state.' I considered that these officers had imposed a dictatorship, so that was high treason according to this definition, so I filed a complaint with the prosecution."[28]

Lykourezos was a young and unknown lawyer at the time. Since then, he has become one of the more famous lawyers in Greece, involved in many high-profile celebrity trials. In an interview in his office the dapper Lykourezos explained that Greek law permits private prosecution in criminal cases; that is, private citizens are entitled to file criminal cases. The state prosecutor is then obliged to investigate the case and see if it has merit. Lykourezos did what any Greek citizen could have done: on September 9, 1974, he filed a criminal suit bringing charges against thirty-five individuals for treason. In early October, other private citizens followed his lead and brought additional suits, this time adding the charge of mutiny to that of treason, and bringing the total number of individuals charged to fifty-five. Lykourezos gained instant celebrity as a result of the suit; people stopped him in the street to congratulate him. It may have even boosted his political ambitions, as he came close to being elected to the new Parliament in the fall 1974 elections. Other individuals would later file similar private criminal suits, also for torture and for the murder of students in the suppression of the uprising at the Athens Polytechnic.

The private suits both forced the government's hand and relieved it of the burden of having to initiate prosecutions itself. Early in October the Karamanlis government issued a decree explicitly excluding the top leaders of the military regime from the benefits of the Amnesty Law, thus paving the way for prosecutions. In a landslide electoral victory in November 1974, the government received support for its position. According to *The Times* of London, "most Greeks call for punishment of the Junta and its henchmen less out of vengeance than to discourage others from imitating them."[29] The disagreements were less about the need for some kind of punishment and more about the type and scale of punishment. In February 1975, the government quelled a military coup attempt against the Karamanlis government that aimed to force the government to grant a full amnesty and to free jailed military officers awaiting trials.[30] Despite unrest in the officer corps, the government moved ahead promptly with the prosecutions.

What were the motivations behind the government's decision to pursue trials? Karamanlis died in 1998, but I hoped his papers could help me understand his motivations for supporting the innovative trials in Greece. I went to the Karamanlis Foundation and Library, situated in a beautiful white building in a residential suburb of Athens. The librarians and historians there told me they had very few papers in the archives about the trials, and none that would help me understand his motivations. This was the first, but far from the last, occasion when I came to understand that the trials were more important to me as a researcher than they were to many people in Greece. In my mind, the trials were one of the key accomplishments and legacies of the Karamanlis administration, but the people at the foundation were rather puzzled by my claim that Greece was a global leader on this issue. Nonetheless, they did arrange for me to meet with Achilles Karamanlis, Constantine Karamanlis's brother and confidant, who still worked with the foundation. Achilles Karamanlis, elderly but alert, did not speak English, so a young historian from the foundation was kind enough to sit with us and translate. Achilles began by explaining why his brother was against the death penalty. This was an indication of something I grasped later: that the innovation the Greeks perceived was not the fact of the trials themselves, but rather the Karamanlis decision to commute the death penalty for those convicted of treason. When asked why his brother supported the trials in general, Achilles responded that "Karamanlis was obeying the feelings of the Greek people" when he agreed to the trials. They wanted everyone to be punished, from the highest to the lowest. Public opinion in favor of trials was very strong. Karamanlis "could not avoid having trials," his brother said. It was like the "common sense" for the period. But his main philosophy was always to calm political extremes, so his actions were aimed at trying to find a compromise between reality and his philosophy.[31]

Others in Greece also stressed that they didn't see the decision to hold trials as particularly innovative or unusual. As Nicos Alivizatos, a prominent lawyer and the co-author of one of the most important articles on the Greek trials, explained to me, there was a long tradition of political trials in Greece.[32] Because of this, many people took it for granted that Karamanlis would try the leaders of the former regime and execute them, as in the past. This was the meaning of the call: "All the guilty to Goudi!" Most famously, five top political leaders and one military leader had been executed in 1922 by a firing squad in the Goudi barracks after a speedy trial for treason amidst a military defeat that led to the withdrawal of Greek troops and refugees from the territory now held by Turkey. This loss of territory is still referred to by the Greeks as "the Great Catastrophe." Greek historical memory was sharp, and 1922 was a vivid point of reference in Greek identity. The 1922 trials, however, were not human rights prosecutions. They were trials for treason, but they were a "parody of justice," without proper due process or testimony from crucial witnesses, and really just political revenge.[33] Yet the 1922 trials stood out in the collective memory and provided a clear reference when the public considered what should happen to the Greek Junta leaders. There were also trials followed by executions after the coup of 1935 and again after World War II for some Nazi collaborators.[34] Greek political history thus provided the conditions that made prosecutions more likely. Important was not only the fact of the ruptured transition but also the memory of the use of political trials.

Karamanlis was well aware of these past trials, but he believed that they had contributed to political instability because those who were tried and executed often became martyrs. One historian of the period, Evanthis Hatzivassiliou, says that "Karamanlis was looking for reconciliation, not as we understand it today, but as an end to the constant cycle of blood."[35] There was a powerful swing to the left during the dictatorship. When Karamanlis came back, he was caught in a bind. On the one hand, given Greece's move to the left and the political tradition of trials, he had to hold prosecutions to legitimize his government and convince people that it was not simply a return to the incomplete democracy of the past. But for Karamanlis, "execution makes blood, and blood makes martyrs."[36] So the solution that Karamanlis arrived at was to hold prosecutions but to stay executions.

This helps explain why Karamanlis held the treason trials, but not why he continued with prosecutions on torture and the Polytechnic uprising. The report by the European Commission of Human Rights may have been important here. Hatzivassiliou suggested the Karamanlis government may have wanted to have the torture prosecutions because the country "was dishonored" by the European Commission report. "For the leadership of the right, there was always the feeling that we must not prove to be unworthy of Europe and the West."[37]

In January 1975, the movie Z was shown for the first time in Greece, and it became the most popular film in Greek history. At the end, when a young investigator indicts four police officials for complicity in the murder of Lambrakis, audiences cheered out loud. The cheers may have reminded Karamanlis that "many Greeks feel that he has not done enough to punish those responsible for more than seven years of dictatorship."[38] Maria Piniou-Kalli later recalled that she had hated Karamanlis because she blamed him for Lambrakis's death. But after the transition, she realized that he had changed—that he was more democratic, maybe because he had learned what it was like to be in exile, to feel betrayed, to lose his freedom. Before, Maria said, Karamanlis was "a servant of the palace," and yet after he returned, he held a plebiscite that led to the abolition of the monarchy. Even so, Maria doesn't give Karamanlis or the state much credit for the trials, which she believes came from the demands of the people.

Three main sets of trials took place in Greece. The first and most important were these treason trials of the top leaders of the military regime in April 1967 for having overthrown the democratic government. They were not, properly speaking, human rights prosecutions, because they were for the interruption of democracy, not for individual violations of human rights. But in the wake of the treason trials came two sets of prosecutions that constituted genuine modern human rights prosecutions—the first for torture; and the second for the murder of students in the bloody repression of the uprising at the Athens Polytechnic on November 17, 1973. The treason trials were the most important: once the major leaders of the regime were imprisoned, tried, and convicted to death for treason, the back of the former regime was broken; it was therefore possible to continue with the other prosecutions. Like the treason trials, the torture prosecutions and the Polytechnic trial were also initiated by private citizens using private prosecution provisions, and were later taken over by the state. Although Greek law at the time did not specifically prohibit torture, the prosecutions were based on accusations of violations of the existing criminal code provisions against abuse of power and bodily damages.

The treason trials against twenty-four members of the military regime took place from late July to mid-August 1975. Foreign and domestic journalists were allowed access, but the public was excluded. Eventually, eighteen of the protagonists of the 1967 coup were found guilty, and the three top leaders of the coup—Generals Papadopoulos, Pattakos, and Makarezos—were sentenced to death. President Karamanlis commuted the death sentences to life in prison, provoking a sharp reaction from opposition political parties and the press. The move was vehemently criticized, especially by the left, who still clamored for revenge for the brutalities of the regime. In response to Karamanlis's decision, Andreas Papandreou said that "with this last act, the government [had] finalized its mockery of the people and of justice and [had] become historically identified with the

Junta."[39] Karamanlis personally had long opposed the death penalty, but he also believed that executions would play poorly in the rest of Europe, and he was committed to gaining Greek membership in the EEC.[40]

Maria Piniou-Kalli introduced me to one of her friends, Cristina Moustaklis, who had testified at the torture trials. Cristina was the wife of a retired Greek officer, Major Spyros Moustaklis, who was left critically injured and mute after being tortured during the dictatorship. Major Moustaklis had received one of Greece's highest military awards, but he was cashiered during the Junta for participating in a resistance movement against the colonels. He was a "star witness" in the torture trial of the EAT-ESA police, but he could barely talk, only gesture and point. In a dramatic appearance, the forty-eight-year-old Moustaklis groaned while he bared his shoulder to reveal the scar of a deep wound—"Muttering 'nai, nai' (yes, yes) and gesturing with his left arm, he tried to show how he had been beaten."[41] His wife Cristina then took the stand. She explained how she had gone every day to the police headquarters, and every day asked for her husband, only to be told that he was not there. Finally, one day, they told her that he was ill and had been taken to the hospital. When she went to the hospital, she found him gravely injured, unable to speak, unable to walk, and with his entire lower body so bruised that it was the color and texture of a liver. The doctors showed her the X-rays. Since she was a dentist, she knew how to read them, and she saw that the date on the X-ray was forty-five days earlier. Every one of those forty-five days when she went looking for him at police headquarters, he was already lying gravely injured. Other witnesses held at the same police headquarters testified that after Moustaklis had suffered a stroke, he was left in a room on the floor for over twenty-four hours without medical attention. One prisoner had been taken to the room and shown the body of Moustaklis—whom he recognized, covered with blood, lying on the floor—as a threat. "Do you want to end up like this—if not, then talk to us now."[42]

Eventually, fifty-five active and retired officers and conscripts were tried in a military court in Athens. In the two major sets of torture trials, thirty-seven of the accused were found guilty, and they were given prison sentences that ranged from the most serious, twenty-three years, to the least serious, three and a half months.[43] In a report on the first trials, Amnesty International commended the government for meeting high standards of jurisprudence and for not allowing the prosecutions to degenerate into show trials. But Amnesty criticized the government for failing to conduct "a thorough, centrally coordinated investigation of the Junta's system of interrogation," and for not following through with more prosecutions.[44] Part of the Karamanlis strategy was to move quickly, so that the main prosecutions ended within a year and a half, and the sentences in the remaining torture trials were often quite lenient. What is extraordinary about the Greek case compared to all the other cases in this book is how quickly the trials moved ahead. The Greeks tried large numbers of individuals, including top leaders of the regime, sentenced many of them, some severely, and finished all this within a year and a half.

The Greek case stands out as the first time that a government held its own officials accountable for past human rights violations. But this is not how the Greek protagonists or scholars remember the prosecutions. When asked why Greece held trials, they continued to say that it was "obvious" that such trials should be held, that there was "no choice," that it was "in the air." It soon became clear that the Greeks did not see these trials as the first example of human rights prosecutions, but rather as a continuation of a long Greek tradition of political trials. This is an example of how movements can use political tradition as a source to create new innovations. When Papandreou said that by commuting the death sentence of the top leaders in the Junta, Karamanlis made a "mockery of justice," he entirely missed the point. When the Greek judiciary insisted on due process and Karamanlis commuted the death penalty, they broke the connection to the old political trials, such as the executions in Goudi in 1922, and set the scene for genuine, modern human rights prosecutions.

Portugal

Although the Portuguese revolution occurred before the Greek transition to democracy, the Portuguese moved more slowly than the Greeks on the issue of accountability, so their story of prosecutions comes historically after the Greek story. When, on April 25, 1974, the rebel officers in Portugal carried out a revolution and initiated a transition to democracy, it was the first transition in what would later be characterized by Samuel Huntington as the "third wave of democratization," when some thirty countries around the world changed from non-democratic to democratic political systems in a short period of time.[45] The young military officers had few models to guide them in how to carry out such a transition. Since Portugal was not a member of the Council of Europe, it had not ratified the European Convention on Human Rights and was not subject to the supervision of the European Commission of Human Rights. Curiously, Portugal did not turn to the Greeks for inspiration. External diffusion of transitional justice was not yet a factor, and internal determinants continued to drive decisions about prosecutions.

Dictator António Salazar had founded the hated political police, PIDE, in 1933. The PIDE headquarters, in what is now the fashionable Chiado district in central Lisbon, was an imposing old structure just down a narrow street from the Brasileira coffeehouse, an Art Nouveau building where writers and intellectuals, including the poet Fernando Pessoa, used to gather. The young military leaders of the revolution had not targeted the PIDE headquarters as a military objective in the first stage of the coup, and no military unit was sent to secure the building. But when the first news of the revolution reached the street in April 1974, a crowd gathered spontaneously and marched to the PIDE headquarters, shouting: "Morte à PIDE!" Eventually, the new government sent in troops to arrest the PIDE officials and carry them away in trucks. Onlookers screamed: "Kill the Assassins!" One man in the crowd shouted: "Don't worry, we won't torture you." On the same day as the revolutionaries freed 77 political prisoners from the notorious prison at Caxias, they filled it up again with 180 PIDE officers.[46]

PIDE's control had extended throughout Portugal and to its colonies. One of the main goals of the revolution of April 25 was to secure a political solution to the colonial wars. By 1974, Portugal was among the last colonial powers with large holdings abroad, its holdings including East Timor, Mozambique, Angola, and Cape Verde. Decolonization thus became one of the main demands of the young military officers who led the revolution, the Armed Forces Movement, or MFA. They had served in the colonial wars, and their experience convinced them that there was no short-term military solution in sight. They wanted self-determination at home and in the colonies, freedom, and the rights of man, but they were divided about the direction in which they wished Portugal to go. Some wanted a transition to liberal democracy; others wanted more radical social and economic change.[47] As a result, unlike almost all the other cases in this book, in the two years after April 25, 1974, Portugal experienced "a revolutionary situation" and a crisis of the state, which was eventually resolved by a transition to democracy. This transition was very unstable: there were two coup attempts, one from the right and one from the left, and constant turmoil as the various factions within the government and within the country vied to control the future of Portugal.[48]

Despite the strong fear and hatred of PIDE in the general population, repression had been relatively selective. A major historian of the Salazar regime, Irene Pimentel, in her meticulously researched history of PIDE, documented that the political police were directly responsible for a total of eleven deaths in custody in Portugal between 1945 and 1974, which was a very small number compared to the thousands killed by the military regimes in Chile and Argentina. This, then, also calls into question the notion that greater repression leads to more extensive use of transitional justice. Portugal had much lower levels of dead and disappeared than Spain, yet Portugal instituted widespread purges and a significant number of prosecutions, while in Spain there was no accountability. Both academics and practitioners agree that PIDE's worst abuses were in the colonies. Torture was widely used by PIDE there, and death under interrogation was a constant reality. Those who survived interrogation were put into prisons and concentration camps, where the terrible living conditions often led to illness and death.[49] No PIDE officials in the colonies, however, were ever brought to trials, in part because many escaped to South Africa after the revolution in Portugal.

PIDE held over 12,000 prisoners between 1945 and 1973, many of whom experienced multiple prison terms.[50] Surveillance of the population was widespread and included tapping telephone lines and intercepting mail. PIDE also had a wide network of collaborators and informers. The perception was that the network was even larger, so the population had the sensation of being under constant surveillance. Torture was common in PIDE prisons, as revealed by later testimony from both victims and PIDE officials. The most common forms included severe beatings, sleep deprivation, simulated executions, and the so-called "statue," where prisoners were forced to stand for long periods of time—some of the same techniques that would later be used by the U.S. military at Abu Ghraib and Guantánamo Bay. Torture was not used on all political prisoners; it tended to be reserved, in particular, for members of the Communist Party.[51] Because levels of repression in Portugal itself were lower than they were in many other cases, and because a relatively small number of PIDE officials were directly involved in torture, there were fewer possible people to prosecute for human rights violations. But many in the population believed that all members of PIDE were guilty of repression.[52] The initial call for "*Morte à PIDE*" became a call of "*Caça aos Pides*" (Hunt PIDE officials). Members began to fear for their safety; some even turned themselves in to the new government because they thought they would be safer in jail than in the streets.[53]

Although the new government had arrested the PIDE officers, it was not clear what it intended to do with them. Most of the top leaders of the regime were permitted to go into exile, mainly in Brazil; thousands of other officials were removed from their jobs, often with little due process. In response to the criticisms of this policy, one of the "Captains of April" who led the revolution, Vasco Lourenço, explained that in the past, instead of purges, new regimes executed those from the past regime. "We didn't want to use executions, so we had to substitute other means of dealing with the past: purges and trials." The new revolutionary regime made very extensive use of purges, but in the end, trials were held only for the PIDE officials, not for other members of the regime. Nonetheless, for some, the PIDE prosecutions "symbolically served to judge the regime in its entirety."[54]

Lourenço claimed that "our intention from the beginning was to judge the crimes of the dictatorship."[55] But Captain Sousa e Castro, another of the "Captains of April," recalls that right after the coup, "no one was thinking of trials. They were thinking of detaining PIDE officials, but not trying them. There was ambiguity in the revolutionary forces." The military government saw the pressure for action from the street as a sign that something had to be done. Trying to come up with this "something," it was seen then as "natural" to submit officials to trials.[56] But trials were simply not an important item in the first years of the Portuguese transition, and human rights was not part of the common discourse at that time. The debate there was not about human rights but about revolution and counterrevolution. The country was polarized between right and left, and by divisions within the left. The new constitution adopted two years later included a specific provision for the prosecution of PIDE officials, largely as a result of the one member of the constitutional assembly from a party of the extreme left.[57] Then, in the hot summer of 1975, a law was passed that retroactively criminalized membership in PIDE. Today, from a human rights point of view, it seems shocking that a government should decide to judge its opponents using retroactive justice that criminalized a whole category of people simply for being members of what was then an official state bureau. At the time, this apparently did not provoke much controversy since many in the population believed that all PIDE officials were guilty.

After a countercoup in November 1975 marginalized the more radical groups and put the centrists in control, Captain Sousa e Castro was named superintendent of the Commission for the Extinction of PIDE. As he took up his new post, Sousa e Castro found that the government was holding about 1,000 PIDE members in prison throughout the country, many of whom had been in jail for over a year without charges and without a trial. In some cases, the conditions were substandard. Family members of PIDE officials started to visit and write Sousa e Castro to complain, saying their relatives were not allowed to read newspapers or watch television, and some had been submitted to abuse and even to simulated executions. Sousa e Castro recounts: "PIDE was the scapegoat." He thought that the law criminalizing PIDE was a "crazy law," but it was the law he had to work with. And he felt that the situation revealed "the great moral problem of the revolution. We had started to treat our enemies in the same manner that the authoritarian regime had treated its enemies." Sousa e Castro believed that it was part of his job to address this moral problem. So he worked to improve the conditions of incarceration of PIDE officials, dismissing many of the jailors believed to be responsible for the abuse. In addition, he asked for and received permission to hire more employees and to constitute new military tribunals just to deal with the backlog of cases. Then, finally, in September 1976 he started the trials.[58]

In most cases, PIDE officials were found guilty but were given relatively light sentences: often they had already served the time of their sentence and were released. These quick trials and light sentences in turn gave the impression to many activists that the new members of the Commission for the Extinction of PIDE were not committed to accountability and justice. The commission became a target of criticism, and Captain Sousa e Castro was called the *defensor dos Pides* (the defender and protector of the PIDEs) in the newspapers rather than the man sent to abolish the organization and deliver accountability. As a result, many individuals who had suffered under PIDE refused to come forward and testify. Some did not want to testify against their torturers and be retraumatized in court; others refused to testify because they said they didn't recognize the legitimacy of the institutions carrying out the process. Because they were convinced that the Commission for the Extinction of PIDE was committed to giving the lightest sentences possible, they refused to cooperate with it. The failure of key witnesses to testify turned these fears into prophecies. The military tribunals were not able to convict without adequate evidence. So, only in a handful of cases like that concerning the murder of General Humberto Delgado, killed in 1968, was sufficient evidence produced to generate a conviction for murder and a long sentence. In this case, the prosecutions were held in absentia, and no one actually went to prison.

The kind of private case that Alexandros Lykourezos filed in Greece could also have been used in Portugal because the legal systems there permit private prosecutions of criminal cases. Yet, in Portugal in the 1970s, individuals did not file private criminal suits to address past human rights violations. None of the sources on the period, nor the scholars who study it, can recall a single case of private criminal prosecution for human rights violations during the authoritarian period. When victims were asked why they hadn't filed private criminal cases, they simply said that it hadn't occurred to them, or they believed that it was more appropriate for it all to be handled in a centralized way by the state through the Commission for the Extinction of PIDE.[59] After almost half a century of authoritarian rule, Portugal simply did not have a liberal rule of law culture or set of practices that would have facilitated such private prosecutions.

The result of this history is that very little is known in Portugal or abroad about the prosecutions of PIDE officials.[60] Having been forgotten by historians, the prosecutions have also been forgotten by the general public, or remembered only with a vague sense that not much was done and that the guilty were let off with the lightest of sentences. Sousa e Castro believes that "because the trials were always seen as too benevolent, with very light sentences and little punishment, the idea stuck that there hadn't been trials at all." Those who did remember the prosecutions remembered them as something that contributed to the whitewashing of the actions of PIDE rather than a process of accountability.[61] Today, finally, this situation is beginning to change. Irene Pimentel, the author of the definitive history of PIDE, is now working on a book about the PIDE prosecutions using the trial archives. Filipa Raimundo, whose MA thesis had been so helpful to my research, is currently working on her PhD thesis on the prosecutions, which will help others become more aware of the topic. In this case, "navigating by sight" led the Portuguese revolution to try out some new processes that were not yet in place around the world. Without any strong external pressure and without defeat in an international war, the Portuguese succeeded, along with the Greeks, in being one of the first nations in the twentieth century to hold some of their own state officials accountable for violations of human rights during a previous authoritarian regime.

Spain

In the cases of Greece and Portugal, prosecutions were possible in part because of a "ruptured" transition. In contrast, the "pacted" transition in Spain was clearly an important part of the explanation for why prosecutions were not possible. Like Portugal, Spain had experienced a very long authoritarian regime, the thirty-nine-year dictatorship of General Franco. But the Spanish experience had been far more violent. Human rights violations were widespread, especially during the Civil War, but also afterwards. A total of between 267,000 and 400,000 prisoners were held in Franquista concentration camps during and after the Civil War,[62] where forced work and executions were commonplace. Recent scholars estimate that the Franco government assassinated approximately 50,000 people *after* the end of the Civil War.[63] Because most of these violations in Spain took place during the Civil War and before the formation of human rights NGOs, there were few definitive reports or campaigns documenting abuse. The severity of the problem, or the absolute number of victims, are thus not convincing factors to explain the trials in Southern Europe. There were clearly more victims in Spain than in either Greece or Portugal, yet most of the Spanish victims had died three decades earlier, so the passage of time made it more difficult for family members to bring cases forward. Further, the passage of time meant that many of the perpetrators were themselves dead or elderly by the time of transition.

Spain had not been a member of the Council of Europe and had not ratified the European Convention on Human Rights, so the commission never worked on the Spanish case. The negotiated transition and the ongoing power and legitimacy of the Franquista forces allowed them to block all efforts at accountability. Franco's supporters were still strong and numerous, and they continued to believe that his regime had saved the country

from godless communism. They watched with alarm as the initially peaceful transition next door in Portugal turned chaotic, and used their remaining power to block any efforts at accountability. Memories of the Civil
War were still vivid, and Spaniards wanted above all to avoid a repetition
of the past. They had had their fill of political trials during the Civil War,
when perfunctory courts-martial often ended in executions and burials
in unmarked graves. During the transition, few in the streets called for
revenge. And after the transition, there were no major purges, no prosecutions, no truth commissions, no museums, nor any other transitional
justice mechanisms. An Amnesty Law was passed in 1977 with almost
unanimous support in the Spanish Parliament.

The Spanish transition was seen as a "paradigm of transition, not only
because of its successful outcome but also because it was carried out
through a democratic, fully inclusive and consensual procedure."[64] But
this paradigmatic transition could not address the human rights violations
of the past. At the time of the transition, it seemed that Spain had put its
past successfully behind it; later, it became apparent that while people had
kept silent, they had not forgotten. Not until 2000 was a group formed
in Spain to call for accountability for the past. The Association for the
Recuperation of Historical Memory estimates that over 30,000 bodies lie
in unmarked mass graves from the Franco period. It has called upon the
government to exhume mass graves, to provide compensation for the families of Franco's victims, and to open all remaining military archives that
include information on executions.[65]

I came to understand the Spanish case better two years after my
research in Greece and Portugal, at a conference organized in 2010 by colleagues at the University of Minnesota on exhumations of mass graves in
Spain. A number of the key protagonists for accountability in Spain came
to participate, including Emilio Silva, the co-founder of the Association for
the Recuperation of Historical Memory. One speaker presented a map of
exhumations in Spain today—showing the country literally covered with
dots representing mass grave sites.

The Spanish presenters stressed the palpable fear about the past, not
only during the Franco regime itself but also decades after the transition
to democracy. This fear intensified in 1981, when right-wing Franquista
forces attempted a coup against the new democratic regime. Two hundred
armed officers burst into the Congress building and held 350 members of

Congress hostage. Only after King Juan Carlos I gave a nationally televised speech in support of democracy was the coup averted. The coup was not provoked by efforts at accountability, but it highlighted the fragility of the new democracy.

Emilio Silva explained that even today in Spain when they go to small villages to talk to the family members of the victims about the exhumations of mass graves, people will close their doors and windows, and speak in a low voice. Silva's grandfather was one of the victims buried in a mass grave, and it was his campaign to locate the body of his grandfather that led him to organize the movement for historical memory. But the fear of speaking of the past was so great even in his own family that Silva never remembers hearing his grandmother mention her husband's death. This unquantifiable fear must be taken into account when we try to explain why some countries can hold prosecutions and others cannot. While we were holding the workshop in Minneapolis, Spanish human rights groups organized the first massive demonstrations in favor of efforts to recuperate historical memory in the nation through exhumations and other judicial means. Sixty thousand people marched in the streets of Madrid. Watching CNN Live from Minneapolis, Silva remarked, "Franco is finally dead," over thirty years after the dictator had died peacefully in his bed.

The regional context of an emerging human rights consciousness, law, and institutions thus formed a permissive context or a regional opportunity structure for human rights prosecutions. All three cases—Greece, Portugal, and Spain—operated within this same structure. Without the regional context, it is unlikely that the trials in Greece and Portugal would have occurred. At the same time, an international legal context was just beginning to emerge for international criminal prosecutions. The Greek domestic trials in 1975 gave a boost to the emerging idea that there should be more accountability for torture. Amnesty International followed the trials closely and translated information about them in Greek newspapers, in the end publishing a report that is still the best concise source on the trials in English or in Greek. Amnesty distributed this report widely, and urged its member sections to try to gain publicity for it.[66] It was serialized in full in at least two Greek newspapers, including a prestigious Athens daily. Amnesty served as a crucial amplifier of the work of Greek civil society and of the state response to its demands. The Greek trials showed that it was possible to hold human rights prosecutions that respected due process without endangering the stability of democracy. Just a few months after the main torture trials in Athens, on December 9, 1975, the countries in the UN General Assembly adopted the Declaration on the Protection of All Persons from Being Subjected to Torture and Other Cruel Inhuman or Degrading Treatment or Punishment (known as the "Torture Declaration"). The Declaration was the starting point for international law on individual criminal accountability for torture, specifically, and for core human rights violations more generally. But the draft declaration mentioned only criminal proceedings under *national* law, making no reference to the possibility of foreign or international accountability. States, ever jealous of their sovereignty, resisted such language, fearing it could encourage international intervention in their affairs. The Greek delegate at the United Nations worked hard to include some language about international implementation because, as he explained, during the dictatorship in Greece "domestic legislation did not suffice," and international condemnation was essential to stop torture.[67] The representatives from the newly democratized governments in Greece and Portugal made important contributions to the UN debates on torture and human rights. The new delegates at the United Nations from Greece and Portugal "were passionate about human rights, and so committed and capable," recalls one Amnesty International staff person who worked in New York in the late 1970s.[68] After approving the Torture Declaration, delegates passed a resolution proposed by Greece, the Netherlands, and Sweden calling on the United Nations to promote further international efforts against torture.[69] They wanted a more binding treaty.

Because these were such early cases of prosecutions, both Greece and Portugal required a set of very fortuitous circumstances to be able to succeed. Navigating without a map, the process succeeded in Greece, floundered somewhat in Portugal, and was completely blocked in Spain. By the 1980s, however, both Greece and Portugal had set a new world precedent by holding some of their own state officials to account for human rights violations. The next chapter focuses on another early adopter of prosecutions, Argentina, where this particular combination of regional human rights institutions, a ruptured transition, and a strong domestic demand for accountability was also crucial. The justice norm was just beginning to emerge.

3

Argentina

FROM PARIAH STATE TO GLOBAL PROTAGONIST

fter the prosecutions in Greece and Portugal during the 1970s, the next major human rights prosecutions took place in Argentina in 1985. On trial were the nine commanders in chief of the armed forces who had served on the Juntas that ruled Argentina from 1976 until 1982.[1] I lived in Argentina during the entire period of the trials against the Juntas, from April 1985 until December of that year. Like my Argentine friends and colleagues, I avidly followed the trials, closely reading the special weekly newspaper, *El Diario del Juicio (The Newspaper of the Trial)*, which was published from May through December 1985. I first saw the young assistant prosecutor for the trials of the three military Juntas in Argentina, a lawyer from the Solicitor General's Office, Luis Moreno-Ocampo, on television. Years later in The Hague, Moreno-Ocampo explained to me that it was a "coincidence" that brought him to work on the prosecutions against the Juntas.[2] Although he was of the same generation as many of the victims of the military regime, he had not been personally touched by the violence. Moreno-Ocampo came from a traditional family in Argentina. On his mother's side, the family was deeply conservative, and the men served in the military. His maternal grandfather had been a general, and his mother's brothers were high-ranking officers. His father was a liberal businessman who had suffered through a bankruptcy when Luis was a young man.

From early in his life Luis showed some entrepreneurial flair; after completing high school, he set up a small furniture company. With the income from his business, Luis supported himself to pursue his real love—the law. He studied at the University of Buenos Aires Law School, specializing in criminal law, and getting to know individuals among the faculty and students who would later play a key role in the trials and in the evolution of transitional justice in Argentina. He entered the judicial system in the 1980s during the dictatorship. In 1984, after the transition, when it became clear that Prosecutor Julio Strassera was going to need help to process the massive number of human rights cases against the military Juntas, he recruited Moreno-Ocampo, one of the few lawyers in the Solicitor General's Office who specialized in criminal law.

Moreno-Ocampo's family background made him aware of what a daunting task the prosecution faced. The prosecutors not only had to convince the judges that the nine Junta leaders on trial, including ex-President General Jorge Videla, had committed crimes and deserved punishment. They also had to convince Moreno-Ocampo's mother and many like her in the Argentine public who didn't believe the military were guilty. Moreno-Ocampo had been working on preparing the case for over six months, but his mother continued to think that he was making a mistake. "I go to church, and I see General Videla there, and I thank him because he saved us from the guerrillas," she would say. His mother's brother, Uncle Bubi, a retired colonel from the army, had personally gone to speak to General Videla when his nephew was assigned to serve as assistant prosecutor. He told Videla that he could not prevent his nephew from working on the trial, but he could give his personal promise to Videla that he would never speak to his nephew again—a promise Uncle Bubi kept until his death.[3]

In Argentina in 1984, just after re-democratization, many people in the population believed either that the military had not committed human rights violations or, if they had, that the violations were necessary in the context of a war against terrorism in which the military had defeated dangerous insurgent groups. They recalled the period just preceding the military coup in 1976 as a time of violence and chaos, when many members of the elite feared that they would be kidnapped by left-wing guerrillas for ransom, or that a bomb would explode in their children's school. Right-wing paramilitary groups had operated with impunity, unrestrained by political authorities. As in the past, civilian elites called upon the military to intervene in politics to establish order. The conservative newspaper *La Nación* editorialized that some military sources believed that if they "continued to abstain from filling the power vacuum," they "could be accused by the judgment of history of criminal neglect."[4] Many ordinary Argentines agreed. What they didn't know was that this military coup would usher in more death and repression than had been experienced at any previous time in modern Argentine history. By 1984, the military were indeed facing the "judgment of history," but not the one they expected. The charge was not criminal neglect but murder, torture, and kidnapping on a scale so large that it was difficult to fathom, let alone prosecute.

Meanwhile, just across the River Plate, Uruguay was undergoing a democratic transition at exactly the same time as Argentina, but events took a different turn on issues of accountability. Uruguay had a "pacted" transition, not a "ruptured" one like in Argentina, and the military were able to impose some conditions. Representatives of Juan María Bordaberry's party, the Colorado Party, and the left-wing coalition, the Broad Front (*Frente Amplio*), negotiated a secret agreement with the military for a transition to democracy. Although the exact contents of the agreement are not known, it is generally agreed that it included some kind of informal guarantee to the military that they would not be prosecuted for human rights violations. When presidential elections were held in 1984, a candidate of Bordaberry's Colorado Party won the presidency, making it less likely that the new government would investigate the abuses of a military government with which it had been associated.

In 1986, the Uruguayan Congress, at the request of the new government, passed a sweeping Amnesty Law that protected the military from prosecution for human rights violations committed during the dictatorship. To the consternation of the human rights advocates with whom he had worked for over a decade in exile, Wilson Ferreira put the support of his wing of the Blanco Party behind the Amnesty Law. He feared, as did many Uruguayans, that the military would carry out a coup if they weren't protected from prosecution. Meanwhile, Uruguayans watched—some with admiration and some with trepidation or disdain—as the Argentines took the chaotic and uncharted path toward accountability with the past. This chapter describes the trials in Argentina and also tries to explain why Uruguayans initially chose a different path.

Phase One: The Argentine Military Regime, 1976–83

After the military coup in 1976, the Argentine military escalated its brutal repression of the opposition, including mass kidnappings, imprisonment without charges, torture, and murder.[5] After re-democratization, the country's truth commission, the National Commission on the Disappeared (CONADEP), initially reported almost 9,000 deaths and disappearances in Argentina during the period 1975–83. The military eventually murdered most of the "disappeared" and buried their bodies in unmarked mass graves, incinerated them, or threw them into the sea.[6]

This massive and systematic use of disappearances was itself a repressive "innovation" on the part of the Argentine armed forces. Disappearances had been used elsewhere, including Nazi Germany; Guatemala during the counterinsurgency war of the late 1960s; and Chile under Pinochet.[7] Nevertheless, the Argentine case marked the most widespread and systematic contemporary use of the practice. Other repressive practices of the Argentine military regime, such as appropriating babies from disappeared women, falsifying their identities, and placing them for adoption in families friendly to the regime, were likewise frighteningly novel.

After failed solitary searches for their loved ones, family members of the disappeared created new human rights organizations. In 1977, the Mothers of the Disappeared (*Madres de la Plaza de Mayo*) and later a group of Grandmothers (*Abuelas de la Plaza de Mayo*) mobilized themselves. The Grandmothers were mothers of disappeared people who were either kidnapped with their children or who gave birth in captivity. The Grandmothers thus sought both their children and their grandchildren.

Along with the groups of Mothers and Grandmothers, a very broad and diverse set of human rights groups developed over time in Argentina, including the Permanent Assembly for Human Rights, the Center for Legal and Social Studies (CELS), the Ecumenical Movement for Human Rights, and the Peace and Justice Service (SERPAJ).[8] All of these groups faced repression, and some of the members were themselves disappeared or imprisoned. These groups had different memberships, strategies and tactics, styles of work, and relationships with other political and social groups. Although they often collaborated, they also disagreed about many aspects of human rights work in Argentina.

When these groups first started working in the mid-1970s, they felt very alone. But over time, they learned to seek help from a handful of international non-governmental organizations like Amnesty International; from the regional human rights institution, the Inter-American Commission on Human Rights; and even from the U.S. government after the election of Jimmy Carter made human rights a priority in U.S.

foreign policy. While working at the Washington Office in Latin America, part of my job was to help these representatives from human rights organizations in Argentina to make contacts during their visits to Washington, D.C. During interviews, they often asked congressional staff to write letters on behalf of their missing or imprisoned family members. Family members in Argentina lived with the constant hope that their disappeared children might still be alive in prisons somewhere in the country. At the time, the goal of the human rights organizations was to locate the disappeared. No one talked about accountability for repression, or retributive justice.

Argentine activists were especially active in relation to the Inter-American Commission on Human Rights (IACHR), which had been founded in 1960 by the Organization of American States (OAS). OAS members had taken a strong stand after World War II: some Latin American states had been among the most persistent advocates of human rights at the San Francisco Conference that drafted the Charter of the United Nations in 1945. Without their support, the Charter might not have had multiple references to human rights. In the OAS, Latin American countries also passed their own American Declaration for Human Rights early in 1948, a few months before the Universal Declaration of Human Rights was approved in the United Nations. Even so, by the 1970s, the OAS was dominated by military regimes, and one commission member referred to it as "a gentleman's anti-communist club."[9] The IACHR was created in response to political events in the region, including the Cuban revolution and the repressive Trujillo regime in the Dominican Republic. In 1969, member states adopted the American Convention on Human Rights, which, when it went into force in 1978, enhanced the role of the commission and created a regional human rights court. Some state actors thought the convention would be a "decoration," believing it would never dare expose actual violations. The Carter administration, however, earmarked funds for the IACHR, which allowed it to hire five new lawyers, buy computers, and establish a specialized library and documentation center. Most important, the commission now had funds for on-site investigations, which it would use to great effect in the case of Argentina.[10]

Yet the new budget and staff would have been for naught without the dynamic commissioners who led the IACHR in the 1970s. There were seven elected members nominated by governments. In the past, these commissioners had mainly been establishment law professors and ex-diplomats who found it hard to condemn governments in the region. But in the seventies a group came together that was unusually committed to human rights. Members from Argentina and Uruguay elected before the military coups were joined by representatives from the few remaining democracies in the region: Venezuela, Costa Rica, Colombia, and the United States. This majority was led first by the Uruguayan jurist Jimenez de Arechaga, and then by the brilliant Venezuelan diplomat Andrés Aguilar, who served on the IACHR from 1972 to 1985 and infused new dynamism into the commission. The IACHR staff, under the leadership of executive secretary Edmundo Vargas Carreño, a Chilean exile, was very committed to human rights. Throughout the 1970s, at least a four-person majority of the seven commissioners turned the commission into an innovator of human rights practice and law. U.S. Commissioner Robert Woodward and his successor, Tom Farer, added their voices to the majority.[11]

Andrés Aguilar was a bon vivant who loved Caribbean music but was also "an eloquent spokesman for democracy." The son of a diplomat, Aguilar held both a law degree from McGill University in Canada and a doctorate in political science. He taught law and served as dean of the law school in Caracas. Aguilar came of age politically during Venezuela's ten-year dictatorship of General Marcos Pérez Jiménez, which was characterized by fraud, corruption, and repression. His sympathy for victims of political repression was heightened by his own experience of being imprisoned in 1956 for opposing the dictatorship.[12] When Pérez Jiménez was overthrown, Aguilar, then only thirty-four years old, became minister of justice of the new democratic government in 1958. He later served as Venezuelan ambassador to the United Nations and as chairman of the UN Commission on Human Rights. He thus arrived at his position as president of the IACHR with wide diplomatic experience. During his early diplomatic career, he saw one Latin American country after another fall to military coups, including the established democracies in Chile and Uruguay. For thirteen years, he applied his considerable charm, and his skill as both a diplomat and a charismatic speaker with a natural ability to give clear and compelling explanations, to the cause of using the IACHR to advance human rights.

In 1979, Aguilar and other IACHR members made an on-site visit to Argentina to gather information for their first major report on the human rights situation there. The commission members and staff met with both government officials and hundreds of victims and their family members; family members stood in long lines for hours in order to talk to them. Argentine human rights activists worked closely with the IACHR to provide testimony for this groundbreaking report. No one was more important for the links between the Argentine human rights groups and the IACHR than Emilio Mignone, whom we first met in Chapter 1.

At 5 a.m. in the morning on May 14, 1976, just two months after the coup, a group of heavily armed men took Mignone's twenty-four-year-old daughter, Monica, from their home in Buenos Aires. The men showed army identification, and Mr. Mignone told his daughter to go with them, saying he would seek her release immediately. Mignone had held a number of influential positions in government, education, and international organizations. Monica was a member of the Peronist Youth organization and was working with a Catholic lay group in a shanty town outside Buenos Aires. At the time, the scale of disappearances was not widely known, and Mr. Mignone had faith in due process. But he and his family never heard another word from Monica. From that time on, Mignone devoted himself to finding his daughter and to pursuing the cause of the disappeared. He was a leader in the Permanent Assembly for Human Rights and a founding member of the Center for Legal and Social Studies, which would later become one of the most important groups working for accountability. Because Mignone had worked in the early 1960s in Washington, D.C., as an official of the OAS, he was a fundamental link between the Argentine human rights community and international organizations, especially the IACHR.

In 1980, the IACHR issued a lengthy country report on Argentina, based on its on-site visit in 1979. The IACHR was the first source to call in print for human rights prosecutions in Argentina. The Argentine military regime initially prevented the report from being distributed in Argentina, but Mignone and CELS helped smuggle many copies into the country to make it available there. In its conclusions, the IACHR twice called upon the government to hold trials, both for deaths and for torture attributed to government officials. Specifically, the IACHR recommended that the Argentine government "initiate the corresponding investigations, to bring to trial and to punish, with the full force of the law, those responsible. . . ."[13]

Today, this seems a simple and obvious recommendation, but it was neither simple nor obvious at the time. Still, this was not the first time that the IACHR had recommended human rights prosecutions. Using quite similar language, the IACHR first proposed that a government prosecute and punish individual perpetrators in its 1974 report of human rights violations in Chile during the Pinochet regime, and then again in a second report on Chile published in 1977.[14] This recommendation was repeated in IACHR reports on El Salvador and on Haiti in 1979.[15] By the time the IACHR made this recommendation in the Argentine case, it was part of the institution's standard repertoire. When the IACHR first recommended trials to Chile in 1974, it did so even before the first domestic human rights trial had been held in Greece. These commissioners were ahead of their time and place in thinking about accountability. They were suggesting something that had never before been done in Latin America: domestic trials of state officials for human rights violations. By one of those unexpected twists of history, the "gentleman's anti-communist club" of the OAS had named commission members so ardent in their mission of promoting human rights that they contributed to the start of the justice cascade.

The human rights groups in Argentina didn't have to wait to read the IACHR report to decide they wanted some kind of justice: many victims shared a desire for trials and retribution. Yet it was still difficult for Argentine citizens to imagine that it was possible to turn their felt need for justice into any practical form, so the IACHR recommendations were important in providing support from a respected international organization.

Even though I had met with individuals from the Argentine human rights movement when I worked at WOLA in the early 1980s, I found it difficult to recall when Argentines began to make the demand for prosecution. In a conversation in an outdoor café in Buenos Aires during one visit, a friend, Carlos Acuña, helped me understand how the demand for trials first appeared in the human rights movement. Today, Acuña is a senior scholar at an important private university in Buenos Aires, but in the late 1970s he was a young member of the Peace and Justice Service (*Servicio Paz y Justicia* or SERPAJ). When the Nobel Committee awarded the 1980 Peace Prize to the head of SERPAJ, Adolfo Pérez Esquivel, it brought great visibility to the organization; but in 1977, when Acuña started working there, it was just one of various human rights organizations struggling during the dictatorship. Acuña attended many meetings with members of other organizations to discuss statements that they would issue in joint petitions and slogans that would appear on banners in their marches. Acuña recalls clearly that before the IACHR report, they had debates about including the demand for "justice" in their petitions.[16] Everyone in the Argentine human rights community agreed that they should include demands for truth and information about the disappeared, but they disagreed, often vehemently, about whether to include demands for justice. "Are you crazy?" asked some. "Are you a provocateur?" Justice was perceived as too dangerous because it implied a demand for punishment of the very leaders who still held power. Activists feared such a demand would bring down the wrath of the regime. SERPAJ and the Mothers of the Plaza de Mayo wanted to include the word "justice," but some of the other groups believed it would be politically irresponsible to be so confrontational with the military. Carlos recalls that while he and his colleagues didn't know exactly what they meant by justice, they did know that they wanted "to throw these guys in jail." In their conversations, they didn't mention other historical precedents like Nuremberg, Tokyo, or Greece. It was truly a local demand. They were criticized for being naive to believe it was possible to hold trials; not many predicted that they would be one of the first countries in the world to prosecute their leaders for human rights violations.

The correspondence of other Argentine activists also reveals that they were hesitant during the dictatorship to demand prosecutions explicitly even in internal letters. In a letter to one of the main groups, a lawyer from CELS denounced the military's position that they had won an irregular war against subversion, and that in such a war, the "victors judge the vanquished, not the other way around." But he did not propose a clear alternative, and only asked, *"Will one ignore the chapter on the responsibility of military authority???"* (emphasis in the original)[17] An internal memo by another CELS advocate, written a year later, in March 1980, after the visit of the IACHR but before the release of its report, was somewhat more explicit. He wrote that one unhelpful way of addressing the issue frequently used at the time was expressed in the question, "Nuremberg: yes or no?" For reasons of "elementary realism," he argued that this was not the right way to pose the question. "The question posed here has a more political character: it is about historical and ethical responsibility, rather than having a purely juridical character." But, while agreeing that there was a pressing need for the human rights movement to "formulate a plan of action," he didn't clarify what exactly that plan should be with regard to prosecutions.[18] Still we learn from this memo that by 1980, the Nuremberg precedent was being discussed in Argentina. It is thus less surprising that General Viola had Nuremberg on his mind when he made his speech in Washington, D.C., early in 1981, claiming that "A victorious army is not investigated. If the Reich's troops had won the last World War, the Tribunal would have been held not in Nuremberg but in Virginia."

Yet by 1983, the demand for "Trials and Punishment for All the Guilty" (*Juicio y Castigo a Todos los Culpables*) became both a slogan and a primary demand of the human rights movement in Argentina. There was another slogan that was also chanted in the demonstrations: *Al paredón, al paredón, ni olvido ni perdon* ("To the wall, to the wall [to be shot by the firing squad]. Neither forgetting nor pardon"). This echoes the Greek and Portuguese street chants to kill perpetrators. Although catchy and rhyming in Spanish, the firing squad chant never achieved the prominence of the slogan for trials and punishment for all the guilty. Argentines in the human rights movement had moved from fear of putting the word "justice" in their slogans to including much more precise words referring to trials and to punishment. They were making the maximalist demand of trials for all the guilty; so here, for the first time, we have citizens chanting a slogan about *human rights* prosecutions.

What had changed to bring this slogan into being, to make it possible to conceive of and demand trials? The IACHR had issued its report, calling for prosecutions and punishment, giving some legal cover to the demands of local groups. But more important, the Argentine military had lost a disastrous war over the Falklands or Malvinas Islands in the South Atlantic in 1982. They had seriously misinterpreted the situation, predicting neither that the United Kingdom would respond militarily to the attack nor that the United States would support its NATO ally. The military were delegitimized not only for their loss in the war but also for their mismanagement of it. Young Argentine conscripts, sent to the Malvinas with inadequate supplies, suffered from cold and hunger to the apparent indifference of their superiors. This delegitimation of the military regime limited the control that the military would have over the conditions of the transition to democracy.

By 1983, human rights advocates in Argentina had settled on the demand for judgment and punishment, and they had begun to flesh out what this would mean in practice.[19] The specifics of the prosecutions emerged after the presidential campaign and the transition to democracy under the new government of Raúl Alfonsín, a centrist politician of the Radical Party. Alfonsín had been a member of one of the key human rights organizations, the Permanent Assembly for Human Rights, during the dictatorship. Initially, however, he did not take a strong position on trials and accountability. Whatever the movement meant by justice and punishment, Alfonsín and his advisers had more modest aspirations. During his electoral campaign, Alfonsín committed himself to seeking justice for human rights violations, but he had to balance this commitment with the desire to integrate the armed forces into the democratic polity and prevent future military coups.

Human rights demands and discourses were a much more prominent part of the Argentine transition than in many other countries in Latin America. Human rights organizations participated actively in the electoral campaigns of various candidates and parties, and huge human rights marches were a constant feature of the transition. On August 19, 1983, for instance, 40,000 people marched in the streets of Buenos Aires to repudiate the military's proposal for a self-amnesty law to protect itself from future prosecution. Alfonsín, already a candidate for the presidency, sent a message of support, but didn't appear at the march. On September 23, the military government signed the complete self-amnesty law for everyone associated with the regime.[20] In a speech on September 30, Alfonsín denounced the self-amnesty and proposed its annulment, saying, "We want the same penalty for the torturer and for the person who commits homicide."[21]

Phase Two: The Alfonsín Government, 1983–89

The transitional justice mechanisms that eventually emerged during the Alfonsín government were the result of interactions between the human rights movement, the government, and the political opposition, each of which was engaged in forms of improvisation in an unfamiliar realm. According to Inés Gonzalez and Oscar Landi, the treatment of human rights violations in Argentina during this period "was a process with a life of its own, the course and results of which escaped the calculations and desires of each of the actors directly involved."[22] After Alfonsín assumed office in 1983, he took a series of key steps to advance the movement toward justice. The most important of these were the revocation of the self-amnesty law; the creation of the National Commission on the Disappeared (CONADEP); and the trial of the military Juntas. There were few historical precedents for each of these moves, meaning the government was essentially inventing new tactics and institutional forms. The terms "truth commission" and "transitional justice," which we use so frequently today, were not yet part of the ordinary lexicon.

Carlos Nino was a brilliant legal theorist who was one of President Alfonsín's advisers on the trials in Argentina. Nino was a philosopher of law, who had taught at the law school of the University of Buenos Aires and received his PhD from Oxford in 1977. In his doctoral thesis, he developed a "consensual theory of punishment which combined retributive and deterrence justifications for punishment."[23] Although the thesis was developed in relation to criminal law and not human rights violations, this model would shape Nino's thinking about the Argentine trials. Nino rejected a pure deterrence model, which only focused on the prevention of future crimes, because it didn't take into account the needs of the victims for retribution. He also rejected a purely retributive model, because to punish everyone responsible for human rights violations ignored the political limits of what was possible.[24]

Nino and his colleague, Jaime Malamud-Goti, were on fellowships at the University of Freiburg in Germany during the last months of the military regime. Watching Argentina from Germany in the midst of the Malvinas/Falklands War, Nino and Malamud-Goti hatched their ideas for human rights trials in Argentina. Perhaps because they were lawyers, they never considered any other form of accountability aside from prosecutions for individual criminal accountability.[25] They took it for granted that if there would be some form of accountability, it would be trials. Upon their return to Buenos Aires in May 1983, the two men set up a series of meetings with political leaders to try to promote the idea of conducting prosecutions. They talked to various candidates, but they hit it off best with Alfonsín. According to Malamud-Goti, they really seemed to "click" with him, perhaps because Nino was a member of Alfonsín's party, and some of Malamud-Goti's family came from Alfonsín's hometown.[26] Over time, a deep respect developed between Nino and Alfonsín, the legal philosopher and the politician.[27] They came to share the same view about the purpose of human rights prosecutions, which focused primarily on the idea of prevention. In his 1996 book, Alfonsín said that the justification for the trials in Argentina was "not mainly punishment, but prevention: to keep this from happening again."[28]

The Alfonsín government had originally planned to give the armed forces sole jurisdiction to prosecute military personnel for human rights violations and then to pardon those sentenced before the end of the administration. But when the government presented its military reform bill to Congress, the opposition added various provisions that hampered the government's ability to limit the scope of trials, including a provision for the mandatory appeal of these human rights cases to a civilian appeals court.[29] When the armed forces failed to make even a minimum good-faith attempt at prosecution, the trials were thus transferred to a civilian court. A leader of the human rights movement and father of a disappeared person, Augusto Conte, was elected as a member of Congress, which allowed him to bring human rights issues directly onto the parliamentary agenda.[30]

No previous trials of the top leaders of authoritarian regimes for violations during their governments had ever been held in Latin America. Thus, when Strassera and Moreno-Ocampo began their work on the trial, they didn't have any road map of how it should be done. Although the Greek trial had been held almost a decade earlier, that model was not present in the minds of the Argentines as they organized their own trial. The Bolivian Congress initiated accountability trials against high-ranking members of the military government of General García Meza in 1984, but the proceedings didn't begin until 1986, and the decisive phase of the trial occurred in 1989–93.[31]

In Argentina, as the trial of the Juntas got underway, the prosecutors used domestic criminal law, not international human rights law, so that they could not be accused of retroactively applying the law. The prosecution relied heavily on the CONADEP truth commission report, which shows that truth commissions and prosecutions are not necessarily two separate mechanisms but can be complementary and mutually reinforcing. The truth commission staff helped do a pre-selection and forwarded 1,500 cases where the evidence could establish the responsibility of the military leaders. Of these, the prosecution decided to focus on just over 700 cases of murder, kidnapping, and abuse for which sufficient evidence was available to establish the responsibility of the top level of the military government.[32] As part of the effort to provide evidence for the trial of the Juntas, forensic experts led a project of exhumation of graves of the disappeared.

The public phase of the trial lasted for seven months in 1985, was attended by large numbers of members of the public and the press, and produced a vast historical record.[33] The prosecutors knew that the eyes of the nation were upon them, so they proceeded carefully. The most powerful cases were presented first, including those of victims who had no connection to the guerrilla movements. Moreno-Ocampo, for example, was particularly moved by the case of Pablo Díaz, one of a group of high school students kidnapped because of their activism. Although the group was called Guevarist Youth, their main activity had been trying to get a discount bus ticket for students. Moreno-Ocampo first met Pablo when he was interviewing hundreds of victims in the early months of 1985 to select the cases they would present at the trial. Pablo was sixteen when he was kidnapped from his home in the middle of the night in the presence of his entire family, taken to a secret detention center, tortured, and eventually detained for three years before being released. He was one of only two survivors of the kidnapped members of his group of students. When the prosecution team asked him if he and his family would be willing to testify publicly, he originally said he couldn't do it.

"I don't know if I want my case to be made public," he said. "Up until now, except my family, nobody knows what happened to me. . . . I don't want to have problems getting work and have people give me strange looks. The other day, the father of my girlfriend was watching a TV program about CONADEP, where different victims told what had happened to them, and he could not believe it. At one point, he asked me, 'Hey, Pablito, do you think this can be true?' I answered yes, that I thought so. Of course, I didn't say anything about what had happened to me. Not even my girlfriend knows."[34] The girlfriend's father, like Moreno-Ocampo's mother, couldn't believe that the Argentine military were capable of committing such crimes. Even the CONADEP truth commission report, and the TV programs based on the report, had not been able to convince them.

Eventually, Pablo and his family agreed to testify. In the courtroom during the first weeks of the trial, he explained that at his kidnapping he was taken from his home blindfolded, thrown to the floor of a car on top of another prisoner, and driven to a secret detention center. When they were questioning him, they said they were going to "put him on the machine." Thinking they meant a lie detector, he said "good," because it would convince them he was telling the truth. He discovered "the machine" meant torture with an electric prod; when they applied it to his lips and gums, and his genitals, he could smell the odor of burning flesh. They kept asking him for the names of his classmates in the group. Later, they tortured him again. He was close to fainting when he felt a terrible pain in his foot; it was his toenail being pulled out with pliers. The pain was so extreme that he asked them to kill him.[35]

The case of the kidnapped high school students later became a cause célèbre in Argentina and the topic of a best-selling book and a film, both entitled *The Night of the Pencils*; but the case was virtually unknown at the time Pablo testified. The prosecution's strategy of stressing the innocent victim—the victim who was not a member of the guerrilla organizations—was underscored by another witness who also testified in the early weeks of the trial. Magdalena Ruiz Guiñazú, a journalist and member of the CONADEP, responded to an aggressive question from a defense lawyer with her own questions. She asked: "Were the 127 disappeared children terrorists? . . . Is it lawful to torture, kill, and make people disappear? No. And for as long as I live, I will continue believing that those who did this are the worst kind of criminal." The room was silent for a moment. You could hear a judge clear his throat. Interviewed later, Prosecutor Strassera considered it "brilliant testimony" because she gave a "moral lesson." Strassera knew that much more than punishment and deterrence were at stake in his trial. This was drama of the highest level, and Pablo Díaz and Magdalena Ruiz Guiñazú were eloquent players.[36]

Hannah Arendt, in her *Eichmann in Jerusalem* (1963), had recognized and criticized this quality of theatricality in trials. The purpose of the trials, she argued, was to produce justice, not to provide a showcase for the suffering of victims. The prosecution team in Argentina, by limiting the trial to seven hundred cases with the best evidence, focused on providing the evidence to do justice. But they knew they had to win the hearts and minds of the public, as well as persuade the judges.

Many of the dead and disappeared in Argentina were members of various guerrilla organizations, in particular the largest Peronist insurgent group: the Montoneros. They too had their day in court, especially when the prosecution turned to the case of the Escuela Mecánica de la Armada, where the head of the navy, Admiral Emilio Massera, had imprisoned a group of Montoneros. The broader point the prosecutors made was that no one could be submitted to torture or summary execution.

In the end, five of the nine leaders of the Juntas were convicted. The two most important leaders of the first Junta, General Videla and Admiral Massera, were sentenced to life in prison. Massera, former head of the navy and Junta member, was, after Videla, the second most powerful leader in Argentina during the most intense period of repression. The remaining three were sentenced to between four and a half and seventeen years in prison.[37]

Two weeks after the trial began, Moreno-Ocampo received a phone call from his mother. "I still love Videla," she said, "but you're right and he has to go to prison." Moreno-Ocampo commented later, "It was the hearings with victim testimonies that convinced her, not her son. The judicial ritual is very important. It is a neutral ritual that gives order to society."[38] If the trials prevent future human rights violations, as Alfonsín and Nino had hoped, it will not only be because they punish the perpetrators. It is also because the ritual or symbolism of a trial, the evidence presented, and the apparent neutrality of the process convinces broader parts of society that the perpetrators deserve punishment. This symbolic element is even more important in human rights prosecutions than it is in ordinary criminal trials.[39] It would have been difficult for the Argentine military to commit human rights violations on that scale without the military coup in 1976. And many Argentines wanted the military coup—indeed, they practically knocked on the doors of the barracks asking the military to intervene. When the repression started, many Argentines didn't want to know what was happening, and made efforts to avoid knowing. Even when the military regime ended, many, like the mother of Luis Moreno-Ocampo, believed the military had saved them from terrorism. So the trials were a national event, a public spectacle that had the purpose of punishing the guilty, reaffirming certain norms, and creating a national understanding of the past.

After the trial of the Juntas was completed, the judiciary continued to work on a wide range of other human rights cases involving lower-level officials. The government had initiated the trial of the Juntas, but most of the new cases were brought forward by victims and their lawyers, using provisions for private prosecution in Argentine criminal law. As a result, the executive couldn't control the process. Instead of just the nine Junta leaders, as Alfonsín had intended, almost three hundred officers faced prosecutions in civil courts. The expansion provoked unrest in the Argentine military and led sectors to carry out coup attempts against the Alfonsín government. Fear gripped the population. As one citizen remarked: "Twenty thousand people disappeared after the last coup. How many will it be this time?" Many inside and outside the government believed that Alfonsín's first task was to preserve democracy, and that the concern with transitional justice had gone too far.

As opposed to the past, this time the great bulk of the civilian population did not support the coups, but instead rallied behind the government. During the coup attempt of Easter week in 1987, hundreds of thousands of people gathered before the Congress building in central Buenos Aires in support of the civilian government.[40] Despite this support, the Alfonsín government believed it had to give in to military pressure to save the democratic government; it passed a law that was essentially an amnesty (the Due Obedience law) that blocked future trials.

This was a formative moment for the global transitional justice movement, because many analysts and politicians concluded from the Argentine experience that domestic human rights prosecutions were not viable because they would provoke coups and undermine democracy. But such an analysis misinterprets the actual sequence of events in Argentina. In Argentina, the nine Junta members were tried, and five were convicted. The coup attempts did not begin until more far-reaching trials against junior officers were initiated. So, to read the Argentine case as an example proving that prosecutions in themselves are not possible is to disregard the successfully completed trial of the Juntas and the degree to which the Argentine military has since been subordinated to civilian control. After Alfonsín left office, the government of Carlos Menem pardoned the convicted military officers in jail. Many interpreted this pardon as still another indication that the trials had been futile. But the pardons did not reverse the trials or the sentences. In the words of two of the most astute observers of the Argentine trials, despite the concessions granted by Alfonsín and Menem, the "high costs and high risks suffered by the armed forces as a result of the investigations and judicial convictions for human rights violations are central reasons for the military's present subordination to constitutional power."[41]

Phase Three: 1989—The Present

Phase Two ended with the Due Obedience law and with Menem's presidential pardons of the members of the Juntas. In many other countries, these kinds of setbacks silenced human rights activists' demands for accountability. Resilient Argentine activists, though, responded with more innovations. It was as if the very act of having their aims opposed and blocked renewed the commitment of Argentine groups to continue their struggle. Interestingly, some scholars have argued that facing such opposition can have the paradoxical effect of multiplying memories of atrocities and thus spurring action.[42]

In addition, existing human rights groups turned to regional and foreign institutions when progress on accountability was blocked in Argentina. In a book on transnational activism that I wrote with Margaret Keck, we discussed something we called a "boomerang effect," where domestic social movements reach out to international allies to gain leverage and to bring pressure to bear on their government from the outside.[43] I first learned about boomerangs watching the Argentine human rights movement form transnational linkages in the 1980s.[44] When Argentine groups were blocked by the amnesty laws from pursuing trials in their domestic courts, they did a judicial version of the boomerang: they sought out judicial allies abroad to pressure their government at home. CELS brought a case to the IACHR, which in 1992 concluded that the Argentine amnesty laws and the pardons issued by President Menem for crimes committed during the dictatorship were incompatible with the American Convention on Human Rights.[45] They also sought judicial allies abroad and brought their cases to foreign courts, especially in Spain, but also in Italy, Germany, and France, opening up some of the first foreign human rights prosecutions.

Meanwhile, domestically, organizations continued their innovative legal challenges. The legal team for the Grandmothers of the Plaza de Mayo worked to hold military officers responsible for the kidnapping and identity change of the children of the disappeared, who in many cases had been given to allies of the military regime. The Grandmothers' lawyers argued that because the crimes of kidnapping minors and changing their identity had not been covered in the amnesty laws, they could be litigated. This legal maneuver became one of the wedges that domestic groups used to breach the amnesty laws. The strategy began to succeed by the mid-1990s, but initially most of those found guilty were lower-level military and some members of the adoptive families.[46]

In 1998, federal judges in Argentina ordered preventive detention for both ex-President General Videla and Admiral Massera. Both had been sentenced to life in prison in the trial of the Juntas, and both had benefited from Menem's pardon. They couldn't be tried a second time for the same offense, but this time they were accused of kidnapping babies and falsifying public documents. The context and timing of both Videla's and Massera's arrests suggests that Argentine judges may have been influenced by foreign trials in France and Spain.[47] To fend off political pressures to extradite many officers to Spain, some Argentine judges apparently decided to place a few high-profile but politically marginalized officers like Videla and Massera in preventive detention.

Perhaps the most challenging of the legal battles was another private prosecution case led by CELS to have the amnesty laws declared unconstitutional. The case was against a member of the Argentine Federal Police, Julio Simón, who was involved in the 1978 kidnapping, torture, and murder of José Poblete and his wife Gertrudis, along with the abduction of their eight-month-old daughter, Claudia, who was stripped of her identity and turned over for adoption to a military family. According to the testimony of survivors, Simón wore a keychain with the swastika symbol and made the detainees listen to Nazi anthems. Although Poblete had lost both his legs in an accident, Simón tortured him and even threw him down the stairs in the detention center. Two CELS lawyers, María José Guembe and Carolina Varsky, litigated the case, using private prosecution to continue to force open the process of accountability. At about five foot one, with long, straight hair that gives her the appearance of a younger woman, María José Guembe doesn't look like someone the Argentine military would have expected to finally break the back of their impunity. But she was already an experienced lawyer by the time she took on the Poblete case. Guembe and Varsky argued that the amnesty laws put the Argentine judicial system in the untenable position of being able to find people criminally responsible for kidnapping a child and falsely changing her identity, but not for the more serious crime, the murder and disappearance of the parents (which gave rise to the crime of kidnapping). Additionally, they argued that the amnesty laws were a violation of international and regional human rights treaties to which Argentina was a party, and which were directly incorporated into Argentine law. Federal Judge Gabriel Cavallo found the arguments compelling, and wrote a judgment that was a lengthy treatise on the significance of international human rights law in Argentine criminal law.[48]

Pablo Parenti, who was working for Judge Cavallo at the time, explained that the importance of the case was not just that it invalidated the amnesty, but that it did so combining arguments from domestic law with arguments from regional human rights law, especially the Inter-American Court and the Inter-American Commission on Human Rights. He was not aware of any precedents of other national courts invalidating an amnesty law in this way.[49]

Argentina offered a propitious environment for this kind of decision because the 1994 Constitution gave international human rights treaties constitutional status, and because the courts had earlier found that customary international law could be applied by domestic courts. CELS solicited international groups to write amicus briefs for their cases, thus succeeding in establishing for the first time in the Argentine judicial system the practice of using foreign amicus briefs. An appeals court supported Judge Cavallo's decision in the Poblete case. In 2003, before the case reached the Supreme Court, the Argentine Congress, with the support of the Kirchner administration, passed a law that declared the amnesty laws null and void.

In June 2005, the Argentine Supreme Court, in a 7–1 majority vote, declared in the Poblete case that the amnesty laws were unconstitutional. The Court cited jurisprudence from the Inter-American Court of Human Rights that limited the ability of member state legislation to enact amnesty laws for crimes against humanity. The Supreme Court also decided that the crime of disappearance was a crime against humanity for which there are no statutes of limitations. The effect of the Court's decision was to permit the reopening of hundreds of cases that had been closed for the past fifteen years. Between 2005 and 2010, these cases have progressed through the courts, leading to multiple convictions. Because Argentine democracy was now more consolidated and the judicial system more experienced, few people argued, as they had in the past, that these trials were threatening to democracy.

While Argentina followed this path of human rights prosecutions, Uruguay and neighboring Brazil, which experienced transitions at the same time, took different paths. The human rights violations of the Uruguayan dictatorship were on a different scale than those in Argentina. Repression in Uruguay was not characterized by legions of disappeared people; instead, the military implemented a program of far-reaching arrests, routine torture of prisoners, and complete surveillance of the population. In 1976, Amnesty International estimated that 60,000 people had been at one time arrested and detained in Uruguay; one out of fifty Uruguayans had been through some period of imprisonment since the coup; and many had been tortured. Yet the military had killed or disappeared fewer people than in the neighboring countries of Argentina and Chile. The unofficial report published after re-democratization, *Uruguay: Nunca Más*, listed 131 people killed by security forces, including 32 cases of death under torture, and 166 disappearances, only 33 of which occurred in Uruguay.[50]

After the Uruguayan Congress passed the immunity law in 1986, Uruguayan citizens and human rights groups organized a campaign to gather a half-million signatures to force a popular referendum on the law. The fact that the campaigners were able to collect so many signatures in a country of only 3 million people speaks to the power of human rights norms in Uruguayan society. The vote took place in April 1989, and the results were a blow to the accountability movement. Nationwide, 54 percent of the population voted to retain the law giving the military immunity from prosecution for human rights violations. In Montevideo, the capital city, with one half of the country's citizens, only 42.5 percent voted for immunity. Many Uruguayans were afraid, given the posture of the military during the referendum campaign, that if the law were overturned, it would lead to another military coup.[51] And their fears were heightened by recent events in Argentina. The 1987 Easter week coup attempt in Argentina had led President Alfonsín to adopt amnesty laws there. How could prosecutions work in Uruguay if they hadn't been able to move ahead in Argentina?

Over time, some human rights groups in Uruguay interpreted the vote as a democratic—and thus legitimate—decision against accountability. As opposed to Argentina, where the self-amnesty was passed by the authoritarian government, here the amnesty law was passed by a democratically elected Parliament, and then ratified by a popular referendum. "*El pueblo habló*" (The people have spoken), Uruguayan human rights activists would sometimes tell me when I asked them about the possibility of prosecutions.

Initially, Argentina had stood alone in the region as the country that attempted extensive human rights prosecutions. Only Bolivia, after another ruptured transition, followed the same path, eventually trying and convicting a number of the main leaders of the military government that had ruled from July 1980 until August 1981, including the former dictator General García Meza. So important was the nature of the transition for the Bolivian process of transitional justice that the main scholar of the trials concluded: "Only with this type of transition, a transition through rupture, or total collapse, as occurred in both Argentina and Bolivia, has it historically been possible to open the space necessary to bring military dictators to justice."[52]

Some aspects of the political context within Argentina made it possible for Argentines to innovate in the area of human rights and transitional justice. The first of these is the level of repression. The Argentine case was unique in that the repression was extreme, but not so extreme as to eliminate all possibilities for activism. The military regime in Argentina killed more people than did the regimes in Chile, Brazil, and Uruguay. Guatemala endured far greater repression than Argentina or any other country in the region, and the repression was so severe that it eliminated or silenced the human rights movement there.[53]

Second, the nature of the transition itself also influenced whether or not activists were able to demand more accountability. Like Greece and Portugal, Argentina experienced a "ruptured" transition, in contrast to Chile, Uruguay, and Brazil, which were all "pacted" transitions. Because the Argentine military regime collapsed after its defeat in the Falklands/Malvinas War, the armed forces were not able to negotiate the conditions of their exit from power. This helps explain why it was possible for Argentina to hold trials for the Juntas almost immediately after the transition, and why it was more difficult to hold such prosecutions elsewhere. Because both Uruguay and Brazil had pacted transitions, which strengthened the position of the former authoritarian leaders to control events afterwards, it was more difficult for them initially to hold prosecutions.

But these two starting points—the level and nature of repression and the type of transition—only get us part of the way in explaining the very high level of Argentine innovation. The Argentine case also illustrates a point frequently made by social movement theorists: political opportunities don't just exist in the abstract but need to be perceived and constructed by activists.[54] The political actors in Argentina faced a more conducive context for their demands after the transition to democracy, yet these groups were also more likely than some of their counterparts in other countries to perceive and create political opportunities.

The early trial of the Juntas in Argentina contributed to an increase in judicialization there. Since 1985, there has been a significant increase in the number of cases submitted to the Supreme Court and to federal and state courts. The trial of the Juntas encouraged "the discovery of law," as ordinary citizens began to perceive the legal system as more viable and legitimate if it could be used to hold the most powerful former leaders of their country accountable for past violations.[55] People observed that if the law could be applied even to the powerful, maybe they could use it to pursue their own goals.

Similarly, the structure of the judicial system in Argentina may have provided more leeway for legal innovation. The Argentine system permits judges to enter into the judiciary at various points in their career. In Chile, by contrast, for many years there was just one career track for becoming a judge, and aspiring judges had to choose it straight out of law school and spend their entire career working their way up the institutional ladder. The discipline and promotion of judges within the institution was controlled by the conservative Supreme Court. As a result, Chilean judges learned that they had to follow the line advanced by the Supreme Court that human rights trials were "political" and thus should be avoided by an ideally apolitical judiciary. Argentine judges had somewhat more autonomy, and this may have given them more room for independent judicial decisions in human rights prosecutions than colleagues elsewhere.[56]

Another institutional feature of the Argentine legal system also appears to be important. Some civil law systems like Argentina's have provisions for "private prosecution" in criminal cases. As a researcher, it took me a long time to understand and even find the right word in English for this practice because in our common law countries, state prosecutors are solely responsible for bringing forward criminal cases. In the United States, for example, victims can be plaintiffs in civil cases for damages, but they do not play a direct role in initiating criminal prosecutions. Common law systems operate this way because they stress that a crime is against the whole society, not just against the victim. But, where the government controls access to criminal prosecutions, unsurprisingly it may be more difficult to initiate cases against government officials. In civil law systems with private prosecution, victims and their allies can help initiate criminal prosecutors or can accompany state prosecutors in these cases. In a judicial system with strong private prosecution provisions, like that in Argentina, victims can insist that a prosecution continue, even when the state prosecutor would like it dropped. The private prosecution option may help explain why more human rights trials occurred in Argentina than in Uruguay, for example. Uruguay remains one of the few countries in the Americas that does not have provisions for private prosecution in criminal cases, and the lack of this provision made it almost impossible for lawyers representing victims to push cases forward when the state prosecutors were unwilling.

Although in the early cases of prosecutions—Greece, Portugal, and Argentina—it was necessary to have a ruptured transition in order to move ahead promptly on prosecutions, *by the 1990s, a ruptured transition was no longer a precondition* for prosecutions, and eventually countries with pacted transitions, such as Guatemala, Chile, and Uruguay, also began to be able to use prosecutions. This illustrates a crucial point in these stories: *the political world is not static.* Human agency has the capacity to transform the conditions within which political action takes place. The very fact that some countries had been able to hold their state officials accountable began to change the terrain of expectations in which other countries operated. Prosecutions were objectively threatening to powerful state officials. But fear of prosecutions was also subjective. People expected prosecutions to be dangerous, so they avoided them. But those expectations were just guesses about what might happen; they were not iron laws. The early cases of prosecutions altered people's expectations about the effects of trials; by altering such expectations, they made it more likely that citizens would be less fearful and more emboldened to demand justice.

Part II

SPREADING IDEAS ABOUT
INDIVIDUAL ACCOUNTABILITY

Interlude

HOW AND WHY DOES THE ARGENTINE
EXPERIENCE SPREAD?

U p to this point, I've been talking about the early emergence of the idea and practice of individual criminal accountability in Greece, Portugal, and Argentina. Now I want to turn to the discussion of how and why these ideas about accountability began to diffuse around the globe. It is appropriate to begin that discussion with Argentina because it was important to the universal spread of the idea of individual criminal accountability.

Argentina has been more than just another case in the literature on transitional justice. Argentina helped invent the two main accountability mechanisms that are the focus of much of the debate on transitional justice: truth commissions and high-level human rights prosecutions. Transitional justice strategies do not have to be homegrown to be effective, but the Argentine case illustrates that important innovations have come and can come from diverse sources. The Argentine model also suggested that mechanisms like truth commissions and prosecutions need not be mutually exclusive options, but can be beneficially combined. Indeed, Argentines innovated a type of trial—the truth trial—that actually combines elements of trials and truth commissions. More recently, Argentine lawyers and judges have innovated judicial strategies for declaring its amnesty laws unconstitutional, thus permitting blocked human rights prosecutions to proceed. Other countries are beginning to follow suit, as evidenced by similar efforts in Chile and Uruguay to undermine the application of amnesty laws.

The three cases discussed in the first part of this book differ in how well their experience with prosecution spread to the rest of the world. The experience of the prosecutions in Portugal didn't diffuse; the idea of the Greek trials spread through some legal, academic, and activist networks, but never reached the broad public; by contrast, awareness of the Argentine prosecutions spread globally, though not necessarily as an example to emulate. The Greek case was important for the European human rights system and for the early work of Amnesty International, but neither the Greek nor the Portuguese case left a lasting impression on Latin America or the world. From time to time, Luis Moreno-Ocampo would claim that the Argentine trials were the first in the world, forgetting to mention the Greek precedent. This may have been because he was so deeply involved in the Argentine trials; but if the Greek case had served as a strong precedent for Argentina, the assistant prosecutor of the Argentine trials would not have failed to mention it. Even Wolfgang Kaleck, a major German lawyer who has been litigating foreign human rights issues in German and other European courts since 1998, understands the Argentine trials to be far more important precedents than the physically closer but much less well known trials in Greece and Portugal.[1]

But why were the Argentines more successful in diffusing their model than the Greeks or the Portuguese had been? First, Argentina was operating in a region where dozens of other countries were undergoing transition at the same time. Thus, the Latin American region was primed to respond to the Argentine experience. Second, the Argentine human rights movement had inserted itself more firmly within the consolidating international movement. In the mid-1970s, when the Greek and Portuguese prosecutions took place, the human rights movement was just getting off the ground. Although Amnesty International helped publicize the Greek trials, there were not many other groups to help disseminate the idea of prosecutions. There were virtually no human rights groups in Greece and Portugal, and perhaps as a result, no one there took up the task of spreading the idea of the trials.

In other words, people spread ideas and practices, and they have to believe in them enough to want to spread them. The Greeks, as we saw, doubted whether their prosecutions were novel practices at all, and the Portuguese were ambivalent about whether justice even occurred. The debates in both countries in the 1970s were mainly framed in terms of the traditional right vs. a more radical left. For the left in both countries, the prosecutions were always too little, too late. For the right, the prosecutions were messy and unnecessary. In Portugal, as we have seen, the experience was almost forgotten. The world was transfixed by the example of the transitional and potentially revolutionary situation in Portugal after 1974, but not by the more mundane practice of trials that came several years after the transition. Few people wrote about the Portuguese trials at any length or talked about the trials as a positive example within Portugal, much less outside.

When I interviewed the major architect of the Portuguese prosecutions, Captain Sousá e Castro, he told me that no foreign journalists or academics had ever interviewed him before about his transitional justice work. He admitted that the Portuguese left remembered him as the defender of the PIDE officials, not the person who brought some limited justice. In Greece, the archivists in the Karamanlis Library couldn't locate any documents for me about the decision to hold prosecutions. The Greek authors of one of the most important articles in English about the trials never translated that article into Greek. It seemed there was just not enough interest. Most of the international awareness of the Greek experience came through the Amnesty International report on the trials, and the discussion of the Greek trials by Samuel Huntington, the brilliant, conservative Harvard political science professor who had named and drawn attention to the global trend toward democracy in his widely cited book, *The Third Wave: Democratization in the Late Twentieth Century.*

By 1985, when Argentina tried its top leaders for human rights violations, the global human rights movement was gaining strength and stability, and diverse groups spread the news of the Argentine experience with prosecutions. Other countries responded both positively and negatively to the Argentine experience. In this sense, the Argentine case created great controversy, and thus drew attention to the model, for better or worse. Finally, individual Argentine citizens and others familiar with the Argentine experience moved around the globe and carried their knowledge with them. In contrast, neither the Greeks nor the Portuguese worked actively to diffuse and normalize their experience.

Argentine human rights activists were not passive recipients of a justice cascade, but the pioneers and propagators of multiple new tactics and transitional justice mechanisms. The human rights innovations are so extensive that I consider Argentine social movement activists and members of the Argentine government to be among the most important protagonists in the area of human rights accountability. Argentines then actively worked to spread their institutional and tactical innovations abroad, though they didn't necessarily do so because they were satisfied or proud of their accomplishments. Often Argentines spread their innovations inadvertently because they were dissatisfied with their shortcomings and sought out international avenues to extend or reinitiate prosecutions.

In most of these endeavors, the Argentine groups didn't work in isolation. There is extensive documentation of the transnational linkages of the Argentine human rights movement.[2] As we saw in Chapter 1, in the late 1970s the legal and institutional framework for human rights was rather new and still quite inert. It existed as a possibility, but its potential had not yet been actualized or set into motion. Activists from countries like Argentina and Chile—with the support of state and non-governmental allies, mainly from Europe and the United States—were crucial in making use of the opportunities presented by these institutions, transforming them from potential into actual mechanisms for change. The single most important international institution in the case of Argentina was the IACHR, which produced a pioneering report on human rights in Argentina that first recommended that state officials be tried and punished for their crimes. The IACHR had made the recommendation before, but Argentina was the first country to follow through on it.

To focus mainly on the transnational dimension of these struggles, though, may sometimes blur the question of where the initiative arises. On many occasions, the impetus for such networking came from inside Argentina. Argentine groups sought out international linkages and brought them into human rights work in Argentina. Thus, the Argentine case makes clear that norm cascades don't only begin in the wealthy North, but can also be initiated by innovative countries in the global South.

The Argentine case set into motion a series of actions and reactions. The Chileans, for example, explicitly designed their justice strategy to avoid what they considered the "mistakes" of the Argentine experience. They would have truth and reconciliation with a truth commission, but not individual criminal accountability through trials. This strategy held firm from 1990 until 1998, when General Pinochet was arrested in London. The South Africans considered the Argentine, Chilean, and Salvadoran examples, and designed an innovative strategy that they hoped would provide a better combination of the search for truth, justice, and reconciliation. The

South African Commission for Truth and Reconciliation was designed to give amnesty only to those perpetrators who came forward and told the whole truth about their involvement in human rights violations. In principle, perpetrators who did not come forward or did not tell the truth could be prosecuted. Transitional justice had become an international affair, and the particular choices that domestic actors made were conditioned but not determined by prior choices elsewhere.

The key ways in which the Argentine human rights movement spread its innovations were through publications, the media, and the actual movement of individuals to new positions. Most important, the Argentine experience illustrates that early diffusion happens through individuals, and in particular, through the networks in which individuals operate. The networks that led to the diffusion of these ideas were like the expanding ripples of raindrops on a lake: each person in the network helped form and connect to new networks that sent the ideas further out into the world. The human rights organizations, the truth commission, and the trial of the Juntas trained a generation of activists and human rights professionals, many of whom went on to innovate and practice their skills elsewhere. Many of these Argentines were later tapped for leadership roles in international activities and became brokers connecting activists in different parts of the world.

Most famously, Luis Moreno-Ocampo is now the chief prosecutor of the International Criminal Court, one of the most important jobs in the international human rights world today. Moreno-Ocampo says that he thought the trial of the Juntas would be his life's work, but he later learned that it was just "training" for his work at the ICC. The legal and political lessons he learned in Argentina now inform his day-to-day work. In particular, in Argentina, he learned to investigate cases without the help of the police, since the police there were often implicated in the crimes. This skill comes in handy at the ICC because the Court does not have its own police force. He also learned how to carry out prosecutions while in the process of constructing rule of law. In developed countries, Moreno-Ocampo says, prosecutors take for granted stability and acceptance of the law. In Argentina and at the ICC, he has learned the more difficult task of prosecuting in a context where new law is under construction. Finally, the Argentine experience prepared him to operate in a context where conflict and criticism are a constant part of his work, which helped him weather the many attacks on the ICC and on his performance.[3]

Juan Méndez, the former political prisoner during the dictatorship who was my mentor in my early work in Washington, D.C., has occupied more important positions in international non-governmental and intergovernmental organizations than almost any other major human rights activist. Méndez moved from top positions in NGOs like Human Rights Watch and the International Center for Transitional Justice, to positions in the Inter-American system and the United Nations. During the fifteen years that he worked at Human Rights Watch, he proved essential in bringing a deep understanding of the trials in Argentina and elsewhere in the region into the premier U.S.-based organization.

The career of another Argentine, Patricia Tappatá de Valdez, is a vivid illustration of how diffusion works through individuals in networks who form bonds of trust. During the Argentine dictatorship, she lived in Peru, and eventually became the director of one of the most important human rights organizations there, the *Comisión Episcopal de Acción Social*. Patricia did not live in Argentina during the period of the truth commission or the trial of the Juntas, but she followed them avidly from afar. Her brother and his family had been imprisoned during the dictatorship, and she felt a deep personal as well as professional connection to the cause of justice and accountability. In 1992, Patricia returned to Argentina to work in a new human rights organization there, *Poder Ciudadano* (Citizen Power), which was led by Luis Moreno-Ocampo, in his main work after the trial of the Juntas.

The United Nations was in the process of setting up the Truth Commission on El Salvador, only the third of its kind in Latin America, and the first ever implemented by the United Nations. When UN officials were looking for a person to head up the staff of the newly formed truth commission, Patricia's name was suggested to a top aide to the Peruvian UN secretary-general, Perez de Cuellar, by a Peruvian human rights lawyer who was working at the UN at the time. The commission itself was comprised of three international commissioners, all senior diplomats and jurists, chaired by former Colombian president Belisario Betancur. But the day-to-day work of the commission was done by the staff, headed by an executive secretary. In 1992, the secretary-general named Patricia executive secretary of the commission. When she arrived in New York to begin the process of setting up the truth commission, Patricia discovered that little preparation had been done. She recalls that they handed her a thin file with the results of a brainstorming session that had included Juan Méndez and a handful of other NGO experts. Her employers at the UN assumed she would know about the Argentine Truth Commission, because she was from Argentina.[4]

Just as members of her network came up with Patricia's name for the United Nations, Patricia in turn drew upon her networks to compose her small staff and to establish trust with the NGO community in El Salvador when she arrived there. She is convinced that her prior work with the Catholic Church human rights networks in Peru gained her the trust of the Church in El Salvador, without a doubt the most important actor in the human rights community there.[5] One of the major cases the Salvadoran Truth Commission would examine was that of the five Jesuit priests and their housekeeper murdered by soldiers in San Salvador in 1989. For her staff, Patricia hired, among others, two young activists from Argentina and Uruguay: Alfredo Forti and Felipe Michelini, the son of Senator Zelmar Michelini, who was assassinated in Argentina in 1976. Forti and his family were victims in an infamous case of disappearances featured prominently in the IACHR report on Argentina in 1980. In 1976, when he was sixteen, Forti, his mother, and his four brothers were already on a plane in the main Buenos Aires airport bound for Venezuela, when armed uniformed men took the entire family off. Forti and his brothers were left on the streets of Buenos Aires, but his mother never reappeared. Like Juan Méndez, Forti came to the United States, where he finished his education and began to work on behalf of human rights. After joining with Valdez on the Salvadoran Truth Commission, Forti later went on to work for the UN Human Rights Verification Mission in Guatemala and for the OAS in its Democracy Promotion Unit. In 2004, he set up his own consulting firm, and among his clients was the government of Peru when it was forming its own Truth and Reconciliation Commission. In the most surprising turn of fate, by 2009, Forti was serving as the deputy assistant secretary of the Defense Ministry for the Argentine government. So Forti went from being disappeared *by* the Argentine military to being one of the people in charge *of* the Argentine military.

After her work with the Salvadoran Truth Commission, Patricia returned to Argentina. In 1992, a Human Rights Watch colleague from her network put her in contact with Alex Boraine, who would later become deputy chair of the South African Truth Commission. Boraine was interested in the Argentine experience, and Patricia helped arrange his visit to Argentina. There he met many of the relevant actors, including my friend, political scientist Catalina Smulovitz, who gave him an overview of the entire transition process in Argentina. When the South Africans were deciding what kind of solutions they should implement, Boraine invited Patricia and Catalina to a conference in South Africa organized by the Institute for Democracy in Africa (IDASA) on how newly democratic regimes can best deal with those responsible for human rights violations committed during the regime. At one of the dinners, Boraine told Patricia, "South Africa is totally connected to Europe, but we don't know anything about Latin America. We have to learn more about Argentina and its transition to democracy." He wanted to organize a visit of South Africans to Buenos Aires. With funding from the Open Society Institute in New York City, Patricia organized an eight-day visit to Argentina for South African academics, members of Congress, and members of the human rights commission. Among the participants was Wilmot James, the executive director of the Institute for Democracy in Africa and a professor of sociology. James later asked Patricia to serve on the board of IDASA. "In South Africa, I met fabulous people, and I learned so much from them," Patricia explains. "We have done exchanges with NGOs there, because they have a lot of resistance to the United States, and they want more connections with Latin America. When they are here, they realize that we can share and exchange experiences, but at the same time, we are so different."[6]

Once again, individuals within networks formed bonds of trust, and this trust was the basis through which ideas and people initially moved, and practices spread. María José Guembe, who litigated the Poblete case before the Argentine Supreme Court, spent time as a visiting scholar at Notre Dame University and contributed chapters on the Argentine transitional justice experience to various works on accountability. Members of the Argentine human rights forensic anthropology team went on to train experts in Guatemala, Bosnia, and elsewhere about how to exhume graves to produce both information for grieving families and evidence for prosecutions. Each of these individuals, and many more like them, acted as "human chains," linking together the Argentine experience with the rest of the world.

This analysis empirically documents Argentine innovations, yet I do not wish to romanticize them. Living in a country at the beginning of the justice cascade has not always been an easy experience for Argentines. Nor do I recommend that other countries should imitate or duplicate all that has been done in Argentina with regard to human rights. So much attention is devoted to demanding accountability for the crimes of the dictatorship that at times this eclipses other important issues. But the Argentine case shows the possibility that a country can move in three decades from being a major violator of human rights to a country whose citizens have made major innovations in the struggle for human rights. It underscores the major contribution of social movements and public innovations from actors in the global South to the international human rights agenda. Above all, the Argentine case demonstrates that the process of diffusion was not passive. Human rights activists and new democratic officials struggled to ensure accountability, sometimes against great odds, and real people worked hard in networks to spread these ideas. It is to this process of diffusion, both regionally and globally, to which we now turn.

4

The Streams of the Justice Cascade

The justice cascade did not have a single source. Rather, we can think of two main streams from different sources flowing in—streams that began to merge at the start of the twenty-first century. By 2010, individual criminal accountability had gained momentum and had been embodied in international law, international and domestic institutions, and in the global consciousness. It is this momentum that makes the metaphor of a "cascade" an apt one.

The first stream began in the Nuremberg Trials in 1945 and 1946, but it temporarily dried up or went underground for almost fifty years until states created the specific ad hoc international institutions—the International Criminal Tribunal for the Former Yugoslavia (ICTY) and the International Criminal Tribunal for Rwanda (ICTR) in 1993 and 1994, respectively. These tribunals in turn put into practice and furthered the doctrine and jurisprudence of individual criminal accountability.

The second stream involved domestic and foreign prosecutions for individual accountability. This is the stream we have been following through Greece, Portugal, and Argentina. But, in its early days, this stream didn't flow directly either, since the example of trials in Portugal and Greece didn't spread broadly. And yet, by 1985, the trials in Argentina had generated broad international attention, and a stream of prosecutions began to flow through Latin America—including Bolivia, Guatemala, Panama, Chile, and Haiti. These prosecutions often moved slowly and were contested, uncertain, and perceived as still dangerous and reversible. When activists were blocked in domestic courts, they sought to use foreign human rights prosecutions for holding perpetrators responsible for violations in other states. By 1998, the Pinochet arrest had become the most vivid illustration of the potential power of the second stream.

Underneath these two streams of prosecutions, states and non-state actors worked to build a firm streambed of international human rights law and international humanitarian law that fortified the legal underpinnings of the cascade, culminating in the Rome Statute of the ICC in 1998. One of the central principles of penal law is that one cannot be punished for doing something that is not previously prohibited by law. As states shored up the legal basis for the justice cascade, they assured that it would not be another ephemeral flow but a sustained political and legal development. The Nuremberg and Tokyo trials did not rest on a sturdy legal foundation, and so they were more open to accusations of victor's justice and retrospective justice. They helped to create new law through their practice, but at times it seems as if they were making up the law as they went along. By the time Pinochet was arrested in 1998, however, a firmer legal foundation for individual criminal accountability had been built up, and even the conservative Law Lords in London concluded that on the basis of law that Pinochet himself had ratified, he *could be* extradited to Spain to stand trial for torture committed in Chile during his regime.

The two streams and the underlying streambed initially appeared to be quite separate from one another (see Figure 4.1). For example, the creation of the International Criminal Tribunal for the Former Yugoslavia owed

Figure 4.1 **The Justice Cascade: Legalization of the Norm of Individual Criminal Accountability**

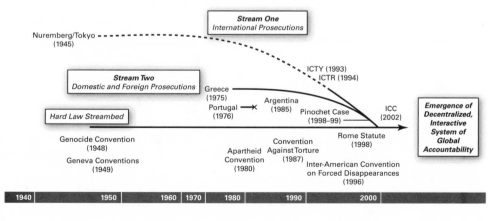

little to the domestic prosecutions that preceded it. The ICTY was seen as the first international tribunal since Nuremberg and Tokyo, and its creators drew their inspiration almost solely from that precedent, not from the domestic prosecutions taking place around them. The stories behind these developments have been told in a series of excellent books and articles,[1] but rarely do all the pieces of this global trend get put together in one place.[2] I wish to paint the bigger picture of phenomena happening through history and around the globe. Sometimes we might think that all of the action happened in Rome in 1998, when the delegates gathered to draft the Statute of the ICC. But Rome was an outgrowth of processes that started in Nuremberg and continued in Athens, Buenos Aires, Madrid, London, and Geneva—accelerating in the last thirty years. When the delegates met in Rome, there was an extensive back story that made the International Criminal Court possible but not inevitable. Each development makes the next more possible, but human agency and choice is constantly present. This chapter describes the course of the various streams of political and legal doctrine and practice that flowed into the justice cascade.

Scholarly literature on diffusion often makes it appear as if cascade phenomena happen through "contagion," as if such change happens without either effort or planning. Instead, at each stage of the cascade, real people are deeply involved in pressing for change. In the case of the justice cascade, these people were part of what I will call the "pro-change alliance" in favor of individual criminal accountability. They included mainly individuals working in like-minded governments, and individuals working within international and domestic human rights NGOs and professional associations. As it is impossible in a single chapter to present everyone who worked tirelessly to press for accountability, the stories of a few of the major actors will have to stand in for the countless individuals and groups that made the cascade happen.

Building the Streambed:
Inserting the Individual into International Law

The first change that needed to occur for the justice norm to advance was that international law had to begin to focus on the individual. Some think of this process as the "criminalization of international law," but it could also be thought of as the "individualization" of international law, because it focused on the individual—both as the perpetrator of crimes and as a victim who had standing to bring forward cases against perpetrators. This change began in the area of international criminal law; it was led by an Egyptian lawyer named Cherif Bassiouni, who did more to help create the ICC than any other single individual. The grandson of a famous lawyer and independence leader in Egypt, Bassiouni learned early the power of law when his grandfather was sentenced to death, only to have his conviction reversed by the British Privy Council. "My grandfather was my model, and there was nothing I wanted more than to be a lawyer and to be in the service of justice; this was my calling in life."

Sent to law school in France and later in Switzerland, Bassiouni became involved in the student anti-colonial movement. He returned to Egypt in 1956 to fight during the siege at Port Said in the brief Suez War, where he was injured and subsequently decorated with the Egyptian equivalent of the Congressional Medal of Honor. After the war, Bassiouni helped train Algerian troops in Egypt for their independence struggle against the French; for this, when he returned to complete his studies in France, the French government detained him and expelled him from the country. While serving on the Egyptian presidential staff, he first discovered that his government engaged in torture. Naively, he recalls, he decided that the president and cabinet must not know about it because, he thought, they could never have signed off on such a policy. But after he denounced the practice, he was placed under house arrest and threatened with the very torture he had just denounced. Bassiouni spent seven months in a darkened room. When he was released, he discovered that the government had confiscated his property and that of his family. It is not surprising, then, that Bassiouni turned to international law. He recalls that "when I left Egypt in 1962, and came to the United States, I was pretty well committed to fighting injustice at the international level."[3] In the United States, Bassiouni completed advanced legal studies and secured a job teaching law at DePaul University in Chicago, where he has taught ever since. He has used this position as a springboard from which to launch an extraordinary career helping to design international legal institutions.

I interviewed Bassiouni in his office at DePaul University, where he proudly pointed to a photograph of his grandfather on the wall as he told me his story. "I understand now your interest in human rights," I said, "but how did you get involved in international criminal law?" The institutional vehicle that brought Bassiouni to international prominence was a little-known professional association called the International Association of Penal Law (AIDP, for its French acronym), which since 1924 had been advocating for an international criminal court. As a young law professor, Bassiouni was given an extraordinary opportunity to represent the U.S. section by presenting a major paper on extradition at an AIDP conference in Europe. In preparing the paper, he was struck by the absence of the individual in all of international criminal law. Bassiouni explained that "everything was established on the basis of a relationship between governments. And I had the image of the individual being a package, you know, that one government wraps up and puts in the mail and sends to the other government. And I said, 'This is ridiculous.' Conceptually this is not right. This is not a bilateral relationship between two governments; this is a trilateral relationship, where the individual is a subject as much as the states are! Now, as strange as that may sound to you, this was the most revolutionary idea to descend on the field of international criminal justice in 1968." Bassiouni was able to persuade the association to take up this theme of the individual in criminal law, and it has been at the center of his life's work ever since.

This conceptual change also reflects the move from state accountability to individual accountability that is at the heart of the justice cascade. The justice cascade involves a dual shift from the state to the individual: individuals are held accountable for violations of the law, and in many countries, individual victims have also gained more standing to bring forward cases when their rights have been violated. The process through which this conceptual change enters the law spans three previously separate fields of law—human rights law, humanitarian law (or the laws of war), and international criminal law—which are eventually united in the Rome Statute.

By the 1970s, states had drafted a number of important human rights treaties, but only the Genocide Convention of 1948 and the Geneva Conventions of 1949 contained specific language about individual criminal accountability. The principles in these treaties, however, had not been invoked to justify prosecutions. The norm of individual accountability was most clearly stated in the Torture Convention, which began (as we saw) with the Torture Declaration passed by the UN General Assembly in 1975. Amnesty International and the governments of Sweden, the Netherlands, and the newly democratic government of Greece were the main protagonists in proposing and passing the Torture Declaration. They continued to be deeply involved in the process of drafting the binding treaty against torture, the Convention Against Torture (CAT). But they were joined by Bassiouni and his group of penal lawyers in ways that would have an important impact on how the norm of individual criminal accountability was articulated in the CAT.

Bassiouni worked with a young lawyer from Amnesty International, Nigel Rodley, and Niall MacDermott, the head of the International Commission of Jurists. Rodley had lost many of his family in the Holocaust. He studied law in the United Kingdom, taught law in Canada, worked at the UN Secretariat, and was pursuing a PhD in law at NYU before coming to work as the first head of the legal office at Amnesty International in 1973.[4] He brought commitment, broad international experience, and a keen legal mind to his task. Rodley and MacDermott worked with Bassiouni to convene a committee of experts in international and comparative penal law to draft an early version of what would later become the Convention Against Torture. By this time, Bassiouni was the secretary general of the AIDP, and he had been increasingly engaged in the work on the United Nations. As part of his work with the association, he had somehow persuaded the ex-president of Italy, a member of AIDP, to set up an International Institute of Higher Studies of Criminal Sciences in the town of Syracuse, on the island of Sicily. Bassiouni explains: "I had this vision that what we needed was sort of an island where people from east, west, and north and south could meet." The president of Italy agreed, and the Siracusa Institute was founded in 1972. It would become the main informal center where the ideas for the ICC were later drafted and discussed; but at this early moment, the institute also played a role in the creation of the Convention Against Torture.

The committee of experts met in Syracuse in December 1977 to prepare a Draft Convention for the Prevention and Suppression of Torture. Bassiouni, Rodley, and MacDermott were there, together with twenty-seven other experts, mainly law professors from Western countries, although some experts also came from Brazil, Egypt, India, Nigeria, and Japan. They explicitly chose to use an international criminal law approach to establish an obligation on states to prosecute or punish offenders or to extradite them to another state willing to do so.[5] Once they had completed the draft convention, the AIDP, under Bassiouni's leadership, presented the Siracusa draft of the Torture Convention to the

UN Subcommission for the Promotion and Protection of Human Rights. The Swedish attorney general was one of the participants at the Siracusa meeting. Probably through his connection, many of the provisions of the AIDP draft found their way into the Swedish draft which was the starting point for the drafting of the CAT. It shows how international NGOs worked directly to influence the content of international law. The fact that an association of criminal law scholars under Bassiouni's leadership was involved in the draft helps explain why this was the first major human rights treaty to put the individual at the center of the treaty, as the perpetrator of torture, and to provide clearly for individual accountability. The draft speaks throughout of "a person," or a state official, as being responsible for committing or instigating torture or failing to prevent it. This draft clearly states that persons believed to be responsible for torture should be prosecuted, and it leaves open the possibility of domestic, foreign, and international prosecutions. An unobtrusive clause making universal jurisdiction possible appears in the AIDP draft for the first time. The Swedish government later submitted a draft incorporating some of these provisions to the Human Rights Commission, since formal drafts must be submitted by governments, and it was the starting point for negotiations on the CAT.[6]

The streambed of international law underpinning the justice cascade was built with the intense collaboration between individuals, NGO, and like-minded states. Thus Bassiouni and his criminal law experts could not have made an impact if diplomats in Sweden and the Netherlands had not taken up many provisions from their draft and incorporated them into the CAT. Similarly, the provision for universal jurisdiction in the draft would not have stayed in the final text of the treaty had it not been for the intense work of Amnesty International to persuade states to accept the language. Nigel Rodley, the legal adviser for Amnesty International at the time, explains that initially most states hated the provision for universal jurisdiction. Even the Dutch were initially uncomfortable with universal jurisdiction, and their position didn't change until the Dutch section of Amnesty International and the International Commission of Jurists promoted a resolution in the Dutch Parliament supporting the idea. So, as Rodley describes, the AIDP and the Swedes were responsible for getting the provision for universal jurisdiction in the draft treaty, but the activists like Amnesty International through their lobbying and persuasion were the ones who helped make sure the provision stayed in the final text.[7]

The efforts of a Swedish diplomat, Hans Danelius, assisted by a Dutch diplomat, Jan Herman Burgers, were particularly important. Burgers explains that Mr. Danelius had "taken a great role" in drafting the Declaration and also the Convention Against Torture. "So you might see him as the father, and me then, as the midwife, helping the baby to be born."[8] Burgers's concern with torture dated to his military service in Indonesia, then a Dutch colony, in 1948–50. Although he never witnessed it personally, he learned that torture was applied there by the Dutch military to extract information from captured guerrilla fighters. He later recalled that "this came to me as a terrible shock," and it left him with an "obsession with this ghastly subject of torture." One way that Burgers worked through his obsession was to dedicate himself to drafting both international law and Dutch foreign policy designed to eradicate torture. Burgers became a member of Amnesty International in the early 1970s. In my interview with him, he stressed that in both the Netherlands and Sweden, the influence of local human rights groups like Amnesty International had been very important in stimulating the governments to work against torture. It is noteworthy that both Burgers and Bassiouni came to the issue as young men who were deeply shocked by the knowledge of their own governments' participation in torture—knowledge that would fuel a lifetime of work.

The final version of the Convention Against Torture called for both state accountability and individual criminal accountability. The CAT refers to various state obligations, but the actual offender in most of the treaty is "a person"—specifically, a public official who either inflicts torture directly or instigates, consents, or acquiesces to it. The convention requires states to ensure that acts of torture are offenses under domestic criminal law; to investigate alleged cases of torture; and to either extradite or prosecute the accused. Most significantly, the final convention preserved language granting universal jurisdiction for torture, which simply said that each state party shall take measures to establish its jurisdiction over torture if the alleged offender is present in its territory, and if it decides not to extradite. In other words, a torturer can be prosecuted by any state that has ratified the convention if the offender is in that country. Universal jurisdiction provided for a system of decentralized enforcement in any national judicial system against individuals who committed or instigated torture. Sweden considered this provision the "cornerstone" of the convention because it was intended to make it hard for torturers to evade domestic prosecution by finding a safe haven in a foreign country. Many countries, including the United States, supported the inclusion of universal jurisdiction in the treaty.[9] Legal experts from Amnesty International were highly involved in proposing and supporting the language about individual criminal accountability and universal jurisdiction in the Torture Convention.[10]

Nonetheless, the provision for universal jurisdiction in the Torture Convention provoked a strong debate. France and the United Kingdom thought it would create problems under their domestic legal systems, while Argentina and Uruguay, still under authoritarian governments, firmly opposed it.[11] But as the negotiations for the treaty drew to an end, countries such as Argentina, Uruguay, and Brazil, which were originally opposed, experienced transitions to democracy. The new Alfonsín government instructed its representatives to work for the passage of the convention. This helped shift the balance in the negotiations in favor of the convention, contributing to its passage by the UN General Assembly in December 1984.[12] The Convention Against Torture was opened for signature in February 1985, and it went into effect in 1987. Among the first twenty states to sign (though not necessarily the first to ratify) were not only well established Western democracies but also a number of the states where early human rights prosecutions were used, including Argentina, Bolivia, Greece, Portugal, and Panama.

For Bassiouni, the success of the Torture Convention indicated that it was now possible to push ahead for the creation of the institution that had long been his dream and the dream of his organization: a permanent international criminal court—"By now you have organizational support. You have the history of the organization. Go for it. That's when I started pushing the association to rekindle interest in the ICC."

But he would take an unexpected detour to the ICC by way of the Apartheid Convention. At the same time the various states were negotiating the Torture Convention in the mid-1970s, African states assumed leadership in drafting another treaty with a strong criminal law component: the Apartheid Convention. The Apartheid Convention begins with the statement that apartheid is a crime against humanity, referring directly to criminal law language from the Nurembeurg Tribunal. Not all human rights advocates or legal experts were aware of the implications of the Apartheid Convention for individual criminal accountability. Cherif Bassiouni recalls that in 1979, he received a call from a member of the AIDP who was then a justice on the Supreme Court of Senegal, and who was also a member of the UN Commission on Human Rights. He asked Bassiouni, "Are you familiar with Article Five of the Apartheid Convention?" and Bassiouni had to admit, "Not really." So his Senegalese colleague said, "Do you know that Article Five is the only article in an international convention that says that there should be an international criminal court?" When his Senegalese colleague then asked him, "Can you draft the statute for the establishment of an international criminal court to prosecute apartheid?" Bassiouni answered, "Sure." In 1980 and 1981, Bassiouni drafted a statute for an international court, one that was never put into effect to prosecute apartheid. But, around fifteen years later, when state delegations at the United Nations started talking again about an international criminal court, Bassiouni's draft statute was there waiting.[13]

Well before the creation of the ICC, the Inter-American Commission on Human Rights and the Inter-American Court of Rights once again played a catalytic role in pushing for individual criminal accountability, this time with regard to disappearances. Disappearances—where governments kidnap their opponents, detain them in clandestine prisons, and often murder them—had been a hallmark of repressive regimes in Latin America, including Argentina, Guatemala, and Chile. The case that came before the Inter-American Court in the mid-1980s involved disappearances in Honduras between 1981 and 1984. Many countries in Latin America had experienced far more disappearances than Honduras. Human rights groups estimate that there were approximately 180 disappeared people in Honduras, compared to over 10,000 in Argentina and over 3,000 in Chile. But Honduras had ratified the American Convention on Human Rights and accepted the compulsory jurisdiction of the Inter-American Court of Human Rights *prior to* the period in which the disappearances occurred. Crucially, this opened the door for legal enforcement against Honduras that was not available with respect to most of the other countries in Latin America. An important precept of positive international human rights law is that states should be held to obligations that they have explicitly accepted by ratifying treaties, and only for human rights violations that occur *after* they have ratified such treaties and accepted their legal obligations.

The Inter-American Court decision in 1988 on a Honduran disappearance case, the Velásquez Rodríguez case, established important precedents regarding the international responsibility of the state for human rights violations. The Court concluded that the American Convention on Human Rights establishes that governments have the obligation to respect the human rights of individuals and to guarantee the enjoyment of these rights. As a consequence of this obligation, the Court found that "states must prevent, investigate and *punish* any violation of the rights recognized by the Convention. . . ."[14] In this landmark decision, a human rights court found for the first time that states had a "duty to punish."

Activists and their state allies drafted a Declaration on the Protection of All Persons from Enforced Disappearance, adopted in 1992, and a regional treaty, the Inter-American Convention on Forced Disappearance of Persons, which entered into force in 1996. The Inter-American Convention contains virtually identical language on universal jurisdiction as the CAT and thus underscores a move toward individual criminal accountability for issues other than torture.[15]

Individual Criminal Accountability for War Crimes

The individual had long been present in another branch of international law—international humanitarian law, or the "laws of war," mainly embedded in the Geneva Conventions and monitored by the International Committee of the Red Cross. But humanitarian law and human rights law had been separate until the 1980s. The laws of war were understood to cover crimes committed between combatant groups in war, whereas human rights law was understood to apply to state treatment of its citizens. In order for humanitarian law to play a role in the justice cascade, it had to be "discovered" and activated by human rights lawyers. Early in the 1980s, human rights lawyers realized that because many human rights abuses were perpetrated by states and armed groups in the context of civil war, the Geneva Conventions offered tools for establishing individual criminal accountability for crimes committed during wartime.

More than any other individual, Aryeh Neier helped to bring together humanitarian law and human rights law. After working for fifteen years with the ACLU, in 1978, Neier helped found a small human rights group, Helsinki Watch, to work on human rights issues in the USSR and Eastern

Europe. When Ronald Reagan was elected president in 1980, Neier says that he was "concerned that Helsinki Watch would get cast in a Cold War light," so "it seemed appropriate to create Americas Watch" as a partner organization to Helsinki Watch in 1980 to focus on the anti-Communist dictators in Latin America as well as the Communist regimes of Europe.[16] After setting up Americas Watch, one of the first people he hired was Juan Méndez. Neier later wrote: "It was Juan who helped me grasp the significance, both in our work and in the evolution of a human rights consciousness internationally, of holding officials accountable for past crimes. . . ."[17] Helsinki Watch and Americas Watch were later combined with other regional watch committees to become Human Rights Watch (HRW). Human Rights Watch in turn would join Amnesty International as another major transnational human rights NGO. In the 1980s, though, HRW was a relatively small and flexible new human rights group with innovative leadership.

In the early eighties, Neier recognized and seized the opportunity to draw more on humanitarian law. Many of the cases in Latin America of interest to the human rights community, especially in El Salvador and Guatemala, were involved with armed conflicts. Governments constantly asked why human rights groups didn't talk about violations "by the other side as well"—that is, by guerillas and insurgent groups. But human rights law at that time was concerned with violations by state officials, not by non-state actors. Violations by non-state groups were technically "domestic crimes," akin to felonies like murder or aggravated assault. As such, it was thought that governments had adequate national criminal law at their disposal to respond to such crimes. This answer, although technically correct, did not resonate well with many internal audiences, who were often persuaded that human rights groups were "biased" because they only criticized governments.

In 1982, Neier and his staff hit upon the idea of monitoring the laws of war, as well as human rights law, which permitted them to talk about violations committed by insurgents as well as the government. To a savvy activist like Neier, using humanitarian law to criticize both guerillas and governments also provided credibility in the contentious atmosphere of Washington during the Reagan administration. For example, having criticized violations of humanitarian law by the guerillas in El Salvador, Human Rights Watch was also able to talk about the violations of the

U.S.-supported insurgent group, the Contras, who were fighting against the Sandinista government in Nicaragua.[18]

Around the same time, in 1982, Amnesty International asked David Weissbrodt, who was on sabbatical leave from his job teaching law at the University of Minnesota Law School, to work in the legal counsel office of Amnesty International in London. Amnesty wanted him to prepare a memo for the organization on humanitarian law as to how it might be applied to situations of grave human rights violations in war. Weissbrodt argued that "more regular use of international humanitarian law could provide Amnesty International with an additional legal foundation for its concerns."[19] Despite his urging, however, Amnesty International did not more fully incorporate humanitarian law in its work until the early 1990s; and even then, it did not initially use it in the way Aryeh Neier was recommending, to hold both insurgent groups and governments accountable.[20]

Human rights organizations working with humanitarian law stressed the importance of using Common Article III of the Geneva Conventions as a cornerstone of their work with the laws of war. Common Article III was so important because it sets out clear standards for humane treatment for both non-combatants and combatants who have surrendered or been taken prisoner in internal wars. In particular, it prohibits—"at any time and in any place whatsoever"—murder, cruel treatment and torture, and "outrages upon personal dignity, in particular humiliating and degrading treatment."[21]

The efforts by HRW and Amnesty International to incorporate humanitarian law into their work foreshadowed the eventual merging of elements of human rights law and humanitarian law in the ICTY and the ICC. This embrace would later put HRW in a position to take leadership in calling for an international war crimes tribunal for the former Yugoslavia.

The Second Stream Accelerates—Domestic and Foreign Human Rights Prosecutions

At the same time the CAT was being drafted and ratified, legal developments were continuing in domestic polities around the world—developments that began to reinforce the idea of individual criminal accountability for state officials for human rights violations. Before the ICTY began working in 1993, prosecutions had taken place in court settings scattered across twenty-three different nations. Many of these were from Latin America, but after the end of the Cold War and the process of transition in the Soviet bloc, they also included countries from Eastern Europe and eventually Africa. Although these courts used different legal reasoning to justify the prosecutions, all were beginning to implement an individual accountability model for human rights violations.

The graph below (Figure 4.2) again shows the trend in domestic and foreign human rights prosecutions from our database, documenting that it was well established and growing dramatically before the establishment of the ICTY in 1994. The graph also suggests that a major expansion of human rights prosecutions occurred after 1989, around the time when the Cold War ended, which reinforces the argument that this helped create the conditions for the diffusion of the justice norm.

In 1990, in his seminal article on the topic of accountability in the *New York Review of Books* entitled "What Should be Done About the Guilty?", Neier drew upon the experience of Latin America to suggest that the path of domestic trials was fraught with danger and complexity.[22] Thus, early in 1990, even one of the foremost advocates of justice, at the foremost human rights organization, was pessimistic about the possibilities for prosecution and punishment in *domestic* courts. This contributed to the decision of HRW to press for international tribunals.

Figure 4.2. **Foreign and Domestic Prosecutions Prior to 1994**

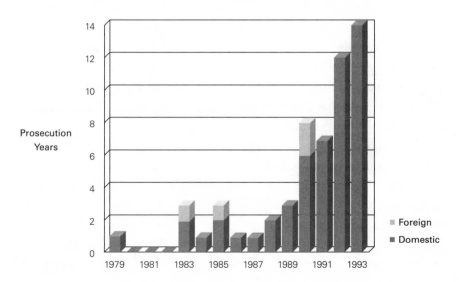

The First Stream of the Justice Cascade Reemerges

The end of the Cold War opened up the political space necessary to begin resurrecting the Nuremberg precedent. Yet the first post–World War II demand for international war crimes trials was made not for the former Yugoslavia but for Iraq. In 1990, after Saddam Hussein invaded Kuwait and seized Western hostages, both British prime minister Margaret Thatcher and President George H. W. Bush mentioned the Nuremberg precedent, endorsing the idea of a war crimes trial for Hussein. The gravest war crimes of the Iraqi regime had been committed during the "Anfal Campaign," in which Iraqi forces killed close to 100,000 Kurds in rural Iraq, including through the use of poison gas. At the time, the United States had supported Iraq in the war with Iran, so it refrained from protest.[23] But a HRW researcher, with the help of a U.S. diplomat, had gotten access to 17 metric tons of documentation about the campaign, shipped all of it back to the United States, and used it to produce an HRW report that concluded that Iraq had committed genocide against the Kurds.

The documentation thus existed to prosecute Hussein for genocide. But at the time, the only international venue that could hear a genocide case was the International Court of Justice (ICJ). The ICJ, like most international tribunals, involved state accountability, not individual criminal accountability, and could only receive complaints from states. HRW staff were unable to find a government willing to bring the case against Iraq before the ICJ.[24] But the idea of trying Hussein for war crimes resurfaced again in 1991, following the emergence of new reports documenting widespread killings of Kurdish civilians. In speeches in 1991, German prime minister Hans-Dietrich Genscher repeatedly raised the possibility of prosecuting Hussein. The idea did not gain much traction until after the United States invaded Iraq in 2003. Nonetheless, the Iraqi case had put the Nuremberg precedent back on the international agenda.

The combination of the end of the Cold War, the existence of genocide once again on the soil of Europe, and the inability of the world to gather the political will to stop that genocide, gave impetus to the creation of the first international war crimes tribunal since World War II.[25] On February 22, 1993, without dissent, the UN Security Council approved a plan submitted by Secretary-General Boutros Boutros-Ghali to establish an international criminal tribunal, the International Criminal Tribunal for the Former Yugoslavia (ICTY), to try those accused of war crimes in the region. But as the first half of this chapter makes clear, by the time the Security Council created the ICTY, members of the United Nations had been working for twenty years, since the Torture Declaration in 1973, to establish in international law the obligation to prosecute and punish state officials for human rights violations.

The first person to advocate publicly for an international war crimes tribunal in the former Yugoslavia was a local journalist, who issued an appeal that appeared in May 1991 in the newspaper *Borba*, under the title "Nuremberg Now!"[26] Shortly thereafter, in July 1992, Human Rights Watch called for the establishment of a tribunal for human rights violations and war crimes in the former Yugoslavia, among the earliest recommendations for individual criminal accountability in the Balkans. Although Bassiouni and the AIDP had been campaigning for many years for an international criminal court, neither Human Rights Watch nor any other prominent human rights group had ever before campaigned to establish an international war crimes tribunal. Researchers from HRW and other organizations were on the ground in the former Yugoslavia, and their reports revealed that the situation continued to worsen: the scope and type of violations in the war in Bosnia-Herzegovina after 1992 made it "appropriate" not only to use the phrase "crimes against humanity," but also to use "the name for the ultimate crime: genocide." As Neier explains in his memoir, "we thought it fitting to call for a tribunal like the one that tried the Nazis to hold accountable those engaged in Nazi-like crimes."[27]

Many have suggested that the Security Council's decision to form a tribunal for the former Yugoslavia instead of other countries with equally serious human rights violations revealed the Eurocentric bias of its members, who were more shocked about genocide in Europe than elsewhere in the world. But few other cases brought together all the conditions present here: an international war, documentation of crimes against humanity and genocide, a long and unsuccessful history of attempting to resolve the conflict by other means, as well as the strong presence of media able to broadcast powerful images around the world.

Only a few days after the appeal by Human Rights Watch for a tribunal for the former Yugoslavia, the media carried the first exposé of concentration camps in the Balkans, with photos of emaciated prisoners in camps that looked all too similar to the Holocaust.[28] The public all over the world responded to the new images and information. On August 13, 1992, states took the first step toward a tribunal when the Security Council set up a Commission of Experts to Investigate Grave Breaches of the Geneva Conventions. The Council appointed Bassiouni as chair. It also requested that states and international humanitarian organizations submit to the Human Rights Commission substantiated information concerning Balkan war crimes. In this first step, decision makers were consciously drawing upon the Nuremberg precedent, which had also started with a request for states to submit evidence on war crimes.

An important turning point came after the Clinton administration took office in January 1993 and appointed Madeleine Albright as the U.S. ambassador to the United Nations. Born in Czechoslovakia, Albright had both a strong interest in Central and Eastern Europe and a commitment to human rights. She became "one of the most tireless supporters of the Court."[29] As Albright liked to say, her "mind-set" was all about the Holocaust and Munich. When the Security Council voted to establish the ICTY, Albright declared: "There is an echo in this Chamber today. The Nuremberg Principles have been reaffirmed. . . ."[30] Many European policy makers, and especially the German foreign minister, also pressed for prosecutions in the case of the former Yugoslavia. And like Albright, observers commonly described the creation of the ICTY as a legal development that flowed almost directly from Nuremberg.

Most individuals involved in the creation of the ICTY cite the Nuremberg Tribunals, the Tokyo War Crimes Tribunals, and to a much lesser extent, the trial of Eichmann in Israel, as the main precedents for their work. They were not for the most part, informed by the practice of domestic human rights prosecutions that had occurred around the world, nor had they been involved in the negotiations for the CAT and other treaties providing for universal jurisdiction.

Some opponents of the ICTY suggested that a better alternative would have been for the United Nations to encourage the new governments in the former Yugoslavia to deal with their own war criminals through domestic prosecutions. But many realized, as Neier wrote in November 1993, that "the prospect that anything of the sort could happen is so remote—indeed, fantastic—that it does not bear comment."[31] Indeed, by 1993, the perceived failure of many efforts at domestic prosecutions had led some to believe that it was unrealistic to expect countries to carry out such trials.

This was a point at which amnesty laws were still blocking prosecutions in Argentina, Chile, Uruguay, and many other countries in Latin America.

Once the United Nations authorized the creation of the ICTY in February 1993, Neier continued to play an important role. That year he moved from his position heading HRW to a new position as the president of the Open Society Institute, the large foundation set up in New York by the investor and philanthropist George Soros. Neier now had considerable funds to put behind his commitment to international justice. The United Nations provided inadequate financial support to Bassiouni's Commission of Experts to allow it to complete its work, but with Neier's help, Bassiouni raised $1.4 million from the MacArthur Foundation and the Open Society Institute—more than had been provided to the commission from the UN.[32]

The Security Council needed to appoint a prosecutor for the new tribunal, and it wanted to do so by consensus. Secretary-General Boutros-Ghali submitted Bassiouni's name as his first candidate to Madeleine Albright, then president of the Security Council. But he failed to win an election on a tied straw vote in the Security Council after the UK delegation criticized the selection of a Muslim to prosecute cases with mostly Muslim victims. Bassiouni speculated that the major powers did not want to appear to favor the Muslim victims and thus displease the Serbs.[33]

Instead, the South African jurist Richard Goldstone was elected as the chief prosecutor of the ICTY. Shortly after his election, he was invited by the British ambassador to a small party in South Africa to meet the former British prime minister Edward Heath, who was on a private yachting holiday in Cape Town. When Heath learned that Goldstone had just been elected chief prosecutor of the ICTY, he asked in a friendly tone: "Why did you accept such a ridiculous job?" Goldstone replied that he thought prosecuting war criminals was important. Heath said something to the effect that "if people wished to murder one another, as long as they did not do so in his country, it was not his concern and should not be the concern of the British government."[34] Heath was perhaps not an unbiased observer. While he was prime minister, the European Court of Human Rights had found the British government responsible for cruel and degrading treatment of IRA prisoners in British jails. Because the European Court used a state accountability model, it never found Heath or any other state official individually responsible, but Heath must have understood the implications of the broadening trend.

Richard Goldstone, like others involved in the tribunal, saw the Nuremberg precedent as the primary source for the work on the ICTY. But he recognized that because it was a pathbreaking decision to create the new tribunal, all the conditions had to be in place, and in the case of the former Yugoslavia all of these factors converged. The conditions included the end of the Cold War, the media images of ethnic cleansing that recalled the Holocaust, and the fact that the national and international NGOs campaigning for the tribunal had "recently acquired the power to influence public opinion."[35] Just as the use of the first national trials in Greece had required a convergence of unusual factors, so too did the creation of the first international tribunal.

The creation of the ICTY in 1993 was a turning point in the campaign against impunity. Once the ICTY was in place and up and running, it became much more possible to set up other domestic and international tribunals. Domestically, the ICTY helped to establish the Bosnian War Crimes Chamber to take over part of its caseload. One scholar notes that "As a hybrid court organized under domestic law, the chamber was thoughtfully designed to enhance local capacity in ways that would endure after international participants were phased out."[36] The ICTY also helped spark the establishment of the International Criminal Tribunal for Rwanda (ICTR) in 1994 to prosecute perpetrators of the genocide there. Eventually, these developments helped mobilize state support for the creation of the International Criminal Court. The momentum from the work of these international courts contributed to the establishment in 2009 of a hybrid court in Cambodia to prosecute members of the Khmer Rouge, more than twenty years after the fall of that regime.

Gary Bass argues that it was possible to pursue international justice because legalistic solutions were much easier and politically more plausible than military intervention to stop atrocities. The establishment of the ICTY was an "act of tokenism" by the world community—"The world would prosecute the crimes that it would not prevent. The tribunal was built to flounder." And flounder it did, for quite a while. Bass argues that these kinds of legal actions "have often been a substitute for real political actions in Bosnia and Rwanda."[37] Richard Goldstone recalled his first press conferences with chagrin, since the international media had also "written off the ICTY as the 'fig leaf' of the international community established to hide its shame for inaction in the former Yugoslavia."[38]

What both Bass and the international media at the time missed is that setting up a tribunal *is* "real political action," and it can offer a cost-effective alternative or complement to military action. A legal solution is slower, and it has a logic of its own. This logic is formal and procedural, rather than outcome-oriented. Once states set up tribunals with autonomy, for example, they can't be sure what the decisions of these tribunals will be. Thus, after a bungled prosecution in 2009, the ICTR had to release Protais Zigiranyirazo, someone alleged to be "a chief architect of the country's 1994 genocide."[39] But slowly, over time, the ICTY and the other international tribunals began to build a momentum and jurisprudence that belied some of their detractors' criticisms.[40]

The Streams Converge: The Creation of the ICC

The end of the Cold War and the institutionalization of the two *ad hoc* tribunals reinvigorated international interest in establishing a permanent international criminal court. Work on that idea first began after World War II, when the newly formed United Nations took up the task of planning for an international tribunal to try war criminals and perpetrators of crimes against humanity. In this period, few countries were deeply committed to the project, and the Cold War and its attendant stalemate at the United Nations disrupted any serious efforts. Bassiouni explains that "major powers discovered that rather than fight international criminal justice in a flagrant way, you do what I call 'guerrilla tactics,' and the best guerrilla tactic you can use is the UN bureaucracy and allocation of resources." The International Law Commission of the United Nations suspended further discussion of the issue in 1953, after it was unable to arrive at a definition of "aggression" as one of the key crimes that the new tribunal would address.

Renewal of these efforts in the early 1990s was spearheaded by a coalition of actors, including international members of the AIDP who had worked for a permanent international criminal court. They were now joined by human rights NGOs, such as Human Rights Watch, the Lawyers Committee for Human Rights, and Amnesty International, which had long pushed for prosecutions of perpetrators and other forms of accountability in the wake of gross violations of human rights. Governments that had internalized the international justice ethic also joined, particularly in Europe and Latin America.

The small Caribbean island state of Trinidad and Tobago got the process started again in 1989 when it proposed an international criminal court to address drug trafficking. In 1990, an NGO committee of experts, chaired by Bassiouni, prepared a draft statute for an ICC that would have jurisdiction for all international crimes. The draft was modeled after the 1981 text Bassiouni had prepared for the implementation of the Apartheid Convention. Germany helped get momentum when the foreign minister, Hans-Dietrich Genscher, who had also been an advocate of the ICTY, appealed to the UN General Assembly to create an international court "where crimes against humanity, crimes against peace, genocide, war crimes, and environmental criminality can be prosecuted and punished."[41]

Although the United States would later be an opponent of the ICC, in the early period, the U.S. government under the Clinton administration was more favorable to the idea of creating an international criminal court. Historically, the United States had been "the leading proponent of international institutions based on principled rules," and for a brief moment in the mid-1990s, "the United States seemed willing and able to play this role again."[42] Michael Scharf, a lawyer in the U.S. Department of State from 1989 to 1993 who crafted the U.S. government's position on the ICC, said that in 1993 the United States significantly changed its stance. Prior to 1993, the policy had been "to prolong without progressing the debate." But in 1993, the United States "committed itself actively to work toward resolving the remaining legal and practical issues" involved with the creation of the ICC.[43]

Scharf claims that a number of factors were important for the United States. First, the American government thought that an international court could be useful in cases like that of the Somali warlord and his soldiers who attacked UN Peacekeepers in June 1993. Both the United States and the United Nations wanted to hold them criminally accountable. The United States, of course, could have attempted to seize the Somali warlords and either tried them on the battlefield for violations of the laws of war, or brought them to the United States to stand trial. But this would have been difficult and controversial. Second, the United States also believed an international criminal court could be used in the case of the Libyans who had downed Pan Am Flight 103 over Lockerbie, Scotland. Libya had rejected a UN Security Council resolution to extradite two individuals to the United States who had been identified as responsible for the attacks, but said it would extradite them to an international court. The United States wanted to call Libya's bluff. But "the most important factor of all" for the change in the U.S. position on the ICC, Scharf argued, was the establishment of the ICTY. In its work on the ICTY, the United States had successfully addressed the "same complex legal and practical issues that it had identified as obstacles" to the ICC.[44]

In this context, then, the United States changed its position, making it easier for the General Assembly to decide to move ahead with an ICC treaty conference. Of course, the Clinton administration expected the negotiations to produce a court the United States would be willing to support—that is, a court over which the United States would have more control. Without U.S. acquiescence in the early stages, it is unlikely that the negotiations for the court would have gotten off the ground.[45] By the time they gained momentum around proposals that the United States would not support, it was too late to stop the process. This shows the strength of the idea of individual responsibility for human rights violations. It was not just too late for the United States to stop the ICC, it was too late to stop the idea of individual criminal accountability. Some participants in the Rome process believed that U.S. opposition to the Rome Statute actually provoked more state support for the ICC than would have otherwise existed.

The International Law Commission (ILC) of the United Nations took up the issue of the ICC again and produced a quite conservative draft statute in 1994 that envisioned a less powerful and independent court than the one eventually created. Even those like Professor Bassiouni who were committed supporters of the idea of an international court did not imagine in their writings at the time that a strong court with compulsory jurisdiction and an independent prosecutor would emerge.

These conservative expectations changed in the four years between the ILC draft and the signing of the Rome Statute in 1998. An Argentine diplomat, Silvia Fernández de Gurmendi, was intimately involved with the process leading up to the ratification of the Rome Statute. Fernández was part of the new generation of post-transition government officials who supported the development of international law. She entered the Foreign Service in 1989, five years after Argentina's transition to democracy.

In 1994, Fernández was assigned to be the legal adviser to the Argentine mission to the UN in New York. She soon became part of a small group of government officials from Canada, the "Nordics," and Italy, who called themselves, "pretentiously, perhaps," the coalition of friends of the international criminal court. At this time, she recalls, there was a kind of "parting of the waters" between those countries that wanted to support the creation of a criminal court, and others that did not accept the proposals.[46] Among those who opposed the idea of an independent court, she pointed out, were all the permanent members of the Security Council (United States, the UK, France, China, and Russia), as well as a number of developing countries, including Mexico and India. "The supporters were able to convince the UN to create two different preparatory committees for the ICC," and Fernández and Bassiouni were named as the two vice presidents of these committees. She became one of the founders of a group that referred to itself as "like-minded" states in support of the court. "At the beginning, we were only about ten countries that met and designed the strategies, but we made a lot of noise and gave the impression that we were a gigantic group. My colleague from the UK would always ask, 'Tell the truth, how many are you?' But we benefited from the fact that there was a silent majority, a bunch of countries that were ready to support us." Particularly important was the parallel NGO group which worked in partnership with the like-minded states. The NGOs organized the Coalition for the International Criminal Court, a global network of over 2,000 NGOs advocating for the ICC and ratification of the Rome Statute.

Throughout the process, whenever the negotiations got difficult, Bassiouni organized informal "intersessional" meetings at the Siracusa Institute in Sicily. Fernández recalls it as a "fabulous place, very beautiful," near the ruins of the ancient Greek city of Syracuse, and surrounded by trees and places to talk. All the delegates stayed in the same hotel, the Grand Hotel Villa Politi, an elegant eighteenth-century building where Churchill had stayed during his vacations while he painted landscapes of the surroundings. The Siracusa meetings were not only for the like-minded but also for opponents of the court. They became increasingly open over time and the last one was open to all states. The like-minded group continued to expand, in part, Fernández said, because "we wanted to create the impression that we were a steamroller, so we weren't very exacting about the entrance requirements." Later, they realized they had to agree upon some specific principles. Even with the new entry requirements, the group still grew, and it reached sixty states by the time of the Rome Conference in 1998. In Latin America, in addition to Argentina, the group came to include Uruguay, Chile, Brazil, and Venezuela. South Africa was also an important member, persuading other African states to join. A crucial turning point occurred when the Labour government of Tony Blair was elected, and the United Kingdom switched sides. The wall of opposition from the permanent five members of the Security Council to the ICC was finally broken. Still, Fernández worried that the Western group continued to be too influential. A significant effort was made to encourage smaller and poorer countries to come to the Rome Conference. A special fund was set up to support the participation of developing countries at Rome and to provide technical assistance to their delegations.

In the summer of 1998, the UN diplomatic conference in Rome finalized the statute for an International Criminal Court. The group of like-minded states and hundreds of NGOs propelled the process and achieved consensus or compromise to produce a comprehensive 128-article statute. The Rome Statute is the clearest statement of the new doctrine of individual criminal accountability. It is explicit: the fact that an individual has been a head of state, or a member of government, "shall in no case exempt a person from criminal responsibility" nor lead to a reduction of sentence.[47] The ICC, as the most recent distillation of new rules, came relatively late and drew upon the experience of other efforts at individual criminal accountability, especially the ad hoc tribunals but also individual country experiences.

In the end, the drafting of the ICC was the product of a transgovernmental network of Foreign Ministry lawyers from a core group of countries, including Canada, Argentina, Sweden, Norway, and the Netherlands.[48] This transgovernmental network was penetrated by what we term an *epistemic community* of criminal law lawyers, some gathered together in the AIDP.[49] The transgovernmental network and the epistemic community, in turn, worked in close collaboration with an NGO advocacy network, supporting and often participating informally in the drafting process of the ICC Statute.[50]

The dramatic change in the draft text between 1994 and 1998 was largely due to the persuasive discursive power of NGOs and the like-minded states. They tipped the balance in favor of a strong and independent court, and created such great momentum that they swept the majority of state parties along, neutralizing opposition from powerful states like the United States, China, and India, which "found their own preferences trumped by a coalition of smaller states."[51] The U.S. position was undermined by the confrontation that sometimes happens between ordinary power politics and the basic logic of law. Legal negotiations are of course infused with power politics, but not just any kind of argument can be made within a legal discourse. The United States was opposed to a court that "would have jurisdiction over U.S. nationals without the case-specific consent of the U.S. government." But as one scholar points out, any treaty language to secure such an outcome was "fundamentally incompatible with the notion that criminal law should apply to everyone equally," and thus "it was ultimately rejected by the 120 nations who voted for the Rome treaty."[52]

This alliance of like-minded states and human rights NGOs promoted the ICC and eventually persuaded a large number of states to sign and ratify the statute, despite strong U.S. opposition to the final draft. The statute opened for signature in 1998; by 2010, 110 states had ratified it. The ICC Statute underscored international commitment to the principle that certain crimes are crimes not only against individuals but against the entire world. In consequence, jurisdiction lies with any state, or the international community as a whole, to prosecute those who engage in them.

Those who focus on the ICC don't fully appreciate how its dramatic success was not only the result of specific moves in the negotiations leading up to the Rome Statute but also of over two decades of work in favor of accountability recounted in the opening chapters of this book. The creation of the ICC was not an isolated event, but drew from the two streams of the justice cascade. It built on not only the obvious international precedents like the ICTY and the ICTR, but also the experience of countries that had previously held domestic human rights prosecutions. Some of the states, NGOs, and numerous individuals present at the Rome Conference had been advocating accountability since the Greek trials in 1975. Some, like Bassiouni, had also been involved in drafting the Convention Against Torture, with its provisions for individual criminal accountability; others, like Fernández, were very familiar with domestic prosecutions in their countries. States, delegates, and NGOs had learned about the possibility of accountability from watching international and domestic human rights prosecutions. But some had become pessimistic about the possibility of accountability if it was limited to domestic courts. Amnesties everywhere were blocking domestic prosecutions. Both state and non-state actors who pushed for the creation of the ICC believed that accountability needed international support, and the ICC seemed to be the institution for the job. Yet they and their opponents had very different expectations about what would be the consequences of creating such a court—a topic I will address in later chapters.

Foreign Human Rights Prosecutions Begin and Accelerate

When delegates completed the Rome Statute in July 1998, it was still only a great promise. Despite the euphoria of having drafted a statute far stronger than any dreamed possible, no one was sure how many states would ratify it, and thus how soon the new court would come into being. NGO representatives thought it would take at least a decade before the required sixty states would ratify and the treaty would go into effect. To their surprise, only four years later, in July 2002, the treaty entered into force. Still, the idea of international justice was hypothetical—a proposition, an idea—not realized yet in practice.

Only a few months after the Rome Conference ended, an event occurred that would begin to embody the idea of international justice. It is difficult to recreate the electricity produced when British police arrested Chilean general and former president Augusto Pinochet in a London hospital on a Spanish extradition warrant for torture and other human rights crimes. Even the most ardent advocates of accountability didn't really believe such an arrest was feasible. The international lawyers knew it was legally possible, but no one believed it was politically possible. Opponents of international justice were outraged. The Pinochet case was so prominent because General Pinochet himself had become the epitome of the modern authoritarian dictator. As opposed to other countries, with faceless juntas or rotating presidencies, Pinochet had kept all the power to himself, and maintained himself as chief executive for seventeen years. He had controlled the transition to democracy to maintain his position as commander in chief of the armed forces, and eventually become a "Senator for life." Pinochet, through his own efforts and those of his opponents, was a global symbol. During his regime, the Chilean opposition in exile around the world had single-handedly created one of the most efficient solidarity networks of modern times. They formed committees in over eighty countries, lobbied tirelessly for sanctions against the Pinochet regime, and publicized his persona so that the photo of his dour face behind dark glasses and folded arms was almost as much an international symbol of authoritarianism as Che Guevara's face on T-shirts had been the international symbol of revolution. Thus, his arrest personified and embodied the struggle over global justice. The world watched, transfixed, over the next two years as the British justice system, and the streets of London and Santiago, played out the drama of the general's detention and trial.

The British courts assiduously confronted the jurisdictional questions posed by the Spanish request, finally determining that the Spanish courts had the ability to try Pinochet for crimes committed in Chile over a decade before. The ruling was based primarily on the positive law of the Torture Convention and the extradition treaties signed by Spain and the United Kingdom. Although the CAT granted universal jurisdiction in the case of torture, this provision had not been used until the Pinochet case in 1998–99, over ten years after the CAT went into effect. The Law Lords (basically the British Supreme Court) determined that a Chilean politician was not immune from extradition to Spain for torture committed while he was head of state since both countries had ratified the Torture Convention recognizing international jurisdiction for the crime of torture. The Law Lords limited their decision only to the Torture Convention because the letter of treaty law ratified by all parties clearly stated that universal jurisdiction existed for torture.

Although British authorities ultimately allowed Pinochet to return to Chile after determining he was too incapacitated to stand trial, the events in Europe had important political repercussions in Chile that rippled across South America and the rest of the world. Once frozen, an unprecedented number of human rights cases started moving ahead in Chile's courts. The Chilean Supreme Court punched holes in Pinochet's self-awarded shield of immunity from prosecution. After his arrest, an upsurge of other foreign prosecutions began, generated by what Naomi Roht-Arriaza has called "the Pinochet Effect."

The Pinochet case galvanized lawyers around the world, as it made them aware of the possibilities of prosecutions. Human rights lawyers in Uruguay told me that it was not until after the Pinochet case that they began to wonder if they had been too passive with regard to their own amnesty law, which encouraged them to think about the new litigation strategies that eventually put ex-President Bordaberry in prison. A human rights lawyer in Germany, Wolfgang Kaleck, who has handled foreign Argentine cases in German courts and who brought a case against Donald Rumsfeld for torture, recalls: "The 1998 Pinochet case: that was the trigger moment. From now on they have to be aware that this is serious, not just raising public awareness."[53]

In this chapter, I have described the global efforts to build the legal streambed of the justice cascade, which started with the Genocide Convention in 1948, the Geneva Conventions in 1949, and the Torture Convention in 1984. These were necessary for later legal action, as the Law Lords would make quite clear in their Pinochet decision. The only bases upon which Pinochet could be extradited to Spain were the actual provisions of positive law, agreed to by all parties. Without the specific provisions of the Torture Convention, and the fact that all the states involved in the case—Chile, Spain, and the United Kingdom—had ratified it prior to some alleged cases of torture, it is highly unlikely that the Law Lords would have agreed to extradition. The same can be said for other crucial decisions leading to the justice cascade, such as those by the European Commission of Human Rights with regard to Greece, or the Inter-American Court on Honduras. The evolution of human rights law and humanitarian law, the proliferation of new treaties with increasingly precise language about individual criminal accountability, and the widespread ratification of those treaties were all necessary conditions for the justice cascade. But they were not in any sense sufficient.

We have seen the crucial role that a handful of individuals also played in the justice cascade, individuals like Cherif Bassiouni, Jan Herman Burgers, Madeleine Albright, Juan Méndez, Silvia Fernández, and Aryeh Neier. These people are not necessarily from powerful states in the North but come from diverse backgrounds. It is interesting that both Bassiouni and Méndez had been imprisoned by their repressive governments, and had gone into exile with a deep desire for justice. Their stories illustrate how ideas and knowledge often travel because people travel. The dictatorships' use of exile backfired, when exiles contributed to the human rights movement not only through their moving personal stories of repression but also directly through their involvement both in the small committees and in the increasingly professionalized organizations that documented and publicized human rights abuses and promoted change.

But these individuals were influential because they created or used institutions that served as organizational launching pads for their ideas. Bassiouni revitalized the AIDP to play a crucial role in securing its oldest dream of creating an ICC, and he created the Siracusa Institute, where North and South could meet. Neier and Méndez turned HRW into a powerful organizational force against impunity. Burgers, Fernández, and Albright show the role that norm entrepreneurs can play within governments. If individuals were essential for initiating the justice cascade, many state and non-state actors needed to be persuaded in order for it to spread. (The theoretical discussion about why these different groups were persuaded to support the move to individual accountability for human rights violations is taken up in the last chapter.)

We now turn to the pressing issue of what difference all this makes. Will the hopes of people like Méndez and Bassiouni be realized? Will individual criminal accountability for human rights violations actually lead to improvements in human rights?

By the turn of the twenty-first century, a backlash had already emerged against the justice cascade. Scholars like Jack Snyder and Leslie Vinjamuri claimed that the "idealists" advocating prosecutions had not considered political realities, and that those advocating prosecutions are actually creating more abuse than they are preventing. One scholar wrote an article entitled "The Rise and Fall of Universal Jurisdiction," in which he concluded that "universal jurisdiction was essentially a post–Cold War discourse and self-feeding hype generated by NGOs, activist lawyers and judges, academic conferences and papers, and mass media."[54] When the ICC started to get underway, its first four cases involved crimes against humanity in Africa. Three of these cases—one against an insurgent group in Uganda, one in the Democratic Republic of the Congo, and one in the Central African Republic—had been referred to the Court by their own governments. The fourth, that of Sudan, was referred to the Court by the UN Security Council. A fifth case, involving Kenya, was the only one that prosecutor Luis Moreno-Ocampo brought to the Court using his independent powers as prosecutor, the very powers that the United States had worked so hard to limit in the negotiations. In December 2010, the prosecutor sought indictments against six Kenyan politicians, including the finance minister, for crimes against humanity during and after the 2007 elections. The

Office of the Prosecutor is now studying other cases, including Colombia, Guinea, Afghanistan, Georgia, and Palestine. But by this point the euphoria had worn off, and the Court born of such high expectations in 1998 had come to be seen by some as a court created by the North to prosecute crimes of the South because all of the early cases involve Africa. Yet this story doesn't reflect the actual creation or the operation of the ICC. Many African countries were supporters of the Court at the Rome Conference, and were among the early and enthusiastic ratifiers of the Rome Statute. Almost one-third of the elected judges on the Court are from Africa, and almost two-thirds are from the developing world. Three of the first four cases were referred by African governments.

How did a court initially opposed by all the members of the Security Council become viewed as a court created by the North? Much of the backlash relied on prior beliefs about the impact of domestic, foreign, and international tribunals. And yet there was a lack of rigorous research to counter this skepticism. It is to this issue that we turn next.

Part III

DO HUMAN RIGHTS
PROSECUTIONS MAKE A
DIFFERENCE?

5

The Effects of Human Rights Prosecutions in Latin America[1]

The Rome Statute and the arrest of Augusto Pinochet had given the human rights movement a reason for optimism, but many policy makers, scholars, and activists disagreed vehemently about the desirability of the justice cascade. Their disagreement was often based on different predictions about the effects or consequences of human rights prosecutions. When Pinochet was detained in London in 1998, the foreign minister of Chile was Miguel Insulza, a leader of the Socialist Party that was once led by President Allende. Insulza, part of a coalition government with the centrist Christian Democrats, called upon the British to free the man who once forced him into exile. " 'The last thing Chile needs is Pinochet as a martyr,' Mr. Insulza said, expressing a commonly held notion that if General Pinochet were somehow hounded to death by his legal problems the country would still explode."[2] The British Conservative leader, William Hague, also called upon the British government to let Pinochet go home to Chile. "It's damaging relations with Chile, a long-standing ally of our country, and causing instability in a country that is now democratic."[3] Some went even further. Margaret Thatcher, the former British prime minister and an old acquaintance of Pinochet's, announced with outrage that his detention amounted to a "judicial kidnapping."[4]

These politicians echoed scholars of transition to democracy in the mid-1980s who concluded that prosecutions for past violations were likely to destabilize new democracies. For example, Samuel Huntington believed that if the trials were undertaken, they had to be carried out immediately after the transition or it would not be possible to hold them at all.[5] Huntington's words carried weight in academic and policy circles, and he was mistrustful of the wisdom of human rights trials. Huntington's incredulity was echoed by younger generations of scholars of transition, who mulled over the potentially negative unintended consequences of such prosecutions. Many feared that prosecutions could weaken already fragile democracies and lead to coups. The noted Argentine scholar Guillermo O'Donnell was co-author of the definitive multi-region study of transitions to democracy with colleagues Philippe Schmitter at Stanford and Lawrence Whitehead of Oxford University. They suggested that in most transitional democracies, holding trials would be very difficult, concluding that "if civilian politicians use courage and skill, it *may not necessarily be suicidal* for a nascent democracy to confront the most reprehensible facts of its recent past."[6] Even Aryeh Neier, executive director of Human Rights Watch at the time, and one of the most eloquent advocates of trials, was pessimistic at the end of the 1980s. "Permitting the armed forces to make themselves immune to prosecution for dreadful crimes seems intolerable," he wrote, "yet it also seems irrational to insist that an elected civilian government should commit suicide by provoking its armed forces." It is interesting that Neier uses the same metaphor as O'Donnell and Schmitter linking suicide and trials.[7]

This literature dates back to the late eighties and early to mid-nineties, right around the time I was making my first foray into the topic of human rights prosecutions. In 2001, I wrote an article with my friend and colleague Ellen Lutz, called "The Justice Cascade," which focused mainly on the foreign human rights prosecutions involving Latin American countries. Ellen and I had met in early 1980 in Washington, D.C., while I was working at WOLA and she was a staff person at the Amnesty International D.C. office. We discovered to our surprise that we had both lived in Uruguay, and now we both worked on Uruguay for our respective organizations. A few years later, Ellen became directly involved in foreign human rights litigation in the United States, serving as one of the lawyers for the plaintiffs in civil lawsuits against former dictator of the Philippines Ferdinand Marcos, and against an Argentine general, Carlos Guillermo Suarez Mason, former commander of Argentina's First Army Corps. Both of these men had taken up residence in the United States when the dictatorships ended in their countries. In the case of Suarez Mason, one of the plaintiffs whom

Ellen represented was Alfredo Forti, who had been forcibly removed from the airplane with his mother and four brothers in Buenos Aires in 1976. Forti and the plaintiffs won their lawsuit, but none ever collected monetary damages on their judgment. One U.S. bank account containing assets belonging to Suarez Mason was seized, but the funds involved were not sufficient even to cover incidental litigation costs.

When we wrote our article together in 2001, Ellen taught me much about human rights litigation. I still recall one day when she called and said that she had been awake all night worrying about how we were addressing the question of the bases of jurisdiction. At the time, I didn't even understand what she meant. Ellen carefully explained the ways in which governments obtain jurisdiction in foreign cases—through the nationality of the victim or the perpetrator, through the territorial location where the crime occurred, or through universal jurisdiction. So, for example, in the human rights cases brought by Argentines in Italy, the victims had dual citizenship in Argentina and Italy, and thus the (part) Italian *nationality* of the victims allowed the Italian courts to have jurisdiction. In a case in the United States involving the murder of exiled Chilean Orlando Letelier and his U.S. assistant in a car bombing in Washington, D.C., U.S. courts had jurisdiction both because of the *territorial* location of the crime and the nationality of one of the victims. Thus, not all foreign courts rely on universal jurisdiction to gain standing for prosecutions. I now understand that jurisdiction is, and continues to be, one of the most important and controversial issues for foreign human rights prosecutions.

Having personally participated in such prosecutions, Ellen was often more skeptical than I was about these cases. She later reflected: "For me the most important lessons learned from the Marcos lawsuit were that whenever possible, justice for human rights crimes must be as accessible as possible to those who suffered most and that the best kind of justice leads to national acknowledgment of the wrongs that occurred and societal involvement in righting them."[8] She did not believe that foreign prosecutions could do an adequate job of discovering and considering evidence; nor did they provide victims with a sense of closure, though she concluded that they were better than no justice at all.

Between 2001 and the present day, much has transpired in global politics. Ellen documented this trend in *Prosecuting Heads of State*, which she co-edited with Caitlin Reiger. The two editors describe a new era of accountability for approximately forty former government officials and heads of state who had been formally prosecuted for human rights violations.[9]

Some scholars of international relations and international law have been especially critical of the increasing use of international and foreign human rights prosecutions. In this chapter and the next, I will spend a lot of time discussing what may seem like tiresome arguments with colleagues. These arguments, however, extend well beyond petty academic debates because they have real policy implications. Stephen Krasner, a respected senior international relations scholar from Stanford University, wrote an op-ed piece which appeared in both the *New York Times* and the *International Herald Tribune* in 2001, saying that "attempts to bring even the leader of an abhorrent regime to trial could make it more difficult to promote democracy by making such leaders and their accomplices more desperate to maintain their hold on power."[10] Writing later with legal scholar Jack Goldsmith, Krasner contended that "a universal jurisdiction prosecution may cause more harm than the original crime it purports to address."[11] Goldsmith and Krasner share a common "realist" perspective that includes a distrust of international law.

The arguments of the trial skeptics are important because, if they are correct, they imply that governments should not be pursuing prosecutions. These are not "just" academic quibbles, but debates with potential real-life consequences for victims and perpetrators, for democracy, for human rights, and for conflict. These academic debates tend to resurface within governments, and the academic positions are echoed, sometimes even cited, by government officials trying to justify their positions. In some cases, the academic actors are also policy actors. Both Krasner and Goldsmith later went to work in the Bush administration. Goldsmith reappears in this book in Chapter 7 as the policy actor who insisted that the Bush administration rescind one of the crucial torture memos. More often, academic debates filter into government debates and influence policy indirectly.

For example, in another influential piece of realist scholarship from 2003, Jack Snyder—Columbia political science professor and, notably, the editor of the series in which this book appears—wrote with Leslie Vinjamuri a rebuttal of the grand claims regarding the consequences of trial justice.[12] They argued on the basis of thirty-two cases from around the world that under certain conditions, human rights trials can themselves increase the likelihood of future atrocities, exacerbate conflict, and undermine efforts to build democracy.[13]

The skeptics have been joined by another group of unlikely allies: culturally aware international lawyers, scholars, and activists concerned that "one size fits all" models of transitional justice will not be sufficiently attentive to different cultural, political, and legal contexts. They question whether it is necessary to put into place "a model that mimics Western legal mechanisms."[14] A single "template" for transitional justice can be problematic, they argue, since what is helpful in one place may be harmful someplace else.[15] Culturally oriented thinkers highlight the use of "traditional" legal and social practices, especially in Africa, to address past human rights violations, finding that such practices may be more appropriate than prosecutions in some settings. For example, they sometimes hold up the local Gacaca processes used in Rwanda after the genocide as a good example of how traditional legal practices may be superior to more formalistic legal prosecutions in the Western mold.

This increased sensitivity to context and history is certainly welcome. It is often accompanied, however, by assumptions that may or may not be adequately supported by empirical evidence. For example, many of the criticisms of prosecutions in Africa are based on the assumption that ordinary Africans don't support demands for justice. So, a systematic survey of 2,700 villagers in northern Uganda, many of whom were victims of insurgent violence of the Lord's Resistance Army (LRA), found that their main priorities were health care, peace, education, and livelihood. Only 3 percent mentioned "justice" as their top priority. But such conclusions sometimes depend on how you interpret responses. In the same survey, 70 percent of respondents said it was important to hold people accountable for human rights violations and war crimes, and 59 percent said that the LRA leaders should be put on trial.[16] It is difficult to interpret these findings as clearly indicating that people in northern Uganda don't care about justice or that legal accountability is an unwelcome Western imposition.

Many arguments against trials are based on the causal assumption that they block efforts to resolve conflict, and thus that people must choose either peace or justice. Given such a choice, people will indeed very often choose peace. But there is not yet systematic empirical evidence that prosecutions do block peace processes or exacerbate conflict. Until such evidence is provided, it is another false dichotomy to ask people if they would choose peace or justice.

Trial supporters have made equally far-ranging predictions about the positive effects of prosecutions, often with relatively little evidence.[17] Human rights prosecutions have been put forward as a means to build democracy, strengthen rule of law, provide justice to victims, and end impunity. However, trial optimists also have had little satisfactory "hard" evidence to support their claims. There was clearly a need to bring in some more data, to stop speculating, and to start testing some of these propositions. Before discussing my conclusions about the impact that trials in fact have, I should explain my method for collecting and weighing empirical evidence.

Building the Database

Collecting comprehensive empirical data on a subject or a series of events requires difficult decision making, engagement with sophisticated data collection techniques, and intensive labor. The first step is choosing a trustworthy source that is available over a long period of time. For my project, I decided to use the U.S. State Department's *Annual Country Reports of Human Rights Practices*, which are generally considered a reliable source of human rights information.[18] These reports include information on human rights practices and domestic judicial activity for 26 years in 198 countries and territories. The reports are not perfect or completely objective; they sometimes reflect the policy and ideological biases of the U.S. government, though they have improved over time. But they are practically the only source in the world that covers human rights issues for such a wide range of countries for so many years.

In the mid-1970s, Congress mandated that the State Department prepare these reports as part of a dramatic set of legislative initiatives that first incorporated human rights concerns into U.S. foreign policy. This legislation called on the United States to refrain from providing military and economic assistance to countries that engaged in gross violations of human rights. And because there were few sources at that time on such violations in the world, *Annual Country Reports* were mandated to document human rights practices and guide U.S. policy. At first, the country reports were thin and of poor quality, but their quality improved, and today, together with Amnesty International's *Annual Reports*, they are routinely used by scholars who need such information on all countries of the world since the late 1970s. My research assistant Carrie Booth Walling and I started reading the early reports for evidence of trials. Carrie was busy working on her own dissertation on humanitarian intervention, but she threw herself into our research with her natural determination and meticulousness.

Carrie and I had long discussions about how we should define and "code" a human rights prosecution. "Coding" is the process of classifying and quantifying information for the purpose of statistical analysis. What is a human rights prosecution? How might we count prosecutions? How do we differentiate between a free and fair trial and a judicial vendetta of one political figure against another? The hardest issue was whether we should code prosecutions wherever they occur or look only at instances of "transitional justice," that is, at human rights prosecutions in countries making a transition to democracy. It is these transitional cases that have been of greatest interest to scholars and that have provoked the heated debate about the impact of moves toward individual accountability. Because all of these countries have recently been ruled by authoritarian regimes, often with grave repression, citizens there have both the greatest hope that prosecutions and truth commissions might end the cycle of state-sponsored violence and the greatest apprehension that there could be another military coup. Transitional human rights prosecutions are those that take place in a new democracy for violations that happened during the previous authoritarian regime. But transitional trials are difficult to code. One must identify the existence of a prosecution, assess whether that prosecution took place *after* a transition to democracy, and then decide if the violation took place *before* the transition, that is, during the prior authoritarian regime.

The answers we provided for these questions ultimately became our "code book"—the instructions we would later provide for student research assistants helping us with the coding. But at the beginning, Carrie and I alone read through page after page of often dry and yet terrible reports of human rights cruelties from around the world. We were searching for the initially infrequent mentions of attempts to hold perpetrators accountable. In the first few reports, Portugal was the only country listed with a trial. To enter into the database, the prosecution activity discussed in the report must inflict costs on a government agent accused of having *individual criminal responsibility* for human rights violations.[19] Some of our prosecutions involve former heads of state and high-level officials, but prosecutions of lower-level officials, including police officers and prison guards, are also included. To avoid erroneously considering political trials, we only coded prosecutions in countries where the *Annual Country Report* suggests that reasonably fair trials with some protections for the rights of the accused could occur. Prosecutions could be initiated either by governments themselves or by individuals or groups. In common law countries, only governments initiate criminal prosecutions; but in some civil law systems, victims and groups representing victims, acting as "private prosecutors," may initiate criminal proceedings either directly or indirectly. This is particularly common in Latin America, and may help explain why Latin America has been a leader in human rights prosecutions.[20]

Since we conceived of human rights prosecutions as a form of enforcement of human rights norms, we did not limit our cases only to those prosecutions that resulted in convictions. We had the idea that the whole process of prosecution—from indictment, to extradition, to preventive detention, to the trials themselves—might make an impact, even when it didn't result in a conviction. So we decided to code this entire "process of prosecution," and not just verdicts or convictions. Our reasoning was that even when prosecutions do not result in convictions and incarceration, they impose not insignificant costs upon individuals, including the financial burden of litigation, the income lost during preventive detention, and importantly for elites, loss of prestige and legitimacy. These costs could in turn deter future rights violations.

Some of our colleagues have criticized our decision to code the entire "process of prosecution" and not only prosecutions that result in conviction. They argue that it is only through convictions that we can know that actual costs were imposed on perpetrators. Others worried that we were overcounting because we were looking at the whole process of prosecution. What if there were countries that dragged on with trials year after year but never produced a conviction? My friend and colleague Leigh Payne independently began another transitional justice data-coding project, using a different source—a digest of news reports from around the world.

Leigh and her team decided to record only those prosecutions that ended in a verdict—a conviction or an acquittal, but at minimum some verdict. This coding decision implies that trials will have an impact only if they are completed.

Leigh and I began a heated but constructive debate on the differences in our coding definitions. I argued that even in the literature on common crime, sociologists claim that the very process of criminal prosecution, even when it does not result in conviction, is a form of punishment.[21] This might be more pronounced for human rights prosecutions of public officials. For example, the detention and prosecution of Augusto Pinochet in London never led to a conviction, and yet most considered it very costly to Pinochet and a cautionary warning for other state officials who had committed human rights violations. Pinochet was once seen as invincible; but when he returned to Chile after being detained in London, he was "a real nowhere man," according to one news story.[22] Even the head of the conservative party associated with Pinochet did not attend the small ceremony in the airport when the general returned. An opinion poll taken around the same time showed that over half of Chileans believed Pinochet should be tried in Chile. I would argue that Pinochet's extradition proceedings in London and the trial of Slobodan Milošević at the ICTY in The Hague were the two most important accountability processes in terms of communicating the significant possibility of enforcement for human rights violations. Yet neither of these prosecutions resulted in a conviction because both of the accused died before they could be convicted. State officials agonize over their reputations, and even the taint of having been involved in a criminal prosecution for human rights violations could be damaging to a political career.

A second decision we had to make concerned how to quantify this information. We decided that the information available in the reports was not fine-grained enough to allow us to count the actual number of trials occurring at any given time in the world. So, we came up with the idea of using what we called "country-prosecution years." Despite the complexity of this term, its meaning is simple: if there was evidence that a cost-imposing prosecution ever occurred in a country in a single year, we coded that country a "1" for that year. If there was no evidence of any process of prosecution, we coded a zero. No matter how many trials a country had in one year, it never received more than a "1." We thought this meant we were using a level of precision in the data coding that was appropriate to the precision of the reports. We also thought it probably meant that we were undercounting the actual number of trials, because I knew of cases—in Argentina, for example—where dozens of trials were moving ahead simultaneously, and yet we only coded Argentina as having one country-prosecution year. Nonetheless, a country that has an active program of human rights prosecutions accumulates over time a score that we call "cumulative prosecution years." This score allows us to distinguish those countries making significant efforts at accountability over time from countries that have held no or few prosecutions. More precise information on the actual number of trials occurring at any one time is only available for a handful of countries.[23]

The coding project took much longer than I had first anticipated. Eventually, though, we produced what we referred to as the Transitional Trial Dataset, and we created the first charts and tables summarizing the data (more advanced and updated versions appear below). Analysis of the dataset confirmed some of my earlier hunches. There was indeed a dramatic increase in prosecutions for individual criminal accountability in the world. As Figure 5.1 demonstrates, the bulk of enforcement in this new model has occurred in domestic courts. The pie chart in Figure 5.2 shows that 66 percent of the prosecution years in the dataset occur in the country

Figure 5.1. **Number of Human Rights Prosecution Years, Separated by Type, 1979–2009**

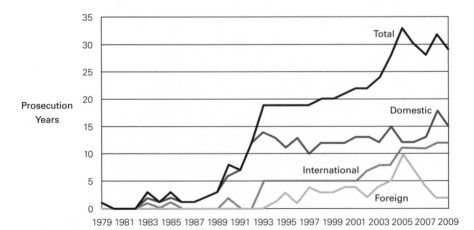

where the crime was committed, and fully 73 percent of trial activity takes place either in domestic or foreign courts. The data also revealed some new facts. For example, it turned out that Argentina was the country in the world with the most country-prosecution years. By following events in Argentina for all those years, I had, without realizing it, been attuned to the global leader in transitional justice, and thus I glimpsed these trends before they were apparent elsewhere.

As soon as we had established to our satisfaction the very existence of the justice cascade, we realized that our data could not only help us understand the trend toward individual criminal accountability in the world but also allowed us to evaluate the impact of these prosecutions. We first attempted to address the question of "effects" using only material from the Latin American cases. Not only did Latin America account for half of the country years in the original transitional trial dataset, but many Latin American countries were among the earliest to use human rights prosecutions as well as truth commissions; more time had passed than in any other region, making it easier to be able to evaluate the impact of these transitional justice mechanisms. But I also focused on Latin America because it was the region I knew best. I felt that I understood the history and politics of the countries where trials were occurring and that this would help me understand the process better.

As the pie chart in Chapter 1 (Figure 1.2) indicated, the trend toward

Figure 5.2. **Percentage Total Human Rights Prosecution Years by Type, 1979–2009**

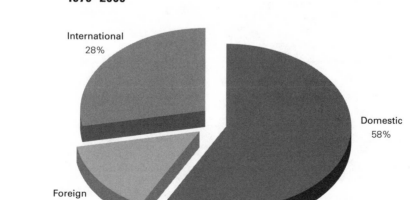

domestic human rights prosecutions has been most pronounced in Latin America, which accounts for 55 percent of total prosecutions, although it is home to approximately 8 percent of the world's population. This higher number of prosecutions is *not* a result of there having been more human rights violations in Latin America than in other regions of the world. Indeed, the single genocidal episode in Rwanda in 1994 accounted for a higher death toll than that registered by all combined campaigns of government brutality documented by truth commission reports in Latin America. Still, Latin American countries account for the majority of domestic prosecutions, and they also are the subject of 53 percent of the foreign human rights trials (shown in Figure 5.3).

Most of the foreign prosecutions in our database were held in the domestic courts of European countries for violations committed largely in the Americas. But these are not European countries acting against Latin American countries. Rather, human rights lawyers representing Latin American victims of violations are "borrowing" European courts when they are blocked from seeking justice in their own judicial systems. The great bulk of these foreign prosecutions have been brought to foreign courts by human rights organizations or private lawyers using private prosecutor provisions and acting on behalf of victims or their relatives. Increasingly,

Figure 5.3. **Regional Distribution of Foreign Prosecutions, 1979–2009**

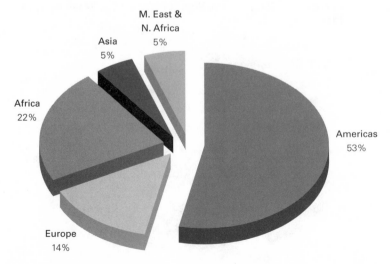

foreign prosecutions are also being held in one Latin American country for violations committed in another Latin American country. But even in Latin America, there is significant variation among different countries in the degree to which they have adopted the new accountability model, and there is also variation within a single country as to when it initiates prosecutions. Brazil has held no human rights trials for violations during the authoritarian government, and Uruguay held no prosecutions for the first fifteen years after the transition, only to begin a handful of prosecutions early in the twenty-first century. We examined all the transitional countries in Latin America, both those that have held transitional prosecutions, and the most important transitional country that has not held prosecutions, Brazil. (Appendix 1 provides a list of all the Latin American countries that have pursued transitional prosecutions.)

As we see in Figure 5.4, although prosecutions sometimes extend for many years after a democratic transition, overall, they cluster in the decade after transition. Most of the transitions to democracy in Latin America happened in the period 1983–93. The total number of country-prosecution years there has two peaks—one in 1992–95 and a second, shorter one in 2002–04. Because there have been no new transitions to democracy in the region since Peru in 2000, eventually transitional prosecutions will decline, almost by definition.

Figure 5.4. **Number of Latin American Prosecutions, 1979–2009**

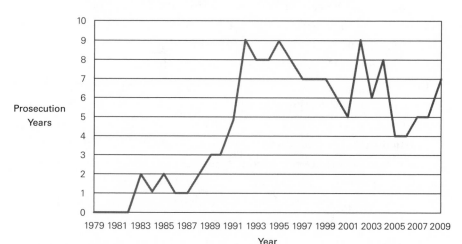

The Nature and the Impact of the Justice Cascade
in Latin America

Carrie and I initially used the data in the transitional database in very simple ways to evaluate arguments advanced by both trial skeptics and trial enthusiasts in the context of Latin America, the region with the oldest and most pronounced record of using human rights prosecutions. Now I also use data to scrutinize a few of the "received wisdoms" in the literature that get repeated so often that it later appears they are true, even though they have not been tested with much evidence. We can distill two such received wisdoms about the nature of human rights trials: (1) human rights trials must happen quickly after transition or they will not happen at all; and (2) transitional justice decisions made in the immediate post-transition period, including amnesties, are durable and mutually exclusive. By mutually exclusive, I mean that the options are always phrased in either/or terms, so it makes it seem as if a country that chooses one option has to forgo the other. So, scholars suggest that a country has to choose truth *or* justice, peace *or* justice, but not both, and that once the choice is made, it is lasting and unchangeable.

In terms of impact, trial skeptics make at least four different claims about the harm of prosecutions: (1) that prosecutions can destabilize democracy and lead to military coups; (2) that human rights prosecutions can increase human rights violations; (3) that prosecutions can increase or prolong conflict; and (4) that prosecutions might impede the consolidation of the rule of law, or that rule of law must be constructed first, before such prosecutions can be attempted. Below, I use both qualitative and quantitative evidence from Latin America to explore the impact of prosecutions and the mechanisms through which they exert an impact.

With regard to the argument that justice comes quickly or it does not come at all, our data clearly indicate that transitional justice continues to be pursued for many years after the transition itself. The average number of country-prosecution years among transitional countries in Latin America is 6.41, and these years are often spread out over a much longer period. Most prosecutions were held in the decade after transition, but in some countries like Argentina, prosecutions were initiated shortly after the transition and continue to be held twenty years later. In other countries, like Chile and Uruguay, few to no prosecutions were held immediately after the transition, but many were held much later.

Samuel Huntington argued that over time, "The popular support and indignation necessary to make justice a political reality fade; the discredited groups associated with the authoritarian regime reestablish their legitimacy and influence."[24] The Latin American cases suggest that popular support and indignation do not necessarily fade, nor do the discredited groups associated with the authoritarian regime reestablish their legitimacy and influence, at least not if they have been the subject of prosecutions. The military and its civilian allies in Argentina, Uruguay, and Chile are far more discredited today than they were after the transition. In Uruguay, a political magazine cover showed a photo of the face of ex-President Bordaberry superimposed on a body behind bars wearing striped prison attire. His son, Pedro Bordaberry, who ran for president in the 2009 elections, barely mentioned his father during the campaign. He lost. In Chile, where a president from the center-right party was elected in 2010 for the first time since the transition to democracy, the candidate went out of his way to distance himself from Pinochet and the repressive politics of the past.

The Latin American cases indicate that there are many possible paths for coming to terms with the past and that no one path is the necessary or feasible one. Political conditions on the ground will make some choices more or less possible at different moments, but they do not definitively close off options. Even amnesties, designed to once and for all erase the option of prosecutions, have failed to do so in most of the countries of the region.

Literature on the perils of prosecutions presented the transitional moment as a time when solid bargains were struck about transitional justice that would endure over time. Observers suggested that countries face mutually exclusive choices between trials and forgiveness, truth and justice, or peace and justice. Huntington, for one, spoke of the decision as "Prosecute and Punish vs. Forgive and Forget"[25] The Spanish case was often held up as an example of a durable solution to forgive and forget. O'Donnell and Schmitter cite the Spanish case as evidence that "The passage of time attenuates the bitterest of memories," and that all political actors can be convinced "not to dig around in the past."[26]

Others argued that the desire for "truth" (truth commissions) and "justice" (prosecution) could and should be separated. José Zalaquett, in particular, maintained in the early period of transition to democracy in Chile that it was preferable to promote the search for truth via truth commissions but to limit the search for retributive justice, and that such an arrangement is more likely to contribute to "reconciliation" than one that uses trials.[27] Not surprisingly, given Zalaquett's subsequent role in the crafting of Chile's transitional strategy, the country decided to have a "National Commission for Truth and Reconciliation" in 1990, but not to hold human rights prosecutions. "Reconciliation" sometimes became a euphemism for "no trials."

But in Latin America at least, transitional justice solutions were neither durable nor mutually exclusive. In the context of a norm shift where prosecutions are becoming more commonplace worldwide, the passage of time has not attenuated demands for justice but rather encouraged victims in other countries to "dig around in the past." Even in Spain, the paradigmatic case of "forgive and forget," people like Emilio Silva have fought for the exhumation of mass graves and set up new organizations for "the recuperation of historical memory."[28]

In Latin America, the transitional justice bargains struck in the immediate post-transition period have varied considerably over time. Transitional countries in Latin America usually have instituted both truth commissions and prosecutions, and they have used them in different sequences. There is simply not a trade-off between truth and justice; to the contrary, the countries in the region that held more prosecutions were also more likely to have a truth commission than countries that held fewer prosecutions. Further, countries that used prosecutions also often employed a range of transitional justice mechanisms, including monetary reparations, removal of abusive officials from office (vetting), memorials, and other forms of memory work. In some cases, one mechanism is used to substitute for or replace another. So, for example, in the Chilean case, initially the truth commission was seen as a truth-telling method that would replace or substitute for prosecution. As we have seen, this replacement would give way with the arrest of Pinochet in London.

Brazil appears to be the only case where a country has so far succeeded in using reparations as a substitute for prosecutions when responding to the demands of victims. Some human rights victims, for example in Argentina, have been critical of reparations precisely because they fear that they are being offered "blood money" to buy their silence and to dampen other demands, such as those for prosecutions, or for locating the remains of their disappeared children. In Chile, after Pinochet's detention in London, the party aligned with him proposed an important expansion of the reparations program that had been functioning for ten years, with the provision that beneficiaries waive any legal claims against perpetrators. The proposal did not prosper, but it illustrates that the idea of reparations as a means to avoid justice is not just paranoia in the minds of victims.[29]

Throughout this book, I have spoken of the connection between amnesty laws and human rights prosecutions. Amnesties have often had a dual purpose: they permit governments to release political prisoners from jail, and they offer reassurances to former government officials that they will not be prosecuted. The Greek amnesty law was worded in an ambiguous manner, and Karamanlis had to clarify that it did *not* cover former government officials before trials could move ahead. In Argentina, one of the first moves of the Alfonsín administration was to lift the self-amnesty law passed by the military government just before it left power. But when Alfonsín was under pressure from the military, he too proposed amnesty laws to limit additional human rights prosecutions. In Uruguay, a majority of the citizens voted to uphold the amnesty law in two different plebiscites on the issue. Particularly striking in Latin America is the combination of amnesties and some kind of human rights prosecutions. Amnesties were used in various forms in virtually all of the transitional countries in Latin America.[30] Leigh Payne's research team was so struck with the prevalence of amnesties that they chose to include amnesties as part of their transitional justice database. They discovered that not only had truth commission and trials increased over time, but so too had amnesties. They wrote that this implied that there was not a uniform move to justice, but a simultaneous increase in amnesty and accountability.[31] Rather than a "justice cascade," Leigh concluded, there was a "justice balance"—a balance between sometimes contradictory mechanisms like trials and amnesties.

One reason amnesty laws have been increasing is because perpetrators of abuse have reacted to the justice cascade. Previously they didn't expect or fear trials, so getting an amnesty would only make them worse off, because it implied guilt. But by the end of the 1990s, their calculus changed because they needed protection from the increased threat of prosecution. I thus disagree with Leigh and her co-authors that an increase in amnesty laws signals an increase in impunity, which in turn implies the justice cascade is not occurring. The increase in amnesties is often a *response* to the justice cascade, not evidence against its existence.[32] Although I equate *blanket* amnesty laws with impunity, not all amnesty laws signal impunity. The combination of amnesty with prosecutions was possible, first, because each amnesty law was different, and some exempted certain actors or actions. For example, the Guatemalan amnesty law exempts genocide and crimes against humanity, while the Uruguayan law only covers the military and not the civilian leaders of the authoritarian regime. These partial amnesty laws can and have co-existed with prosecutions, and thus are consistent with some forms of individual criminal accountability.

Second, amnesty laws often faced challenges in courts that led to their later erosion or reversal. Judicial interpretations of amnesty laws in various countries eventually concluded that the crime of disappearance is an ongoing crime ultimately unprotected by amnesty laws. But these judicial interpretations didn't emerge spontaneously. They were often proposed by lawyers for victims litigating human rights cases who sought innovative legal strategies around amnesty laws. In Argentina, as we saw earlier, when faced with amnesty laws that blocked judicial cases about disappearances, groups pushed forward on cases that involved the kidnapping of the babies born in captivity to disappeared women. We coded the kidnapping cases as human rights prosecutions, and it was these prosecution years that contributed to giving Argentina such a high number of prosecutions. Sometimes, governments or judicial branches had reasons of their own for undermining amnesty law. In Chile, for example, the Supreme Court decided in 1998 that the amnesty law didn't include disappearances, which it redefined as an ongoing crime until the body was located. The decision permitted the judicial system to reopen cases that had been closed for years. Although we don't know for certain the motivations of the justices, the decision lent credibility to the Chilean government's claim that human rights cases could be prosecuted in domestic tribunals in Chile, and thus that Pinochet should be allowed to return home from his detention in the United Kingdom. Finally, regional and national jurisprudence is pushing toward the reversal of amnesty laws. In 2001, the Inter-American Court of Human Rights declared the Peruvian amnesty law to be contrary to the American Convention on Human Rights, and in 2005, the Argentine Supreme Court declared its amnesty laws unconstitutional in the Poblete case.

Only in Brazil and El Salvador have amnesty laws continued to have the desired effect of blocking prosecutions. Even in Brazil, in March 2009, the Public Ministry filed the first criminal complaint against the military for disappearances during the dictatorship. The case involved the disappearances of two Argentines in a Brazilian town near the border with Argentina, as part of "Operation Condor." One of the two men was of Italian descent, and his case was included in a larger case in Italian courts about the Condor Plan.[33] In 2007, an Italian judge issued arrest warrants for 140 Latin Americans suspected of involvement in the Condor Plan, including 13 Brazilians. As in other cases, the demand for foreign prosecutions appears to have contributed to the initiation of the first domestic criminal trial for disappearances in Brazil. In December 2010, the Inter-American Court of Human Rights determined that the Brazilian amnesty law was invalid and said the government must conduct criminal investigations of disappearances.

This use of multiple and changing transitional justice mechanisms contradicts the notion that bargains in the post-transitional period are stable and mutually exclusive. It also makes it very difficult to isolate the impact of any particular factor on later developments. Snyder and Vinjamuri, for example, argue that amnesties "have been highly effective in curbing abuses when implemented in a credible way, even in such hard cases as El Salvador and Mozambique."[34] But at least in Latin America, there is no evidence that amnesties alone are highly effective because amnesties are almost a constant. It is difficult to untangle their impact from that of other mechanisms. For example, El Salvador passed multiple amnesty laws, had a truth commission, carried out a major reform of the police, and held some human rights prosecutions before the amnesty law was passed.[35] El Salvador has seen a significant improvement in its human rights record, but it is not clear which of these is behind the improvement: amnesties, the truth commission, police reform, prosecutions, redemocratization, or the end of the civil war. There is no evidence that the amnesties in El Salvador or anywhere else in the region were effective *by themselves* in curbing abuses. At least in the Latin American cases, no generalization can be made at all about the impact of amnesty laws except that they have not for the most part been effective in preventing human rights prosecutions.

Leigh Payne and her team of researchers, using their different coding criteria, have produced the most persuasive yet puzzling finding about the effects of amnesties. They find that only when amnesties and trials are combined do they produce positive moves toward human rights protections. This is consistent with the data discussed here on Latin America because virtually every country that used prosecutions also had amnesty laws. But Leigh and I also have an ongoing discussion about the impact of amnesties. I argue that most amnesties are designed to prevent trials. Thus, if prosecutions occur, it is usually because the amnesties have been circumvented—often through creative litigation strategies by human rights organizations, or innovative maneuvering by judges. I argue that it is the prosecution, not the amnesty, which is doing the work of deterring future abuses. Leigh responds that her quantitative analysis shows that trials in isolation do not prove to have a statistically significant impact on human rights improvements, but that when combined with amnesties, trials increase the likelihood of positive change.[36] She and her team propose that perhaps amnesties help calm the military or police who are the targets of prosecution, thus buying time for other transitional mechanisms to exert a social effect. Since many amnesties exclude some crimes (e.g., genocide) or some perpetrators (e.g., junior officers), they divide the opposition to prosecutions, and prevent a united front of perpetrators from forming. Also, they argue, amnesties help limit unhealthy expenditures on costly trials, thus assisting the transitional regime in attaining economic stability during a turbulent time.

1. Prosecutions and democracy

What impact do human rights prosecutions have on democracy? Do prosecutions undermine democracy and lead to military coups, as the pessimists claim? If we compare regions that have made extensive use of prosecutions to regions that have not, we find that Latin America, which has made the most extensive use of human rights prosecutions of any region, has also made the most stable democratic transitions of any region. During the twentieth century, political instability and military coups were endemic in Latin America. Since 1980, however, the region has experienced the most profound transition to democracy in its history, and there have been very few reversals of democratic regimes. Ninety-one percent of the countries in the region are now considered democratic, well above the level for

Eastern Europe and the former USSR (67 percent), Asia and Pacific (48 percent), or Africa (40 percent).[37]

Since 1983, when the first prosecutions were initiated in the region, there have been only four successful anti-democratic coups in Latin America, and none was provoked by human rights prosecutions. These include the "self-coup" in 1992 in Peru, and coups in Haiti in 2004, Ecuador in 2000, and in Honduras in 2009, all of which have since reverted back to democracy. The remaining countries that used prosecutions have not had a successful coup attempt since the initiation of prosecutions, and in many cases, they are increasingly considered "consolidated" democratic regimes. No government in Latin America "committed suicide" by carrying out human rights prosecutions. The argument that prosecutions undermine democracy came largely from observations of a single case: the early coup *attempts* in Argentina against the Alfonsín government, after it completed the trial of the Juntas for past human rights violations and embarked upon far-reaching prosecutions of lower-level officials. But almost twenty years have passed since those failed coup attempts, and Argentina has had more transitional prosecutions than any other country in the world, all while enjoying the longest uninterrupted period of democratic rule in its history and weathering at least two major economic crises.

Some trial skeptics now argue that it is acceptable to hold prosecutions in "consolidated" democracies, but not in transitional democracies.[38] This argument is difficult to test because political scientists don't have a good definition of when a democracy is consolidated. By whatever definition, it is clearly easier to wait until democracy appears to be strong and irreversible before a country holds prosecutions. For the most part, this is what Chile and Uruguay chose to do. But some Latin American countries like Argentina, Guatemala, and Peru have chosen to hold prosecutions before their democracies were consolidated, and there is not evidence that this choice undermined their path toward a stronger democracy. One could even argue that prosecutions *helped* consolidate democracy, by warning spoilers (leaders who use force to undermine political change) of the possible costs to them of another coup and an authoritarian interlude.

Looking at the Latin American cases, it is difficult to maintain the argument that human rights prosecutions destabilize democracy. Nor, it should be noted, do we yet have indisputable evidence indicating that human rights prosecutions promote or enhance democracy. Virtually all of the countries in the region, for complex reasons, have made a transition to democracy that appears to be sustained. All quantitative studies of the causes of repression show that democratic rule is clearly associated with the protection of human rights.[39] We assume it is democratic practices that are responsible for the improved human rights scores in much of the region. Brazil, however, which is the only major transitional country in the region not to hold prosecutions for past violations, presents an interesting outlier among the Latin American cases. For example, Brazil's level of democracy is considered relatively high, and similar to that of Argentina, Peru, and Mexico, but its human rights record is not as strong as this would seem to suggest. I believe that Brazil's failure to hold state officials accountable may help explain why its human rights situation has not improved as much as some other countries in the region.

2. Prosecutions and human rights

To explore the impact that prosecutions have on human rights, Carrie and I initially examined very simple repression scores in countries before and after prosecutions to see if we could discern any impact of prosecutions. To measure repression, we used averages from a scale created by other researchers called the Political Terror Scale (PTS). This scale was compiled using codings both from the Amnesty International annual reports and State Department annual reports.[40] It aims to measure the level of a core set of human rights violations—torture, summary execution, disappearances, and political imprisonment—which are often called "physical integrity rights." The scale ranges from 1 to 5, where "1" means virtually no violations of physical integrity rights and "5" means violations are very widespread and are used against the whole population. To gauge the impact that prosecutions had on human rights, we examined the conditions prior to prosecutions and after prosecutions in all of the Latin American countries in our database.[41] Table 5.1 shows that countries with more years of prosecutions have, on average, human rights scores that are better than the regional average, while those transitional states that did not pursue prosecutions had a score that was worse than the average. Since human rights abuses are measured from 1 to 5, one can say that a change of 0.87, like that shown between countries with no prosecutions and those with more than ten years of prosecutions, represents a 17 percent decrease in

Table 5.1. **Comparison of Human Rights Scores of All Transitional Countries in Latin America, 1976–2004**

	Avg. regional HR score*
All transitional countries in Latin America	2.91
Countries with:	
No prosecutions	3.15
Between 1 and 5 years of prosecutions	2.88
Between 5 and 10 years of prosecutions	2.49
Over 10 years of prosecutions	2.38
N = 338	

Higher scores indicate worse human rights practices, with 5 as the maximum and 1 as the minimum.
Source: Taken from Political Terror Scale (Amnesty International) data. See www.politicalterrorscale.org.

overall human rights abuses. This 17 percent corresponds to a great deal fewer instances of personal torture, disappearances, and unlawful killings at the hands of state forces.

One problem that social scientists constantly fret over is what they call in statistics jargon "spurious correlation," which refers to the possibility that the relationship between two social facts—in this case between human rights trials and lessened repression—might be attributable to some unnoticed third factor. It has been suggested that one such factor is previous democratic experience, meaning that those countries that were democratic at some point in the past are more likely to have trials *and* better human rights practices. If this is correct, it suggests that previous experience with democracy, not human rights prosecutions, leads to improvements in human rights. Another talented and quantitatively inclined research assistant, Geoff Dancy, investigated this by counting cases in our database and figuring baseline averages. In the end, Geoff found that this particular theoretical argument does not seem to stand up to the empirical record. While previously democratic countries are slightly more likely to hold trials after transition, they are no more likely to show improvements in average human rights scores, compared to other countries with prosecutions. Transitional countries with trials, compared to those without trials, are much more likely to show average improvements, but previous democratic experience does not seem to *explain* human rights improvements.[42]

The simple analysis in Table 5.1. also cannot distinguish if the improvements in human rights are due to the democratic institutionalization or to numerous variable factors other than prosecutions. This is difficult to test because there is only one major transitional country—Brazil—that did not hold prosecutions. However, if we first look at Brazil before and after transition to democracy in 1985, we see that its average score on the Political Terror Scale worsened for the ten years after transition. The Brazil case suggests that transition to democracy, in and of itself, does not guarantee an improvement in basic human rights practices. But it is still possible that some as yet unknown factors that prevent trials *also* cause the continuing rights abuses.

A second way to partially isolate the effects of prosecutions from the effects of transition to democracy is to observe the differences between transitional countries that had a greater number of prosecutions and those that had fewer prosecutions. All fourteen countries that held prosecutions went through processes of democratic transition. And yet the countries that held more prosecutions had a higher average improvement in human rights than the countries that had fewer prosecutions. So, the seven countries in the region that had more prosecutions experienced an average improvement of 0.9 on the 5-point PTS, while the seven countries that had fewer prosecutions had an average improvement of 0.4 on the PTS.[43]

A third piece of this puzzle concerns truth-seeking. Countries in Latin America that held more prosecutions were also more likely to have a truth commission. The countries that had both truth commissions and a high number of prosecutions had better repression scores than countries that just had prosecutions. These results, together with the evidence from Brazil, suggest that the use of transitional justice mechanisms, in themselves, may have some independent effect separate from that of transition to democracy. It could be possible that there is some other factor doing the work here rather than the prosecutions—perhaps the political will to hold perpetrators accountable for past human rights violations. It is not clear, however, how one could separate out the political will to hold prosecutions from the existence of prosecutions themselves. The take-home point is this: regardless of which part of the human rights improvement comes from transition to democracy, from political will for accountability, or from prosecutions, in the face of this data it remains hard to sustain that human rights prosecutions actually led to more atrocities in the Latin American cases.

These initial findings were suggestive but unpersuasive to most social scientists. Colleagues pointed out, correctly, that we weren't able to control for other factors, and that the effects we observed could be produced by all sorts of other factors that were not included in our discussion. But for our purposes, this early research helped us start to rule out the notion that prosecutions in Latin America were associated with any worsening in human rights scores. Yet the ongoing skepticism encouraged us to undertake the full quantitative analysis with controls that is presented in the next chapter.

3. Prosecutions and conflict

Another key claim circulating primarily among security specialists is that human rights prosecutions can lead to more conflict. Quantitative studies have demonstrated that civil war is the best predictor of violations.[44] That is, if a country is embroiled in an armed internal war, innocent people are likely to be the target of systematic violence. Conflict indeed leads to human rights violations, but it is not clear that human rights prosecutions lead to an increase in conflict. This returns us to the "peace vs. justice" debate discussed above, where these two outcomes are presented as mutually exclusive. For example, some argue that Ugandans prefer peace and reconciliation to retributive justice (i.e., prosecutions), and since you can't have both, peace and reconciliation is the better and more culturally appropriate option. But this argument rests on the as-yet-unproven causal claim that prosecutions undermine peace—a causal argument that is not supported by evidence from Latin America.[45]

Latin America experienced many internal conflicts between 1979 and 2008—the years for which we have data on prosecutions. Seventeen Latin American countries experienced some form of internal or international conflict (from a minor conflict to a full-fledged war) in the period 1970–2008.[46] In most cases, judicial proceedings followed rather than preceded violence. There is not a single transitional trial case in Latin America where it can be reasonably argued that the decision to undertake prosecutions extended or exacerbated conflict. Snyder and Vinjamuri argue that the decision *not* to hold more prosecutions in El Salvador contributed to less fighting there, but their argument—that if prosecutions had been undertaken, more conflict would have ensued—is not supported by evidence from other countries in the region. Figure 5.5 charts the number of conflict years in Latin America compared to the number of human rights prosecution years. We see that as prosecutions (the black line) increase in the region, the number of conflicts (the gray line) decreases. We can't make any causal claims that the rise in prosecutions leads to the decline in conflict; indeed, it could be the other way around, that the decline in conflicts has made it easier for countries to hold human rights prosecutions. But in the light of this trend, it is difficult to sustain that human rights prosecutions have led to an *increase* in conflict.

The striking feature of Latin American politics, in addition to the increase in democracy, is the overall decline in conflict in the region. After a history of fairly extensive internal conflict for decades, the region is now largely free of internal and international wars. With the dramatic regional trend toward human rights prosecutions, and only a single case (Colombia) where significant conflict continues to date, it is difficult to sustain the argument that prosecutions have entrenched conflict in the region.

4. Prosecutions and the rule of law

Most scholars recognize that for human rights violations to decrease, countries need to strengthen their rule of law systems. There are as many

Figure 5.5. **Regional Conflict Years and Prosecutions Years, 1979–2006**

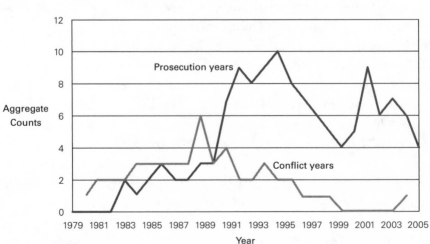

definitions of rule of law as there are of justice. The oldest is the idea that rule of law means "government of law and not of men." In other words, rule should not be arbitrary, but governed by well-established and clearly defined laws and procedures. A component of virtually every definition of rule of law is the idea that "nobody is above the law," and in particular, that public officials too are bound by the law. Some scholars argue that rule of law needs to be established *prior to* the effective use of prosecutions or truth commissions.[47] This raises the crucial issue of how to build the rule of law in countries where it is not yet strong.

Latin America has been undergoing a process of judicial reform and promotion of the rule of law over the last twenty years that parallels the spike in human rights prosecutions described earlier. Rather than see the construction of rule of law as a process separate from human rights prosecutions—or as one that must precede prosecutions—it should be recognized that building rule of law has coincided with human rights prosecutions in much of the region.[48] Indeed, the rise of the field of rule of law aid in the 1990s in large part grew out of the human rights movement of the 1970s and the 1980s. As the movement pushed for transitional justice mechanisms, it "raised the profile of law and legal institutions as a cause of external attention and internal reform in the region. As such, it paved the way for the current nature of rule of law aid in the region."[49] The leading promoters of judicial reform recognize this mutual reinforcement.[50]

Specific prosecutions can also help build rule of law, as they did in Argentina. The trial of the Juntas in 1985 encouraged "the discovery of law," as ordinary citizens perceived a system of law as more viable and legitimate if it could be used to hold the most powerful former leaders of their country accountable for past violations.[51] Again, a crucial ingredient of a rule of law system is the idea that no one is above the law. Government officials cannot ignore the law or act outside of it. As such, it is difficult to build such a system while simultaneously ignoring recent gross violations of political and civil rights, and failing to hold past and present government officials accountable for those violations. Of course, human rights prosecutions are only one of various ways to strengthen rule of law. But the Latin American cases illustrate that prosecutions and strengthening rule of law can be two simultaneous and mutually reinforcing processes.

Unfortunately, there is no good data on rule of law to test these propositions more rigorously, in part because defining and measuring rule of law is extremely difficult. One measure called a "Law and Order score" looks at the strength and impartiality of the legal system, as well as crime rates and the number of illegal strikes. As harsh authoritarian regimes and civil wars came to an end throughout the region, unemployed "men with guns" contributed to an increase in violent common crime. Such crime rose in many Latin American countries after the transition to democracy. Even so, ten of the fourteen transitional countries in Latin America that have held prosecutions have seen improvements in their Law and Order scores from the year they held the first trial to 2006. Brazil, the only Latin American country in the Law and Order database without human rights prosecutions, has seen a decrease in its Law and Order score. These kinds of data do not allow us to make any causal claim that human rights prosecutions build rule of law. However, they call into question the notion that rule of law is a necessary *precondition* for human rights prosecutions. Many Latin American countries had quite low scores in the years that they initiated prosecutions, and yet they managed to improve rule of law and hold prosecutions simultaneously. Ten of these transitional countries have held human rights prosecutions and have seen their scores improve, suggesting that holding prosecutions is compatible (not in conflict) with the process of strengthening rule of law.[52]

We have seen the impact of prosecutions on human rights practices, democracy, rule of law, and conflict. It is not enough, however, simply to establish that the predictions of the trial pessimists have not been confirmed by the evidence in Latin America. I also want to think about the mechanisms through which prosecutions and truth commissions actually work.

Mechanisms of Social Impact

Prosecutions and the subordination of the military to civilian control

One of the ways in which prosecutions can influence human rights is through the effect they have on civil-military relations. In Latin America, to strengthen democracy and avoid future military coups, it was essential to subordinate the military to civilian control. Scholars who have explored the history of military intervention in politics in the region have pointed to the problems created by institutional structures and military ideology, which encouraged the military to act as a guardian—independent of civilian leadership—charged with defending the "fatherland" from internal and external threats. Given this history, subordinating the military to civilian control is a difficult task.[53] Accountability for past human rights violations, however, is one of various measures that Latin American states have used to get the military under control.

Of the fourteen countries in Latin America that used human rights prosecutions, eleven have seen a decrease in the involvement of the military in politics, and in some cases witnessed a sharp decrease.[54] Five countries—Chile, Guatemala, Honduras, Panama, and Peru—all with ten or more country-prosecution years, have witnessed over time a decrease in the role of military in politics by at least 3 points on a 6-point scale. Three transitional countries have not seen greater subordination of the military to civilian control: Mexico, Haiti, and Ecuador. Two of these, Mexico and Haiti, are the only two transitional countries that have also seen their human rights practices worsen. This suggests that the control of the military may be a mechanism through which prosecutions in Latin America have led to improvements in human rights practices.

A comparative study by Acuña and Smulovitz of the civil-military relations in three Latin American countries after democratization—Argentina, Brazil, and Chile—found that the military forces in Argentina were more subordinated to constitutional power than in the other two countries, as a result of their defeat in the Falklands/Malvinas War and of the prosecutions of the Juntas. The subsequent civilian governments established clearly that the president is commander in chief of the armed forces, and eliminated the "historically established large quotas of power and autonomy of the military elite."[55] Brazil and Chile, on the other hand, are examples of transition to democracy "under military tutelage." Since that study was published, the Chilean government has taken steps to bring the military under greater civilian control, but this did not happen until after the detention of General Pinochet in London and his subsequent prosecution in Chile. This reinforces the argument that human rights prosecutions can contribute to the process of establishing civilian control over the military.

The one remaining transitional country in Latin America that has not held any human rights prosecutions—Brazil—has not always taken forceful measures to subordinate military and other security forces, including the police, to civilian control. In August 2008, the minister of justice, Tarso Genro, announced publicly that he believed that the Amnesty Law did not cover the crime of torture, opening the debate about the possibility of initiating transitional human rights trials in Brazil. The military reacted openly: both active and retired military officers participated in a public event at the Military Club that protested against any trials and punishment for torturers. The organizers threatened that they would discuss the "terrorist past" of members of the government of President Lula da Silva, including Minister of Justice Genro. The participation of active-duty military officers in this event, including a general who was the head of the Eastern Command, was clearly a political *action* against the policies of civilian leaders of the government, something not tolerated in systems where the military is fully subordinated to civilian control. The day after, Genro felt obliged to announce: "We aren't under military tutelage," using exactly the same terminology as the study by Acuña and Smulovitz; but events belied his words. In a system where the military was subordinated to civilian control, it would have been appropriate for the minister of defense to have disciplined active-duty officers for participating in public political events. Instead, members of the military called upon the minister of defense to defend the military position, and the minister felt obliged to say that the army "has no historical responsibility" in relation to these human rights issues, and continues to have "an irreproachable national reputation."[56]

Cultures of impunity

When state officials have never been punished for past violations, it can contribute to a culture of impunity, which conditions a country's approach to human rights. This may sound tautological, but the argument here is that the failure to prosecute (impunity) leads to a particular set of expectations—a culture of impunity that in turn can rebound back into more violations. In Brazil, for example, the lack of any punishment for past state officials for violations during the dictatorship may have contributed to an atmosphere of impunity that feeds continuing high levels of violations there today. Brazil is one of the few democratic countries in the region that receives worse human rights scores today than it did during the military government. This is mainly attributable to police officers, who routinely kill suspected criminals at rates so high that they are often seen as summary executions rather than legitimate uses of force: in the state of São Paulo alone, state officials were responsible for 334 deaths in 2006.[57] One source estimates that police have committed 10 percent of the homicides in the São Paulo metropolitan area in the past fifteen years, and are thus co-responsible for abnormally high levels of urban violence.[58] This level is very high even compared to urban centers in the United States, where lethal police violence outpaces that of other developed countries. For example, in 1991, 1,171 people died in the city of São Paulo during "confrontations with the police," compared to 27 in New York City.[59] Although the causes of police violence in Brazil today are very complex, it is possible that the full amnesty for past human rights violations continues to feed a culture of impunity that makes police violence more likely.

I may be too critical of Brazil here. In all fairness, one problem Brazil faces with these measures is that human rights organizations in Brazil and elsewhere have expanded their focus over time from a narrow concentration on direct government responsibility for the death, disappearance, and imprisonment of political opponents to a wider range of rights, including the right of people to be free from police brutality and the excessive use of lethal force. The Brazilian police have become notorious for their high level of lethal force, with wide-scale killings of poor and marginal populations living mainly in the slums of major cities.[60] So, it is not that the federal government of Brazil is involved in more human rights violations than during the military government. Rather, the federal government has been unable to restrain human rights violations by state and municipal security forces. But this expansion in the focus of human rights reporting has occurred throughout the world, and yet other countries in Latin America still see improvements in their scores. So, I continue to believe that a culture of impunity in Brazil is fueling these violations at the state and local levels.

This research calls into question some basic assumptions and received wisdoms in the transition literature about the nature and effects of prosecutions. Our evidence shows that in Latin America—the region most experienced in justice—prosecutions do not increase human rights violations, exacerbate conflict, or threaten democracy; and amnesties by themselves do not produce peace or deter future human rights abuses.

Our research suggests that we need to pay more attention to how the conditions for prosecutions change with the passage of time. We show that whereas trials were considered impossible in many transitional countries immediately after a transition, conditions changed and prosecutions became not just possible but likely. Most observers could not anticipate that prosecutions would become more likely because they believed that the relative strength of actors would remain constant and that norms and attitudes wouldn't change. In other words, theorizing on transitional justice has dealt insufficiently with the possibilities of change and the mechanisms through which change occurs.

The Latin American experience is important because many of the former dictators in the region, such as Videla, Viola, Fujimori, Bordaberry, and Alvarez, have now been prosecuted and convicted for human rights violations. These leaders lost power—sometimes before prosecutions, but more often during or as a result of trials. Latin America has experienced profound transformations, including a shift in norms about transitional justice. These transformations diminished the influence of once powerful actors and made prosecutions more likely over time. The decrease in power of such "veto players" is due to both material and normative factors. These leaders eventually retire, losing their material control over troops and budgets, and are replaced by a new generation of military leaders who may or may not be beholden to past leaders. Pablo Parenti, the prosecutor involved in the human rights trials in Argentina, explained to me that when they first started issuing subpoenas for military officers, they had to send people into the military barracks to deliver the subpoena, a frightening prospect against a military that had disappeared over 10,000 people. More recently, they send the people with subpoenas into the residential suburbs of Buenos Aires, where they deliver them to their retired recipients, who are at home watching television.

The changed context alters how political actors think about their interests. Past state officials who are being prosecuted for human rights violations are less valuable allies than they were formerly. Other political actors often want to distance themselves from officials whose involvement in repression has been revealed. In Latin America, new generations of military and civilian leaders have come to believe that their careers will be advanced by criticizing former repressors rather than by associating with them.

Blackmailers continue to be at work in many parts of the world. Joseph Kony, the head of the Lord's Resistance Army in northern Uganda, has refused to sign a peace agreement until the ICC withdraws its arrest warrant for him. He has reinitiated a brutal civil war in which thousands are being killed and young people are abducted to be his soldiers. President al-Bashir of Sudan has likewise hinted that the security of UN Peacekeepers and aid workers is in peril because the ICC has issued an arrest warrant for him. In both cases, blackmail is the technically correct term, I believe, for what is going on. The trial skeptics say that the "problem" is the ICC, or the demand for prosecution. But objectively, the "problem" is the blackmailer. The ICC—or, more accurately, the demand for prosecution—just makes the problem manifest. The realists say that these are simply the "political realities" of the world, and to ignore them is to be a naive idealist.

What the Latin American cases help us understand is that *political realities are not permanent or inevitable, but are constantly being reaffirmed or reconstructed through political discourse and activity*. For many years, analysts of Latin American politics believed that the constant cycle of weak democracy, military coups, and increasingly violent authoritarian regimes was the ineluctable political reality of the region, born of its history, its stage of capitalist development, its class structure, its Iberian culture, or some other persistent feature of its political and economic condition. But with all the continuing problems faced by fragile democracies in the region, Latin America has taken a turn toward democracy. And has done so in the context of the biggest wave of human rights prosecutions in the history of the world.

In Latin America, countries have not had to choose between truth or justice, peace or justice, or between prosecutions and democracy. Instead, they have faced more complex issues, such as under what conditions can prosecutions contribute to improving human rights; under what conditions can they contribute to enhancing rule of law systems; and what sequencing or combination of transitional justice mechanisms can help build democracy and resolve conflicts.

Facing what seem to be positive results in the Latin American region, skeptics will no doubt question Latin American exceptionalism: maybe the justice cascade has been good, but only in this one region? To respond to this challenge, in the next chapter, the scope of this inquiry widens from one single region to the entire globe.

6

Global Deterrence and
Human Rights Prosecutions

For Maria Piniou-Kalli, whom we met in Chapter 2 when she was welcoming the fall of the Greek Junta in the streets with her son, the Greek trials in 1975 were vitally important both within Greece and in the world. They revealed a detailed picture of how torture functioned in this country and what its results were for both victims and torturers. The trials showed her that "it is possible to convict torturers for their crimes adhering to a just procedure, a fact that was not self-evident at the time."[1] Maria was the daughter of a resistance leader in Greece who was arrested and imprisoned. The first torture victim Maria ever saw was her own father.[2] Shortly after completing medical school, Maria herself was imprisoned during the military dictatorship for her political activity. After the return to democracy, she founded and directed the Center for the Rehabilitation of Torture Victims in Greece. Drawing on her experience treating victims of torture, and her background in the Greek classics, Maria came to believe that the Greek dictatorship and its widespread use of torture was a deep tragedy in the country's history. According to Aristotle's ancient definition, tragedy only ends with catharsis, which is associated with punishment. For Maria, the trials of the torturers provided such a catharsis for victims and for the Greek society as a whole. Catharsis, in the Greek tradition, results not only in relief but also in knowledge.[3]

Some of her friends do not share Maria's vision. Maria put me in contact with Cristina Moustaklis, the wife of Colonel Spyros Moustaklis, who was rendered mute by torture. Cristina, who spoke haltingly but persistently in English, told me her long and painful story. Asked about the impact of the trials, Cristina responded: "Trials, what trials?" Although her husband's torturers were given severe sentences of twenty-three and twenty-one years respectively, by the time we talked, they had been out of prison for ten years and walked freely on the streets of Athens. The trials could not return her husband to her. After he was tortured, he never spoke again. She spent years with him, first in the hospital, then traveling to the United States and elsewhere to seek out treatment. She movingly described her belief in human rights and her hopes that others will not suffer what she suffered. Yet, like many of the victims, and especially the family members of victims, Cristina remembers the trials as important, necessary—and utterly inadequate.

The question of the impact of human rights prosecutions is fraught with such contradictions. Again, "justice" means so many things to different people that trials inevitably fall short of expectations. Cristina represents the positions of many family members of victims in that she was supportive of the prosecutions and wished deeply that they might prevent a reoccurrence of the tragedy she had lived. She cooperated with the trials as a key witness. And yet, like so many family members of victims, she believes the trials were also hollow because they could never restore her loved one, nor could any punishment seem commensurate to the crimes.

Here we continue to address the question of the effectiveness of prosecutions. This book does not systematically *evaluate* justice from the point of view of the victims like Cristina and her husband. That would take a very different approach, focused on fewer cases and involving in-depth interviews with victims and their families.[4] Yet all the victims and their families with whom I have spoken over the years wish to prevent future torture, disappearance, and other forms of repression. Their desire to prevent human rights violations is the common denominator they share with scholars, policy makers, and practitioners. This common denominator is the focus of this chapter. But the needs and wants of victims and survivors are far more complex than this, and I am left unable to evaluate whether those needs and hopes have been met. Nevertheless, I hope that this research will be of some comfort to victims, since it indicates that although human rights prosecutions often cannot repair personal losses, they can help prevent such violations in the future.

Defining Effectiveness

We judge the effectiveness of prosecutions by measuring their consequences against some kind of yardstick or criterion. There are three different yardsticks that people frequently use to evaluate the consequences of prosecutions. The first is an ideal of justice. Since there are so many different ideals, these yardsticks differ from one another, but they share the characteristic of being a "comparison to the ideal"—a comparison between what actually happened and what should have happened in an ideal world. Comparison to the ideal can be either explicit or implicit.

Human rights activists often engage in comparison to an explicit human rights ideal. The activists in Argentina, for example, were not satisfied with the historic prosecutions of their Juntas in 1985. Only five of the nine Junta members were convicted, and only two of them received a life sentence. Activists had the explicit ideal that the punishment should be on par with the crime, and they stated that all the Junta members should have been convicted and that more of them should have received life sentences. Other activists have criticized the ICTY for giving Slobodan Milošević the chance to represent himself, thus providing yet another opportunity for him to traumatize his victims, this time when he questioned them in the courtroom after they testified against him. Because these flaws offend the sensibilities of those committed to justice, they make the argument that it would have been better to have no prosecutions at all than to have the ICTY's flawed prosecutions. This is often the job of human rights activists: to be a voice of conscience and to constantly remind us of the distance between our practices and our ideals.

Scholars also engage in comparisons to the ideal when it comes to international and national justice. I once asked participants on a panel on international justice at an academic conference to specify the ideal of justice that they were using as a yardstick to evaluate international tribunals. One said that he believed the capitalist system should have been put on trial. Some scholars believe that human rights prosecutions, for example, should not only look at legal responsibility for deaths and disappearances but also at legal responsibility for hunger or homelessness. As long as prosecutions address only some human rights but not others, they seem inadequate. Other scholars are critical of any prosecution involving excessively harsh punishment because they believe in restorative rather than retributive forms of justice. Activists, on the other hand, are often critical of prosecutions because the sentences are too lenient.

No situation has been more subject to comparison to the ideal than the ICTY and subsequent trials in the Balkans. So, for example, some scholars have argued that it was unfair to prosecute Milošević for human rights violations in the Balkans but not to prosecute NATO forces for the people killed by the air raids on Kosovo. Others find that the ICTY has erred on the side of appearing even-handed by trying to prosecute individuals from all sides, when the main aggressors were the Serbs. Still others highlight the ways in which political actors have made strategic use of trials. In her insightful commentary on the Balkans, *Hijacked Justice*, Jelena Subotić criticizes local efforts at applying global norms. "Although international organizations may initiate international justice projects for all the noble reasons," she writes, "their effects may be quite different when they are strategically adopted by local political actors. . . ." She goes on, "Only when postconflict societies choose to talk about the horrors that happened, the state and societal complicity in the atrocities, and begin to change the way the past is taught will we be able to say that justice has been done."[5] While these are worthy goals, few attempts at accountability can be expected to accomplish such feats, at least in the short term.[6]

Comparison to the ideal is an important form of ethical reasoning. We need to keep the ability to hold our actual practices up to our ideals and constantly measure where they fall short. Such reasoning is a powerful pressure for change in the international system. It is one of the main tools that advocacy groups use in the world. But it is also important to be careful how we use this form of the ideal comparison, and to distinguish it clearly from systematic empirical comparison. Most important, comparison to the ideal should be explicit rather than implicit. The analyst should clarify that the practice or institution in question is being compared *not* to an empirical example in the world but to a set of ideals of what such a practice or institution should look like, and those ideals should be explicitly stated and defended. For example, if an author believes that the ideal would be a trial of the capitalist system, the reader is entitled to know that this is the ideal against which the current tribunal is being compared. If the implicit ideal is a universal and completely impartial system of international justice, which would operate unfettered by existing power realities, it would also be useful for a reader to know this.

A counterfactual is a second kind of yardstick sometimes used to measure the effectiveness of human rights prosecutions. Some argue that if the ICC had not indicted President al-Bashir, the human rights situation in Sudan would be better than it is today. This is a classic counterfactual argument, where the first part of the statement (if the ICC had not indicted Bashir) is not true, so the speaker is referring to a hypothetical or imagined outcome.[7] Our world is full of counterfactual reasoning; all of us think in this way from time to time. But counterfactuals can be tricky because different people can imagine different hypothetical outcomes, as we see in the case of arguments about the impact of the International Criminal Court.

Scholars and practitioners use counterfactual reasoning very often when referring to the impact of the ICC, perhaps because the institution is so young, and not enough time has elapsed to do a full empirical analysis. The first indictment was in a case referred to the Court by the Ugandan government against the leaders of a particularly violent armed insurgent group, the Lord's Resistance Army (LRA). The Court has since issued an arrest warrant for three of the top leaders of the LRA, including Joseph Kony, its commander in chief. The case has provoked controversy, much of which involves counterfactual reasoning. For example, Adam Branch, among many others, has argued that the ICC's intervention may prolong the conflict and intensify the government's militarism: the ICC, "in a quest for effectiveness, may end up not only undermining its legitimacy but also lending support to violent and anti-democratic political forces." There are many parts to this argument. Because the Ugandan government is not fully democratic, some argue that to accept a referral from it reinforces the legitimacy of authoritarian forces within the country. Another claim cited by Branch is that "justice will in fact be made more difficult by the ICC intervention, since it precludes the possibility of community reconciliation by spiriting away key perpetrators, those who most need to be reconciled or dealt with by their communities."[8] Virtually all of these criticisms have the implied counterfactual that if the ICC had not intervened, the situation in Uganda would be more peaceful than it is with ICC intervention, and they do so on the basis of hypothetical evidence.

Other scholars make contrary assertions. One, for example, argues that the political pressure arising from the ICC led Sudan to eliminate LRA bases in the south, which Kony's forces had been using as safe havens to launch attacks into Uganda. This in turn significantly weakened Kony, forced him to demand an amnesty, and so diminished LRA atrocities.[9] This too is a counterfactual argument, but in this case, the claim is that if the ICC had not intervened, the situation in Uganda would be more violent. So, we have two almost opposite counterfactuals about the same situation, and it is difficult to determine which is the more valid.

Over time, it will be possible to study many more ICC cases and to perform a systematic empirical comparison of serious conflict situations in the world, contrasting those where the ICC has intervened to those where it has not. Such a systematic comparison would be a more persuasive way of evaluating the ICC's effectiveness. For the time being, readers need to be aware when they are reading counterfactual arguments, and to understand that very different alternative counterfactuals may be equally plausible.

Because of the problems with comparisons to the ideal and counterfactual reasoning, I prefer systematic comparative empirical research. This involves choosing cases that are sufficiently similar for the comparison to be valid, and trying to compare them rigorously. On the basis of such research, I argued in the previous chapter that the countries in Latin America that used human rights prosecutions have better human rights records than countries in the region that did not use such prosecutions, or used them less frequently. I don't say that these prosecutions met my ideals of justice, but simply that countries that used them appear to be better off. Sometimes such comparisons lead in turn to the use of counterfactuals. So, for example, I used the empirical comparisons to generate a counterfactual about Brazil: if Brazil had carried out human rights prosecutions, it might have seen a reduction in the level of violence. Systematic empirical comparisons are neither straightforward nor easy. As we have seen, many scholars were not persuaded by the arguments about trials that Carrie Booth Walling and I were making because we didn't use a more sophisticated statistical analysis to control for other intervening factors. These scholars point out, reasonably, that we claim that trials are improving state practices; but what if there are other factors we are not taking into account that actually drive the human rights progress, factors such as the level of economic development or the strength of democracy?

I knew that to be more persuasive, I would have to do more complete statistical analysis, but I didn't have the necessary quantitative skills. By full statistical analysis, I mean one that accounts for other factors that may explain what we see as the outcome of prosecutions—these include controls for level and persistence of democracy, the presence of civil war, and a country's economic wealth, among other things. Luckily, one of my advanced graduate students, Hunjoon Kim, had both a deep knowledge of issues of transitional justice and an excellent command of quantitative analysis. He was working on a dissertation on the origins and effects of transitional justice that included both a large quantitative study and a qualitative study of the origins of truth commissions in South Korea. Hunjoon agreed to work with me on a joint quantitative article on the impact of human rights prosecutions in the world. He was interested in perfecting and using our trial database for both our joint project and his dissertation.

This chapter summarizes the results of this large statistical study that I co-authored with Hunjoon Kim, published recently in the *International Studies Quarterly*.[10] Hunjoon and I decided to use a large study of many countries to test four different propositions that had emerged out of previous research. First, we wanted to test the proposition that human rights prosecutions are associated with general improvements in human rights. Second, we wanted to explore whether prosecutions contribute to human rights because they impose punishment on state officials, or because they communicate and dramatize norms. Third, we wanted to test if prosecutions in one country can contribute to improvements in other countries; in other words, if it is possible to have deterrence across borders. Finally, we wanted to answer the main question raised by trial skeptics: Do prosecutions in situations of internal or civil war exacerbate human rights conditions?

Proposition #1: Human rights prosecutions are associated with improvements in human rights

To try to test all of these propositions, Hunjoon Kim and I used an expanded version of the same database that I had prepared with Carrie Booth Walling. We wanted to examine both the impact of domestic prosecutions and the added effects of any foreign and international prosecutions on human rights practices. To gather information on the latter, we had to supplement the U.S. State Department data with information gathered from human rights groups, non-governmental organizations, and intergovernmental institutions. Because foreign and international prosecutions exist for only a relatively small number of countries, we could not test to see if these trials had a separate, independent effect on human rights. Instead, we put international and foreign prosecutions in a single category called "international," and added the international prosecutions to those of domestic human rights prosecutions. Even so, domestic prosecutions make up the great bulk of total prosecutions in the database.

We used these data to explore the impact of human rights prosecutions. We tested the argument of recent realist discussions of trials, in particular the argument that prosecutions lead to more violations.[11] We also examined the alternative deterrence argument that domestic prosecutions represent an increase in the probability of punishment for human rights violations and, as such, would be expected to lead to a decrease in violations.

Proposition #2: Prosecutions lead to improvements in human rights practices both through punishment (deterrence) and by communication norms (socialization)

Hunjoon and I didn't only want to figure out *if* human rights prosecutions had an effect on human rights practices; we wanted also to learn more about *why and how* human rights trials make a difference. We wanted to understand the theoretical mechanisms through which prosecutions lead to change. There are a number of theories about why such prosecutions might contribute to change, but they can be grouped into two general arguments: rational theories that focus on the role of deterrence or enforcement; and social-psychological theories that look at the contributions that prosecutions make toward socializing security forces and state officials and internalizing new norms.

Many advocates for trials stress that they support prosecution because they believe they could prevent human rights violations in the future. In other words, people want prosecutions not necessarily for retribution but to deter future crimes. But these advocates don't usually clarify the mechanisms through which they expect transitional justice to work. Sometimes, there is the assumption that just telling the truth and revealing the facts will have an effect in itself. The truth commission report in Argentina was called *Nunca Más* ("*Never Again*"), partly to convey this idea that truth-telling could help prevent a repetition of the crimes. But more often, advocates embrace some version of deterrence theory; explicitly or implicitly, they believe that some kind of punishment is most likely to deter future human rights violations.

This proposition relates to many larger debates about whether enforcement or sanctions are necessary for states to comply with international rules.[12] Many commentators have long claimed that we shouldn't expect human rights norms to have any important effects because they don't have any enforcement or teeth. But I believe that human rights prosecutions can be conceptualized as a form of enforcement or sanction for violations of domestic and international criminal and human rights law. If enforcement is necessary to get countries to comply with the law, we would expect prosecutions to lead to better practices.

This argument draws on an important literature on deterrence in domestic legal systems which explores whether increases in punishment lead to declines in common crime. Within this literature there are contentious and still-unresolved debates among criminologists. One of the most controversial issues involves the death penalty—and particularly whether the death penalty deters crime. Indeed, at least in the United States, the debate over the death penalty is so prominent that many people believe that deterrence arguments are themselves discredited because we have little evidence showing that harsh penalties deter crime. But deterrence focuses on two different factors: (1) the probability or likelihood of punishment; and (2) the severity of punishment. Arguments about the death penalty are only about the severity of punishment. There is little evidence that an increase in the severity of punishment leads to lower levels of crime. Studies have shown, however, that increasing the *likelihood* of punishment *can* deter crimes within countries.[13]

To date, there are few parallel studies to test these arguments about deterrence in the international system. Hunjoon and I applied them to international politics to see if human rights prosecutions lead to a decrease in human rights violations. We did not explore the issue of the severity of punishment, although many people, like Cristina Moustaklis and the victims in Portugal, saw the length of the prison term as the main indication of the seriousness of trials. Some of the human rights organizations observing the trial of ex-President Alberto Fujimori of Peru in 2009, for example, decided that they would protest the results if Fujimori received a sentence of less than twenty-five years. Human rights prosecutions have sometimes led to quite severe sentences. Fujimori did receive twenty-five years, and the Argentine Adolfo Scilingo received a sentence of more than six hundred years at his trial in Spain. Human rights prosecutions virtually never use the death penalty, since it is increasingly believed to be contrary to human rights law. As research on domestic crime rates has not clearly shown that more severe punishment deters crime, it is not likely that we will find that severe punishment deters human rights violations. Indeed, I believe that activists may place too much emphasis on the severity of punishment in such prosecutions. I suspect that the fact that Fujimori was held legally accountable is more important than whether he was sentenced to fifteen years or twenty-five years of imprisonment.

Our database indicates that what has changed dramatically in the realm of international human rights is the likelihood of individual punishment for state officials responsible for violations. Prior to the 1970s, there was virtually a zero percent chance that heads of state and state officials would be held accountable, either during the repressive regime or after the transition to a democratic regime. Indeed, the international realm may provide some kind of natural experiment for deterrence theory, since a key variable—the likelihood of punishment—has moved from zero to a positive number in a relatively short period of time in many states. The likelihood of punishment varies from country to country and from region to region, and we would expect those countries that have more trials to see a greater deterrence effect.

Applying a deterrence model to the realm of human rights implies a rational assumption that state leaders choose repression in light of the costs and benefits it is likely to yield.[14] At first, it may seem odd to think of state officials who engage in unspeakable atrocities as rational actors who calculate the costs and benefits of their behavior. Clearly there are sadists, psychopaths, and extreme ideologues among those who engage in repression, yet studies of repressors have long suggested that they are, for the most part, ordinary people with common motivations. Some state officials carry out repression because it brings them specific political, ideological, or economic benefits; for example, repression often allows officials to confront and punish their political opponents, prolonging in the process their own regimes and careers. Repression may also permit state officials to emphasize their role as saviors of the nation from external or internal threats, thus enhancing their political power and reputation.

Finally, repression can provide economic payoffs for the repressors. Nazis confiscated the wealth and possessions of the Jews they murdered; today, families continue work to recover the stolen art or the bank accounts of their relatives. Reports of disappearances in Argentina reveal that when state officials kidnapped their opponents, they often also ransacked their homes, stealing money and goods, which they later divided among themselves. Studies of genocide in Rwanda also document that neighbors often used the ethnic killings as a cover to settle old accounts and confiscate land and property. In situations where human rights violations provide significant benefits to repressors and impose few costs, one doesn't have to be a die-hard rational choice theorist to understand that it will be difficult to stop repression.

The alternatives to the rationalist deterrence model are social, psychological, or normative models, which posit that sometimes both repression and compliance occur mainly for reasons that have more to do with culture and beliefs than with a rational calculation of costs and benefits. These psychological or norm models stress the logics of "appropriateness" and obedience to authority. Lower-level state officials may carry out human rights violations because they are ordered to do so, and they lack the moral compass or the verbal formula that permits them to refuse. Hannah Arendt's famous point about the banality of evil in her book on the trial of Adolf Eichmann, the German bureaucrat who deported millions to the death camps in Nazi Germany, was that Eichmann was not a monster, but rather a "thoughtless" man, who was concerned about his career advancement and incapable of telling right from wrong.[15] Similarly, the Yale psychologist Stanley Milgram found in his experiments in the 1960s that most people were willing to give electric shocks to strangers in another room if ordered to do so. They received only five dollars for participating in the study and no punishment if they dropped out. Nonetheless, many of the participants administered what they believed to be electric shocks to people, apparently because they thought it was the appropriate thing to do in the context of the experiment, and they lacked a reason or a way to say no.

It wasn't just that Adolf Eichmann was a thoughtless man who couldn't tell right from wrong. Rather, as Arendt tells us, "his conscience spoke with a respectable voice, with the voice of respectable society around him." Since respectable society in Nazi Germany supported the Final Solution, his conscience was at ease. At one point in his trial, Eichmann claimed that no one ever told him that what he was doing was wrong—"The most potent factor in the soothing of his own conscience was the simple fact that he could see no one, no one at all, who was against it."[16]

An international relations scholar would say that Eichmann and the people in Milgram's experiments were following "logics of appropriateness." In other words, they weren't doing a cost-benefit analysis to decide how to act, but rather they were asking themselves, "In this situation, what kind of behavior is appropriate?" and acting in accordance with that. In extreme conditions, even genocide can be seen as the appropriate behavior.

Human rights prosecutions allow respectable society to speak with a different voice. Such prosecutions are not only instances of punishment or enforcement but also high-profile symbolic events that communicate and dramatize norms and socialize actors to accept those norms. After such prosecutions, no future perpetrators could later claim that they didn't know what they were doing was wrong. Prosecutions are an expression of social disapproval; the informal social sanctions that follow from the formal legal sanctions can have important effects in political arenas where reputation is essential.[17] Because state officials care about their reputation and esteem, and the reputation and legitimacy of their state, they may change their behavior in response to processes involving the mobilization of shame by advocacy networks and international organizations.[18] As norms become more deeply internalized in society, certain options are no longer even considered.

My colleague, the sociologist of law and criminologist Joachim Savelsburg, maintains that the main way law has an effect is by becoming embedded in collective memory. "Law steers collective memory," he argues, and it does so "directly but selectively." "Trials produce images of the past," yet those images are not an objective portrayal of the truth, but rather a ritualized presentation of evidence of the kind required by the legal system. Savelsburg studies such collective memory by looking at the media and at textbooks to see how they record the past.[19] In a recent book, *Crime and Human Rights: Criminology of Genocide and Atrocities*,[20] he contends that scholars have often ignored the large literature in criminology when we think and write about human rights. When I first got interested in deterrence theory, Joachim helped direct me to the relevant studies about deterrence in criminology. Now he worries that I am focusing too much on the deterrence side of the equation and am not paying enough attention to how trials might affect culture and society, especially through collective memory.

These social and psychological literatures suggest that enforcement may not be necessary in all circumstances and that behavioral change might be possible in the absence of strong enforcement mechanisms. They *do not necessarily say* that stronger enforcement is counterproductive for compliance, just that it may not be necessary. Thus, while sociologists and international relations theorists disagree about whether enforcement is necessary for compliance, few argue that stronger enforcement is counterproductive.

There is a psychological literature that has now been developed by legal scholars which suggests that material incentives like punishment can sometimes have negative or unintended effects on behavior because they "crowd out" other, more positive processes of change.[21] If this argument is relevant to our cases, however, we would have seen that human rights prosecutions make the situation worse rather than better.

To help us better understand the mechanisms through which prosecutions affect human rights practices, Hunjoon Kim and I decided to contrast the impact of human rights prosecutions with the impact of truth commissions. Truth commissions are high-profile processes about past human rights violations that seldom involve any punishment. Truth commission reports rarely give the names of perpetrators, and even when they do, such naming does not lead to a material sanction. Because a truth commission does not result in any material punishment of individuals, if only material costs matter, truth commissions are unlikely to have any independent effect on human rights practices. If, however, both social and material costs are important, we would expect to see that both prosecutions and truth commissions have a positive impact.

If Joachim Savelsburg is right and trials work primarily through their effects on collective memory, we shouldn't expect them to have a rapid or direct effect on future perpetrators. The effects of any trial will depend on how it becomes embedded in collective memory. For example, since the trials in Portugal are barely remembered by anyone, we wouldn't expect them to have much of an impact; the trials in Argentina or Chile, however, would have a much greater effect because they have become embedded in collective memory through the media, and in textbooks, films, and fiction.

Proposition #3: Human rights prosecutions lead to "deterrence across borders"

Although prosecutions are likely to have the biggest deterrent effect in the country where they occur, there is also the possibility for more general prevention or deterrence. Assuming that repressive actors pay attention to both the likelihood of punishment in their own societies *and* to the possibility of punishment in nearby countries, an increase in prosecutions in the region as a whole could lead to a decrease in repression in other countries nearby. Since individuals pay more attention to legal developments in those countries closer to them, we might expect that prosecutions in one country will have an impact on repression in other countries in the same region.

We decided to test this argument by examining whether countries in regions with more human rights prosecutions see a greater impact on repression than countries in regions with low cumulative totals. So, for example, the trials of members of the military in Argentina in 1985 were likely to exert influence on the military in Chile and Uruguay, even though trials were not yet occurring in these countries. There are sufficient similarities among these countries that perpetrators could seriously consider that the fates of their colleagues in Argentina might have some implications for their own situation. High-profile international and foreign prosecutions that receive international press coverage may have a more general effect in a wide range of countries around the world. Even in this case, regional similarities may continue to matter. Although the extradition hearings for Pinochet in London might have had a global deterrent effect, I believe that Latin American militaries, in particular, were influenced by Pinochet's experience. Because of common history and language, other Latin Americans identified with Pinochet and thus saw his fate as linked to their own. I found some anecdotal evidence of this phenomenon from interviews I conducted in Guatemala shortly after Pinochet was arrested in London. The Guatemalans I interviewed were distinctly aware of the Pinochet arrest, and they readily made connections between perpetrators in their own country, especially former President Ríos Montt, and Pinochet. Ríos Montt, who was president during the genocide in the early 1980s, had also been indicted in a Spanish court. Shortly after his indictment, he stated publicly that he was not afraid of the Spanish arrest warrant and had every intention of continuing his travels as before. Yet every person I spoke with pointed out that Ríos Montt had not set foot outside of Guatemala since the Spanish indictment.

The literature makes few references to deterrence from punishments that happen outside the borders of a country. That makes sense for common crime, since the common street criminal is unlikely to be reading the newspaper and paying attention to arrests and punishments elsewhere. It is much more plausible to assume that state officials pay attention to what happens to officials in neighboring countries. There are two possible kinds of "deterrence across borders." First, a potential perpetrator may see prosecutions in neighboring countries and modify his behavior because he fears that similar trials could soon take place in his country. This is the case of the Uruguayan watching what happens in Argentina and changing his behavior accordingly. Such deterrence across borders is more likely to happen within regions or areas with common cultures or languages. They speak the same language, so the Uruguayan can listen to Argentine television news and keep up to date on what is happening there. Because the two countries share a border and had military dictatorships at the same time, it is plausible that what happens in Argentina might someday happen in Uruguay.

A second kind of cross-border deterrence happens with foreign prosecutions, where security forces or government officials watch a foreign trial and imagine that they, too, in the future could be arrested and tried abroad. They can do what General Ríos Montt of Guatemala did and protect themselves from foreign prosecutions by not traveling. But they can't completely rule out that their own governments might someday give in to extradition requests and actually arrest them and extradite them abroad to stand trial.

If there are deterrent effects across borders, the decentralized system of enforcement will be more effective than if the effects are limited to the perpetrator's home country. This would lead to a multiplier effect, where those regions that use prosecutions more frequently produce a broader positive impact on human rights beyond their borders. Some countries in the region may be in fact "free-riding" on the prosecutions in their region, benefiting from the deterrence effect without having to take the political risks and costs of holding their own prosecutions.

We can examine whether there appears to be a cross-border deterrent effect by seeing if the cumulative number of prosecutions in a region appears to have any effect on practices in other countries in that region. Although various mechanisms could lead to such an outcome, it is plausible that cross-border crime reduction is at work.

Proposition #4: Prosecutions during civil and internal wars exacerbate human rights practices

But if the effects of deterrence do cross borders, other cross-border effects may be equally plausible. So, for example, it is just as plausible that military governments, watching what happens to their colleagues put on trial in nearby countries, would be unwilling to give up power because they fear trials. Thus, human rights prosecutions in one country could lead to greater longevity for authoritarian regimes in other countries. This is a scenario that scholars such as Jack Snyder and Stephen Krasner have suggested. Not only could authoritarian governments become more entrenched, but so could insurgent groups that commit human rights violations. When these groups see prosecutions of insurgents happening in nearby countries, they may decide not to engage in peace negotiations and lay down their arms for fear that they, too, will face human rights trials and punishment. It is hard to test this argument because it involves counterfactuals about how long an authoritarian regime would have lasted without the threat of prosecutions compared to how long such regimes are lasting in practice.

At least in Latin America, where the threat of prosecutions has been greatest, there is no evidence that the threat of trials led either authoritarian leaders or insurgent groups to entrench themselves. But such fears are very real for a whole set of countries in Africa today where civil wars continue to rage, such as Sudan, the Democratic Republic of the Congo (DRC), and Uganda. These cases are quite different from those in Latin America. The Latin American cases involve prosecutions after a transition to democracy for violations during a previous authoritarian regime. The cases of Uganda and the DRC involve international indictments of non-state insurgent groups during a civil war, while the Sudan case involves the indictment of the president and other high-level state officials of an authoritarian regime for genocide and crimes against humanity. Many scholars and practitioners have criticized the International Criminal Court for indicting suspected war criminals in these countries. If the threat of prosecution prolongs civil wars, Krasner and Goldsmith argue that such indictments could actually be causing more human rights violations than they prevent. We try to address these issues by consulting our quantitative data to see if the presence of civil war affects the impact of prosecutions.

The Statistics

In this chapter (and the article on which it is based) we use our data on human rights prosecutions in transitional countries during the period 1980–2004 to explore the four research propositions stated above. We look at transitional countries because the entire transitional justice literature tells us that transitional societies are in a state of instability and fluctuation; choices about accountability made during such periods could have an enduring impact. Important new work by Beth Simmons also demonstrates that human rights law has had more impact in a subset of transitional societies than in either fully authoritarian or fully democratic countries.[22] Simmons, however, does not examine the impact of human rights prosecutions, as we do here. There is no corresponding theoretical literature which posits that prosecutions will have an important impact on the already high level of human rights protections in fully democratic societies, or in fully authoritarian societies.

We included all states that experienced a transition between 1974 and 2004. This includes the countries from the beginning of what Huntington has called the "third wave" of democratization.[23] This seems appropriate since the first cases of domestic prosecutions after the World War II trials began are in those countries that led the third wave: Greece and Portugal. We considered all countries undergoing three types of transition: democratic transition; transition from civil war; and transition by state creation. Democratic transition occurs when a country moves from a repressive and closed regime to an open and decentralized government. Transition from civil war occurs when a state recovers from the instability and turmoil of a domestic armed conflict. And transition by state creation happens when new countries (such as those that emerged after the breakup of the Soviet Union) also change from repressive and closed regimes into more open and democratic governments. We found one hundred transitional countries from 1980 to 2004. (A list of these countries is in Appendix 3.)[24]

We created two measures for prosecutions: the first, called human rights prosecutions (HRP), tracks whether a country had a prosecution at any point after transition. The second, called cumulative human rights prosecutions (CHRP), is a measure of the cumulative number of prosecution years in any country, which captures the persistence and frequency of prosecutions. Our cases cover forty-eight countries with at least one human rights prosecution, including thirty-three with two or more cumulative prosecution years. (A list of countries and a battery of summary statistics appears in Appendices 3–4.)

Figure 6.1 provides a snapshot of our sample and independent variables. The gray line shows our entire sample of all the countries experiencing transition between 1980 and 2004. We see a steady increase in the number before 1989 and a sudden rise between 1989 and 1992, reflecting the collapse of the Soviet Union and the Eastern European regimes. The lower, black line shows the gradual increase of states with human rights prosecutions after 1980. Basically, what made our research systematic was that we did not choose to examine only those countries that had already decided to use human rights prosecutions, but rather all the countries that are represented by the gray line (those in transition that could have used prosecutions). Some did use them and some did not. This, then, allowed us to make the comparisons between those countries that used prosecutions and those that did not, as well as comparisons between countries that used more prosecutions and countries that used fewer prosecutions.

Figure 6.1. **The Number of States with Transition and Human Rights Prosecutions**

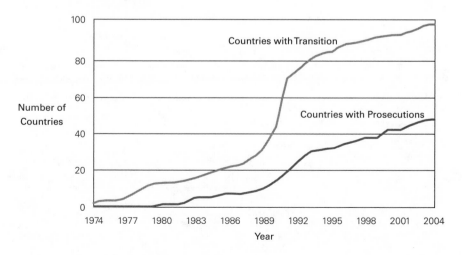

Figure 6.2 shows the change in the average cumulative prosecution years over time globally and by region. This is just another version of the table in Chapter 1 that depicts an increase in human rights prosecution, but this time, we also break it down by region over time. The larger graph on the left shows the global cumulative prosecution years, and the smaller graphs on the right break that trend down by region. They show that Latin America certainly is leading the trend, but average cumulative prosecution years in Africa and Europe are also moving upward over time.

Next, we explored the impact that human rights prosecutions and truth commissions have on a core set of violations—torture, summary execution, disappearances, and political imprisonment—which we refer to as "repression" or as "physical integrity rights." Human rights prosecutions mainly address executions, torture, disappearances, and genocide, so we should look for impact on these physical integrity rights. We measured it using a physical integrity rights index developed by David Cingranelli and David Richards.[25] We also cross-checked our findings using an alternative

Figure 6.2 **Changes in the Average Cumulative Prosecution Years (CHRP) Over Time, by Region**

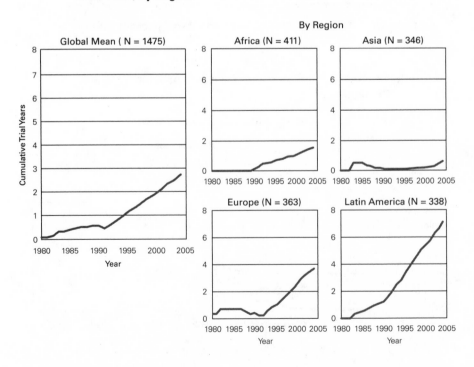

measure—the Political Terror Scale (PTS) discussed in the previous chapter, coded both from Amnesty International reports and State Department reports.[26] Our findings were basically the same whether we used the physical integrity index or the PTS.

Figure 6.3 summarizes this physical integrity measure over time in the world and in different regions. Using the physical integrity scale from 0 to 8, where "8" represents the highest level of human rights violations and "0" the lowest, it shows changes in the mean score of repression of physical integrity rights in transitional societies over time. This is a kind of snapshot of changing levels of basic violations in all the transitional countries in the world and in the various regions. The graph in the left panel represents the mean score of all transitional countries. The average level of repression is fairly constant, but we can see a slight drop over time; moreover, there are visible discrepancies when we examine the mean level of repression by region. While the European countries show quite stable, low levels of repression, we witness a substantial decrease in the levels of repression

Figure 6.3. **Change in the Average Level of Repression Over Time, Globally and by Region**

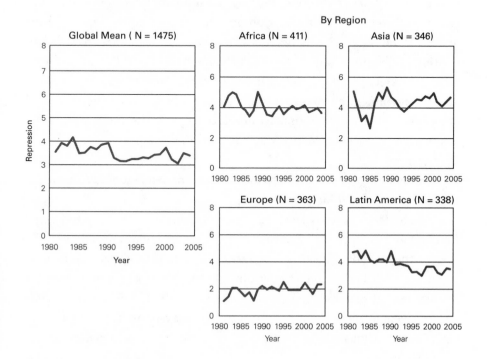

over time in Latin American countries, with levels of repression in Africa appearing to decrease slightly as well.

Once the data had been gathered, Hunjoon used three different statistical methods to explore the interactions between the independent variable (human rights prosecutions) and the dependent variable (level of human rights violations). The benefit of this kind of analysis, as compared to the simpler analysis in the previous chapter, is that it allowed us to control for many other factors and thus better isolate the effects of prosecutions from any other factors that might affect the level of repression. Previous studies point to eight other factors that typically influence the level of human rights violations. These include, most importantly, the level of democracy, the level of development, and the presence of international wars or civil wars. In other words, we know from previous studies that wealthier and more democratic countries have fewer human rights violations than poorer undemocratic countries. We also know that one of the biggest predictors of whether or not a country will engage in violations is whether or not it is engaged in a civil or an international war. During wars, governments feel more threatened, and they may respond with rights violations in the name of national security. Some other studies have shown that the fact that a country has ratified an international human rights treaty as well as the population size and population growth of the country can also have an impact on human rights practices. We expected that these factors will continue to be important, so we took them into account. Previous studies have not explored the impact of human rights prosecutions, so our study adds a new dimension to statistical analyses in the field. We also explored the impact of truth commissions because they are the most often cited alternative transitional justice mechanism in addition to prosecutions.[27] Truth commissions publish ample data on past violations but do not lead to punishment, so they permit us to look at the independent effect of normative processes of naming and shaming.

One challenge in statistical analysis is to understand which factors came first and are really the ones causing the effects we are interested in studying. In the case of transitional countries, so many things are happening at once that it is difficult to sort out what matters. Many countries are simultaneously experiencing a transition to democracy, which corresponds to improvements in liberty and in their judicial systems, as well as human rights prosecutions. For this reason, we compare transitional countries without prosecutions to those with human rights prosecutions, and we use statistical techniques that try to address a possible reciprocal relationship among our variables and pinpoint which factors are doing the work of reducing repression.

Evidence

Figure 6.4 provides a simple visual representation of the basic findings of the study—that countries with human rights prosecutions tend to have lower levels of repression than countries without human rights prosecutions. It shows the changes in the average repression score of countries with different experiences with prosecutions. On the left-hand side is the measure of repression: the higher the number, the higher the level of violations. Within both graphs, a black line indicates the global means, that is, the changes in the yearly mean of the repression score for all the countries in the analysis (both those that experienced prosecutions and those that did not). In the top graph, we compared this global mean repression score of countries with prosecutions (a light gray line) to those without

Figure 6.4. **Changes in Mean Score of Repression by Human Rights Prosecution Experience**

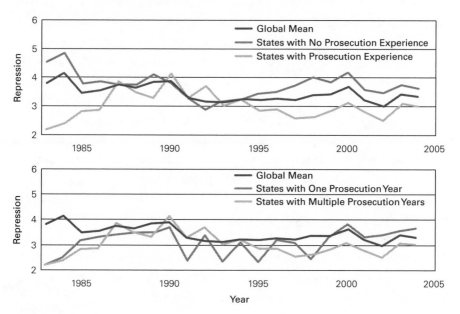

any prosecutions (a dark gray line). The distinction between the two lines becomes clear and remains stable after 1994. The mean repression scores of the group of countries without prosecutions are constantly above the average global level of violations, while the mean repression scores of the group of countries with prosecutions are below the average. The graph (Figure 6.4) compares the mean repression scores of countries with one prosecution year (dark gray line) to those with multiple (2 to 20) prosecution years (light gray line). While countries with one prosecution year for most of the time period have a below-average mean repression, states with multiple prosecution years tend to have more stable and lower repression scores than the average after 1994. These are still just averages, and the reader who wishes to see the regression tables should look to Appendix 4. Basically our findings are similar to those in the previous chapter, but this time we were able to control for the other important factors that might also have an impact on repression.

In many ways, our findings are consistent with previous studies. Democracy, civil war, economic standing, population size, and past levels of repression all have a statistically significant and substantively important impact on the level of repression. But in addition, human rights prosecutions also have a strong and statistically significant downward impact. When controlled for all the other relevant factors, the level of repression in countries which have had a prosecution is lower than that of countries which never had a prosecution. Moreover, not only prosecution experience but also the persistence and frequency of prosecution matters. The level of repression decreases as the number of years with human rights prosecutions increases in a country. If a country were to move from the minimum (0) to maximum possible number of prosecution years (20), this would bring about a 3.8 percent decrease in the whole repression scale.

The truth commission variable was included in the model both as a control variable to estimate the true effect of human rights prosecutions and as an independent variable to test whether truth commissions have an independent effect on repression. The fact of a truth commission being present also contributes to improved human rights protection in transitional societies. Our model shows that a truth commission brings about a 0.19 point decrease in the repression score in the short term and a 0.43 point decrease in the long term. If a country were to have both a human rights prosecution and a truth commission after transition, that would bring about a 0.35 point decrease in the repression score in the short term and a 0.8-point decrease in the long term. This provides some support for the social and psychological explanations for a decrease in repression. Our finding suggests not only that punishment matters but that truth-telling matters as well. This may imply that prosecutions function not only through rational deterrence but also through communicating and drama-tizing societal norms.

In sum, we found that countries with human rights prosecutions have better human rights practices than countries without prosecutions. In addition, transitional countries that have experienced more prosecutions over time (and thus a greater likelihood of punishment for past violations) have better practices than countries that have had no or fewer prosecu-tions. Contrary to the arguments made by some scholars, human rights prosecutions have not tended to exacerbate human rights violations.

The main criticism of such prosecutions by some scholars is that they can lead to greater repression, especially in situations of civil war, because the demand for prosecution can delay a peace agreement. Since civil war in particular is associated with human rights violations, anything that prolongs the war could have the effect of exacerbating abuses. In our sample, 53 countries—265 country years (18 percent)—were recorded to have a minor or major civil strife after transition.[28] In addition, 16 countries—124 country years (8.4 percent)—had gone through a transi-tion from a civil war. We were able to use these variations within our sample to examine the different effects of prosecutions in the context of past or current civil wars.

We found that the independent effects of prosecutions on repression are still significant in situations of civil war. Civil wars continue to be associated with worsening human rights, as previous studies have shown, but human rights prosecutions under civil wars do not make the situation worse. Basically, controlling for war, our results show that prosecutions in countries with civil war transitions do not have a different impact on repression than those in countries with other types of transitions.

This finding provides counterevidence to the argument that prosecu-tions in civil war contexts are less effective. Athough the involvement in civil war certainly exacerbates governmental repression, the experience of prosecution still appears to have a positive impact on human rights pro-tection in those situations, compared to other civil conflict states with no such prosecutions. In addition, the independent effect of truth commissions also holds true under various civil war–related scenarios.

We also tested whether human rights prosecutions might have a possible deterrence effect across borders. We already know that countries are more likely to use prosecutions if they are already being used by other countries in the region.[29] This is why the prosecutions show a strong regional clustering. But what happens if a country in a region doesn't use human rights prosecutions even though many of its neighbors do? Does it benefit from a deterrence effect from its neighbors' use of prosecutions?

Our analysis shows that the presence of human rights prosecutions in geographically proximate countries surrounding a particular country significantly decreases the level of repression for that country, which suggests a possible deterrent effect beyond borders. A transitional country with no human rights prosecution activity at all can achieve a similar effect as a country with its own prosecutions if four or more of its neighbors already have prosecutions.

This research calls into question the claim by trial skeptics that human rights prosecutions aggravate poor human rights practices. Recall that we conceptualize prosecutions as an increase in the enforcement of existing human rights norms. This kind of enforcement involves individual criminal sanctions for state officials who engaged in violations. The prosecutions database shows that there has been an increase in enforcement and in the costs of repression, which is likely to be perceived by government officials who make choices about how much repression to use. We cannot distinguish these costs, but we believe they are both the economic and political costs of the formal sanctions (lost wages, litigation fees, inability to participate in elections while on trial or in jail, etc.) and the informal social and political costs that arise from the publicity surrounding the prosecutions (loss of reputation or legitimacy, and the resulting loss of political and social support). At the same time, there is no reason to believe that the benefits of repression have increased. So, if the benefits of repression have remained constant, and the formal and informal costs of repression have increased, the economic theory of crime predicts a decrease in crime, which is what we see in the countries that have experienced more cumulative country-trial years. We also found that truth commission experience has a positive impact on human rights. This suggests that the mechanisms through which transitional justice measures influence human rights involve not only a calculation of the possibility of punishment but also a response to processes that provide information and communicate norms.

Protecting and improving human rights practices requires that transitional countries make substantial structural changes in the nature of their domestic institutions. Such changes are not easy to make. Human rights prosecutions are only one of the many forces that can contribute to positive change. They are not a panacea for human rights problems; they appear to be one form of sanction that can contribute to the institutional and political changes necessary to limit repression.

These findings are still preliminary and have been contested by other scholars. As we have seen, Leigh Payne and her team also produced a dataset on human rights prosecutions, amnesties, and truth commissions, using codings from different sources of information. They did not count the entire process of prosecutions, as we did, but only actual verdicts in human rights trials, either acquittals or convictions. They also used somewhat different statistical methods. Leigh and her team found that human rights verdicts, in themselves, did not lead to a statistically significant improvement in human rights practices. They also found that truth commissions, by themselves, actually were associated with worsening human rights, not improvements. But, when human rights verdicts were combined with amnesty laws, they found that they did lead to improvements in human rights, and when all three—verdicts, amnesties, and truth commissions—are combined, they are also associated with improvements. In this sense, Leigh and her team agree with Hunjoon and me that trials can lead to improvements in human rights; but we differ about the conditions under which this happens.

To try to resolve these differences, Leigh and I have begun to merge our databases in order to continue to explore *how* transitional justice leads to human rights improvements, and especially, *through what processes or mechanisms* trials and truth commission can lead to greater respect for human rights.

We all agree that prosecutions appear to be having an impact, but we don't yet understand well enough the ways in which trials work. We dispute the claims of trial skeptics that prosecutions are exacerbating human rights violations in the world. We suggest, to the contrary, that it appears that prosecutions lead to *improvements* in human rights. But until we resolve some of our differences, we won't have more precise theoretical statements or clearer policy recommendations. We can't yet sort out clearly whether trials work mainly through deterrence and punishment or through socialization and collective memory. We also can't say yet whether it is better to combine prosecutions with amnesties, or to annul amnesties. We suspect that the answers, like most in the social world, are complicated: that prosecutions work both through deterrence and socialization; that prosecutions combined with some kinds of partial amnesties may be a good solution; and that blanket amnesties should be avoided.

In the last two chapters I have endeavored to provide an empirical response to those who advance a generally negative reading of human rights developments and their expression in legal action. I have done so on the basis of evidence from countries around the world. But, to this point, I have left unaddressed a question that is on the minds of many scholars and policy makers: What about powerful states like the United States, Russia, or China? Will the justice cascade ever make a difference there? In an attempt to answer this question, we turn now to the U.S. case.

7

Is the United States Immune to the Justice Cascade?

Scholars of international relations and global civil society have long said that the real test of international law and new norms will be their ability to influence the actions of even the most powerful states. Thus, no discussion of the impact of the justice cascade would be complete without a consideration of its implications for the United States. In particular, I want to focus on U.S. non-compliance with the prohibition on torture and cruel and degrading treatment during the administration of George W. Bush. What effect, if any, did the prior history of the justice cascade have on Bush administration policy? Did domestic and international demands for accountability, and the initiation of national and foreign human rights prosecutions, have any influence on decision makers in the upper echelons of American government? In the short term, the U.S. case illustrates a central point of the realist theory of international politics: powerful states are able to disregard international rules at will. In the longer term, however, this case shows that even the United States is not totally beyond the reach of the international human rights laws and humanitarian law it helped to codify.

I had already started the research for this book when I first began to learn about the human rights violations of the Bush administration after 9/11: I still recall an e-mail from an Argentine colleague asking me whether they were starting to "disappear" people in the United States. At the time, I thought she was referring to Middle Easterners residing in the United States who were being detained for long periods without charges in the period after 9/11. I wrote back to say that although this was indeed arbitrary detention without trial, these people were not disappeared. We now know that I was wrong. By 2002, the Central Intelligence Agency was indeed taking detainees to "black sites," secret detention centers where they were tortured and interrogated. American officials were denying that they knew the whereabouts of these detainees, and they did not allow the International Red Cross to visit them. This fits the technical definition of disappearance.[1] UN experts have clarified that international law completely prohibits such secret detention.[2]

By the spring of 2004, after the photos of torture and degrading treatment of inmates in Abu Ghraib prison in Iraq appeared, and the report of General Antonio Taguba investigating the abuse was leaked to the press, I walked into the last human rights class of the semester and said to my students: "I have been teaching this class for over ten years, and I have to stand up and say something today that I have not said before. We have clear proof that the United States government has engaged in torture and cruel and unusual punishment of detainees."

The proof came from the Taguba Report, an internal report from the U.S. military. The report stated that "several U.S. army soldiers have engaged in egregious acts and grave breaches of international law"; it continued: "Between October and December 2003, at the Abu Ghraib Confinement Facility (BCCF), numerous incidents of sadistic, blatant and wanton criminal abuses were inflicted on several detainees. This systemic and illegal abuse of detainees was intentionally perpetrated by several members of the military police guard force. . . . The allegations were substantiated by detailed witness statements, and the discovery of graphic photographic evidence."[3] Later, we learned that the practices described in the Taguba Report went far beyond the actions of a handful of individuals; they were the result of a concerted policy set at the highest levels of the U.S. government.

Starting in 2005, I began to present research in a series of conference papers, lectures, and eventually a chapter in a book entitled *Bringing Human Rights Home*.[4] But in all these earlier versions, I assumed that U.S. officials *could not* have fully understood the implications of the justice cascade, because *if* they had understood, they wouldn't have adopted policies that were criminal under both U.S. and international law. Since that time, additional interviews and a wealth of new publications have helped me realize that Bush administration officials understood the law. They didn't use this understanding to ensure good-faith compliance, but they did use it to craft legal strategies to protect themselves from the possibility of future prosecution.

Between 2002 and 2008, the United States was in violation of the Torture Convention's prohibition on torture and cruel and degrading treatment.[5] In recent years, new books by Bush administration insiders and journalists have revealed more completely the inner workings of the administration's policy of torture and detention. These works confirm that the post-9/11 approach to torture was the product of a relatively small group of allied policy makers in the executive branch of the government, led by Vice President Dick Cheney; his legal adviser, David Addington; and a team of lawyers in key positions in the administration, in particular, John Yoo, deputy director of the Office of Legal Counsel of the Justice Department. Addington and Yoo wrote relevant legal memos that justified the policies, often using extreme legal positions. Almost from the start, and throughout the process, they were warned by allies, by military lawyers, and by individuals both within and outside the administration that their policy was illegal and likely to cause grave consequences for rule of law, for the image of the United States, and for themselves. But they disregarded these warnings and marginalized the messengers.[6]

At first, these legal memos seem puzzling. Why would the U.S. government put in writing its controversial justifications for practices considered human rights violations? The so-called "torture memos" are almost unprecedented in recent world history. If the U.S. government wished to carry out illegal activities, why didn't it just do so, without leaving a "paper trail" of legal justifications? Wouldn't written documentation generate internal controversy and make it harder for top-level officials later to deny that they condoned illegal practices?

I now believe that the very production of these memos was a response to the rise in national and international human rights prosecutions. The tipping point in the global justice cascade came somewhere between 1998—when the Rome Statute of the ICC was completed and opened for signature and Pinochet was arrested in London—and 2001, when Milošević was turned over to the ICTY and the ICC went into effect. U.S. field operatives became increasingly aware that they could be prosecuted for violating human rights, and they asked for legal cover and political assurances that would protect them from such prosecution. In this sense, the memos themselves are indications, however perverse, of the impact of the justice cascade. Before the cascade began, state officials and human rights activists literally couldn't imagine individual criminal accountability for human rights violations. Yet in 2002, CIA officials repeatedly sought guidance from top Bush administration officials about legally acceptable interrogation techniques. In a sworn statement in federal court, one CIA official said that the "requests for advice were solicited in order to prepare the CIA to defend against future criminal, civil, and administrative proceedings that the CIA considered to be *virtually inevitable*."[7] What happened between the 1970s, when such an outcome was unimaginable, and 2002, when it was considered virtually inevitable?

U.S. torture policy had a particularly virulent effect—and not just for its victims. Because of the power and influence of the U.S. government, its practices are watched, cited, and imitated by repressive governments throughout the world as justification for their own practices. By the later years of the second term, the Bush administration was obliged to moderate some elements of its policy by withdrawing the most controversial legal memos; but to its very last days in office, the administration continued to seek immunity from prosecution for state officials. Since coming into office, the Obama administration has focused on halting the use of torture, but has avoided holding anyone legally accountable for it. President Barack Obama, like many other leaders we have seen in this book, wanted to look forward, not backward. Like other governments around the world, though, the Obama administration has discovered that the legal demands for accountability might not be so easy to ignore.

U.S. Legal Commitments to the Prohibition of Torture

What does it mean to say the United States was not "in compliance" with prohibitions on torture? Compliance includes both what states do (behavior) and also what they say about their behavior. Are they aware of norms and laws, and do they refer to them as justification for behavior?[8] Thus, an examination of U.S. compliance with the prohibition on torture needs to look both at U.S. behavior and U.S. justifications for its behavior. There are many reasons why we might expect a powerful state like the United States not to be in compliance with international law. Because it is the hegemon in the international system, other states find it difficult to sanction the

United States for flouting the law. The United States also has particularly difficult treaty ratification rules, and an ideological tradition of isolationism and skepticism about international institutions. Furthermore, with a federal government and a common law system, the United States may face additional procedural and institutional obstacles to ratifying and implementing international law.[9]

Although it faces these difficulties, the United States also has a long history of commitment to human rights, a democratic system that allows for checks and balances by the judicial and legislative branch on excesses of executive power, and a strong civil society, including many non-governmental organizations working on human and civil rights. The U.S. military has a tradition of concern for the laws of war going back to the Lieber Code of the Civil War era, and it employs well-trained military lawyers, including the Judge Advocate Generals (JAG) Corps. Democracies are more likely to face internal pressure generated by lobbying, media exposure, and litigation to abide by their international treaty commitments. If these countries fail to comply, they may face sanctions from their domestic constituencies as well as from the international community. Thus, once democracies commit to international legal obligations, these internal processes should produce higher levels of compliance with their commitments.[10]

The United States has long accepted the prohibition on torture and cruel and unusual punishment, both in domestic law and in its international law commitments. The Eighth Amendment to the U.S. Constitution, part of our Bill of Rights, prohibits the federal government from inflicting "cruel and unusual punishment." There are many debates about what constitutes cruel and unusual punishment, but it has never been in doubt that torture is prohibited. In the 1972 case of *Furman v. Georgia*, Justice William J. Brennan wrote that the "essential predicate" of the prohibition was "that a punishment must not by its severity be degrading to human dignity."

The United States has ratified a number of treaties that clearly state its international legal obligation never to use torture and inhuman and degrading treatment under any circumstances, including the Geneva Conventions of 1949, the International Covenant on Civil and Political Rights of 1976, and the Convention Against Torture. America was deeply involved in the process of drafting these treaties, and worked to make the prohibition on torture and cruel and degrading treatment more precise and enforceable. During the drafting of the CAT, the U.S. delegation clearly supported treaty provisions on universal jurisdiction with regard to torture.[11] At one point in the negotiations, Argentina, still under the dictatorship, objected to the provision on universal jurisdiction. The U.S. delegate responded by saying that

> Such jurisdiction was intended primarily to deal with situations where torture is a State policy and, therefore, the State in question does not, by definition, prosecute its officials who conduct torture. For the international community to leave enforcement of the convention to such a State would be essentially a formula for doing nothing. Therefore in such cases universal jurisdiction would be the most effective weapon against torture which could be brought to bear.

The delegate added that "it could be utilized against official torturers who travel to other States, a situation which was not at all hypothetical."[12]

At the same time as the Torture Convention was being negotiated in the early 1980s, the idea that torture was a violation of international law that could be prosecuted anywhere in the world was underscored by the case of *Filártiga v. Peña-Irala* in the United States. The case involved a young man, Joelito Filártiga, who was tortured to death by Américo Norberto Peña-Irala, the chief of police in Asunción, Paraguay, in 1976. It was brought forward by Joelito's father, Dr. Joel Filártiga, and his sister, Dolly, who had tracked Peña-Irala down in Brooklyn, New York, where he had overstayed a tourist visa. The Filártigas believed there had to be some way to seek justice, so they contacted lawyers at the Center for Constitutional Rights (CCR), an NGO devoted to civil rights litigation. The CCR lawyers came up with the novel idea that they could use a jurisdictional statute called the Alien Tort Claims Act—which was drafted in 1789, largely to address piracy—as a basis for suing a Paraguayan torturer in the United States. Their argument was accepted on appeal in 1980 by a U.S. federal court judge, who decided that, by 1980, there was a customary international legal prohibition against torture, and declared that "the torturer has become—like the pirate and slave trader before him—*hostis humani generics*, an enemy of all mankind."[13] This case opened the way for human rights civil cases in U.S. courts, and the Alien Tort Claims Act became the primary way that foreigners could sue for damages in U.S. courts for human rights violations.

The administration of George H. W. Bush submitted the CAT treaty to the Senate in 1990 and supported ratification. A bipartisan coalition in the Senate, including the conservative senator Jesse Helms of North Carolina, worked to ensure that the Senate gave its advice and consent for ratification. The Senate Foreign Relations Committee voted 10–0 to report the convention favorably to the full Senate. When she spoke in support of ratification, Kansas Republican senator Nancy Kassebaum said, "I believe we have nothing to fear about our compliance with the terms of the treaty. Torture is simply not accepted in this country, and never will be."[14]

When the United States ratified the Torture Convention in 1994, U.S. lawyers went through it with a fine-toothed comb; as a result, the United States presented reservations against various provisions of the convention that might come into conflict with domestic law. It did not, however, make a reservation against the provision calling for universal jurisdiction.

Increasingly, U.S. jurists argue that international human rights treaties are not "self-enforcing" and thus must be implemented in domestic law in order to have effects in U.S. courts. The Geneva Conventions were implemented in domestic legislation in 1996, when overwhelming majorities in the Congress passed the War Crimes Act, which makes it a criminal offense for U.S. military personnel and nationals to commit grave breaches of the 1949 Geneva Conventions, including torture and cruel and degrading treatment. Congress passed the law mainly so that the United States could prosecute war criminals from other countries, especially the North Vietnamese, who had tortured U.S. soldiers during the Vietnam War. The bill's sponsor, one of the most conservative members of the House, Representative Walter B. Jones (R–NC), also intended the law to be for use against future abusers of captured U.S. troops in countries such as Bosnia or Somalia. The Pentagon recommended at the time that the legislation include breaches of humanitarian law by U.S. soldiers as well, because the United States generally followed the Geneva Conventions and this would set a high standard for others to follow. The statute gives access to civilian courts for victims of war crimes, and it provides for heavy penalties for such crimes, including the death penalty.[15] It does not provide for universal jurisdiction, so U.S. courts would get jurisdiction in more standard ways— because the victim or the accused are U.S. nationals, or because the crime took place on U.S. territory.

After the Senate had ratified the Convention Against Torture in 1994,

Congress enacted a new federal anti-torture statute to implement the requirements of the convention.[16] It makes torture a felony and permits the criminal prosecution of alleged torturers in federal courts in specified circumstances. A person found guilty under the act can be incarcerated for up to twenty years or receive the death penalty if the torture results in the victim's death. Not surprisingly, Bush administration officials were particularly concerned about the possibilities of prosecution under these two statutes. This is not evidence, however, that they were only concerned about domestic law and not international law. Rather, they were most concerned about those aspects of international law that had been fully implemented within the domestic statutory law of the United States.

In 1999, in its initial report to the UN Committee Against Torture, the U.S. government stated that

> Torture is prohibited by law throughout the United States. It is categorically denounced as a matter of policy and as a tool of state authority. Every act constituting torture under the Convention constitutes a criminal offence under the law of the United States. No official of the Government, federal, state or local, civilian or military, is authorized to commit or to instruct anyone else to commit torture. Nor may any official condone or tolerate torture in any form. *No exceptional circumstances may be invoked as a justification of torture. United States law contains no provision permitting otherwise prohibited acts of torture or other cruel, inhuman or degrading treatment or punishment to be employed on grounds of exigent circumstances (for example, during a "state of public emergency")* or on orders from a superior officer or public authority, and the protective mechanisms of an independent judiciary are not subject to suspension. The United States is committed to the full and effective implementation of its obligations under the Convention throughout its territory.[17]

As this statement makes clear, there was little ambiguity in U.S. legal and ethical commitments to the prohibition on torture and cruel and unusual punishment prior to 2002. While there is evidence that some parts of the government condoned torture in U.S. training programs in the past, there are important differences between past and present practices.[18] Before 2002, high-level policy makers did not publicly condone or justify practices that can be considered torture and cruel, inhuman, and degrading treatment. In the 1970s, for example, when members of Congress learned of accusations that U.S. personnel were complicit with torture in Brazil and Uruguay through a USAID project called the Public Safety Program, the executive agreed to close it down.[19] And in the 1990s, when critics found training manuals used at the Army School of the Americas that gave a green light for torture, the Pentagon decided to discontinue the use of the manuals.[20] But the Army did not discipline any of the individuals responsible for writing or teaching the lesson plans, nor were any students retrained.

After 9/11, some in the United States began to make arguments similar to those used earlier by the governments of Greece, Portugal, and Argentina to justify the use of torture and repression. Those regimes saw leftist and Communist groups as posing the major security threat to the nation and said repression was necessary to confront subversion. Many in the United States now argued that Islamic terrorism was the major security threat to the nation and that torture was justified to confront terrorism. They did not seem aware of the history showing that such justifications led to large-scale human rights violations.

Although general awareness of U.S. use of torture began after the publication of the photos of Abu Ghraib prisoners in April 2004, the use of torture and cruel and degrading treatment began in the so-called CIA "black sites" and in the U.S. detention center at Guantánamo Bay in 2002. Many official reports and secondary studies documented the widespread use of such practices directly by the CIA and by U.S. troops and personnel.[21] Perhaps never before in the history of debates over torture and cruel and degrading treatment has so much information been available about the different techniques used by specific individuals and units. Much of this information comes from sources within the U.S. government, but there are also numerous reports from national and international non-governmental organizations.

When photos were first released from Abu Ghraib prison, officials characterized the depictions as isolated aberrant acts by a few low-level soldiers during a short time period. However, since the story initially broke, reports from the International Red Cross and a barrage of leaked reports from within the U.S. government reveal that the practice of torture and inhuman and degrading treatment was far more widespread and long-standing, occurring not only in Abu Ghraib but also in other detention centers in Iraq, in Afghanistan, and in Guantánamo Bay, including the black sites. A widespread practice in multiple locations implies an institutional policy, not human error.[22] Investigators from the International Committee of the Red Cross (ICRC) visited Guantánamo in June 2004, and in a confidential report later made public described how the military there had used coercive techniques that were "tantamount to torture." Specifically, the ICRC said its investigators found a system of "humiliating acts, solitary confinement, temperature extremes, use of forced positions. . . . The construction of such a system, whose stated purpose is the production of intelligence, cannot be considered other than an intentional system of cruel, unusual and degrading treatment and a form of torture."[23]

By 2004, the Defense Department had identified twenty-six specific cases where detainees had died in U.S. custody and fourteen cases where the cause of death was not "natural." These figures are supported by documents, including autopsy reports, that the Defense Department has now made public.[24] However, the U.S. government still has not permitted a full independent investigation to establish the exact circumstances surrounding these deaths and responsibility for them. Journalists and human rights organizations have documented that in many cases these individuals died as a result of torture.[25]

The debate still continues about exactly which techniques constitute torture and which constitute cruel, inhuman, and degrading treatment, and about what the Geneva Conventions mean when they refer to "humane treatment." But the existence of documented deaths of detainees in U.S. custody as a result of torture leaves no doubt that U.S. officials violated both international and domestic law prohibiting torture and war crimes.

Bush Administration Efforts to Evade the Prohibition of Torture

Much has been written about the Bush administration's interrogation policy. Here I focus on one specific question that has not been fully addressed elsewhere: What impact, if any, did awareness of the possibility of individual criminal prosecution have on Bush administration officials as they embarked upon and carried out this policy? At first glance, it would seem that these officials were oblivious to global developments on the criminalization of torture. On closer inspection, however, many crucial policy moves on interrogation only make sense when seen as a direct response to the threat of future prosecution. In particular, Bush administration policy makers feared the possibility of domestic prosecution under the U.S. War Crimes Statute of 1996 and the federal anti-torture statute of 1994, rather than the possibility of foreign prosecutions. Jack Goldsmith, who worked in the Bush administration Department of Justice, confirms that administration officials were very worried about "criminal law, investigation, and possibly, jail."[26] The discussion below examines chronologically four key policy moves that provide support for the argument that the prospect of domestic prosecution was a key determinant of Bush administration behavior. These policy moves or plans are (1) the early CIA request to the Justice Department for an "advance pardon" for torture; (2) the drafting of various memos on defining torture narrowly and on the applicability of the Geneva Conventions to the conflict; (3) the insistence on inserting specific language into U.S. legislation to provide prosecutorial protection for officials who had engaged in interrogation; and (4) the destruction of evidence, such as the CIA videos of interrogations.

Plan A: Request a pardon in advance

In March 2002, just a few months after Coalition forces occupied Afghanistan, CIA lawyers made a request to the Justice Department—a request which reveals that they knew the interrogations their field agents were being asked to perform might be illegal. These lawyers sought legal protection for those they represented against prosecution. They requested something called an "advance declination," or what we might call a future immunity or pardon for interrogation practices.

Human rights researcher John Sifton first explained to me about the advance pardon for torture, a story he broke in an article for the online magazine *Slate* in March 2010. Sifton, who used to work for Human Rights Watch, has set up his own legal research business. He carries a backpack instead of a briefcase, but his relative youth is belied by the wealth of information he has amassed on U.S. government interrogation policy, much of it from interviews with U.S. sources. Sifton wrote that early in 2002, the CIA asked for an "advance declination" from the criminal division of the Justice Department "for proposed interrogation techniques for Abu Zubaydah, the CIA's first detainee, including mock burial, binding in painful positions, deprivation of sleep for multiple days, being thrown into walls, and water-boarding."[27] Declinations have typically been used in cases of white-collar crime where a company under investigation and wishing to reassure its stockholders might ask the Justice Department whether or not it is going to indict. It is for events that happened in the past, not those that will happen in the future. As Sifton explained: "With, say, a client under investigation for using a dodgy tax shelter, a lawyer might say: 'Hey, let's ask the prosecutors about you, if they're formally *declining* to prosecute, we'll get something in writing—a *declination* letter—and you can sleep at night.'"[28] Sifton pointed out that the Justice Department had never previously issued an advance declination, which would have effectively been a Get Out of Jail Free Card or a promise of immunity that no CIA agents in the future would be targeted for criminal activity.

The Department of Justice criminal division refused to sign any advance declinations on policy grounds; there was simply no precedent for such an action. But the fact that the CIA requested one tells us something about the agency's state of mind in early 2002. It contradicts Bush administration officials who assert that they believed that what they were doing was legal, and instead suggests that from the beginning, institutional actors sought legal tools to protect themselves from prosecution for acts they understood would potentially provoke criminal liability. The failure to secure advance criminal immunity for interrogations made "Plan B" for preventing prosecutions all the more important.

Plan B: Try to define torture so narrowly that no U.S. official could ever be prosecuted for it

Bush administration officials began offering explicit justifications and authorization for torture to military and intelligence agencies, collectively forming a series of now public legal memos and reports prepared by the Department of Justice and the Department of Defense between January 2002 and September 2003. These memos offered general signals about the need for and acceptability of harsher interrogation methods sent down from high levels of the administration. General signals were then "translated" on the ground into a wide range of techniques, some explicitly approved and others not explicitly approved from above.

John Yoo, a law professor at UC Berkeley, was the deputy chief of the

Justice Department's Office of Legal Counsel responsible for writing many of these memos. While at Berkeley, Yoo had gained a reputation for his provocative conservative views about expansive presidential powers during war. He shared these views with the man who turned out to be the most influential lawyer in the Bush administration, David Addington, Vice President Dick Cheney's legal counsel. Both Addington and Yoo believed that the president had virtually unlimited authority during wartime, an authority that neither the Congress nor the Supreme Court could effectively challenge. It is perhaps not surprising that lawyers with such views also did not believe that international law could limit presidential discretion.

In these memos and documents, the Bush administration made three main arguments that helped justify and authorize torture and cruel and degrading treatment. The first was that the Geneva Conventions on the Treatment of Prisoners of War did not apply to the conflict with Al Qaeda and the conflict with the Taliban in Afghanistan; thus, the detainees from those conflicts would not be considered prisoners of war but rather "illegal combatants," a term that does not exist in the Geneva Conventions. This decision is problematic with regard to the laws of war, and it carried with it implications that opened the door to torture. The Geneva Conventions absolutely protect *any* detainee from torture. Thus, a decision that the Geneva Conventions don't apply to a conflict could be understood as saying that torture is therefore permitted. That some U.S. soldiers read these signals this way is clear from their comments and testimony. Two journalists with the *New York Times* noted in May 2004 that "One member of the 377th Company said that the fact that prisoners in Afghanistan had been labeled 'enemy combatants' not subject to the Geneva Conventions had contributed to an unhealthy attitude in the detention center." On the record, the soldier stated: "We were pretty much told that they were nobodies, that they were just enemy combatants. I think that giving them the distinction of soldier would have changed our attitude toward them."[29] And military intelligence officials and interrogators at Guantánamo said that "when new interrogators arrived they were told they had great flexibility in extracting information from detainees because the Geneva Conventions did not apply at the base."[30]

But the argument that the Geneva Conventions didn't apply is equally important for limiting the possibility of prosecution. The War Crimes

Statute of 1996 specifically criminalized under U.S. law grave breaches of the Geneva Conventions. This is why one of the first confidential memos, dated January 25, 2002, cited the threat of prosecution under the act as a reason to declare that detainees captured in Afghanistan were not eligible for Geneva Conventions protections. If the detainees were not covered by Geneva, the memo implied but did not say, then torturing them would not be a grave breach of the conventions, and thus the War Crimes Statute would not apply and could not be used to prosecute U.S. officials.

A *Washington Post* journalist was referring to the War Crimes Statute when he argued in July 2006 that this "obscure law approved by a Republican-controlled Congress a decade ago has made the Bush administration nervous that officials and troops involved in handling detainee matters might be accused of committing war crimes, and prosecuted at some point in U.S. courts." Since September 2001, Bush administration officials "have considered the law a potential threat to U.S. personnel involved in interrogations."[31]

Second, the Bush administration made strenuous efforts to reinterpret the definitions of torture and to redefine American obligations under the Geneva Conventions and the Torture Convention so that the United States could use whatever interrogation techniques it wanted. A now-infamous memorandum, signed by Assistant Attorney General Jay Bybee, but largely written by John Yoo, used a definition of torture that was outside any standard definition, including the one embedded in the federal anti-torture statute. First, it suggested that "physical pain amounting to torture must be the equivalent in intensity to the pain accompanying serious physical injury, such as organ failure, impairment of body function, or even death." Nowhere in the history of the drafting of the Torture Convention, nor in U.S. legislation implementing the convention, does this conceptualization appear: that to be counted as torture, the pain must be equivalent to death or organ failure. Second, the Bybee memorandum said that in order to qualify for the definition of torture, "the infliction of such pain must be the defendant's precise objective."[32] The Bybee memorandum attempts to create such a narrow definition of torture that only the sadist (for whom pain is the "precise objective") who engages in a practice resulting in pain equivalent to death or organ failure is a torturer.[33] In other words, the memo creates an absurd and unsustainable definition—a definition contrary to the language of the law and common sense. The memo sought such a definition not just to permit the use of certain techniques, but more important, to make it almost impossible to prosecute and convict anyone for torture.

Third, the memos claimed that the president's role as commander in chief of the armed forces granted him the authority to supersede international and domestic law and to authorize torture. Again, this runs contrary to the language in Article 2 of the Torture Convention, which states plainly: "No exceptional circumstances whatsoever, whether a state of war or a threat of war, internal political instability or any other public emergency, may be invoked as a justification of torture" and: "An order from a superior officer or public authority may not be invoked as a justification for torture."[34] It also runs contrary to standard U.S. constitutional practices, which have never left the executive branch completely unfettered by the other branches, even in times of war. But the memo would have provided additional legal cover against prosecution, since defendants could argue that neither international nor domestic law applied in these circumstances.

The Bush administration could persuade neither key legal advisers in its own State Department nor many legal experts within the branches of the military of its interpretations in the legal memos. Opposition to the decision that the Geneva Conventions didn't apply in Afghanistan and to the revision of interrogation techniques surfaced early. One day after the memorandum issued by Attorney General Alberto Gonzales recommended that the administration not apply POW status under the Geneva Conventions to captured Al Qaeda or Taliban fighters, Secretary of State Colin Powell wrote to Gonzales urging in the strongest terms that the policy be reconsidered.[35] Lawyers within the Bush administration warned of the possible legal consequences officials could face if they insisted on these policies. In a memo dated January 11, 2002, State Department legal counsel William Taft IV noted that "if the U.S. took the war on terrorism outside the Geneva Conventions, not only could U.S. soldiers be denied the protections of the Conventions—and therefore be prosecuted for crimes, including murder—but President Bush could be accused of a 'grave breach' by other countries, and prosecuted for war crimes." Taft also sent a copy of the memo to Gonzales, hoping it would reach Bush.[36] Alberto Mora, general counsel of the U.S. Navy, also warned his superiors of the possibilities of prosecutions if they continued to disregard the prohibition on torture and cruel and degrading treatment, but his warnings were ignored.[37] The

Bush administration did not see these admonitions as a reason to reconsider its policies. But members apparently did heed them enough to craft a legal strategy that could address the possibility of future human rights prosecutions. This may explain why the subsequent memos read more like defense lawyers' briefs, preemptively defending their clients against the charge of torture.

The torture memos reveal no principled or legal commitment to the prohibition on torture. Not until twenty-nine months after the first memo, in a last-minute memo prepared explicitly for public consumption just before the confirmation hearing for Alberto Gonzales as U.S. Attorney General, did the Bush administration state that "Torture is abhorrent both to American law and values and to international norms."[38] Before this, the primary concern throughout the memos is with how to protect U.S. officials from possible future prosecution, not how to adhere to the principles of the law.

The memos were a direct response to requests from the CIA to get direction on the limits to interrogation, as a form of legal cover for actions for which officials knew they could be prosecuted. In early January 2002, the CIA was already meeting with Bush administration officials demanding guidance. At these early meetings, Addington alluded to the fact that crossing "this dangerous line" could provoke future prosecutors to bring criminal charges against interrogators. A top lawyer at the Pentagon had similar concerns. But George Tenet, head of the CIA at the time, wanted "political as well as legal backing," and so from 2002 until 2005, Tenet held meetings with Cheney, Condoleezza Rice, Donald Rumsfeld, Colin Powell, and John Ashcroft to decide which torments would be inflicted on specific high-value detainees. Similar demands for legal cover came from the military. A commander at Guantánamo completed a twelve-page request for permission to use more aggressive forms of interrogation, including water-boarding. His lawyer noted that members of the armed forces who used these techniques could be committing crimes under the Uniform Code of Military Justice, but that this might be solved with high-level legal permission or immunity.[39]

The justice cascade was thus very much on the minds of Bush administration officials as they prepared their memos. But rather than decide how they could comply with domestic and international law, they believed they could craft legal opinions that would allow them to avoid it. One of the basic tenets of the neoconservative ideology pervading this administration was a disdain and skepticism for international institutions and international law.[40] They believed that law is voluntary and malleable, and that it didn't apply to powerful states like the United States.

Some officials went a step further, framing international law as part of the problem. For them, international law restricting U.S. sovereignty should not only be ignored but actively resisted and, if possible, rolled back. The Department of Defense report on *National Defense Strategy of the United States*, released in March 2005, noted that "our strength as a nation state will continue to be challenged by those who employ a strategy of the weak using international fora, judicial processes, and terrorism."[41] Jack Goldsmith, who worked as the director of the Office of Legal Counsel late in the Bush administration, asks: "Why would the mighty U.S. Defense Department include international organizations and judges as threats on par with terrorism? Who are 'the weak' and why would the department worry so much about its legal tactics?"[42] He clarifies that U.S. officials used the term "lawfare" to describe "the strategy of using or misusing law as a substitute for traditional military means to achieve an operational objective." Goldsmith attributes such extreme hostility to universal jurisdiction to Henry Kissinger. In a number of books and articles Kissinger had been accused of being the intellectual author of various human rights violations and war crimes, and there were calls for his prosecution. Judges in France and Spain had summoned him to be a witness in various foreign prosecutions, especially about Operation Condor, summons he avoided by leaving those countries and making careful decisions about travel.[43]

But Kissinger was "livid" when he discussed the issue with an old friend from the Ford administration, by then secretary of defense in the Bush administration Donald Rumsfeld. Rumsfeld came to see universal jurisdiction claims as just another form of lawfare used by the "enemy" against the United States. But in this case, the "enemies" were European and South American allies and the human rights movement. Rumsfeld took it personally because he was near the top of the chain of command in a nontraditional war against terror using questionable methods. He wanted to find a solution to what he called "the judicialization of international politics," using a term common in academic writings on the topic.[44]

Thus, one important impact of the justice cascade was that it led the Bush administration to instruct its lawyers to draft legal memos that would attempt to protect U.S. officials from prosecution. Policy makers understood that there was a threat of prosecution, but they believed that they were protected from it by secret and often extreme legal opinions from a small group of lawyers. Ironically, the care they took to avert prosecution resulted in the unprecedented production of evidence concerning the direct complicity of top U.S. officials in decisions to torture. Courts in Argentina, Chile, or Spain would have been amazed to have the wealth of documentation about the direct involvement of such high-level policy makers in decisions about torture that was eventually assembled in the first years of the so-called "war on terror" in the United States.

The memo strategy, however, ran up against some problems from both inside and outside the administration. By 2005, a clear consensus was starting to emerge among jurists that the memos were faulty as a matter of law, and would not hold up under legal scrutiny. This fear led the administration not to change its interrogation policy, but to begin what I call Plan C in their legal maneuvers to avoid prosecution.

Plan C: Legislate retroactive immunity from prosecution

Vice President Cheney personally spearheaded a move to demand and secure legislation that provided retroactive immunity for past interrogation crimes for all U.S. officials. The White House first insisted that immunity language be included in the Detainee Treatment Act of 2005, later modified in the Military Commissions Act of 2006.[45] The Detainee Treatment Act was originally designed by John McCain and other members of Congress with an eye toward prohibiting cruel, inhuman, and degrading treatment of persons under American custody. This legislation was a principled legal response to the human rights violations of the Bush administration. The White House fought bitterly against the legislation, and at one point Bush threatened to veto it when it arrived on his desk, which would have been the first veto of his presidency. The Senate nevertheless passed the bill by a margin of 90–9, offering a defeat to the administration's interrogation policy. But the final version of the bill included language imposed by a bargain with the White House. In exchange for securing the prohibition of certain forms of interrogation, Congress agreed to include explicit legislative legal protections from prosecution for U.S. personnel who engaged in interrogations.

The legislation provides for "protection of United States Government personnel" in any civil action or criminal prosecution arising out of their detention and interrogation of aliens "believed to be engaged in or associated with terrorist activity." It specifies that U.S. officials cannot be prosecuted as long as they believed that the interrogation practices they used were lawful. How are they to know that what they are doing is lawful? The legislation states: "Good faith reliance on advice of counsel should be an important factor." The law thus indirectly refers to the torture memos. The Office of Legal Counsel, after all, is the highest executive branch office for determining the law, and during the period from 2002 until 2008, it was the "counsel" who told state officials that what they were doing was lawful.[46]

John Sifton called this little noticed legislative language "very intelligent, very shrewd." He explains that if you were a prosecutor in the United States trying to initiate a prosecution against officials engaged in torture, "you'd know what a pain in the ass it is going to be to get a conviction, because there is statutory law saying that as long as they thought they were acting according to the law they can't be convicted."[47]

Around the same time, in a series of crucial decisions, the U.S. Supreme Court upheld the rights of detainees to humane treatment and to the protections offered by the rule of law, both domestic and international. In June 2006, in *Hamdan v. Rumsfeld*, the Supreme Court rebuked Bush administration policy and its legal interpretations. The Court ruled that the military commission system set up to try accused war criminals in Guantánamo Bay violated both U.S. laws and the Geneva Conventions. In what is now considered a landmark decision about the limits of executive power, the Court said that even during war, the president must comply not only with U.S. laws established by Congress but also with international law.[48] The Court directly contradicted the legal theories put forward by President Bush's legal advisers—that the president has broad discretion to make decisions on war-related issues—which in turn they used to claim the president could authorize torture. In this sense, although *Hamdan* did not directly address torture, it addressed the legal claims in the torture memos in two central ways. First, it determined that the Geneva Conventions applied to detainees in Guantánamo; and second, it undermined the claim of exclusive executive authority upon which the torture arguments had been based. In a subsequent detainee case, *Boumediene v. Bush*, in

2008, the Supreme Court ruled that prisoners in Guantánamo had the right of habeas corpus and could challenge the legality of their detention in U.S. federal courts.

Both the military and civil society were actively involved in bringing these cases to the Supreme Court. For example, in the *Hamdan* case, Salim Hamdan was successfully defended by his military-appointed defense lawyer, in cooperation with volunteer lawyers from the academic world and private law firms. Some forty amicus curie briefs were filed in support of the *Hamdan* brief by human rights organizations, retired military officers, diplomats, and legal scholars.[49] The *Hamdan* and *Boumediene* cases weren't human rights prosecutions, but they were cases about the rights to challenge their detention in courts. Hannah Arendt has said that the most important right is the "right to have rights." Essentially, what the U.S. Supreme Court was deciding was the right of U.S. detainees to have rights. The decision in *Hamdan*, that the Geneva Conventions applied to the treatment of the detainees, further intensified the Bush administration's anxieties about prosecution. If Geneva applied to the detainees, the "enhanced interrogations" could be war crimes, and U.S. officials might be prosecuted under the War Crimes Statute.

After the *Hamdan* ruling, once again, the administration didn't respond by changing its interrogation policy, but by further ramping up its efforts to provide an ironclad legal protection from prosecution. Bush administration officials pressed Congress to pass the Military Commissions Act of 2006, which contained language strengthening the protection already included in the Detainee Treatment Act. The new legislation also required the government to provide legal counsel and pay court costs, bail, and other expenses incurred by prosecution of a government official for interrogation practices. It clarified that the law pertained to prosecutions or investigations in "U.S. courts or agencies, foreign courts or agencies, or international courts or agencies"; and defined that it applied to any action occurring between September 11, 2001, and December 30, 2005, when the original Detainee Treatment Act was signed.

Plan D: When all else fails, destroy the evidence

Finally, the fear of prosecution led to the destruction of evidence that could have been used in future prosecutions. The CIA destroyed hundreds of hours of videotapes of the likely 2002 water torture of three men, allegedly involved with Al Qaeda, by its agents. Michael Ratner, the president of the Center for Constitutional Rights, argues that "This fear of prosecution for torture is the best explanation as to why these tapes were destroyed. They would have been vivid and compelling examples of the violation of laws against torture—laws that in the U.S. carry a life sentence or the death penalty if the victim is killed. Laws in most European countries make such violations of the convention against torture a universal crime, prosecutable no matter where the torture occurred or where the torturer resides."[50]

Hard-nosed policy makers in the Bush administration prided themselves on their realistic understanding of international politics. They believed their strategy of seeking legal memos and protections in legislation would protect U.S. officials from domestic prosecution. But although they thought that law has little autonomous impact, and that power can define the law, they hedged their bets by taking all the necessary moves to keep the possibility of prosecutions at bay.

The Effectiveness of the Bush Administration Responses to Domestic and Foreign Prosecutions

Initially, the worldview of the neoconservatives in the Bush administration was confirmed. There were apparently few domestic or international political costs to their violations of domestic and international law. The negative publicity generated by the release of the Abu Ghraib photos was not sufficient to end the practices. The American public did not demand more accountability for the use of torture. Despite the fact that the graphic revelations came in an election year, torture did not become a campaign issue in the elections that followed either in 2004 or in 2006.

Not only was the administration undeterred by domestic and international criticism of its practices; it actively promoted many of the individuals most closely associated with the torture policy. Mr. Bybee, whose name was on the first controversial torture memo (although it was actually written by Yoo), was appointed to the Ninth Circuit Court of Appeals. White House legal counsel Alberto Gonzales, who solicited and approved the memos, was nominated and confirmed for the post of U.S. Attorney General. John C. Yoo said that President Bush's victory in the 2004 election, along with the lack of strong opposition to the Gonzales confirmation, was "proof that the debate is over." He claimed: "The issue is dying out. The public has had its referendum."[51]

But, contrary to Yoo's prediction, the issue did not die out. The strategies did not succeed in making the issue go away. Some of the secret legal memos were so troubling that they generated fierce opposition even within the administration. When Jack Goldsmith took over at the Office of Legal Counsel, he realized that he would have to withdraw some of the memos of that office, an almost unprecedented move. This was especially noteworthy since Goldsmith is a conservative legal thinker who had supported many Bush policies.

Individuals associated with the military accused members of the Bush administration of "endangering troops," "undermining the war effort," "encouraging reprisals," and "lowering morale," not to mention "losing the high moral ground." Military sources criticized the administration for failing to seek the advice of the military's highest legal authorities, the Judge Advocate General's Corps.[52] Military and FBI officials not only disagreed with Bush administration insiders about the legality of torture but also about its *effectiveness*. The entire Bush administration strategy was premised on the idea that torture is a necessary and effective tool in the war against terrorism. The investigative journalist Jane Mayer, writing in *The New Yorker*, has said that "the fiercest internal resistance" to the administration's policies came from people who were previously directly involved in interrogation, including veteran FBI agents and military personnel. "Their concerns are practical as well as ideological. Years of experience in interrogation have led them to doubt the effectiveness of physical coercion as a means of extracting reliable information."[53] FBI complaints about harsh interrogation practices began in December 2002, according to released internal documents. In late 2003, an agent protested that "these tactics have produced no intelligence of a threat neutralization nature to date."[54]

Precisely because of the extreme opposition the memos generated within the Bush administration, they were eventually leaked to the press. Once they became public, they generated a controversy and provided detailed information that fed the opposition to Bush administration policy. Without the memos, it might have been possible for the administration to maintain its initial story that the mistreatment of detainees was the result of a few "bad apples." But the memos and other leaked documents made clear that the impetus for harsh interrogation came from the very highest levels.

As a result of these policies, the Bush administration gave damning advice and signals to operatives in the field. Officials led them to believe that they were operating under the cover of law and that the power of the government could protect them from retribution. The U.S. government continues to try to protect individuals involved in torture from prosecution, and it will succeed in many cases. But it is unlikely to succeed in all.

Domestic Prosecutions

Early in the process, U.S.-based NGOs called for accountability for Bush administration officials who condoned or engaged in torture. The first demand of the human rights movement was to revoke and repudiate all existing orders and legal opinions that authorized cruel interrogations or secret detention. The second major demand was to close the Guantánamo Bay detention facility. But human rights organizations also called for accountability. Elisa Massimino, Washington director of Human Rights First, argued that "without accountability up the chain of command, there won't be deterrence, and the torture and abuses we've documented likely will continue."[55] While mainstream human rights organizations like Human Rights First stressed accountability, two domestic civil rights organizations with long experience litigating in U.S. courts took the lead in pursuing domestic lawsuits: the American Civil Liberties Union and the Center for Constitutional Rights. For the most part, these lawsuits were civil suits for damages, not criminal cases, because U.S. law does not permit private prosecution of criminal cases. None of these cases has developed fully. Judges in the first instance used a variety of justifications to dismiss them. Because this book focuses on individual criminal accountability, I will not include a long discussion of these civil cases here. These groups were crucial, however, in bringing forward a series of habeas corpus cases, some of which eventually reached the U.S. Supreme Court and had extensive repercussions.

In addition, the U.S. military has continued to prosecute a series of cases involving the abuse of detainees. As of 2006, Human Rights Watch found that U.S. authorities had opened investigations into about 65 percent of the 600 cases involving U.S. personnel implicated in approximately

330 cases of detainee abuse in Iraq, Afghanistan, and Guantánamo Bay. Of seventy-nine courts-martial, fifty-four resulted in convictions or a guilty plea; another fifty-seven people faced non-judicial proceedings involving punishments of minimal or no prison time.[56] Although many cases were not investigated, and no senior officers have been held accountable, this is not an insignificant degree of accountability and punishment.

The definition of torture in the Torture Convention focuses on pain or suffering "inflicted by or at the instigation of or with the consent of acquiescence of a public official or a person acting in an official capacity." In the drafting of the treaty, the United States itself proposed the wording "or with the consent or acquiescence of a public official."[57] To date, U.S. sanctions have focused only on torture committed "by" public officials, and have disregarded the issues of instigation, consent, or acquiescence of other higher-level public officials. Almost all (95 percent) of the military personnel who have been investigated so far are enlisted soldiers, not officers. Three officers were convicted by court-martial for directly participating in detainee abuse, but no military officer has been held accountable for criminal acts committed by subordinates.[58]

Foreign Prosecutions

U.S. policy makers are learning the same lesson that Chileans and Argentines previously learned: internal attempts to protect state officials from prosecution cannot bind the hands of foreign judiciaries. So, while the memos and legislation might temporarily protect U.S. officials from domestic prosecution, they cannot necessarily protect them from foreign courts like those in Italy, which became the first courts to convict American citizens for crimes committed as part of the war on terror during the Bush administration.

In November 2009, a trial in Italy resulted in convictions in absentia of twenty-three Americans and two Italians for kidnapping an Egyptian terror suspect off the streets of Milan. An Italian judge decided that what the U.S. government called "extraordinary rendition" fit the Italian criminal code definition of "kidnapping." Milan prosecutor Armando Spataro was the man behind the first major legal blow to the CIA's extraordinary rendition program. The Torture Convention makes it clear that states cannot "expel, return ('refouler') or extradite a person to another State where there are substantial grounds for believing that he would be in danger of being subjected to torture." But the policy of "extraordinary rendition," as practiced by the Bush administration, was exactly that: it sent people to other states, with the added complication that these individuals were in some cases actually kidnapped from one country in order to be sent to a third. Human rights advocates say renditions were the CIA's way of "outsourcing" the torture of suspected terrorists.

For Prosecutor Spataro, however, if a man is kidnapped off the streets of Milan, that is a crime that deserves investigation, just like any other crime, even if it was committed by the CIA in collaboration with the Italian Secret Service. The Italian government under Silvio Berlusconi was one of the main European allies of the Bush administration, and it called Spataro a "red robe" or left-wing judge. Yet Spataro sees the law as one of the primary tools in the fight against terrorism. Armando Spataro is a loquacious gentleman, with white hair and courteous manners. Eating his spaghetti carbonara at an outdoor café, he blends in with the surrounding Italian businessmen on their long lunch breaks. But as he tells his story, it becomes clear that one shouldn't underestimate his determination or experience. Spataro started working in the anti-terrorism division of the Milan Prosecutor's Office in 1978, when Italy was beset by internal terrorism of the Red Brigades and other violent leftist insurgent groups whose bombings and murders created chaos and fear around the country. After 9/11, U.S. officials sometimes acted as though they were the first to grapple with the problems of terrorism. But Spataro has devoted almost his entire professional life to the fight against terrorism and the Mafia. When he hears from U.S. officials and from members of the Italian government that the only way to fight terrorism is to go outside the law, Spataro recalls his early encounters with leftist terrorism.

As a young prosecutor in the Milan office, Spataro worked with his colleague, Judge Guido Galli, in the prosecution of the Red Brigades and other terrorist groups. In addition to his work as a judge, Galli also taught law at Milan University. On March 19, 1980 (Spataro recalls the date exactly without having to think), Galli was shot and killed by left-wing terrorists as he left the university after giving a lecture on criminal law. Spataro, who on account of his full-time position as magistrate had a police escort that Galli shared when they were together, had declined an offer to speak to Galli's class that day.[59] Instead, he arrived at the crime scene to see Galli's body on the floor, with multiple bullet wounds to the head, his hands still gripping the copy of the Italian criminal code that he had used in the lecture. Every time Spataro hears people say you can't fight terrorism with the law code, he thinks of Galli. He recalls defiantly: "We overcame terrorism in Italy using the law." The last trial of a member of the Red Brigades was in 1990, and Italy has not been plagued by internal terrorism since that time. After 1990, Spataro was transferred to the anti-Mafia division of the Milan Prosecutor's Office, where he used the same tools to confront a different kind of secretive, violent group.

Ernesto Sabato, the writer who was the chair of the Argentine Truth Commission, wrote in the prologue to the commission's report *Nunca Más* of the Italian government's struggle against violent groups like the Red Brigades: "Never at any time, however, did that country abandon the principles of law in its fight against these terrorists, and it managed to resolve the problem through the normal courts of law, guaranteeing the accused all their rights in a fair trial. When [former Prime Minister] Aldo Moro was kidnapped, a member of the security forces suggested to General Della Chiesa that a suspect who apparently knew a lot be tortured. The General replied with the memorable words: 'Italy can survive the loss of Aldo Moro. It would not survive the introduction of torture.' "[60] Spataro shares the sentiments of General Della Chiesa. For Spataro, it is a matter of principle, and also of efficacy. The Bush administration thinks that "trials are an obstacle to fighting terrorism," Spataro said. "We think we need to use the same system, the same methods we used to fight the Mafia in Italy. To fight terrorism, we need the cooperation of the Islamic community in our democratic countries. In order to get their cooperation, we have to demonstrate that we are a full democracy and that the same rules apply to everyone."[61]

The Bush administration might see Spataro's work within the rubric of lawfare, used by the weak to challenge American strength. Yet Spataro sees law as one of the primary tools against terrorism, and has his experience using law to fight the Red Brigades to back him up. When Spataro says that the same rules apply to everyone, he means the U.S. government, the Italian government, and the CIA. So, if the Italian criminal code prohibits kidnapping, that includes the CIA. It doesn't matter if the victim, in this case Nasr Osama Mostafa Hassan, a.k.a. Abu Omar, was an Egyptian refugee who was already a terrorism suspect in a case carefully followed by the Milan Prosecutor's Office. Indeed, the reason the prosecutor's office knew immediately that Abu Omar had been kidnapped was that they were tapping his phone as part of their own terrorism investigation. After he was kidapped, they intercepted a call from his wife to a friend saying he was missing. The prosecutor's office did not initially know that the CIA was involved; it took years for them to put the case together, using cell phone records, e-mail messages, hotel reservations, car rentals, and other information that the CIA agents left in a relatively clear trail.

Spataro's office eventually determined that on February 17, 2003, Abu Omar was kidapped in Milan around noon by a group of CIA agents with a van, who took him to Aviano, an air base about four hours from Milan that is used by the U.S. Air Force. While the CIA agents were on their way to Aviano, they used a cell phone to make calls to the Milan CIA station chief Robert Lady, to the Aviano air base, and to CIA headquarters in Langley, Virginia. In Aviano, Abu Omar was transferred to a private plane sometimes rented to the CIA, which then flew to Ramstein Air Base in Germany, and eventually on to Cairo, where Abu Omar was handed over to Egyptian authorities. During the nearly four years Abu Omar was in Egyptian custody, his lawyer said that he was subject to torture, including rape, electric shock, and repeated beatings.

The most surprising part of this entire story is the independence with which the Milan Prosecutor's Office has operated. Of course, Spataro admits, there are judges in Italy who are not as independent, who, in Italian slang, might "put the dossier under the sand." One suspects that Spataro is putting rather too much of a positive gloss on the system, that the pressures to drop the case must have been intense. This case could have easily been lost in red tape, as it clearly was for the first year before Spataro took it over. But that is not Spataro's style. Asked if he worries about the problems created by a case against both the CIA and the Italian government, Spataro laughs and says that after trying cases against the Red Brigades and the Mafia, he is not likely to be frightened by the CIA.

Spataro needed all the independence he could get because Prime Minister Berlusconi pressured him to stop prosecution. The government filed a motion to end the trial because the issue is covered by the Italian State Secrets law; the Constitutional Court agreed that some of the testimony Spataro elicited was covered by the law and could not be used. The fact that relatively few Italians were convicted is the result of Spataro's inability to use this testimony. Meanwhile, a member of Parliament (and Berlus-coni's attorney) asked the Superior Judicial Council to punish Spataro, and another senator and former president of Italy accused Spataro's office of being infiltrated with terrorists and requested an investigation of agents of terror networks behind the prosecution.

All of the convicted Americans are believed to be CIA agents, but Spataro was not even certain if, in all cases, they had their real names, since they used assumed names as part of their covert activities in Italy. The Americans were put on trial in absentia, a type of criminal trial permitted by the Italian judicial system but not in the United States. They were tried in absentia because the Italian governments refused to follow through on the prosecutor's extradition requests. But even if the Italian govern-ment had issued an extradition request, the United States would not have extradited the officials to stand trial. It is quite possible that none of the convicted Americans will go to prison. Still, the process of prosecution in this case constitutes a significant form of punishment. At a minimum, these officials will have to be very careful about all travel, especially in or through Europe. A former CIA official said that if Italian prosecutors were successful in getting an international arrest warrant, "the convicted spies would probably face the threat of arrest anywhere outside the United States for the rest of their lives."[62] In addition, we can presume that the prosecution has dramatically complicated their careers. It is difficult to be an undercover agent when you have been the subject of a highly public prosecution. Many of the accused and convicted officials have since retired from the CIA.

These costs are reflected in the decision of one of the convicted officials, Sabrina De Sousa, to sue the U.S. State Department for its failure to grant her diplomatic immunity. De Sousa was accused of having worked closely with Robert Lady, the CIA station chief in Milan. But the United States only has a consulate in Milan, not an embassy, and consular officials are not granted diplomatic immunity. As such, neither Lady nor De Sousa was protected from prosecution. De Sousa's lawyer has said that she would amend her lawsuit against the State Department, adding as defendants Mr. Lady and the CIA, because "according to news reports, they were responsible for this alleged abduction."[63] In addition to damaging careers, these prosecutions have personal and social costs. Robert Lady, who by all accounts was a genuinely personable and relaxed man during his tenure as

CIA chief in Milan, has lost his Italian country home, has gone through a difficult separation, and has quietly taken up residence in Abita Springs, Louisiana. Asked by an Italian reporter what effect the CIA indictments had on him, Lady responded: "I love Italy. I decided to live my life in Italy. My whole family loves Italy. I thought that I could serve there profession- ally, and then at sixty-five I'd be making my own Barbera in my grand house near Asti—ten acres of vineyards, a stupendous place. Instead, I had to flee." As for his wife's leaving him, "Lady said he could not blame her: he was powerless, frustrated, and had little to offer."[64]

Other foreign human rights prosecutions against U.S. officials for tor- ture have been proposed, but they have not developed very far. In late October 2007, Donald Rumsfeld agreed to speak in France at a closed and confidential breakfast meeting organized by *Foreign Policy* magazine. The meeting was held in a building right next door to the U.S. Embassy in Paris. The day before the meeting, the American-based Center for Con- stitutional Rights and the Paris-based International Federation for Human Rights filed a complaint for torture against Rumsfeld before a Paris pros- ecutor. The next morning, Rumsfeld calmly walked outside to his confer- ence, perhaps not yet aware that the case against him had been filed. But he never reappeared to face the journalists and human rights activists who gathered outside the building during the day. Michael Ratner explains: "The big difference with this case and the other cases is Rumsfeld is actu- ally in France. And when an alleged torturer goes into a country, but par- ticularly France, the obligation on the prosecutor to begin an investigation is much stronger than in other cases of so-called 'universal jurisdiction.' We brought two cases in Germany; one of those is still on appeal. There's a case in Argentina, and there's a case in Sweden. I think the point of all of this is to really give Rumsfeld no place to hide."[65]

Ratner is exaggerating the possibility of prosecution here. After a French judge dismissed the complaint in November 2007, the Center for Constitutional Rights appealed the decision to the General Prosecu- tor of Paris, who, in February 2008, dismissed it, arguing that Rumsfeld was immune for actions he completed while in office. In France, later in the same year that the Rumsfeld case was dismissed, a judge convicted a Tunisian ex-diplomat for torture committed while he was a police chief in Tunisia in the 1990s. The contrast between the two cases suggests that French judges may have a double standard, one for lower-level officials from weaker countries and a second for high-level officials from a powerful country like the United States. Nonetheless, Rumsfeld will have to keep abreast of such cases, study the likelihood that they could advance, and plan his future travel accordingly. For a powerful man like Rumsfeld, it must be infuriating, just as it is for his friend Henry Kissinger.

A similar case against Rumsfeld and others in Germany was also dismissed by German judges, who said it was up to the United States to investigate the issue. CCR and its allies filed the complaints under a special law Germany enacted to bring it into compliance with the Rome Statute of the ICC. The law provides for universal jurisdiction for war crimes, crimes of genocide, and crimes against humanity, allowing the German federal prosecutor to investigate and prosecute such crimes irrespective of the location or nationality of the defendant or plaintiff. In April 2009, a regional appeals court dismissed the appeal, and the groups filed a motion for reconsideration in May 2009. Besides Rumsfeld, the defendants in the German complaint also included former CIA director George Tenet and other high-level U.S. officials, as well as some of the lawyers who wrote the memos justifying torture.

Another foreign case is now looking into those public officials who "instigated" the policy. In March 2009, the Audiencia Nacional, the Spanish court that initiated the Pinochet case, took the first steps toward opening a case against six Bush administration lawyers who wrote the memos providing the legal justification for the use of torture: Alberto Gonzales, John Yoo, Jay Bybee, David S. Addington, William Haynes, and Douglas Feith. The complaint, filed by a Spanish human rights group, the Association for the Dignity of Prisoners, is based on the testimony of five Spanish citizens or residents who were prisoners in Guantánamo Bay. The court assigned the case to Judge Baltasar Garzón, who accepted it and assigned it to a prosecutor.[66]

It is quite unprecedented to file criminal charges against lawyers for the policies of their government. Most torture cases have targeted those who actually committed torture or their superiors in the chain of command. In some cases, the principle of command responsibility—whereby the leaders who give the orders are held to a higher standard of accountability than those who actually carry out the crimes—pertains. Donald Rumsfeld, for example, not Dick Cheney, is the object of the cases in France and Germany because he is in the direct chain of command; John Yoo and Alberto

Gonzales were never in the chain of command. Many feel it would be a bad precedent essentially to prosecute a lawyer for giving legal advice. Yet the voluminous documentary evidence in the form of various leaked and released memos might permit the Spanish court to think seriously about what the Torture Convention means when it calls upon state parties to ensure that acts which constitute "complicity" in torture should be offenses under criminal law, and subject to universal jurisdiction.

Judge Garzón, however, faces opposition not only from the U.S. government but also from his own government, currently under the control of the Socialist Party. The Spanish Parliament passed legislation in 2009 limiting wide-ranging Spanish jurisdiction over extraterritorial acts by introducing the requirement of "a link or connection to Spain," either because the accused are on Spanish territory or the victims are Spanish. The new law will not be applied retroactively, however, and there were Spanish victims in Guantánamo, so the future of the case against the Bush lawyers remains uncertain.[67] The U.S. government is unlikely ever to extradite its officials to Spain; but Spanish arrest warrants would require Gonzales and other lawyers to avoid travel in some parts of Europe.

In 2011, political groups and human rights organizations, including Amnesty International and the Center for Constitutional Rights, pressured the Swiss government to open a criminal investigation against former president Bush for personally authorizing waterboarding of terrorism suspects. Although the case had not yet been opened, the former president canceled a trip to Switzerland to be a keynote speaker at a charity dinner in February 2011. A spokesperson for the group that invited Bush stated that he had canceled his trip because of security concerns arising from planned protests, but the human rights groups said they had no doubt he canceled his trip to avoid their criminal case.[68]

Michael Ratner recognized that it would be difficult to convict Rumsfeld, but he also said that the aim of the legal complaints was to demonstrate "that we will not rest until those U.S. officials involved in the torture program are brought to justice."[69] While many of these judicial processes will eventually stall or lead to dismissals or acquittals for political or legal reasons, they can nonetheless undermine the peace of mind, financial security, and reputation of suspected perpetrators. In the next few decades, if little else, former Secretary of Defense Donald Rumsfeld, John Yoo, and others who advocated the policy of explicit non-compliance with the

Geneva Conventions and the Torture Convention may find themselves in a difficult position when they go abroad. Before they initiate any international trip, they may need to make inquires about the state of prosecutions in any country where they intend to travel. There is also some evidence that lawyers involved in torture decisions have encountered restricted job opportunities.[70]

On his second day in office, President Barack Obama ordered the CIA to close down secret overseas prisons and called on the Pentagon to close the Guantánamo Bay prison within a year. The president also revoked the previous Bush administration executive orders and regulations on interrogation that were contrary to U.S. treaty obligations and law. In April 2009, the Obama administration released four secret Bush-era memos detailing legal justification for the CIA interrogation program. But at the same time as he released the memos, the president also issued a statement guaranteeing that no employees would be prosecuted for their role in the interrogation program, as long as they did not exceed the techniques authorized in the memos.

The Obama administration reversed U.S. policy on torture, although through its failure to curtail the practice of extraordinary rendition and seek prosecutions in the United States it continues to be in violation of certain provisions of the Convention Against Torture. On the unwillingness to pursue prosecutions, President Obama has said that he wishes to look forward, not backward. The United States has now entered into the debate that has been going on throughout the world for the last thirty years about the desirability of accountability. But because U.S. actions involved citizens from many countries, and took place on a global scale, the debate about accountability is a global debate. In the U.S. case, not only was there no "ruptured" transition that undermined the power of the leaders of the previous regime, but the officials from the Bush administration, especially former Vice President Cheney, continue to be powerful actors in politics and the media. Human rights prosecutions have had greatest support where there are large numbers of national victims, willing to march in the streets demanding accountability for violations. In the United States, no one was marching in the streets. The victims of the human rights violations of the Bush administration were for the most part foreigners, with foreign names, and without large or active constituencies in the United States.

Even the most committed advocates and experts believe the chance that U.S. administration officials will be held legally responsible for torture is small. "I think these guys did unauthorized stuff, they violated the War Crimes Act, and they should be prosecuted," said Michael Ratner. But he added that prosecutions are improbable because the Justice Department, which has consistently asserted that such rough interrogations are legal, is unlikely to bring them. American officials could argue in any event that they were following policies they believed to be legal, Ratner said, and "a judge would most likely say that is a decent defense."[71]

One of the journalists who did the most to uncover the torture story, Jane Mayer, has said that "I may be wrong, but I personally doubt there will be large-scale legal repercussions inside America" for those who devised and implemented the torture policy. "At the very least, as a journalist, I hope that the records are opened, and all the legal memos released (several crucial ones remain secret) so that the country can learn its own history here. My guess is that the real accountability for President Bush will be in the history books, not the courtroom." Mayer was basing her predictions for the future on what she had seen in the past, as someone who had "covered politics in Washington, D.C., for two decades."[72]

Some aspects of the American legal system make it less likely that there will be criminal prosecutions here than in other countries. In the U.S. criminal system, victims do not have private prosecution provisions that allow them to bring forward criminal cases; in other words, individual victims do not have standing to initiate criminal cases in the United States. As a result, we are likely to see more civil cases for damages in the United States, where individual plaintiffs can bring cases, than criminal cases, where initiating such prosecution is completely in the hands of public prosecutors. Still, there is reason to be cautious. The efforts of Maher Arar—a Canadian whose rendition to Syria has been widely reported— were recently rebuffed by the U.S. Supreme Court.[73] Members of both the Bush and Obama administrations have tried to prevent his case from being heard.

The interesting question is whether a long-term lack of criminal accountability for higher-level officials who condoned or instigated torture will eventually lead more foreign criminal prosecutions to flourish. For the time being, with the exception of the case in Italy, foreign prosecutions against Rumsfeld and other officials have not succeeded, in part because foreign judges have argued that the United States is making efforts at accountability and should be allowed to do so first.

But the issue has not gone away; in fact, it has started to pose significant costs on the individuals associated with the policy as well as for the U.S. government. Human rights trials in other countries around the world reveal that the demand for justice does not disappear with the passage of time. To the contrary, many politicians who believed that they would not and could not be held accountable have, to their surprise, sometimes found decades later that they were wrong.

The people whose positions carried the day within the Bush administration believed they were operating in a realist world where international law and institutions are quite malleable to exercises of hegemonic power. In the short term, their beliefs were confirmed. In the longer term, they will find that this misreading of the nature of the international system is personally and professionally costly to them, not to mention costly to the reputation of the U.S. government. The policy has already proven costly for U.S. soft power and claims to leadership in the area of democracy and human rights.

Part IV

CONCLUSIONS

8

Policy, Theory, and the Justice Cascade

n the spring of 2010, I traveled to Uruguay shortly after the election of the new president, José Mujica. A former leader of the Tupamaro guerrilla movement, Mujica belongs to the same leftist coalition, the *Frente Amplio*, or Broad Front, as the assassinated Zelmar Michelini. Mujica is part of a generation of political leaders in Latin America who have suffered personally from repression, like Michelle Bachelet, the former president of Chile and the daughter of a former army general who died under torture during the Pinochet dictatorship. If anyone should want revenge and be in a position to deliver it, it would be Mujica. During the dictatorship, Mujica spent thirteen years in prison, where he was tortured, held in solitary confinement, and deprived of the most basic human needs.

Shortly before Mujica's election, ex-President Bordaberry, who was president when Mujica was taken prisoner and during the worst period of his ill-treatment, was sentenced to twenty-five years in prison for human rights violations during his dictatorship. Juan María Bordaberry, now eighty-one and ill, is also the father of Mujica's main political opponent, Pedro Bordaberry, of the traditional Colorado Party. Mujica, at seventy-five a portly and streetwise politician, nevertheless said that he hoped to introduce into Congress a bill saying that all convicted defendants over the age of seventy should be allowed to serve their sentence in house arrest rather than a prison. If passed, Bordaberry would be one of the first prisoners to benefit from the new policy. Mujica's proposal is a reminder that forgiveness and leniency can come at the same time as justice, and they can come from unexpected places. Once again, practitioners in Latin

America are in the vanguard in thinking about the next stage of the justice cascade.

It is appropriate to talk about policy recommendations at this point. I don't have one simple recipe to offer for transitional justice. First, foreign prosecutions and international tribunals can be cost-effective alternatives to military intervention. Policy makers and the general public have become all too eager to embrace military intervention as a tool for addressing human rights violations in other countries. But military intervention to promote human rights is enormously costly, in both financial and human terms. Moreover, social scientists have little evidence that such costly military intervention actually leads to improvements in human rights. Prosecutions cannot stop human rights violations in the short term, but in the long term they may be a much less costly and less violent solution to the problem. Remember that international and foreign prosecutions do not operate in isolation, but are a backup system to domestic courts, where most accountability takes place.

As regards domestic prosecutions, each country will find its own way, and craft its unique response, as Uruguay is now doing. But I can offer some preliminary advice, both from many years of observing countries make choices about how to address the human rights violations that happened in the past, and from our analyses on the effectiveness of trials.

I believe that my advice is directly relevant to the United States as we grapple with questions of accountability for torture. The United States is only exceptional in the sense that it has a much less fragile political and judicial system than the transitional countries that are the main focus of this book. The most striking facts that stand out in all the research here is that demands for justice have been remarkably resilient, and yet it has not been easy for any country in the world to confront its past. Almost all leaders, originally faced with the dilemmas of accountability, have wanted to turn the page and look toward the future, not the past. Even in countries like Greece and Argentina where there were strong popular demands for accountability, leaders have faced agonizing choices that they feared could lead to military coups.

As the United States confronts the legacies of Bush administration violations, we sometimes act as if we were the first country in the world to face this dilemma, and that our political system is too fragile to cope with accountability. Many claim that any effort to seek accountability for the people responsible for abuses is only giving comfort to terrorists. These are exactly the dilemmas faced by governments all around the world when they hold prosecutions for human rights violations. The U.S. political system is far less vulnerable, and our judicial system far more capable, than those of the new democracies that have coped with similar problems. Demands for justice are robust, and countries have grappled with these same problems and come away often stronger as a result. Real human rights prosecutions—where the rights of both unpopular victims and the unpopular accused remain protected—are never easy. As the Uruguayans learned, human rights prosecutions don't win plebiscites.

When they are making tough decisions about accountability, governments should keep in mind the results of systematic empirical research. First, there is now strong reason to believe that the use of prosecutions in transitional countries is associated with improvement in human rights. Scholars still don't agree entirely about the conditions under which those improvements occur, but most research has found correlations between the use of prosecutions and improvements. Second, governments shouldn't rely on the unsupported "wisdom" that is often driving decisions about transitional justice. While crafting their own unique response to past violence, governments should feel free to disregard unconfirmed but commonly repeated truisms. Many of these take the form of arguments that certain transitional justice mechanisms are mutually exclusive. I can say with certainty that governments *do not* have to choose between *either* truth or justice. Some of the countries that have rebounded most vibrantly from authoritarianism are exactly those that have focused on partial truth and partial justice—in the words of an important report by Juan Méndez—as well as on reparations to victims, and the most diverse forms of memory work. It appears that most transitional justice policies are complementary, not mutually exclusive. This does *not* mean that government must or even should immediately launch truth commissions and far-reaching prosecutions. It just means that over time successful transitional societies have usually used combinations of restorative and retributive justice, and that these have been more likely to be complementary strategies than mutually exclusive ones.

Second, the received wisdom that justice must come quickly or it will not come at all is simply wrong, and we should finally put that red herring to rest. Our cases show that the desire for justice is very persistent, and that if political conditions for prosecutions are not right immediately after transition, such prosecutions can be held later. Countries (and victims) don't have to choose to forgive *or* to punish. Indeed, many survivors of human rights violations, like José Mujica, may find it easier to forgive if there has been some kind of accountability. Most important, we do not have clear evidence yet that governments have to choose between peace and justice. This is still the most controversial dispute in the scholarly literature. What I wish to underscore is that those who argue that justice and peace are mutually exclusive have based their positions on counterfactuals that are contested by other at least equally persuasive counterfactual arguments. Certainly with regard to the International Criminal Court, it is simply too early to sort out which of these counterfactuals is true. At least in Latin America, our evidence has shown that trials do not inadvertently promote atrocities, increase human rights violations, exacerbate conflict, or threaten democracy. It is time to put false dichotomies behind us and begin a more nuanced debate about the conditions under which trials can contribute to improving human rights and enhancing rule of law systems, and about what sequence or judicious combination of transitional mechanisms can help build democracy and resolve conflicts.

For too long, governments have thought that human rights treaties were "cheap talk"—that they could casually ratify them to gain legitimacy or win time, and then disregard them at will. The rise of foreign and international prosecutions has added some less discretionary methods of enforcement, and governments are well advised to treat their legal commitments to international human rights law the way they treat their other legal commitments. In other words, they should read the fine print and not enter into commitments they don't intend to keep. This was the lesson the Law Lords had for Pinochet, who had ratified a treaty calling for universal jurisdiction for torture and then was surprised to be detained in London. The United States is in a similar predicament because it ratified the Convention Against Torture, failed to reserve against universal jurisdiction, implemented it fully in domestic law, and then went ahead and knowingly broke the law. This is also the situation of a handful of regimes in Africa that ratified the Statute to the ICC, in two cases referred cases to the Court, and now are shocked and angry to find that the prosecutor is trying to do his job. These treaties say either you hold people accountable in your domestic courts, or the possibility will always exist that they will be tried in foreign courts.

Ethics and Human Rights Prosecutions

In the debate over human rights prosecutions, the empirical question about the impact of trials has important ethical and policy implications. And yet it is often difficult for political scientists, indeed for any scientist, to talk about ethics. Political scientists sometimes believe that if you take an explicit ethical stance on an issue, it calls into question your scientific objectivity, and thus undermines the credibility of your research. But political scientists may also shy away from normative theorizing because we have not found satisfactory ways to combine our ethical commitments with our empirical research. As long as the appeals to address ethics essentially said, "Stop being a researcher and become a moral philosopher," it wasn't very attractive to me. I had neither the training nor the inclination to engage in abstract moral philosophy. I only decided to address ethical issues when I identified an approach that let me combine attention to both normative issues and empirical research findings.[1]

Ethical theorizing is typically divided into two main approaches: rule-based and consequentialist. In other words, when we make ethical judgments, should we be concerned with how well our actions and the actions of others conform to preexisting moral or legal rules, or should we take into account primarily the consequences of those actions? A purely rule-based approach might say that providing justice for victims of human rights violations and accountability for perpetrators is such an important principle that countries should proceed with prosecutions regardless of the consequences. While I understand and respect that argument, I'm not willing to make it myself. I agree that providing justice and accountability are worthy goals that should be pursued. However, in this case, I believe that knowledge of the expected consequences is important for helping to make hard ethical choices.

In the case of human rights prosecutions, it is not enough to ask, Is it right or good to hold human rights prosecutions? We also want to know what impact prosecutions have on actually protecting human rights. The answer to the second question—What impact do human rights prosecutions have?—could affect the answer to the first question—Is it right or good to hold human rights prosecutions?[2]

If critics are right and, under certain circumstances, human rights prosecutions can lead to more atrocities, sustain conflict, and undermine democracy, a consequentialist reading would suggest that countries *should not* carry out such prosecutions.[3] If, to the contrary, as I have argued here, there is little empirical support for the argument that prosecutions lead to more atrocities, sustain conflict, or undermine democracy, then the ethical balance tips to the other side.

This may help clarify why, for me, careful empirical research, using the best tools at our disposal, is not just a professional obligation but also an ethical one. Many ethical judgments require some knowledge of reasonable expectations about consequences. Good research is the only way to have some understanding of the possible consequences of our actions. In this sense, I believe high-quality empirical research is necessary for ethical judgment.

Three Research Questions

In this final part of the book, I return to the three main questions posed: (1) What are the origins of new ideas and practices about individual criminal accountability for human rights? (2) How and why do these ideas and practices become norms and diffuse regionally and internationally? and (3) What are the effects of human rights prosecutions? Each of these questions requires a somewhat different explanation, although certain factors, such as the key role for advocacy groups, are present in the answers to all three. Finally, the relationship of these answers to broader international relations and political science theory must be considered, especially where they may change international politics.

I have argued that the emergence and diffusion of the justice cascade is the result of the intrinsic power of a new norm, put forward by a coalition of like-minded states and NGOs who are in favor of change, and embedded in law and institutions. Central to explaining all the streams that flow into the justice cascade are ideas about the need to hold individuals accountable for past human rights violations. This norm is powerful and persuasive in itself—not just because of the power of the states that advocated it, or the financial power of the foundations that supported the human rights NGOs, but because the idea is inherently appealing to a broad range of individuals. These appealing ideas were taken up by a "pro-change coalition," consisting of smaller, like-minded states like Sweden, the Netherlands, Argentina, Germany, Canada, and Jordan, working together with legal epistemic communities and NGO networks to press for accountability. Sometimes these efforts had the support of powerful states like the United States and the United Kingdom—but sometimes they were in direct opposition to them. In addition, the coalition had been working for decades to build a web of human rights treaties, along with the corresponding organizations that provided the legal and institutional underpinnings for the practice of individual criminal accountability.

Despite their intrinsic power, though, the new norms could not have won ground against the powerful reigning orthodoxy of immunity without some unique background conditions. The position of the pro-change coalition was aided by structural changes in the world system, in particular, the "third wave" of democracy and the end of the Cold War.

In terms of effectiveness, I maintain that human rights prosecutions are associated with improvements in human rights, probably through a combination of deterrence and socialization. Some actors change their behavior because prosecutions help dramatize and communicate new norms. But widespread diffusion of the norm of individual criminal accountability, when it is embedded in law and institutions, also alters the strategic game for key actors because it imposes new costs on those individuals who violate human rights. This new set of incentives can help prevent or deter violations in the future.

These arguments may seem simple and straightforward, but they run contrary to the main theories in international relations that focus on power, constructivism, and interest as the main explanations for political change. Let us first consider these main alternatives.

Coercive Power

Power is an essential part of the story of the justice cascade, because it is the main factor in explaining why it has taken so very long for individuals to hold state officials accountable for crimes. As we saw at the beginning of this book, one of the great puzzles is that for centuries, judicial systems in countries around the world have held individuals criminally accountable when they committed murder, kidnapping, or aggravated assault; but if state officials committed the same crimes on a much larger scale, they were virtually never held accountable. Power and coercion help us understand this puzzle. The idea of immunity has been the reigning orthodoxy largely because powerful state officials benefited from being protected from prosecution, and they used their power to avoid accountability. Sometimes, state officials made explicit use of coercion or the threat of coercion to protect themselves. For example, General Pinochet warned the new democratic government in Chile that "the day they touch one of my men, the rule of law ends."[4] In 1993, the Chilean armed forces, faced with the possibility of investigations for both corruption and human rights, simulated a coup, during which heavily armed soldiers surrounded the armed forces building while Pinochet and his generals, dressed in fatigues, held a high-level meeting. Although these former repressors have resisted all forms of accountability, they have been much more forceful in rejecting individual criminal accountability than state accountability. While their motives may include a mixture of ideological and material concerns, it is not difficult to understand why these officials would prefer to avoid trials and individual punishment.

Power, in its more obvious coercive forms, helps explain why it took so long for state officials to be held criminally accountable. Power is also important to my explanation because I argue that it is only when the power of perpetrators is diminished that early adopters can engage in human rights trials. What power cannot help us understand well, however, is why all this started to change in the first place. It cannot explain how and why the idea of individual criminal accountability came to be applied in a world where many perpetrators still hold the monopoly on violence.

Powerful states did not lead the trend toward such accountability, and in some crucial instances, they actively opposed it. Except in a handful of cases, like in the former Yugoslavia today, powerful states also did not force other states to use domestic prosecutions. Nor did powerful states lead the trend toward international and foreign prosecutions. The United States supported the Torture Convention, and in time ratified it, but it was not a leading force behind the development of the treaty. That role was played by Sweden and the Netherlands, with star supporting roles by countries emerging from authoritarian regimes like Greece and Argentina. A U.S. endorsement was crucial for creation of the ICTY and the ICTR, but it has been the major opponent of the ICC, the main embodiment of the new criminal accountability model.

Power is useful for understanding why accountability is unevenly applied, but not why individual accountability emerged. Thus, power helps us understand why French judges find Argentine or Tunisian officials guilty of human rights violations in foreign trials, but have refused to move ahead in a case against Donald Rumsfeld. But it can't tell us how it became possible in the first place to hold foreign human rights trials in French courts.

The culminating point of the justice cascade was the creation of the International Criminal Court, a legal development opposed initially by all five powerful permanent members of the UN Security Council—the United States, Russia, China, France, and the United Kingdom—as well as by large and influential newly industrializing countries like India, Mexico, and Indonesia. The ICC was eventually created through a campaign led by the pro-change coalition of small like-minded states and NGOs, many in Europe, but including others from around the world, with important leadership from former authoritarian countries like Argentina and South Africa. China and the United States voted against the Rome Statute. In the entire history of human rights lawmaking, by far the most coercive moment occurred quite late in the game, when the United States first opposed many parts of the Rome Statute of the International Criminal Court; and it then later tried to undermine Rome by seeking bilateral agreements with as many countries as possible saying that they would not submit U.S. citizens to the Court's jurisdiction. Here, the United States expended significant power resources to secure such agreements: providing additional aid, threatening to cut military economic aid and training, and then actually cutting such aid. There is no other example that I am aware of in the history of human rights law where a powerful country expended such resources to secure a particular legal outcome. But note that this example runs *counter* to the argument that the powerful impose international law. In this case, the most powerful state in the system tried to block the implementation of human rights law precisely because it had failed in its efforts to control the drafting process. Moreover, the U.S. campaign against the ICC was oddly ineffective, and the United States ended it after admitting it had been counterproductive to other U.S. interests.

Structural Power

Power is exercised at different levels, and direct coercion or compulsion is only the most obvious form. Michael Barnett and Raymond Duvall have reminded us that worldviews also have structural power and that actors' worldviews are often directly shaped by their social positions, such as their class position or geopolitical location in a wealthy country.[5] For example, the ideas and perspectives underpinning the justice cascade are about empowering the individual vis-à-vis the collective and the state. An individualist perspective is indeed inherent in a Western liberal legal and philosophical tradition, hegemonic in the world today and at the time most human rights law was drafted. Thus, the move to individual criminal accountability could be seen as the result of the structural power of the hegemonic Western worldview. But empowering such an individual vis-à-vis his or her state runs deeply counter to the structural power of states in the state system. So, human rights law presents a quandary for scholars of structural power. We might expect that when state power comes up against liberal ideas of individual rights asserted against the state, state power would win. But, as we have seen in this book, the idea of the individual sometimes wins over the ability of state officials to protect themselves from prosecution.

Some scholars of structural power have argued that the power of the individual is an idea associated with the ascendant capitalist worldview. Some even chalk up human rights trials to this increasingly dominant capitalist ideology. When I was in graduate school, however, capitalism was also used to explain the rise of military coups and repressive governments.[6] I don't think scholars of structural power can claim that capitalist ideology is behind both the move to authoritarian regimes and the move to democracy and human rights trials. Rather, it appears that the capitalist economic system and ideology have co-existed with both labor repression and human rights prosecutions. We need to find more focused explanations for the rise of the idea of individual accountability.

I believe that power, in both its coercive and structural forms, is the most important explanation for why accountability was kept *off* the agenda for so many years, and why even people harmed by human rights violations rarely considered the possibility of prosecuting repressive state officials. Why did Wilson Ferreira, after seeing that his closest colleagues had been tortured and murdered, and almost being killed himself, still write a letter to General Videla where he doesn't even mention the possibility of accountability? Why wouldn't Ferreira say, for example, that Uruguay should either extradite Videla to stand trial in Argentina or prosecute him in Uruguay, but offer him the kind of fair trial that he denied to his victims? The answer is because Ferreira couldn't imagine such a scenario, and part of the reason he couldn't imagine it was because of the operation of structural power, which entrenched the worldview of state officials: that they were simply above the ordinary operation of the law. Why did Carlos Acuña's colleagues in the human rights movement in Argentina at first think he and his group SERPAJ were crazy when they wanted to put the word "justice" in their petitions and slogans? They thought he was crazy because they knew the word "justice" by itself was a direct provocation to the powerful state officials who still ruled their country, and who would do everything possible to keep accountability from being realized.

The Argentine human rights movement could begin to imagine justice, and, as Carlos said, they knew it meant that they wanted to "throw these guys in jail." But the political scene was permeated by power, which meant that the word "justice" was seen as a dangerous tool that could not yet even be mentioned. When could the Argentines start to mention justice? Not until the military lost the war in the Malvinas, when its power was not broken but at least temporarily constrained. Finally, how is it possible that the structural power of a Francoist worldview pervades parts of Spain today so strongly that family members still talk in a low voice within closed doors when they mention the unmarked graves where their relatives were buried during the Civil War sixty years earlier? In what is one of the clearest examples of ideational power, the Spanish Fascists had years of civil war and authoritarian rule in which to instill fear so deeply in the families of the victims that Emilio Silva's grandmother never once mentioned the fate of her husband, even in the privacy of her family.

Structural Constructivism

Power helps explain why it took so long for individual criminal accountability to be adopted, but it cannot explain why the new trend emerged and spread. Constructivism is a theoretical approach that takes seriously the role of human consciousness—including beliefs, ideas, and norms—in social life. The most influential version of this approach is what I call "structural constructivism," which focuses on the deep ideational structures that guide state behavior. But structural constructivism is also not helpful in explaining the emergence of the justice cascade. It does not assume, as do arguments about structural power, that worldviews derive from class or geopolitical social positions. In many situations, these constructivists argue, states don't make rational choices about what to do but instead are guided by almost automatic understandings of what is appropriate behavior in particular circumstances. Constructivists call this form of action a "logic of appropriateness," and it can be contrasted with an alternative model of behavior—a "logic of consequences"—where rational actors weigh the costs and benefits of outcomes and choose their actions accordingly.

This approach shows how the factors that condition international outcomes are not only material power or wealth, but also ideas that are taken for granted and yet shape international politics in equally powerful ways. Just like the power argument above, structural constructivism helps us understand why it was so difficult to initiate individual criminal accountability in the world; but it has trouble explaining why and how change was possible. Change was blocked by beliefs taken for granted not only by leaders but also by the general population, who could not imagine that it would be possible to hold leaders accountable. So, this approach is useful in helping explain why it took so long for individual accountability for violations to emerge. But this approach is not good for understanding why and how change occurs in structures and rules.

Change cannot be understood without seeing how new ideas emerge and spread. These new ideas often challenge the older ideas that constitute the international system. For example, with respect to prosecutions, the old ideas about sovereignty and sovereign immunity maintained that high-ranking state officials should not and could not be prosecuted. The new ideas about individual criminal accountability for human rights violations stress that state officials should and could be held accountable. These new ideas "catch on" through logics that are not captured either by a "logic of consequences" or a "logic of appropriateness." When the Argentine activists first pushed for criminal trials, they were not following any logic of appropriateness. They were being consciously and explicitly "inappropriate"—and they knew it, which was why it was such a frightening thing to consider at first.

These new logics can be explained by "agentic" constructivism, which is basically the approach I take in this book. Like constructivism but more broadly, this is concerned with the role of human consciousness in international politics; but unlike structural constructivism, it is not mainly interested in how deep structures constrain imagination and action. Rather, agentic constructivism is concerned with how agents—that is, real people and organizations—promote new ideas and practices. If successful, such new ideas may catch on and over time create new logics of appropriateness and new logics of consequences. In other words, they will create new understanding of the ways in which states ought to behave, and new understandings of the national interests of states.

Competition/Interest

Interests are by no means absent from my agentic-constructivist argument, but in order to understand interests, we need to unpack the state, and consider how context and ideas shape the way that different actors interpret their interests. The interests of actors don't exist in the abstract, but change over time in relation to the changing institutional and ideational context in which they are operating. Unless victims can imagine prosecutions, they can't calculate that it would be in their interests to pursue them. The interests of states, agencies within states—including the judiciaries and the military and police perpetrators of human rights violations—and victims of violations and their NGO allies all need to be considered. We will see how perceptions of their interests for some of these groups change as the context changes.

As Stephen Krasner has reminded us, the ratification of human rights treaties is an exercise of one form of sovereignty, since only sovereign states can ratify treaties, even as that erodes another kind of sovereignty.[7] In this sense, we can say that states "invited" the process of individual criminal accountability, even if they were often later unpleasantly surprised with the results of their actions. Perhaps the most puzzling part of this story is why state officials would have (more or less voluntarily) relinquished this privilege.

We first need to distinguish between the motivations of different types of state actors. For government officials or members of the security forces who have already carried out human rights abuses, the strategic landscape is initially straightforward: it is in their interest to prevent prosecution for past human rights violations. These spoilers are often willing to go to great lengths to prevent prosecution. Given a choice, they will always prefer no transitional justice at all, guaranteed if necessary by an amnesty. They very often succeed in preventing domestic trials, at least initially, through threats, coup attempts, or blocked peace processes.[8]

Although state officials accused of perpetrating human rights violations oppose trials, some democratic and transitional states have helped create law and ratify the treaties that underpin the idea of individual criminal accountability. The motivations of other state actors are more complex. Newly democratic governments are primarily interested in stability, continuity, and political survival. The new democratic government of Chile, faced with the threats from Pinochet and his allies, believed that human rights prosecutions would undermine stability by provoking a military coup. But President Karamanlis in Greece apparently believed that rapid prosecutions would limit the power of veto players and thus promote stability, so he eventually worked to promote the trials of the military. New democratic governments also have both internal and external constituencies to satisfy, who may support or oppose prosecutions. These diverse motivations of new governments thus cannot easily explain outcomes on prosecutions.

States have drafted and ratified the main treaties providing the legal underpinnings for individual accountability for human rights violations. Of the three treaties that form the backbone of individual criminal accountability, 146 countries have ratified the Torture Convention, 136 countries have ratified the Genocide Convention, and 110 countries have ratified the Statute of the ICC, which was only opened for ratification in 1998. This includes fewer states than those that have ratified other human rights treaties, such as the Convention on the Rights of the Child with 193 ratifications, which include no provisions for individual criminal accountability. Yet, only nineteen countries have not ratified at least one of the three treaties that underpin the move toward individual criminal accountability.[9] Even more states have ratified the core treaties that call on them to ensure rights and provide remedies—phrases increasingly interpreted as implying an obligation to investigate and prosecute.

The relatively high number of ratifications of the ICC is especially significant since under the Bush administration the U.S. government carried out a campaign against the Court, using political and economic sanctions against countries that ratified the treaty and refusing to sign bilateral agreements promising not to turn U.S. personnel over to the Court. Thus, we could argue that it was in the interests of states *not* to ratify the ICC Statute and thereby avoid possible sanctions.[10] Some states didn't ratify for this reason; others ratified the Statute and then signed a bilateral agreement with the United States.

It is possible that not all states understood that the ratification of the Genocide Convention and the Convention Against Torture began to create the legal conditions for individual criminal accountability for human rights violations. This can no longer be the case with the ICC, however, since the Court is focused only on individual accountability, and the U.S. campaign against the ICC could not leave doubt in any state's mind of the implications for individuals.

It appears that the great majority of states supported the development of general legal underpinnings for the individual criminal accountability model. Why would states do this? Why would they voluntarily remove the historical protection state officials had from prosecution? It seems possible that most states believed that individual accountability would be reserved for individuals in other states, not their own (this, for example, was the position of the United States in the drafting of the Torture Convention). And since the ICC can only examine violations that occur after a country has ratified the statute, current state officials know that they are safe from ICC prosecution for any past crimes. So, the Argentine armed forces supported the move toward the ICC because it allowed them to support the cause of human rights without any fear that it would exacerbate their prosecution for past violations.[11]

Even so, it is difficult to find a strong interest-based motivation for why states would have supported the move toward individual accountability for human rights violations. Some state officials believed in ideas about justice, and some may have believed that there are relatively low costs to treaty ratification. When we look at the list of early ratifiers, it is hard to separate out which states fully understood and accepted the implications of their actions. Any norm cascade includes a significant handful of countries that ratify treaties because they believe in them. But there is also a second set of countries that ratify because they think they will not be costly and find later to their dismay that they were mistaken. By then, it may be too late to withdraw or backtrack. Elsewhere, Thomas Risse and I have called this "self-entrapment."

Why would some state officials underestimate the implications and possible costs of their actions? States were basing their calculations of the future on what happened in the past. Thus, in a period of rapid flux, states may misunderstand the implications of their actions. They make mistakes. I'm not arguing that this is a consistent feature of the international system. In general, states are skilled at interpreting their interests. But in a period when norms and corresponding practices are changing rapidly, states can't be expected to anticipate the implications of their actions. No one entirely understood the implications of the universal jurisdiction article in the Torture Convention. There were those, like Jan Herman Burgers, who hoped that it would lead to prosecution for torture, and there were others, like Augusto Pinochet, who couldn't imagine that he would ever be held accountable, and certainly not under the aegis of a foreign court. Thus, I now argue that self-entrapment is a phenomenon characteristic of the early stages of a norm cascade where the implications of the actions are as yet unclear. The costs of ratification of the Torture Convention were not clear to most states until the UK judiciary decided in 1999 that Pinochet could be extradited to Spain to stand trial, basing its decision explicitly on the universal jurisdiction provision of the Torture Convention. Again, the potential costs of the ratification of the Rome Statute may not have been clear until 2007 or 2008, when the ICC began to issue indictments and arrest warrants for individuals suspected of war crimes and crimes against humanity. Thus, a series of African countries that were early ratifiers of the Rome Statute found themselves self-entrapped when they discovered to their dismay the full implications of their ratification decisions.

Although states may have misunderstood the implications of ratifying particular treaties, they have usually viewed foreign and international prosecutions directed at their own officials as contrary to their interests. In virtually all cases of foreign and international prosecutions, the targeted governments have argued, often vehemently, that foreign or international prosecutions for individual criminal accountability are either illegitimate or unnecessary or both. Their arguments varied, but generally the arguments were *not* against the *concept* of individual criminal accountability per se, but against individual criminal accountability in foreign or international courts. This often has led these governments to advocate individual accountability in domestic courts, even if they had not initially taken this position. After Pinochet was detained in London the Chilean government argued forcefully that he could and should be tried at home, even though such trials were initially blocked by domestic amnesty legislation. Although the Ugandan government first referred the case to the ICC for war crimes by the Lord's Resistance Army, it later set up a war crime division of its high court and passed legislation allowing it to try its own war criminals, especially lower-level officials that the Court is unlikely to indict. In both Chile and Uganda, the possibility of domestic trials increased after cases were initiated in foreign or international courts.

The interests of state actors thus often changed when individual criminal accountability moved from being a one-level to a two-level game.[12] Let's suppose that the former members of a repressive government think they are sitting at a single negotiating table with their domestic opponents. If their opponents propose to hold them criminally accountable, the military may be able to threaten to carry out a military coup. This is what the military in Argentina actually did to convince President Alfonsín to pass an amnesty law. When Pinochet thought that he was just in a domestic game, it was clear that his interest (and those of his military colleagues) was to block domestic prosecutions at all costs, and he was able to do so with threats of coups and shows of military strength. When he was arrested in London on the basis of an arrest warrant from Spain, it became clear that he was operating in a more complicated two-level game. The Chilean government was sitting at two different negotiating tables, one with domestic opponents and one with other international actors. The threat of Pinochet's internal allies to carry out a coup didn't have the same impact at the international negotiating table as it did at the domestic one. Indeed, once Pinochet was arrested in London, if his followers had carried out a coup, it would only have made it more likely that Pinochet would be extradited to Spain, convicted, and imprisoned. The Chilean Foreign Ministry was unable to use the standard tools of diplomacy to get him released. It was at this point that the interests of some of those who opposed trials in Chile began to change. It was no longer a question of trials or no trials (in Chile), but now a question of trials in Spain, trials in the United Kingdom, or (perhaps) a trial in Chile. Under these circumstances, the option of a trial in Chile started to look better than before. This is why the possibility of international and foreign trials is a necessary backup system in the accountability model. The legal rule at stake is that states must either try or extradite those accused of crimes. It is hard for a state that has ratified any of these treaties to argue that its officials should not be tried abroad *and* that they will not be prosecuted at home either.

It is this dynamic that converts the one-level prosecution game into a more complicated two-level game and *changes the interests* of the players in question. In these circumstances, foreign and international prosecutions may alter the calculations of past and current members of the security forces to make them more favorable to domestic prosecutions than they would otherwise have been.

The threat of extradition to Spain also led to new prosecutions in Argentina, and the threat of extradition of Uruguayans to Argentina to stand trial gave impetus to the first human rights prosecutions in Uruguay. In January 2008, an Italian judge issued arrest warrants for at least 140 former Latin American officials charged with the deaths of 25 Italian citizens as a result of Operation Condor. These two-level trial games also give leverage to advocates of prosecutions within domestic governments. So, for example, the Brazilian national secretary for human rights, Paulo Vannuchi, said he welcomed the Italian charges, and used them as a reason to call on the government to repeal an amnesty law enacted in 1979, which has been interpreted as granting full immunity to government officials for human rights violations committed during military rule.[13] Whether as a result of the Italian warrants or not, a handful of civil prosecutions against torturers started moving ahead in Brazil after the decision by the Italian judge.[14]

The trend toward individual accountability has added international and domestic criminal courts and individual litigants to the cast of actors. The role of lawyers, judges, and courts in the justice cascade is complex. As parties interested in the growth of rule of law, we might expect such actors to support legal accountability over other forms of accountability. Resolving accountability issues in courts could contribute to the power, wealth, and influence of the judicial sector and increase its autonomy vis-à-vis the executive. Despite the animosity that his arrest warrants provoked with the conservative Spanish government, Judge Garzón became an international celebrity as a result of his involvement in human rights prosecutions. In general, judicial actors will stress legal accountability in domestic courts, but their actions are affected by specific domestic institutional and ideological factors. In some countries, taking up a human rights case or trial could be dangerous and could undermine one's career. For example, during and after the dictatorship in Chile, involvement in such prosecutions had a negative effect on judicial careers, and thus judicial actors tended to shun trials.[15] It is less clear why lawyers and judges would support either foreign or international prosecutions, since these do not promote the interests of national judicial sectors, except to the extent that they can jump-start or contribute to domestic prosecutions.

We can assume for purposes of simplicity that victims of human rights violations usually prefer accountability. Victims are important because they are often the litigants who bring human rights cases to the courts, at least in those civil law countries with provisions for private prosecutions in criminal cases. In most countries, without individual litigants using private prosecution provisions, few human rights cases would be presented to national courts.[16] Victims and their families want accountability; but it is not obvious why they should prefer a criminal accountability model to a state accountability one. From the point of view of material benefits, a state (civil) accountability model would be more likely to provide financial compensation to a victim. Nevertheless, in most of the countries where I have conducted field research, including Argentina, Chile, Greece, Guatemala, Portugal, and Uruguay, victims and their families were at the forefront in demanding individual *criminal* accountability, while some have rejected financial compensation, or accepted it with hesitance and guilt. There are some other countries, however, such as Brazil, where victims have not initially demanded far-reaching criminal accountability. There may be some cultural or regional difference in victims' preferences, as I discussed earlier, but there is not yet systematic empirical evidence that this is the case. I argue that victims generally prefer individual criminal accountability (retributive justice) and that these are "ideational" preferences rather than "material" ones: they are moved to act by their beliefs, not by what would benefit them most financially.

Victims, in turn, had NGO allies that also showed strong preferences for accountability. In many countries, victims become litigants because they are represented by lawyers associated with human rights NGOs and a network of activist lawyers. This network had strong ideational preferences for accountability but not necessarily for individual criminal accountability. Its members were equally at home working on cases in regional human rights courts (state accountability) and for criminal human rights prosecutions in foreign courts. But since the network prefers more accountability, the addition of individual criminal accountability to existing state models allowed them to expand their legal reach dramatically. To the extent that the continued existence of these groups depended on the continuation of human rights prosecutions, we could say that these groups of lawyers had both strong beliefs in favor of trials and also a material interest in trials.

The main point of this section is that interests are relevant; but just like power, interests primarily help explain why it has taken so long for the individual accountability model to be adopted. In addition, we have to break down the understanding of interests to look at the interests of diverse actors within and outside the state. Thus victims, human rights NGOs, some parts of some governments, and parts of international organizations and tribunals form the "pro-change alliance," in favor of greater individual criminal accountability for human rights violations. The inclusion of litigants, litigators, and some judges and courts in the alliance multiplies by hundreds the number of potential actors who could intervene in core human rights issues. But even with these additions to its numbers, the alliance is still a relatively weak coalition in the traditional ways that political scientists usually talk about power, and it is mainly motivated by ideas about justice, and changing understandings of interests shaped by those ideas. Thus, any explanation of the justice cascade must move beyond a narrow concept of interests. We can now return to our three main research questions, and answer them in greater detail.

Question 1: What are the origins of new ideas and practices about individual criminal accountability for human rights?

The first part of this book demonstrated that the justice cascade follows the general pattern of a "norm life cycle."[17] The main norms at stake here come directly from domestic legal systems. The individual criminal accountability model is the dominant model in domestic legal systems. So, the model of justice is not just spreading from one country to another; rather, ideas from the domestic criminal system dealing mainly with common crime are being used to address the more extraordinary crimes committed by state officials. Scholars have long recognized the importance of powerful domestic norms. In some cases, these domestic norms may have a prominence that makes them likely candidates for international norms.[18] The new norms studied here originated in domestic settings in countries in the semi-periphery where they were promoted by norm entrepreneurs, including NGOs, regional human rights organizations, and members of transitional governments. But the domestic model had been available for a long time. What happened in the mid-1970s that made it possible for some countries to consider using it for state officials?

First, all the early adopters of prosecutions had experienced a severe "shock" to the reigning orthodoxy of the impunity model. During the previous authoritarian regimes, these countries had some of the most serious human rights violations in their history. In many countries in Latin America, such as Argentina or Guatemala, not since the colonial period had governments killed as many people as they did in the 1970s and early 1980s. These human rights violations were a *shock* that created pressure for new forms of accountability. Shocks are often necessary to break the grip that a reigning orthodoxy has on the imagination, and they can lead to processes of learning where people seek alternatives.

In this case, when people looked for alternatives, they found a model close at hand in their own domestic criminal justice system, which existed to hold individual perpetrators criminally accountable. I agree with Gary Bass that one cannot understand the emergence of the model of individual criminal accountability "without reference to ideas drawn from domestic politics."[19] Bass also argues that domestic trials are the most sincere indication of the strength of ideas and norms, since it is more difficult to put one's own leaders and soldiers on trial than those of another country, especially one vanquished in war.[20]

Second, the power balance between the leaders of the previous authoritarian regime and the leaders of the new transitional regime affects the choices governments make about prosecutions. Countries that had experienced a "ruptured" transition to democracy, which weakened the power of the military and other groups associated with a repressive regime, were initially more able to use human rights prosecutions. But as the momentum for prosecutions increased, it became possible over time to hold prosecutions even in some of the countries that had negotiated transitions, as Pinochet and Bordaberry discovered in Chile and Uruguay. Even so, the balance of power between old and new elites still continued to be important because prosecutions were often held only after previous office holders had stepped down from their positions of power and had lost the ability to overturn the new democratic regimes.

The early adopters and innovators of trials were largely unaware of one another, and they were not drawing on international models. They chose to use prosecutions because of domestic pressures, not because they were told or obliged to do so by other powerful countries or institutions in the North. In both Greece and all the early adopters in Latin America, regional human rights commissions wrote crucial country reports on human rights violations during the authoritarian regimes that provided evidence and encouragement for such prosecutions, while not in any sense determining the outcomes. Early adopters of transitional polices then acted as "laboratories of justice," which innovated and experimented with new and different transitional justice practices.[21] Eventually, some of these practices served as models that could be used in other countries. But those countries didn't uncritically adopt them; often they modified them substantially to address what they considered to be the problems or errors of these very early models.

Question 2: How and why do these ideas and practices become norms and diffuse regionally and internationally?

The case studies and quantitative evidence presented in this book suggest that active *domestic* entrepreneurship was essential to norm emergence, while a combination of *transnational* emulation and transnational norm entrepreneurship contributes to diffusion.[22] But before this norm entrepreneurship could succeed, certain background conditions had to be in place, including the third wave of democracy, the end of the Cold War, and the entry into force of the main legal tools for accountability.

As we have seen, the diffusion or cascade period coincides with the end of the Cold War and the flowering of the third wave of democracy. The breakup of the USSR created a new group of democratizing states in Eastern Europe that would adopt transitional justice measures, including prosecutions. More important, by taking attention away from a polarized struggle between communism and anti-communism, the end of the Cold War also created a more permissive atmosphere for holding former repressive leaders of whatever ideological stripe accountable for past human rights violations.

The third wave of democracy is a necessary factor to explain both the emergence and diffusion of the norm of individual criminal accountability.[23] But democracy is not in any sense a sufficient condition, since the earlier, second wave of democratization was not accompanied by human rights trials, and even in the third wave, fewer than half of the countries that experienced democratic transitions used human rights prosecutions. The related trends of democratization and the end of the Cold War are thus important for understanding the justice cascade, but they only provide the background conditions, not a fully satisfactory explanation.

An additional necessary factor was the gradual building up of the legal streambed underpinning the justice cascade. States and NGOs had been building human rights law for various decades, but not until human rights law and institutions had reached a certain level of maturity was it possible for the justice cascade to move forward. By 1990, when the diffusion period began, the human rights issue area was highly legalized and highly institutionalized. These treaties and institutions provided possibilities for action; but when the early prosecutions were held, such possibilities had not yet been activated. The activists who helped launch the human rights prosecutions engaged and activated the existing but still dormant human rights institutions.

Once practices of individual criminal accountability had emerged and started to spread, the most important predictor for adoption of prosecutions was what neighboring countries were doing. Hunjoon Kim found, for example, that the single most important determinant for whether a country will use a truth commission or human rights prosecutions is the number of other states in that region that have previously used a truth commission or prosecutions.[24] Early norm adoption is the result of domestic political struggle and norm entrepreneurs, but later adoption is the result of a combination of internal demands and external diffusion of models.[25] This is what the norm life cycle argument originally suggested. The research on human rights prosecutions and truth commissions, however, adds a strong regional dimension to the theory. Norms emerge and diffuse first within regions; only later are they able to jump from one region to another and go global.

For these reasons, the spread of the justice norm has been, and will continue to be, regionally uneven. Because the justice cascade has followed the global wave in democratization, it *will not* extend to regions of the world where democratic transitions have not taken root, for example, in the Middle East, or where democratic reversals are occurring, as in

Russia and Central Asia. After Europe and Latin America, I expect Africa to be the region where prosecutions will continue to be prominent; but justice will be neither rapid nor easy there, just as it was not rapid or easy in Europe or Latin America. In our database, Africa has had more domestic prosecutions than any region except Europe and Latin America. The trend should continue, in part because Africa is the only other region in the world with regional human rights law and institutions in place. These institutions played an important role in supporting prosecutions in both Latin America and Europe, and may also serve as a kind of proxy for regional human rights consciousness. The African Commission for Human Rights was inaugurated in 1987; the African Court on Human and People's Rights was set up in 2004, and had its first meeting in 2006. In this sense, it is similar to the Inter-American Commission of Human Rights, originally set up in 1959, and the Inter-American Court, established twenty years later, in 1979. Although the African system differs from the European and Inter-American Human Rights systems, particularly in its emphasis on collective or people's rights, it is likely to play an important role in accountability in the future. But this is not likely to happen immediately, since in the case of both the European and the Inter-American system, only decades after the institutions were established did they develop the expertise and authority to play a key role in regional human rights practices.

Africa also has institutions available to it that were not available to the Southern European or Latin American countries when they were passing through their transitions to democracy, in particular, the International Criminal Court, as well as some international and hybrid tribunals like the ICTR and the Special Court for Sierra Leone. African countries have widely ratified the Rome Statute of the ICC, and although they are increasingly disenchanted with the Court, it has nonetheless had an impact on actions concerning accountability in the region. For example, Uganda referred the very first case to the ICC, that of the Lord's Resistance Army, but later had some second thoughts about the wisdom of the referral in the context of an ongoing civil war. Nevertheless, in response to international and domestic pressures, Uganda has since set up its own war crime division for its high court, which is poised to begin a case against a lower-level LRA official already in custody. The new war crime tribunal in Uganda was set up in 2010, and at the time of the publication of this book had not yet seen its first case. It took courts in Argentina and Chile almost twenty years after transition to reopen and make strong headway on human rights prosecutions. We should anticipate that accountability will also be an arduous process in Uganda and elsewhere in Africa.

Asia experienced relatively few democratic transitions during the third wave, does not have regional human rights institutions, and Asian countries have ratified the Rome Statute at a lower rate. As a result, we would expect the process of accountability to be slower in Asia than in Europe, Latin America, and Africa. Our database has very few examples of domestic human rights prosecutions in Asia, and Ellen Lutz and Caitlin Reiger record only two Asian heads of state prosecuted for human rights violations, both of them from South Korea. Regional cultural attitudes about accountability may also play a role. Hunjoon Kim's dissertation on truth commissions includes an excellent discussion of truth commissions in South Korea which persuaded me that victims of human rights violations in that country had somewhat different cultural attitudes toward accountability than victims in Latin America. In particular, Hunjoon showed that South Koreans were very concerned with the honor of their families, so South Korea made some choices to restore the honor of victims, rather than to promote deterrence or retribution.

The ideas and practices of transitional justice moved in multiple directions. Practices of individual accountability used in the domestic legal system to address common crime were applied within these same domestic systems to state officials accused of human rights violations. These practices then spread from one country to another in a process scholars call "horizontal diffusion." Thus, when the Uruguayans started using prosecutions, they were often drawing on models that diffused horizontally from neighboring Argentina and Chile.

"Vertical diffusion" also occurred, and it took two forms: bottom up and top down.[26] Bottom-up vertical diffusion occurs when an idea or practice moves from one specific country to an international organization or an international NGO. So, for example, when Juan Méndez wrote a report about the trials in Argentina, and later used his knowledge about those trials to inform his work for accountability at Human Rights Watch, this is an example of bottom-up vertical diffusion. Top-down vertical accountability occurs when practices of individual accountability move from international actors to national ones, for example, when international or regional tribunals encourage states that have not yet used individual criminal accountability to do so in their domestic legal systems.[27]

I talk about some top-down vertical diffusion in this book, but my main argument is that the justice cascade started in domestic politics in the semi-periphery and diffused outwards and upwards through horizontal diffusion from one country to another, and then via bottom-up vertical diffusion from individual countries to international organizations and international NGOs. Another main argument here is that specific individuals working in networks diffused the ideas of the justice cascade. "Diffuse" is not a passive verb in this book. Ideas do not diffuse through the air like viruses; rather, individuals actively diffuse ideas through their networks. As we saw in Chapter 3, the ideas of transitional justice in Argentina spread as specific individuals moved on, through exile and employment, to construct and connect to new networks. Human rights NGOs, working domestically and linked together in transnational networks, were active in promoting the new model of individual accountability.

Scholars of international politics, sociology, and international law have paid much more attention to top-down vertical diffusion. Indeed, there is an entire school of thought in sociology called "sociological institutionalism" that is premised on the notion of top-down vertical diffusion from global culture to domestic societies. Some scholars have disciplinary and geographical "blinders" that sometimes lead them to assume that all diffusion is top down, from global culture or international institutions to domestic politics, or that all diffusion moves from the North to the South. Because international lawyers study international law, not comparative domestic law, they often don't pay attention to prosecutions unless they are happening in an international format. For the most part, they have missed the other forms of diffusion discussed here.[28] For them, the entire justice cascade story moves from Nuremberg to the ICTY to the ICC, and then into domestic legal systems through the legal changes made to implement the Rome Statute. I argue that this is just one of the "streams" that runs into the justice cascade, but it is not the whole story. The post-Nuremberg trend toward individual criminal accountability for human rights violations started twenty years *before* the ICTY, and it started in the domestic courts of individual countries in the semi-periphery where human rights violations had occurred.

The explanation for the justice cascade thus needs to be attentive *both* to developments at the international level and to explanations at the domestic level. Domestically, first in Southern Europe, then in Latin America, developments in regional law and domestic politics permitted human rights activists to press for greater accountability; and in particularly fortuitous situations, they made individual criminal accountability possible. Multiple domestic experiences with individual accountability thus created the backdrop against which the international community developed new legal doctrines and fashioned new international tribunals, especially the ICC.

Horizontal diffusion occurs more forcefully within regions than between regions. So, it is easier for activists to diffuse ideas horizontally from Argentina to Uruguay than from Argentina to Cambodia. Bottom-up vertical diffusion happens from innovative regions to international institutions. Which region is innovative varies somewhat by issue-area; in the area of transitional justice, Latin America has been one of the most innovative regions in the world. I would maintain that ideas about human rights prosecutions diffused through bottom-up vertical diffusion from Latin America to international NGOs and international organizations. Those institutions and INGOs in turn diffused practices to countries in less innovative regions or with more intractable national political situations.

International relations theorists have increasingly called attention to the role of region in world politics,[29] and scholars have identified strong regional diffusion effects.[30] But awareness of the importance of region has not been fully integrated into norm theory or diffusion theory, nor do we understand well the mechanisms through which regional diffusion operates. Region often explains important variations in quantitative models, but here "region" may be a proxy for something else, such as shared language, religion, culture, or history. The notion of an early adopter or late adopter is region-specific, not global. Models diffuse first within regions. Later, there are some country cases that permit horizontal diffusion from one region to another. The Greek prosecutions did not become a model that could jump regions. The South African Truth and Reconciliation Commission, on the other hand, diffused horizontally within the African region and also diffused horizontally to other regions.

In addition, bottom-up vertical diffusion from South Africa to INGOs also occurred. South Africa's truth commission, for example, was instrumental in the emergence and practices of the world's main transitional justice INGO, the International Center for Transitional Justice, in 2001. Alex

Boraine and Paul van Zyl, two of the three co-founders of the ICTJ, were the deputy chair and the executive secretary of the South African Truth and Reconciliation Commission under its chairman Archbishop Desmond Tutu. Alex Boraine is the person who first visited Patricia Valdez in Argentina to learn about the Argentina transitional justice experience, and who then invited Patricia, Catalina Smulovitz, and José Zalaquett from Argentina and Chile to share their experiences with South Africa as it made plans for transitional justice.

Some see the ICTJ as an example of top-down diffusion, where a "one size fits all" model of transitional justice is being exported from the New York offices of the NGO to countries around the world. They miss, however, the actual historical path of the truth commission model associated with the ICTJ. Truth commissions started in Argentina in 1983 as an autonomous innovation by policy makers in coordination with the human rights movement there. The Argentine experience in turn influenced the Chilean Truth Commission, and both Argentines and Chileans were invited to South Africa to share their experiences. But each new truth commission was not simply a copy of what came before; rather, it was consciously crafted to try to avoid earlier problems or to fit the particular situation of a transitional country. South Africans designed their own unique version of a truth commission, building off both the Argentine and the Chilean experiences, but adding important new tools, such as the provision that perpetrators would receive amnesty if they provided truthful testimony to the commission. This model was very appealing globally, in part because it embodied the ethos of restorative justice but did not rule out prosecutions for the unrepentant.[31] In practice, the South African process has not led to prosecutions, but this has not limited its influence.

Eventually, transnational actors became deeply involved in the justice cascade. These actors were sometimes human rights groups and other international NGOs that formed advocacy networks.[32] Individuals in these groups often act as "brokers," linking two or more previously unconnected networks or sites.[33] The transnational justice network was not just your garden-variety social movement, however, because its central members were lawyers with appreciable technical expertise in international and domestic law, who systematically pursued the tactic of human rights prosecutions.[34] Very often, human rights groups pursued justice in the face of governmental indifference or recalcitrance; at other times, they formed alliances with government officials committed to rule of law and to human rights. These government officials, whom Anne-Marie Slaughter has defined as "transgovernmental networks," often included judges and lawyers in the judicial branches of governments.[35] National judicial authorities cooperated both with human rights NGOs and with international and regional courts. These linkages were especially strong in Europe and in Latin America. What I call the "pro-change coalition" thus brought together transnational advocacy groups, expert groups of lawyers, and transgovernmental groups of like-minded state officials.

There was not one single transnational justice network, but various regional networks that occasionally overlapped and connected into global networks. Some regions, especially Asia and the Middle East, were underrepresented. Countries and regions with few domestic human rights NGOs or those with few international linkages were often absent. The Latin American justice network shared for the most part a common language (Spanish) and met occasionally in informal workshops around the hemisphere as well as during the annual meetings of the General Assembly of the OAS, especially when it was going to consider important reports issued by the Inter-American Commission on Human Rights. The Latin American network had strong contacts with U.S.- and European-based NGOs that worked on human rights and transitional justice; but it had weak connections with NGOs based in Eastern Europe, Africa, Asia, or the Middle East. Likewise, there is a European justice network, focused on transitional justice questions primarily in Europe.

The role of such networks in instigating the justice cascade and contributing to its diffusion comes through quite clearly in all of the qualitative research on the topic, including that presented in Chapters 3 and 4 of this book. It is difficult to test quantitatively because we have no measures, or poor measures, of transnational and transgovernmental networks. Nonetheless, Hunjoon Kim has shown that the presence of domestic human rights groups has a positive and highly significant effect on the repeated use of human rights prosecutions.[36]

Learning occurred both at the adoption stage and at the diffusion stage of the norm cascade. For more general diffusion to occur, the existing model of handling human rights abuses had to be perceived as inadequate or broken in some way. Before World War II, there had been no accountability for past human rights violations. The Holocaust revealed the dramatic failures of the sovereign immunity model and led states to construct the human rights regime, with its state accountability model. But while naming and shaming and the state accountability model had some successes, they were often inadequate in dealing with the most repressive states.

This was especially heightened by the conflict in the Balkans, since the shock of the discovery of concentration camps and genocide in the heart of Europe fifty years after World War II suggested that the existing accountability model had failed. The ineffectiveness of the international response to the genocide in Rwanda in 1994 proved yet another example of the failure of the old orthodoxy to prevent major human rights violations. These crises or shocks called in question *both* the reigning orthodoxy of state immunity *and* the new model of state accountability, and they provoked a move toward an individual criminal accountability model at the international level, when the UN Security Council set up the ICTY and the ICTR. The cascade of the accountability norm began in the 1990s in response to these perceived failures of the reigning orthodoxy. Policy makers are particularly open to new ideas after great crises, such as wars or depressions, and other policy failures. This argument, that new policies are adopted in the context of perceived crisis or failure of existing models, has long been a staple of the literature on ideas.[37] In the case of the justice cascade, it would appear that it was the perception of past failure, rather than the perception of success or the hope of gaining any competitive edge, that drove policy innovation. The very slogan of the transitional justice movement, "*Nunca Más*," speaks to this perception of failure that must not be repeated.

But, of course, neither failure nor success is fully obvious, and the perception of the failure of the old model was in part a reaction to publicity efforts by human rights activists, who drew attention to the failures in Rwanda, the former Yugoslavia, and elsewhere. The work of norm entrepreneurs was also essential for first imagining that it would be possible to hold state officials accountable for past violations, then struggling to create specific instances of accountability in domestic and foreign courts, and eventually in the newly created international tribunals.

The ideas that underpin both international and domestic prosecutions are mainly liberal ideas about human rights, due process, and, in particular, individual responsibility for human rights violations. These ideas are indeed associated with liberalism and the West, but they are not in any way limited to it. The idea that violent crimes involving bodily harm such as murder are wrong can be found in every legal system and culture in the world. Although the legal cultures of countries around the world differ significantly from one another, virtually all include prohibitions of murder, rape, and other forms of violence. Not only are violent crimes prohibited, but there is also a globally shared notion that victims are entitled to a redress of wrongs, and that there should be some form of sanctions for wrongs against the community.[38] Margaret Keck and I argued over a decade ago in our book *Activists Beyond Borders* that issues involving bodily harm are most likely to lead to transnational activist campaigns because such wrongs resonate across cultures and societies. The crimes for which individual criminal accountability is sought involve exactly this subset of violent bodily harm crimes.

The justice cascade implies not only that such crimes are wrong, but that the perpetrators of such crimes should be held accountable and punished, even though they are state officials. Once again, there is some cross-cultural research which suggests that the idea of basic "fairness" exists in a wide range of cultures and societies. Psychologist Stephen Pinker argues that humans have a common "moral instinct" that includes the "basic hallmark of moral reasoning that people deserve to be punished for breaking moral rules." Since prohibitions of murder, rape, and other violent crimes exist in the criminal law of virtually all societies and cultures, they are obvious moral rules for which people believe that punishment is deserved. Not only do people feel that those who commit immoral acts deserve to be punished, but they often believe it is wrong to "let them get away with it."[39] The power of these cross-cultural beliefs—both the universal prohibition on murder, rape, and other forms of violence and the idea that people deserve to be punished for breaking moral rules—forms an important part of the explanation for why the justice cascade diffused so rapidly. People have long believed that everyone, including state officials, deserved punishment when they broke moral and legal rules; but the continuing power of state officials (and legal doctrines of sovereign immunity) protected them from prosecution and punishment.

The justice cascade involves yet a third key idea: that suspected perpetrators are at the same time bearers of rights, and have to be protected by guarantees of due process, and increasingly, by the prohibition on the death penalty. It is this third set of ideas about protecting the accused that separates the justice cascade from the political trials of the past. People have long been outraged about governments committing violence against citizens, and occasionally, in moments of crisis, they have held their government officials "accountable"; but such accountability often looked more like revenge or even lynching because the rights of the accused were not protected. This third and final piece of the justice cascade is the least popular and the least engrained. The people in the streets of Greece were furious with Karamanlis when he commuted the death penalty for the Junta leaders. Human rights are always least popular when they are used, in the words of many Brazilians, "to protect criminals." And yet if we speak of a true human rights trial, the rights of the accused must be respected.

But even this third unpopular set of ideas about fair trials is present not only in modern human rights law but also in most criminal law in countries around the world. Different judicial systems have different concepts of what constitutes a fair trial. Nonetheless, a common core of practices that most countries believe constitutes a fair trial, including protections of the rights of the accused, exists in domestic criminal law systems almost everywhere, and is consistent with international law.[40]

There were various counter-ideas to individual criminal jurisdiction. First, the reigning orthodoxy, the immunity/impunity model, did not disappear, but continues to co-exist with the new criminal accountability model. Although impunity was ever more often called into question, the increasing use of amnesty laws around the world shows that immunity is still alive and well. But changing ideas about the desirability and possibility of some form of accountability for human rights violations made it more difficult to advocate pure impunity, and immunity is now often combined with some form of restorative justice. Nor did the state accountability model disappear. It continues to be the main model used by the UN system and the regional human rights courts, and often complements criminal accountability. So, what we have at present is *not* a replacement of one model by another, but a layering of multiple models.

The most powerful counter-idea to that of individual criminal accountability was the idea that countries should focus on "restorative justice," through truth commissions and reparations, but should eschew "retributive justice" through human rights trials. The proponents of restorative justice claim it can promote reconciliation and satisfy victims with truth and reparations, without causing divisions and rancor through retributive trials. The South African case, with its Truth and Reconciliation Commission, is sometimes held up as the paradigm of how restorative justice should function.

One of the most interesting characteristics about the justice cascade is the confrontation and convergence of two new and powerful international norms: criminal accountability and restorative justice. The restorative justice idea also has a strong alliance behind it. It includes activists like José Zalaquett who feared that retribution against still powerful veto players would undermine democracy. The restorative justice model finds strong support too from activists and legal scholars who have long criticized harsh retributive punishment in their domestic legal systems as counterproductive. But the argument here is that the restorative and retributive justice models have not in practice been mutually exclusive. Rather, restorative justice, like truth commissions and reparations, has often been used very effectively together with retributive justice, such as domestic and foreign prosecutions. So, although some advocates like to stress the differences between them, it is perfectly legitimate both theoretically and practically to see these as complementary ideas that form part of the broader movement for accountability for past human rights violations.

Question 3: What are the effects of human rights prosecutions?

The entire first part of this book outlined a norm emergence story that places emphasis on explanations involving individual agency, ideas, and learning. But in the second part of the book, on effectiveness, the role of rationality came more fully into play. Once the new prosecutions and tribunals were up and running, they started to alter the strategic landscape within which state officials operated, and a more standard strategic story began to unfold alongside the norms story.

The results of the analysis summarized in Chapter 6 provide some of the first quantitative support for the existence of a deterrence effect in the realm of human rights. In our research, both human rights prosecutions and truth commissions are associated with improvements in human rights protection, and prosecutions in neighboring countries have a deterrence impact beyond the confines of a single country.

Our findings generally support deterrence theories which posit that an increase in the enforcement of norms and in the likelihood of punishment should lead to a decrease in actual human rights violations. In the past, state officials faced few costs for committing violations; now they face more, especially in those countries that have been persistent in carrying out such prosecutions. This suggests that there has been an increase in enforcement, which, in turn, heightens the expected costs of repression for government officials who make choices about how much repression to use. During the period examined here, the benefits that state officials receive from repression have remained constant, and the formal and informal costs of repression have increased. It thus appears that prosecutions may deter future human rights violations by increasing the perception of the possibility of costs of repression for individual state officials.

But our findings are also consistent with the norms literature, which has stressed that both normative and coercive factors are important for human rights change.[41] Human rights prosecutions are not only instances of punishment or enforcement but also high-profile symbolic events that communicate and dramatize norms. Because trials involve simultaneous punishment and communication, it is hard to know which is doing the work in bringing about improvements in human rights. Are future perpetrators deterred by the fear of punishment, or have they been socialized by the normative process of observing the trials? We looked at the effects of truth commissions too to help us explore this question. Since truth commissions don't involve punishment, if only punishment mattered, we wouldn't expect truth commissions to lead to any improvement in human rights. The fact that our research shows that both truth commissions and prosecutions are associated with improvements suggests that transitional justice works through a normative mechanism like socialization as well as through deterrence.

The threat of prosecution sends a particularly unambiguous message. Precisely because the model of individual accountability is drawn from domestic judicial systems, the meaning of the threat of prosecution is clear to all involved. The association is made between human rights violations and common crime. As such, the threat of prosecution may be a more effective form of communication than foreign policy statements by states.

Much of the earlier work on enforcement of human rights law, including my own, has examined the role of NGOs and states in bringing pressure to bear on countries that violate rights. But the foreign policies of major states have multiple goals, and they frequently give mixed signals on their commitments to human rights. Repressive regimes are often ideologically invested in repression and embrace ethnic or political ideologies that portray them as the saviors of the nation. When they receive mixed signals, they are inclined to "hear" or receive those messages that are most consistent with their worldview and self-perception.[42] A threat of human rights prosecution, however, is harder to misinterpret that the standard foreign policy statement. When the ICTY issued an arrest warrant for Milošević, it sent a much clearer message than when European countries condemned him for human rights violations in Bosnia.

Even in the face of such unambiguous communication, for individual leaders and security forces that have already carried out human rights abuses, the strategic landscape continues to be straightforward: it is in their interests to prevent truth-telling and especially prosecution for past human rights violations. Indeed, as realists have suggested, the threat of prosecution could entrench them in power. States can only affect their actions by preemption: by physically removing them from power through detention or imprisonment.[43] Spoilers will always prefer no transitional justice at all, preferably guaranteed by an amnesty. They often succeed in blocking domestic prosecutions, through threats, coup attempts, obstructed peace processes, and the like. This group has been the main concern of scholars like Snyder and Vinjamuri, who point out the obvious difficulties of such a strategic situation. What they miss, however, is the bigger and longer strategic and norms game that prosecutions can set in motion.

In the longer term, future human rights violations can be prevented through the impact of prosecutions on the new generations of military and police officers, and on civilian political leaders. Young officers who were not involved in the last round of repression may look at past leaders and draw conclusions about their future choices. They observe former leaders, perhaps imprisoned as a result of domestic prosecutions, or with tattered international and domestic reputations. Future military officers may decide that prosecutions have made repression and coups too costly. Of course, how these leaders calculate such costs may vary. Thus, some may interpret the costs of prosecutions mainly in terms of the costs to the reputation and honor of the military, the police, or the party as an institution; others may calculate in a more individualist fashion. Prosecutions and truth commission create sanctions that did not exist before, including not only the possibility of imprisonment but also of damage to one's honor and national and international reputation. Some of these officers will be socialized and some will be deterred. At this time, it is difficult to sort out which mechanism is the more prominent. The main point is that there are some future leaders who can and will be socialized, but there are some who will only be deterred. Thus, any system to prevent future human rights violations must include the possibility of punishment so that it will deter those who are only concerned about the logic of consequences.

Prosecutions for individual criminal accountability *publicize* the new norms. But not all prosecutions publicize equally. Prosecutions of well-known and high-level officials have a much greater publicity effect than prosecutions of lower-level and unknown officials. Thus, the prosecutions of Pinochet, Milošević, and the military Juntas in Argentina had a much greater effect than the prosecutions of lower-level police officers in Portugal after the revolution there in 1974. The impact of the prosecutions of lower-level officials in the ICTY had a lower publicity effect than the trial of Milošević or Karadžič. The type of prosecution may be less important than the fame and level of the official being tried. This is not to say the trials of low- to mid-ranking officials are insignificant; just that they may be less important in publicizing new norms nationally and internationally. Indeed, the prosecution and removal of low- to mid-ranking officials may change local power dynamics and publicize norms to local audiences for whom national politics remain remote.[44]

In order for the publicity effect to be "received," the potential recipient of the message must see himself as somehow similar to the individual being prosecuted. This is why the trial of General Pinochet had a greater impact on other military officers in Latin America than it did on U.S. officials in Washington, D.C. Geographic, cultural, and linguistic proximity can all contribute to the perception that actors are similar to those being tried.

This book proposes a theoretical story about norm emergence and norm effects that I believe is of relevance to other issues of change in world politics. The argument integrates various approaches to international relations, incorporating existing theories about norm emergence, diffusion, and rational action. It maintains that rather than constantly struggling in the paradigm wars between theoretical models, we need to ask ourselves which theoretical mechanism is appropriate at which political moment or stage we are studying.[45] But I would go further than saying that we need to mix theoretical models. I propose a specific sequencing of theoretical mechanisms, connected to the life cycle of the norm. Most politics is "normal politics," with existing norms and clear sets of incentives in place for rational action. Such normal politics takes place both within deep (but accepted and internalized) norm structures, and common rules of the game for rational action. Standard theories of international relations can tell us much about how to analyze these situations. Rational choice provides tools to analyze short-term interactions, and structural constructivism helps us understand how ideas structure the very understandings that make the game possible.

But neither rational choice nor structural constructivism can help us understand how and why dramatic changes sometimes happen in world politics. How do new ideas emerge, catch on, and spread? One way that new ideas catch on is through what Thomas Risse has called a "logic of arguing," where the best argument can sometimes win out. But although some new ideas catch on through this more cerebral process of evaluating the best argument, others catch on through less cerebral processes, involving struggle, pressure, and trend-following.

The single most difficult issue to explain is why certain ideas at certain moments in certain places resonate, grab attention, and become possible. I believe that we will never answer this question unless we are prepared to go beyond explanations that stress the cerebral processes of the logic of arguing, and the politics that make prosecutions a rational response to public pressure. I believe that which ideas catch on is also related to deeper ideational instincts in the human brain. The idea of justice and the need for punishment for those who violate societal norms is deeply embedded in many societies around the world. So there is an initial receptivity to demands for justice. While psychologists can speak of such a "moral instinct," this is still heresy for a political scientist. It is perfectly acceptable for political scientists to suggest that all humans have an innate drive for power or wealth, but many scholars shun the suggestion that humans intrinsically find certain human rights ideas appealing. Yet it does not strike me as particularly odd to suggest that almost everyone would prefer to be alive than dead, free than imprisoned, secure than tortured, fed than hungry. Core human rights norms have resonated so profoundly in the world in part because of this intrinsic appeal. It is surprising to watch how uniformly human beings—even those embedded in cultural scenarios that tell them otherwise—believe that they are entitled to something better.

By the end of 2009, some parts of the international justice network appeared more precarious. The International Center for Transitional Justice was cutting its staff and program after a budget crunch in the wake of the U.S. financial crisis. The Supreme Court in Spain worked to rein in the power of crusading judges like Baltazar Garzón. Luis Moreno-Ocampo faces frequent attack for his work as prosecutor at the ICC. Meanwhile, U.S. denial and backlash on the concept of accountability have yet to be fully reversed. The rapid expansion of the doctrine of individual criminal accountability appears to be slowing down. Maybe the justice cascade will be remembered as just a brief moment of possibility between the end of the Cold War and the beginning of the war on terror. On the other hand, in late 2010 the newspapers and the Internet carried stories almost every day of yet another development in human rights prosecutions. In an interesting reversal of the pattern established when Spanish courts heard cases on human rights violations in Argentina and Chile, in October 2010 an Argentine judge said that if the Spanish courts were unable or unwilling to investigate the crimes of the Spanish Civil War, Argentine courts might try the cases.[46] In November 2010, the Uruguayan Supreme Court found once again that Uruguay's Amnesty Law was unconstitutional and that human rights cases involving the murder of nineteen individuals could continue to move ahead in Uruguayan courts. In December 2010, an Italian appeals court upheld the convictions of the CIA agents for the kidnapping of Abu Omar, and ordered even harsher sentences.

The fact that the justice cascade is embodied in both domestic and international law and in domestic and international institutions makes it unlikely that the trend will be reversed. The possibility of individual criminal accountability has provided useful but imperfect tools to activists, victims, and states to help diminish future violations. These human rights prosecutions will continue to fall far short of our ideals of justice, but they represent an improvement over the past. This past, a world without any accountability for major episodes of human rights violations, is finally receding. The new world of greater accountability that we are entering now, for all its problems, offers hope of reducing violence in the world.

ACKNOWLEDGMENTS

So many people and institutions have inspired, informed, helped, and supported me as I researched and wrote this book that it is impossible to thank and acknowledge all of them sufficiently. I have learned more than I can convey from interviews conducted over many years with the protagonists and observers of the justice cascade, many of whom are characters in the book or listed in the notes.

A Fulbright fellowship supported field research in Argentina, and the John Simon Guggenheim Foundation sustained the final research and writing of the book manuscript.

In addition, an entire academic and personal support network mobilized to help me produce the book. I am especially obliged to those who read the entire manuscript, or substantial portions of it, and provided written comments, including Alison Brysk, James Dawes, Barbara Frey, Roby Harrington, Douglas Johnson, Peter Katzenstein, Margaret Keck, Robert Keohane, Ronald Krebs, Walter Landesman, Ellen Lutz, Juan Mendez, Leigh Payne, Naomi Roht-Arriaza, Joachim Savelsberg, Jake Schindel, Beth Simmons, Jack Snyder, Sidney Tarrow, and David Weissbrodt. Among my greatest debts are to colleagues and friends from Argentina and Uruguay who have stimulated and sharpened my thinking and writing about justice and human rights over the years, especially Catalina Smulovitz, Elizabeth Jelin, Carlos Acuña, Patricia Valdez, Luis Moreno Ocampo, Maria Jose Guembe, Marcelo Ferrantes, Silvina Ramirez, Carolina Varsky, Julieta Parellada, Monica Hirst, Roberto Russell, Anibal Marinoni, Beatriz

Cabrera, Patricia Lema, Virginia Bonnelli, and Alfredo Nieto. I am very grateful to Carrie Booth Walling and Hunjoon Kim for their contributions to my work on these issues, and for permission to use material in Chapters 5 and 6 that draws on our co-authored journal articles, including tables and figures that they originally helped prepare. And in the process of completing the book manuscript, Geoff Dancy, Darrah McCracken, and Brooke Coe served as more than my research assistants; they were a genuine team who helped me finish the manuscript and get it out the door. Their work improved the overall argument, the figures, the writing, and the evidence.

Over the years, I have presented draft chapters of the book to many groups and individuals in diverse countries who provided invaluable comments and feedback, including the Department of Political Science and International Relations at the Universidad Torcuato Di Tella, the Centro de Estudios Legales y Sociales, and the Núcleo de Estudios sobre Memoria at IDES, all in Buenos Aires, Argentina; the Faculty of Social Sciences at the University of the Republic, Montevideo, Uruguay; the Department of Political Science at the University of São Paulo, Brazil; the International Criminal Court, The Hague, Netherlands; the Pompeu Fabra University in Barcelona, Spain; the Institute for the Study of the Americas, University of London; Nuffield College, University of Oxford; the Department of Political Science at the University of British Columbia; and the Successful Societies Program of the Canadian Institute for Advanced Research. In the United States, I have benefited from comments provided by participants in international law workshops at Yale Law School, New York University School of Law, and the University of Chicago Law School; the SSRC Workshop on International Criminal Accountability, Washington, D.C.; the Princeton University International Relations Colloquium; the G. Theodore Mitau Lecture, Macalester College; the Department of Philosophy at the University of Arizona; and the Power of Human Rights workshop at the University of Wyoming. At the University of Minnesota, colleagues gave helpful feedback in presentations to the Department of Sociology, the Distinguished Faculty Lecture Series, the Minnesota International Relations Colloquium, the Institute for Advanced Studies Lecture Series, and the IAS Transitional Justice and Collective Memory Collaborative. Many individuals at these institutions and others provided critical feedback and suggestions on particular chapters or arguments, including Philip Alston, Ben Ansell, Michael Barnett, Gary Bass, Tanja Boerzel, Ann Clark, Antonio Costa Pinto, Thomas Christiano, Nicole Dietelhoff, Raymond Duvall, Peter Evans, Songying Fang, Ryan Goodman, Peter Hall, Rebecca Hamilton, Oona Hathaway, Lisa Hilbink, Harold Koh, Ron Levi, Brian Loveman, Glenda Mezarobba, David Morrill-Richards, Eric Posner, Richard Price, Tonya Putnam, Filipa Raimundo, Thomas Risse, Rossana Rocha Reis, James Ron, David Samuels, Kim Scheppele, Henry Shue, Chandra Lekha Sriram, Ann Towns, Shawn Treier, and Leslie Vinjamuri. I also am very grateful to Tuba Inal, Susan Kang, Patricia Gainza, Augustín Territoriale, Hunjoon Kim, Julia Kasper, Andrew Grover, and Carrie Booth Walling for research assistance. Finally, my editors at Norton, Roby Harrington and Jake Schindel, were efficient, encouraging, and consultative while they helped me pursue my goal of writing for a broader audience beyond academia.

The book is dedicated to the memory of my dear friend and colleague Ellen Lutz, a tireless activist, scholar, and teacher, who devoted her life to the study and practice of human rights. She was the co-author of my first article on human rights prosecutions in 2001 (where we first used the title I later gave to this book) and taught me so much about law and justice over many years. Ellen co-edited a pioneering book on the topic of human rights prosecutions, *Prosecuting Heads of State* (Cambridge University Press, 2009). She read a full draft of the manuscript of *The Justice Cascade*, and gave me vital comments, even as she was battling metastatic breast cancer. From 2004–2010, Ellen served as the executive director of the indigenous rights organization Cultural Survival. Ellen died on November 4, 2010, at her home in Cambridge, Massachusetts. Part of the advance and the royalties of this book will be donated to the Ellen L. Lutz Indigenous Rights Award and Fund, set up in her memory at Cultural Survival.

APPENDIX 1

Latin American Countries with Transitional Human Rights Prosecutions and Truth Commissions

Country (Chronologically by 1st trial)	Prosecutions Dates	Cumulative Prosecution Years	Truth Commission Date
Argentina	1983–90 1993–96 1998–06	21	1983
Bolivia	1983 1993 1995	3	1982
Peru	1985 1990 1993–95 2001–06	11	2001
Haiti	1995–97	3	1995
Guatemala	1988 1991–94 1996–2003	13	1997
Paraguay	1989 1991–92 1994–99 2002–04	12	2003
El Salvador	1990–92 1998	4	1992
Chile	1991–2006	16	1990
Panama	1991–99 2002 2004	11	2001
Ecuador	1992–95	4	1996
Honduras	1992–93 1996–97 1999–2002 2004–05	10	—
Nicaragua	1992–96	5	—
Mexico	2002–2004	3	—
Uruguay	2002 2006	2	1985

Source: Author database.

APPENDIX 2

List of Countries with Transitions

Democratic transitions (66 countries)

Portugal 1974–
Greece 1974–
Spain 1975–
Thailand 1977–91, 1992–
Burkina Faso 1977–80
Peru 1978–92, 1993–
Ghana 1978–81, 1996–
Dominican Republic 1978–
Nigeria 1978–84, 1998–
Uganda 1979–85
Ecuador 1979–
El Salvador 1979–
Honduras 1980–
Bolivia 1982–
Argentina 1983–
Turkey 1983–
Guatemala 1984–
Brazil 1985–
Uruguay 1985–
Haiti 1986–91, 1994–
Philippines 1986–
Republic of Korea 1987–
Hungary 1988–
Chile 1988–
Cambodia 1988–97
Pakistan 1988–99
Poland 1989–
Paraguay 1989–
Czechoslovakia 1989–92
Panama 1989–
Romania 1989–
Benin 1990–
Nicaragua 1990–

Comoros 1990–95, 1996–
Bulgaria 1990–
Fiji 1990–
Mongolia 1990–
Nepal 1990–2002
Albania 1990–96, 1997–
Republic of Congo 1991–97
Mali 1991–
Central African Republic 1991–2003
Niger 1991–96, 1999–
Bangladesh 1991–
Madagascar 1991–
Zambia 1991–96
Guinea-Bissau 1991–98, 1999–
Azerbaijan 1992–
Guyana 1992–
South Africa 1992–
Taiwan 1992–
Lesotho 1993–98, 1999–
Malawi 1993–
Mexico 1994–
Mozambique 1994–
Sierra Leone 1996–97, 2001–
Iran 1997–2004
Armenia 1998–
Indonesia 1998–
Djibouti 1999–
Cote d'Ivoire 1999–2002
Senegal 2000–
Serbia and Montenegro 2000–
Kenya 2002–
Macedonia 2002–
Algeria 2004–

Transition from civil war (16 countries)

Chad 1984–

Lebanon 1990–

Ethiopia 1991–

Angola 1993–

Rwanda 1994–

Bosnia and Herzegovina 1995–

Burundi 1996–

Comoros 1996–

Liberia 1996–

Afghanistan 1996–

Guinea-Bissau 1999–

Lesotho 1999–

Sierra Leone 2001–

Iraq 2003–

Democratic Republic of Congo 2003–

Solomon Island 2003–

Transition of state creation (28 countries)

Namibia 1990–

Yemen 1990–

Germany 1990–

Georgia 1991–

Croatia 1991–

Slovenia 1991–

Serbia and Montenegro 1991–

Belarus 1991–

Moldova 1991–

Azerbaijan 1991–

Kyrgyzstan 1991–

Uzbekistan 1991–

Estonia 1991–

Latvia 1991–

Lithuania 1991–

Tajikistan 1991–

Macedonia 1991–

Armenia 1991–

Turkmenistan 1991–

Ukraine 1991–

Kazakhstan 1991–

Bosnia and Herzegovina 1992–

Russia 1992–

Czech Republic 1993–

Slovakia 1993–

Ethiopia 1993–

Eritrea 1993–

East Timor 2002–

APPENDIX 3

List of Countries with Human Rights Prosecutions and Truth Commissions

Countries with transitional human rights prosecutions (48 countries)

Argentina 1983–90, 1993–04
Benin 1991–93
Bolivia 1983, 1995
Bosnia and Herzegovina
   1993–2004
Bulgaria 1993, 1994, 1996
Burundi 1996
Cambodia 2003–04
Chad 2000–03
Chile 1989, 1991–2004
Croatia 1992–2004
Czech Republic 1997, 1998, 2001
Democratic Republic of Congo 2004
East Timor 2002–04
Ecuador 1992–95, 1997
El Salvador 1990–92, 1998
Eritrea 1991, 1993
Ethiopia 1991–92, 1994–2003
Guatemala 1988, 1991–94, 1996–2003
Haiti 1986–87, 1989, 1995–97
Honduras 1992–93, 1996–2002, 2004
Hungary 1993, 1999, 2000–01
Indonesia 2000–04
Iraq 2003–04
Republic of Korea 1996

Lithuania 1997–2002
Macedonia 1993–2004
Malawi 1995
Mali 1991, 1993
Mexico 2002–04
Namibia 1990
Nicaragua 1992–96
Niger 1992
Panama 1991–99, 2002, 2004
Paraguay 1989, 1991–92, 1994–99,
   2002–04
Peru 1985, 1990, 1993–95, 2001–04
Poland 1990, 1993–94, 1996–2001
Portugal 1980
Romania 1990
Rwanda 1994–2004
Senegal 2000–04
Serbia and Montenegro 2000–04
Sierra Leone 2002–04
Slovenia 1993–2004
South Africa 1992
Spain 1982, 2000
Thailand 1998
Turkey 1983
Uruguay 1998–2000, 2002, 2004

Countries with truth commissions (28 countries)

Argentina 1983
Bolivia 1982
Burundi 1996
Central African Republic 2003
Chad 1990
Chile 1990
Democratic Republic of Congo 2004
East Timor 2002
Ecuador 1996
El Salvador 1992;
Germany 1992
Ghana 2002
Guatemala 1997
Haiti 1995

Indonesia 1999
Republic of Korea 2000
Liberia 2003
Nepal 1990
Nigeria 1999
Panama 2001
Paraguay 2003
Peru 2001;
Philippines 1986
Serbia and Montenegro 2002
Sierra Leone 2002
South Africa 1995
Uganda 1986
Uruguay 1985

APPENDIX 4

Summary Statistics and Data Sources

Summary Statistics

Variable	N	Mean	SD	Min	Max
Dependent variable					
Repression	1393	3.45	2.19	0	8
Independent variable					
Human rights prosecutions	1475	0.39	0.49	0	1
Cumulative prosecution year (ln)	1475	0.51	0.75	0	3.04
Hr prosecutions in neighbors	1475	2.46	2.14	0	7
Hr prosecutions in neighbors (ln)	1475	1.56	1.32	0	4.23
Control variable					
Truth commission	1475	0.18	0.38	0	1
Repression t-1	1353	3.45	2.21	0	8
Democracy	1434	4.08	5.50	-9	10
International conflict	1475	0.06	0.37	0	3
Civil conflict	1475	0.35	0.82	0	3
Treaty ratification	1475	2.06	1.04	0	3
GDP per capita (ln)	1470	6.92	1.27	4.02	10.4
Economic growth	1471	2.71	7.99	-50.2	106.3
Population (ln)	1471	7.03	0.55	5.66	8.34
Population change	1446	1.56	1.49	-6.13	10.7
Africa	1475	0.28	0.45	0	1
Oceania	1475	0.01	0.11	0	1
Asia	1475	0.23	0.42	0	1
Europe	1475	0.25	0.43	0	1
No. of years	1475	15.93	5.79	0	24

Data Sources

Variable	Data Sources
Repression	CIRI human rights database
Democracy	Polity IV Project
International and civil conflict	PRIO/Uppsala armed conflict dataset
Human Rights Treaty ratification	UN OHCHR
GDP per capita, annual GDP growth rate, population, annual population growth rate	UN Common Database (except Taiwan, for which we used the National Statistics data of Taiwan, http://eng.stat.gov.tw/mp.asp?mp=5)

Source: Hunjoon Kim and Kathryn Sikkink, "Explaining the Deterrence Effect of Human Rights Prosecutions for Transitional Countries," International Studies Quarterly *54 (December 2010), p. 960.*

Table 1: Baseline Models: Impact of Human Rights Prosecutions on Repression

	Model 1 (Base)		Model 2a (HRP)		Model 2b (CHRP)	
	Coef. (Std. Err.)	p-value	Coef. (Std. Err.)	p-value	Coef. (Std. Err.)	p-value
Prosecution Experience			-0.160 (0.079)	0.041		
Cumulative Prosecution Years (*ln*)					-0.113 (0.055)	0.038
Truth Commission Experience			-0.186 (0.098)	0.065	-0.175 (0.098)	0.074
Repression *t-1*	0.569 (0.024)	<0.001	0.562 (0.024)	<0.001	0.562 (0.024)	<0.001
Democracy	-0.058 (0.008)	<0.001	-0.055 (0.008)	<0.001	-0.056 (0.008)	<0.001
International Conflict	-0.162 (0.087)	0.063	-0.164 (0.086)	0.057	-0.593 (0.087)	0.068
Civil Conflict	0.458 (0.052)	<0.001	0.478 (0.053)	<0.001	0.474 (0.052)	<0.001
Human Rights Treaty Ratication	0.068 (0.046)	0.141	0.079 (0.047)	0.092	0.083 (0.047)	0.073
GDP per capita (*ln*)	-0.089 (0.041)	0.030	-0.075 (0.042)	0.079	-0.078 (0.042)	0.064
Annual GDP Growth Rate	-0.008 (0.006)	0.163	-0.009 (0.006)	0.130	-0.009 (0.006)	0.130
Population (*ln*)	0.541 (0.075)	<0.001	0.563 (0.076)	<0.001	0.563 (0.078)	<0.001
Annual Rate of Population Change	0.013 (0.038)	0.731	0.026 (0.039)	0.501	0.028 (0.039)	0.474
Africa	-0.430 (0.136)	0.002	-0.489 (0.135)	<0.001	-0.533 (0.137)	<0.001
Oceania	-0.481 (0.208)	0.021	-0.633 (0.212)	0.003	-0.647 (0.214)	<0.001
Asia	-0.208 (0.118)	0.077	-0.312 (0.118)	0.008	-0.347 (0.122)	0.004
Europe	-0.501 (0.120)	<0.001	-0.598 (0.125)	<0.001	-0.621 (0.125)	<0.001
Year	0.010 (0.007)	0.154	0.014 (0.007)	0.050	0.017 (0.008)	0.030
Constant	-1.671 (0.493)	0.001	-1.872 (0.502)	<0.001	-1.863 (0.502)	<0.001
R^2	0.686		0.688		0.688	
X^2	3509.76		3519.46		3520.71	
N	1314		1314		1314	
Number of states	95		95		95	

Note: Table entries are OLS regression estimates corrected for panel-specific autocorrelation and p-values in Stata 9.2/SE. Panel-corrected standard errors are included in the parentheses; t–1=h; lu=h.

Source: Hunjoon Kim and Kathryn Sikkink, "Explaining the Deterrence Effect of Human Rights Prosecutions for Transitional Countries," International Studies Quarterly 54 (December 2010), p. 952.

Appendix 4

Table 2: Fixed-effects Models: Impact of Human Rights Prosecution on Repression

	Model 3a (HRP) Coef. (Std. Err.)	p-value	Model 3b (CHRP) Coef. (Std. Err.)	p-value
Prosecution Experience	-0.425 (0.153)	0.006		
Cumulative Prosecution Years (ln)			-0.383 (0.102)	<0.001
Truth Commission Experience	-0.514 (0.175)	0.003	-0.445 (0.176)	0.012
Repression t–1	0.279 (0.026)	<0.001	0.272 (0.026)	<0.001
Democracy	-0.048 (0.013)	<0.001	-0.047 (0.013)	<0.001
International Conflict	-0.345 (0.096)	0.001	-0.333 (0.096)	0.001
Civil Conflict	0.535 (0.069)	<0.001	0.524 (0.069)	<0.001
Human Rights Treaty Ratification	0.154 (0.068)	0.024	0.133 (0.068)	0.052
GDP per capita (ln)	-0.043 (0.141)	0.761	-0.004 (0.141)	0.979
Annual GDP Growth Rate	-0.016 (0.005)	0.003	-0.016 (0.005)	0.003
Population (ln)	-3.793 (1.434)	0.008	-3.555 (1.428)	0.013
Annual Rate of Population Change	-0.049 (0.052)	0.337	-0.046 (0.051)	0.370
Year	0.038 (0.015)	0.011	0.044 (0.015)	0.003
Constant	29.051 (10.358)	0.005	27.082 (10.315)	0.000
R^2	0.255		0.259	
N	1314		1314	
Number of states	95		95	

Note: Table entries are fixed-effects regression estimates with standard errors in parentheses and p-values in Stata 9.2/SE.

Source: Hunjoon Kim and Kathryn Sikkink, "Explaining the Deterrence Effect of Human Rights Prosecutions for Transitional Countries," International Studies Quarterly 54 (December 2010), p. 954.

Table 3: Impact of Human Rights Prosecution on Repression (Two-stage Estimations)

	HRP instrumented Model 4a (2SPLS)		CHRP instrumented Model 4b (G2SLS)	
	Coef. (Std. Err.)	p-value	Coef. (Std. Err.)	p-value
Prosecution Experience (instrumented)	-0.209 (0.079)	0.009		
Cumulative Prosecution Years (instumented *ln*)			-0.476 (0.184)	0.010
Truth Commission Experience	-0.139 (0.099)	0.165	-0.103 (0.112)	0.036
X^2	173.19		2273.20	
N	1281		1281	
Number of states	94		94	

Note: Table entries are OLS regression estimates corrected for panel-specific autocorrelation and p-values in Stata 9.2/SE. Panel-corrected standard errors are included in the parentheses. To conserve space, we do not report the control variables or constant terms for the regressions.

Source: Hunjoon Kim and Kathryn Sikkink, "Explaining the Deterrence Effect of Human Rights Prosecutions for Transitional Countries," International Studies Quarterly 54 (December 2010), p. 954.

Table 4: Impact of Human Rights Prosecutions on Repression Under Civil Conflict Situations

	Model 5a (HRP) Coef. (Std. Err.)	p-value	Model 5b (CHRP) Coef. (Std. Err.)	p-value
Prosecution Experience	-0.166 (0.087)	0.055		
Civil War x Prosecution Experience	-0.059 (0.090)	0.509		
Civil War Transition x Prosecution Experience	0.139 (0.329)	0.674		
Cumulative Prosecution Years (ln)			-0.113 (0.058)	0.049
Civil War x Cum. Prosecution Years			-0.159 (0.076)	0.038
Civil War Transition x Cum. Prosecution Years			0.168 (0.188)	0.369
Truth Commission Experience	-0.215 (0.117)	0.067	-0.215 (0.118)	0.068
Civil War x Truth Commission	-0.064 (0.106)	0.549	-0.085 (0.106)	0.422
Civil War Transition x Truth Commission	0.282 (0.354)	0.425	0.244 (0.340)	0.474
Civil Conflict	0.501 (0.072)	<0.001	0.542 (0.069)	<0.001
Transition from Civil War	0.296 (0.153)	0.153	0.325 (0.208)	0.119
R^2	0.691		0.692	
X^2	3606.59		3595.06	
N	1314		1314	
Number of states	95		95	

Note: *Table entries are OLS regression estimates corrected for panel-specific autocorrelation and p-values in Stata 9.2/SE. Panel-corrected standard errors are included in the parentheses. To conserve space, we do not report the control variables or constant terms for the regressions.*

Source: *Hunjoon Kim and Kathryn Sikkink, "Explaining the Deterrence Effect of Human Rights Prosecutions for Transitional Countries,"* International Studies Quarterly 54 *(December 2010), p. 955.*

Table 5: The Effect of Prosecutions on Repression Under Various Civil War–related Situations

	Effect of HR Prosecutions			
	Coef.	Std. Err.	p-value	Number of Cases (Country-Years)
No Civil War Transition with No Civil Wars	-0.16	0.09	0.005	1106
No Civil War Transition with Minor Civil Wars	-0.23	0.10	0.029	61
No Civil War Transition with Major Civil Wars	-0.35	0.26	0.179	57
Civil War Transition with No Civil Wars	-0.03	0.33	0.933	104
Civil War Transition with Minor Civil Wars	-0.09	0.31	0.775	32
Civil War Transition with Major Civil Wars	-0.21	0.34	0.544	19

Note: Cell report conditional coefficients and standard errors for effect of prosecution on repression drawn from Model 3a.

Source: Hunjoon Kim and Kathryn Sikkink, "Explaining the Deterrence Effect of Human Rights Prosecutions for Transitional Countries," International Studies Quarterly 54 (December 2010), p. 956.

Table 6: Impact of Human Rights Prosecutions in Neighboring Countries on Repression

	Model 6a (HRP)		Model 6b (CHRP)	
	Coef. (Std.Err.)	p-value	Coef. (Std.Err.)	p-value
Prosecution Experience	-0.160 (0.079)	0.041		
HR Prosecutions in Neighbors	-0.043 (0.023)	0.068		
Cumulative Prosecution Years (ln)			-0.103 (0.055)	0.062
Cumulative Prosecution Years in Neighbors (ln)			-0.093 (0.044)	0.034
Truth Commission Experience	-0.204 (0.097)	0.036	-0.205 (0.098)	0.037
R^2	0.689		0.689	
X^2	3515.35		3518.41	
N	1314		1314	
Number of states	95		95	

Note: Table entries are OLS regression estimates corrected for panel-specific autocorrelation and p-values in Stata 9.2/SE. Panel-corrected standard errors are included in the parentheses. To conserve space, we do not report the control variables or constant terms for the regressions.

Source: Hunjoon Kim and Kathryn Sikkink, "Explaining the Deterrence Effect of Human Rights Prosecutions for Transitional Countries," International Studies Quarterly 54 (December 2010), p. 957.

NOTES

Chapter 1: Introduction

1 César di Candia, "Angustias y Tensiones de Tres Políticos Uruguayos Condenados a Muerte," reprinted from "Qué Pasa," supplement of *El País*, November 13, 2004, in *Brecha*, "Documentos: Para el Juicio de la Historia," October 20, 2006, pp. 7–8, translation by the author.

2 "Carta de Wilson Ferreira Aldunate a Jorge Rafael Videla," Buenos Aires, May 24, 1976, reprinted in *Brecha*, "Documentos," pp. 31–39, translation by the author.

3 From an end of year speech by Bordaberry cited in *Brecha*, "Documentos," p. 5, translation by the author.

4 For more on the Pinochet case, see Naomi Roht-Arriaza, *The Pinochet Effect: Transnational Justice in the Age of Human Rights* (Philadelphia: University of Pennsylvania Press, 2005).

5 See, e.g., Ellen L. Lutz and Caitlin Reiger, *Prosecuting Heads of State* (New York: Cambridge University Press, 2009), and Naomi Roht-Arriaza and Javier Mariezcurrena, eds., *Transitional Justice in the Twenty-First Century: Beyond Truth versus Justice* (Cambridge, UK: Cambridge University Press, 2006).

6 Ellen L. Lutz and Kathryn Sikkink, "The Justice Cascade: The Evolution and Impact of Foreign Human Rights Trials in Latin America," *Chicago Journal of International Law* 2 (2001). We borrowed the term "cascade" from the legal theorist Cass Sunstein, who spoke of "social norm cascades." A norm cascade, in his words, is "a rapid, dramatic shift in the legitimacy of norms and actions on behalf of those norms." See Cass Sunstein, *Free Markets and Social Justice* (New York: Oxford University Press, 1997).

7 For a generous extension of this metaphor as it pertains to the Rome Statute of the International Criminal Court, see Benjamin N. Schiff, *Building the International Criminal Court* (Cambridge, UK: Cambridge University Press, 2008), esp. pp. 14–15. He writes: "A cascade is an area of turbulence and transition in a longer ripar-

ian metaphor. Such a stage seems to have been reached in the area of international justice in the 1990s. The river has normative tributaries, eddies, currents, and dams, as well as a cascade or two already, and it is reasonable to imagine that more of these will be reached."

8 Testimony before the U.S. Congress, House Committee on Foreign Affairs, *The Phenomenon of Torture: Hearings and Markup Before the Committee on Foreign Affairs and Its Subcommittee on Human Rights and International Organizations.* 98th Congress, 2nd sess. H.J. Res. 606, May 15–16; September 6, 1984 (Washington, DC: GPO, 1984), p. 204.

9 Telephone interview with Juan Méndez, April 26, 1996.

10 March 22, 1981, cited in Iain Guest, *Behind the Disappearances: Argentina's Dirty War Against Human Rights and the United Nations* (Philadelphia: University of Pennsylvania Press, 1990), p. 277.

11 Malcolm Gladwell, *The Tipping Point: How Little Things Can Make a Big Difference* (New York: Little, Brown, 2000); for a discussion of "the life cycle of international norms," including norm "tipping points," see Martha Finnemore and Kathryn Sikkink, "Norm Dynamics and Political Change," *International Organization* 52, no. 4 (Autumn 1998).

12 See, e.g., John Rawls, *A Theory of Justice* (Cambridge, MA: Belknap Press/Harvard University Press, 1971); Amartya Sen, *The Idea of Justice* (Cambridge, MA: Belknap Press/Harvard University Press, 2009).

13 See David S. Weissbrodt, *The Right to a Fair Trial Under the Universal Declaration of Human Rights and the International Covenant on Civil and Political Rights: Background, Development, and Interpretations, Universal Declaration of Human Rights* (Cambridge, MA: Martinus Nijhoff, 2001).

14 Judith N. Shklar, *Legalism: Law, Morals, and Political Trials* (Cambridge, MA: Harvard University Press, 1986), p. 149.

15 Lavinia Stan, "Neither Forgiving nor Punishing? Evaluating Transitional Justice in Romania." Paper presented to the conference on *Transitional Justice and Democratic Consolidation*, Oxford University, October 16–17, 2008.

16 Ruth Grant and Robert O. Keohane, "Accountability and Abuses of Power in World Politics," *American Political Science Review* 99, no. 1 (February 2005), pp. 29–43.

17 Although I focus on individual *criminal* legal accountability, there is also an increase in individual *civil* legal accountability, especially in U.S. courts, where individuals found guilty of human rights violations are required to pay damages to their victims. These are cases brought mainly under the Alien Tort Claims Act, which permits tort claims for violations of international customary law.

18 I borrow the term "reigning orthodoxy" from Jeffrey Legro, *Rethinking the World: Great Power Strategies and International Order, Cornell Studies in Security Affairs* (Ithaca, NY: Cornell University Press, 2005).

19 There were isolated examples of accountability in ancient Greece and in revolutionary France, but no sustained attempts at domestic human rights prosecutions until after World War II. See Jon Elster, *Closing the Books: Transitional Justice in Historical Perspective* (New York: Cambridge University Press, 2004). At the international level, various pre–World War II attempts at accountability for war crimes and mass

atrocities fell short of establishing the necessary institutions—Gary Bass, *Stay the Hand of Vengeance* (Princeton: Princeton University Press, 2000).

20 Thomas Risse, Stephen C. Ropp, and Kathryn Sikkink, eds., *The Power of Human Rights. International Norms and Domestic Change* (Cambridge, UK: Cambridge University Press, 1999).

21 These include rights from only two or three of the twenty-seven substantive articles of the International Covenant on Civil and Political Rights, those protecting the right to life and prohibiting torture. The new model also provides enforcement of the Genocide Convention, the Convention Against Torture, and those parts of the Geneva Conventions prohibiting war crimes.

22 Ratner and Abrams refer to four interrelated bodies of law that underpin the move toward individual accountability for human rights violations: international human rights law, international humanitarian law, international criminal law, and domestic law—Steven R. Ratner and Jason S. Abrams, *Accountability for Human Rights Atrocities in International Law: Beyond the Nuremberg Legacy*, 2nd ed. (Oxford and New York: Oxford University Press, 2001), pp. 9–14.

23 Legal scholars talk about "global administrative law," or transnational legal orders or processes, to describe what is going on in diverse fields, including trade, finance, and the environment as well as human rights. See Nico Krisch and Benedict Kingsbury, "Introduction: Global Governance and Global Administrative Law in the International Legal Order," *European Journal of International Law* 17, no. 1 (February 2006), pp. 1–13. See also Geoffrey Shaffer, "Transnational Legal Process and State Change: Opportunities and Constraints," Minnesota Legal Studies Research Paper No. 10-28 (2010), available at SSRN: http://ssrn.com/abstract=1612401; and Harold Koh, "Transnational Legal Order," *Nebraska Law Review* 75, no. 181 (1996). See also Robert O. Keohane, Andrew Moravcsik, and Anne-Marie Slaughter, "Legalized Dispute Resolution: Interstate and Transnational," *International Organization* 54, no. 3 (2000), pp. 457–88.

24 See Charles Beitz, *The Idea of Human Rights* (New York: Oxford University Press, 2009), and Charles R. Epp, *The Rights Revolution: Lawyers, Activists, and Supreme Courts in Comparative Perspective* (Chicago: University of Chicago Press, 1998).

25 Epp, *The Rights Revolution*, pp. 2–3.

26 Elizabeth Jelin, *State Repression and the Struggle for Memories* (London: Social Science Research Council, 2003).

27 See Ruti Teitel, "Transitional Justice Genealogy," *Harvard Human Rights Journal* 16 (2003), pp. 69–94.

28 Charles Call, "Is Transitional Justice Really Just?" *Brown Journal of World Affairs* 11, no. 1 (2004), p. 101.

29 International relations theory suggests there is a "great divide" between domestic society, seen as "rulebound," and the international system, seen as anarchy—Ian Clark, *Globalization and International Relations Theory* (Oxford: Oxford University Press, 1999), p. 16.

30 Stephen Macedo, ed., *Universal Jurisdiction: National Courts and the Prosecution of Serious Crimes Under International Law* (Philadelphia: University of Pennsylvania Press, 2004); Roht-Arriaza, *The Pinochet Effect*.

31 William A. Schabas, *An Introduction to the International Criminal Court* (Cambridge, UK: Cambridge University Press, 2001), pp. 13, 67.

32 Orentlicher calls this "domestic enforcement with an allowance for 'fallback' international jurisdiction," and Naomi Roht-Arriaza refers to foreign trials as a "backstop" for domestic justice. See Diane F. Orentlicher, "Settling Accounts: The Duty to Prosecute Human Rights Violations of a Prior Regime," *Yale Law Journal* 100 (1990–91), pp. 2537–2618; Roht-Arriaza, *The Pinochet Effect*, p. 200.

33 Helena Cobban, "Think Again: International Courts," *Foreign Policy* (March–April 2006).

34 For a discussion of the inability of international relations theories to explain major changes in world politics, see Peter Katzenstein, ed., *The Culture of National Security: Norms and Identity in World Politics* (New York: Columbia University Press, 1996).

35 Kathryn Sikkink and Carrie Booth Walling, "The Impact of Human Rights Trials in Latin America," *Journal of Peace Research* 44, no. 4 (July 2007). We created two sets on human rights prosecutions, one for all prosecutions and one for human rights prosecutions in transitional countries. The data reported here is from the dataset for transitional human rights prosecutions. See http://www.tc.umn.edu/~kimx0759/thrp.website/home.html or www.transitionaljusticedata.com.

36 On the spread of democracy, see Kristian Gleditsch and Michael Ward, "Diffusion and the International Context of Democratization," *International Organization* 60, no. 4 (2006), pp. 911–33, and Scott Mainwaring and Aníbal Pérez-Liñán, *The Emergence and Fall of Democracies and Dictatorships: Latin America Since 1900* (Cambridge, UK: Cambridge University Press, (forthcoming); on neoliberal economic reforms, see Beth Simmons and Zachary Elkins, "The Globalization of Liberalization: Policy Diffusion in the International Political Economy," *American Political Science Review* 98 (2004), pp. 171–89; on pension reforms, see Kurt Weyland, "Theories of Policy Diffusion: Lessons from Latin American Pension Reform," *World Politics* 57, no. 2 (2005), pp. 262–95.

37 Beth Simmons, Frank Dobbin, and Geoff Garrett, "The International Diffusion of Liberalism," *International Organization* 60, no. 4 (2006), p. 787.

38 See Laurence Whitehead, "Three International Dimensions of Democratization," in Whitehead, ed., *The International Dimensions of Democratization: Europe and the Americas* (Oxford: Oxford University Press, 1996), pp. 3–25. See also Harvey Starr and Christina Lindborg, "Democratic Dominoes Revisited: The Hazards of Governmental Transitions, 1974–1996," *Journal of Conflict Resolution* 47, no. 4 (2003), pp. 405–519.

39 Graham, et al, also argue that scholars need to pay more attention to who affects diffusion, including specific people who have varying preferences, goals, and capabilities. See Erin Graham, Charles Shipan, and Craig Volden, "The Diffusion of Policy Diffusion Research," unpublished manuscript, December 2008.

40 Naomi Roht-Arriaza, "State Responsibility to Investigate and Punish Grave Human Rights Violations in International Law," *California Law Review* 78, no. 2 (March 1990), pp. 449–513; Juan Méndez, "In Defense of Transitional Justice," in A. James McAdams, ed., *Transitional Justice and the Rule of Law in New Democracies* (Notre Dame, IN: University of Notre Dame Press, 1997).

41 Samuel Huntington, *The Third Wave: Democratization in the Late Twentieth Century* (Norman: University of Oklahoma Press, 1991); Guillermo O'Donnell and Philippe C. Schmitter, *Transitions from Authoritarian Rule: Tentative Conclusions about Uncertain Democracies* (Baltimore, MD: Johns Hopkins University Press, 1986).

42 José Zalaquett, "Balancing Ethical Imperatives and Political Constraints: The Dilemma of New Democracies Confronting Past Human Rights Violations," *Hastings Law Journal* 43 (August 1992), pp. 1428–29.

43 Julian Ku and Jide Nzelibe, "Do International Criminal Tribunals Deter or Exacerbate Humanitarian Atrocities?" *Washington University Law Quarterly* 84, no. 4 (2006); Jack Snyder and Leslie Vinjamuri, "Trials and Errors: Principle and Pragmatism in Strategies of International Justice," *International Security* 28, no. 3 (Winter 2003–04), pp. 5–44; and Jack Goldsmith and Stephen D. Krasner, "The Limits of Idealism," *Daedalus* 132 (Winter 2003). Political scientists Snyder and Vinjamuri argue that human rights trials will not deter future violations and that, in some circumstances, they will actually lead to an increase in repression or to humanitarian atrocities.

44 Quoted in Lara J. Nettelfield, *Courting Democracy in Bosnia and Herzegovina: The Hague Tribunal's Impact in a Postwar State* (New York: Cambridge University Press, 2010), p. 130.

45 Steven C. Poe and Neal C. Tate, "Repression of Human Rights to Personal Integrity in the 1980s: A Global Analysis," *American Political Science Review* 88 (1994), pp. 853–900; Steven C. Poe, Neal C. Tate, and Linda Camp Keith, "Repression of the Human Rights to Personal Integrity Revisited: A Global Crossnational Study Covering the Years 1976–1996," *International Studies Quarterly* 43, no. 2 (1999), pp. 291–315.

Chapter 2: Navigating Without a Map

1 Here I am bracketing the "successor trials" that followed the Nuremberg and Tokyo tribunals.

2 Filipa Alves Raimundo, "The Double Face of Heroes: Transitional Justice Towards the Political Police (PIDE/DGS) in Portugal's Democratization, 1974–1976," MA thesis, University of Lisbon, Institute of Social Sciences, 2007.

3 Nicos C. Alivizatos and P. Nikiforos Diamandouros, "Politics and the Judiciary in the Greek Transition to Democracy," in A. James McAdams, ed., *Transitional Justice and the Rule of Law in New Democracies* (Notre Dame, IN: University of Notre Dame, 1997).

4 A number of non-governmental organizations in favor of European unification, which had sprung up after the war, united in 1948 to form the International Committee of the Movements for European Unity. The resolutions and the "Message to Europeans," which issued from a Congress of the International Committee held in 1948, were "bursting with the two concepts of democracy and human rights"— Ralph Beddard, *Human Rights and Europe* (London: Sweet & Maxwell, 1980), p. 17.

5 A. H. Robertson, *Human Rights in Europe*, 2nd ed. (Manchester: Manchester University Press, 1977), p. 254.

6　Thomas Hammarberg, "The Greek Case Became a Defining Lesson for Human Rights Policies in Europe," April 4, 2007, Viewpoint, www.coe.int/commissioner/viewpoints/070418asp.

7　Sheldon Carroll, e-mail message to the author, February 15, 2008. See also James Becket, *Barbarism in Greece* (New York: Walker & Co., 1970).

8　Reprinted in *The Hellenic Review* (1968), p. 22.

9　Interview with Cees Flinterman, professor of international law, Limburg University, Maastricht, Netherlands, November 8, 1993.

10　Ann Marie Clark, *Diplomacy of Conscience: Amnesty International and Changing Human Rights Norms* (Princeton: Princeton University Press, 2001).

11　Interview with Theo C. van Boven, Maastricht, Netherlands, November 8, 1993.

12　Ibid.

13　Interview with Jan Herman Burgers, The Hague, Netherlands, November 13, 1993.

14　Interview with Donald Fraser, Minneapolis, MN, March 18, 1991.

15　Council of Europe, European Commission on Human Rights, *The Greek Case, Report of the Commission* (Strasbourg, 1970), Vol. 2, part 1, p. 422.

16　Robertson, *Human Rights in Europe*, pp. 178, 255.

17　Amnesty International, "Amnesty International Conference for the Abolition of Torture: Final Report," Paris, December 10–11, 1973, p. 14.

18　"The Growing Lobby for Human Rights," *The Washington Post*, December 12, 1976, p. B1.

19　C. M. Woodhouse, *The Rise and Fall of the Greek Colonels* (London: Granada Publishing, 1985).

20　Steven V. Roberts, "The Caramanlis Way," *New York Times*, November 17, 1974, p. 326.

21　Dan Georgakas, "Two Greek Commentaries," *Chicago Review* 12, no. 2 (1969), pp. 109–14.

22　Interview with Constantina Botsiou, Athens, Greece, June 27, 2008.

23　Mary Anne Weaver, "Karamanlis Rules Greece with a Strong Hand," *The Washington Post*, November 23, 1976.

24　Interview with Maria Piniou-Kalli, Athens, Greece, June 22, 2008.

25　See Alivizatos and Diamandouros, "Politics and the Judiciary in the Greek Transition to Democracy."

26　Steven V. Roberts, "Greece Restores 1952 Constitution with Civil Rights," *New York Times*, August 2, 1974, p. 57.

27　Alivizatos and Diamandouros, "Politics and the Judiciary in the Greek Transition to Democracy."

28　Interview with Alexandros Lykorezos, Athens, Greece, June 23, 2008.

29　"Memories of Oppression Haunt Greeks as They Go to the Polls," *The Times* (London), November 16, 1974, p. 14a.

30　*The Times* (London), February 27, 1975.

31　Interview with Achilles Karamanlis, Karamanlis Foundation, Athens, Greece, June 24, 2008.

32　See Nicos C. Alivizatos, *Les Institutions Politiques de la Grèce à Travers les Crises 1922–1974* (Paris: Librairie Générale de Droit et de Jurisprudence, 1979).

33　Interview with Constantina Botsiou, Athens, Greece, June 27, 2008.

34 Ibid.

35 Interview with Evanthis Hatzivassiliou, Athens, Greece, June 25, 2008.

36 Ibid.

37 Ibid.

38 Steven V. Roberts, "Greece Sees 'Z' and Gets Excited," *New York Times*, January 13, 1975, p. 6.

39 Quoted in Alivizatos, *Les Institutions Politiques de la Grèce à Travers les Crises 1922–1974*, p. 48.

40 Interview with Constantina Botsiou, Athens, Greece, June 27, 2008.

41 "Mute Shows Trial How His Torturers Crippled Him," *The Times* (London), August 19, 1976, p. 4n.

42 Interview with Cristina Moustaklis, Athens, Greece, June 24, 2008.

43 Alivizatos and Diamandouros, "Politics and the Judiciary in the Greek Transition to Democracy."

44 Amnesty International, *Torture in Greece: The First Torturers' Trial 1975* (London: Amnesty International, 1977).

45 Samuel Huntington, *The Third Wave: Democratization in the Late Twentieth Century* (Norman: University of Oklahoma Press, 1991).

46 Denis Herbstein, "Portugal Junta Frees 200; Airports Opened," *Sunday Times* (London), April 28, 1974, p. 1.

47 I'm indebted to Margaret Keck for her extensive comments and suggestions on this chapter, and in particular on the Portuguese revolution, of which she was a close observer at the time.

48 Paul Manuel, *Uncertain Outcome: The Politics of the Portuguese Transition to Democracy* (New York: University Press of America, 1994).

49 Dalila Cabrita Mateus, *A PIDE/DGS na Guerra Colonial (1962–1974)* (Lisbon: Terramar, 2004).

50 Irene Flunser Pimentel, *A História da PIDE* (Lisbon: Circulo de Leitores, 2007), pp. 53, 419.

51 Ibid.

52 Interview with Col. Sousa e Castro, Sintra, Portugal, July 11, 2008.

53 Interview with Irene Flunser Pimentel, Lisbon, Portugal, July 1, 2008.

54 Interview with Vasco Lourenço, Lisbon, Portugal, July 4, 2008.

55 Ibid.

56 Interview with Col. Sousa e Castro, Sintra, Portugal, July 11, 2008.

57 Filipa Alves Raimundo, "The Double Face of Heroes," MA thesis, University of Lisbon, Institute of Social Sciences, 2007.

58 Interview with Col. Sousa e Castro, Sintra, Portugal, July 11, 2008.

59 Interview with Irene Flunser Pimentel, Lisbon, Portugal, July 1, 2008.

60 Raimundo, "The Double Face of Heroes."

61 Interview with Col. Sousa e Castro, Sintra, Portugal, July 11, 2008.

62 Javier Rodrigo, *Los Campos de Concentración Franquistas: Entre la Historia y la Memoria* (Madrid: Siete Mares, 2003).

63 See Emilio Silva and Santiago Macias, *Las Fosas de Franco: Los Republicanos Que el Dictador Dejó en las Cunetas* (Madrid: Ediciones Temas de Hoy, 2003).

64 Julian Santamaria, "Spanish Transition Revisited," in Marietta Minotos, ed., *The*

Transition to Democracy in Spain, Portugal and Greece Thirty Years After (Athens: Karamanlis Foundation, 2006).

65 Silva and Macias, *Las Fosas de Franco.*

66 Amnesty International, *Torture in Greece: The First Torturers' Trial 1975.* An Amnesty internal memo, "Publicity for Greek Report," dated April 19, 1977, directed to all national sections of Amnesty, urged them "to make a special effort to obtain publicity for this AI report," including feature articles and book reviews in national newspapers.

67 Nigel Rodley, *The Treatment of Prisoners under International Law,* 2nd ed. (Oxford: Oxford University Press, 1999).

68 Interview with Margo Picken, Ann Arbor, MI, October 2, 2010.

69 Herman Burgurs and Hans Danelius, *The United Nations Convention against Torture: A Handbook on the Convention against Torture and Other Cruel, Inhuman or Degrading Treatment or Punishment* (Dordrecht, Netherlands: Martinus Nijhoff, 1988), pp. 13–18.

Chapter 3: Argentina

1 This chapter draws on two previously published essays: Kathryn Sikkink, "From Pariah State to Global Human Rights Protagonist: Argentina and the Struggle for International Human Rights," *Latin American Politics and Society* 50, no. 1 (Spring 2008); and Kathryn Sikkink and Carrie Booth Walling, "Argentina's Contribution to Global Trends in Transitional Justice," in Naomi Roht-Arriaza and Javier Mariezcurrena, eds., *Transitional Justice in the Twenty-First Century: Beyond Truth versus Justice* (Cambridge, UK: Cambridge University Press, 2006). I thank Carrie Walling for her permission to use some of that material here.

2 Interview with Luis Moreno-Ocampo, The Hague, Netherlands, November 10, 2008.

3 Ibid.

4 *La Nación,* February 13, 1976, quoted in Marcos Novaro and Vicente Palmero, *La Dictadura Militar (1976–1983): Del Golpe de Estado a la Restauración Democrática,* 1st ed., *Historia Argentina* (Buenos Aires: Paidós, 2003), p. 19.

5 Disappearances in Argentina began during the elected government of Isabel Perón, but increased dramatically during the military government.

6 Comisión Nacional Sobre la Desaparición de Personas (CONADEP), *Nunca Más: Informe de la Comisión Nacional Sobre la Desaparición de Personas* (Buenos Aires: Editorial Universitaria, 1984).

7 Ann Marie Clark, *Diplomacy of Conscience: Amnesty International and Changing Human Rights Norms* (Princeton: Princeton University Press, 2001).

8 Alison Brysk, *The Politics of Human Rights in Argentina: Protest, Change, and Democratization* (Stanford, CA: Stanford University Press, 1994); Emilio Fermín Mignone, *Derechos Humanos y Sociedad: El Caso Argentino* (Buenos Aires: Centro de Estudios Legales y Sociales, 1991).

9 Klaas Dykmann, *Philanthropic Endeavors or the Exploitation of an Ideal? The Human Rights Policy of the Organization of American States in Latin America (1970–1991)* (Frankfurt: Vervuert Verlag, 2004), p. 14.

10 Ibid., pp. 71–73.

11 Ibid., p. 84.

12 "The UN's Five Wise Men," *Time* magazine, March 3, 1980; www.time.com/time/magazine/article/0,9171,95028.

13 OAS, Inter-American Commission on Human Rights, *Report on the Situation of Human Rights in Argentina*, OEA/Ser.L/V/II.49 Doc. 19, corr.1 (1980).

14 OAS, Inter-American Commission on Human Rights, *Third Report on the Situation of Human Rights in Chile*, OEA/Ser.L/V/II.40 Doc. 10 (1977).

15 OAS, Inter-American Commission on Human Rights, *Report on the Situation of Human Rights in Haiti*, OEA/Ser.L/V/II/46 (1979); Inter-American Commission on Human Rights, *Report on the Situation of Human Rights in El Salvador*, OEA/Ser.L/V/II.46 (1978).

16 Interview with Carlos Acuña, Buenos Aires, Argentina, November 22, 2006.

17 Letter from Boris G. Pasik to Sr. Don Jaime Schmirgeld, Secretary of the Permanent Assembly for Human Rights, June 3, 1979—CELS Library, Buenos Aires, translation by the author.

18 Unpublished memo, written by Augusto Conte, March 3, 1980, to the Permanent Assembly for Human Rights—CELS Library, Buenos Aires, translation by the author.

19 Elizabeth Jelin, "La Política de la Memoria, el Movimiento de Derechos Humanos y las Construcción Democrática en la Argentina," in Carlos Acuña et al., *Juicio, Castigo y Memoria: Derechos Humanos y Justicia en la Política Argentina* (Buenos Aires: Nueva Vision, 1995).

20 Horacio Verbitsky, *Civiles y Militares: Memoria Secreta de la Transición*, reprint (Buenos Aires: Sudamericana, 2006).

21 Nuria Becu, "El Filósofo y el Político: Consideraciones Morales y Políticas en el Tratamiento a los Autores de Crímenes de Lesa Humanidad Bajo la Presidencia de Raúl Alfonsín (1983–1989)," Universidad Torcuato de Tella, Departamento de Ciencias Politicas, 2004, translation by the author.

22 Oscar Landi and Inés Gonzalez Bombal, "Los Derechos en la Cultura Política," in Acuña et al., eds., *Juicio, Castigo y Memoria: Derechos Humanos y Justicia en la Política Argentina*.

23 Carlos Nino. "Strategy for Criminal Law Adjudication," unpublished PhD thesis, 1977; rev. Spanish translation, "Los Límites de la Responsabilidad Penal," Buenos Aires, 1980.

24 Becu, "El Filósofo y el Político."

25 See Carlos Santiago Nino, *Radical Evil on Trial* (New Haven: Yale University Press, 1996).

26 Interview with Jaime Malamud-Goti, Buenos Aires, Argentina, November 28, 2006.

27 Becu, "El Filósofo y el Político."

28 Raúl Alfonsín, *Democracia y Consenso* (Buenos Aires: Ediciones Corregidor, 1996), p. 87.

29 Carlos Acuña and Catalina Smulovitz, "Guarding the Guardians in Argentina: Some Lessons about the Risks and Benefits of Empowering the Courts," in A. James

McAdams, ed., *Transitional Justice and the Rule of Law in New Democracies* (Notre Dame, IN: University of Notre Dame Press, 1997).

30 Emilio Ariel Crenzel, "Génesis, Usos y Resignificaciones del *Nunca Más*: La Memoria de las Desapariciones en Argentina," PhD thesis, Faculty of Social Sciences, University of Buenos Aires, 2006.

31 Rene Antonio Mayorga, "Democracy Dignified and an End to Impunity: Bolivia's Military Dictatorship on Trial," in McAdams, ed., *Transitional Justice and the Rule of Law in New Democracies*.

32 "Como se Preparó la Acusación," *Diario del Juicio* 1, May 27, 1985.

33 See, e.g., *El Diario del Juicio*, the weekly newspaper published during the entire period of the trial of the Juntas, with transcripts of testimony, interviews, and legal and political analysis.

34 Luis Moreno-Ocampo, *Cuando el Poder Perdió el Juicio: Cómo Explicar el "Proceso" a Nuestros Hijos* (Buenos Aires: Planeta, Espejo de la Argentina, 1996), pp. 13–14, translation by the author.

35 "Testimonio del Señor Pablo A. Diaz," *Diario del Juicio* 3, June 11, 1985, p. 63.

36 "Los Testigos Claves según Strassera," *Diario del Juicio* 3, June 11, 1985.

37 "La Sentencia," *Diario del Juicio* 29, December 11, 1985.

38 Interview with Luis Moreno-Ocampo, The Hague, Netherlands, November 10, 2008.

39 See Mark Osiel, *Mass Atrocity, Collective Memory, and the Law* (New Brunswick, NJ: Transaction Publishers, 1997).

40 Horacio Verbitsky, *Civiles y Militares: Memoria Secreta de la Transición*, reprint (Buenos Aires: Sudamericana, 2006).

41 Acuña and Smulovitz, "Guarding the Guardians in Argentina."

42 See Elizabeth Jelin and Susana G. Kaufman, "Layers of Memory: Twenty Years After in Argentina," in Graham Dawson, T. G. Dawson, and Michael Roper, eds., *The Politics of War Memory and Commemoration* (London: Routledge, 2000).

43 Margaret E. Keck and Kathryn Sikkink, *Activists Beyond Borders: Advocacy Networks in International Politics* (Ithaca, NY: Cornell University Press, 1998).

44 This is similar to the process Tarrow refers to as "scale shift," where local groups reach out to include broader targets, new actors, and institutions at new levels— Sidney Tarrow, *The New Transnational Activism* (New York: Cambridge University Press, 2005).

45 Leonardo Filippini, "Truth Trials in Argentina," unpublished manuscript, 2005.

46 Interview with Alcira Rios, Legal Director, Grandmothers of the Plaza de Mayo, Buenos Aires, December 12, 2002.

47 Interview with Martín Abregú, former executive director, Center for Legal and Social Studies, Buenos Aires, July 20, 1999.

48 Gabriel Cavallo, "Resolución del Juez Gabriel Cavallo," *Juzgado Federal* 4, Caso Poblete-Hlaczik, March 6, 2001.

49 Interview with Pablo Parenti, Buenos Aires, Argentina, December 6, 2002.

50 Most Uruguayans disappeared in Argentina, probably as a result of a collaboration between Uruguayan and Argentine security forces.

51 For a fascinating discussion of this campaign and debate, see Lawrence Weschler,

A Miracle, a Universe: Settling Accounts with Torturers (New York: Pantheon Books, 1990).

52 Mayorga, "Democracy Dignified and an End to Impunity."

53 Stephen Ropp and Kathryn Sikkink, "International Norms and Domestic Politics in Chile and Guatemala," in Thomas Risse, Stephen Ropp, and Kathryn Sikkink, eds., *The Power of Human Rights: International Norms and Domestic Change* (Cambridge, UK: Cambridge University Press, 1999).

54 See, e.g., Donatella Della Porta and Sidney Tarrow, eds., *Transnational Protest and Global Activism* (Lanham, MD: Rowman & Littlefield, 2005).

55 Catalina Smulovitz, "The Discovery of Law: Political Consequences in the Argentine Case," in Yves Dezalay and Bryant G. Garth, eds., *Global Prescriptions: The Production, Exportation, and Importation of a New Legal Orthodoxy* (Ann Arbor: University of Michigan Press, 2002), pp. 249–75.

56 Lisa Hilbink, *Judges Beyond Politics in Democracy and Dictatorship: Lessons from Chile* (New York: Cambridge University Press, 2007).

Part II
Interlude

1 Interview with Wolfgang Kaleck, Berlin, Germany, June 6, 2010.

2 See Margaret E. Keck and Kathryn Sikkink, *Activists Beyond Borders: Advocacy Networks in International Politics* (Ithaca, NY: Cornell University Press, 1998); and Alison Brysk, *The Politics of Human Rights in Argentina: Protest, Change, and Democratization* (Stanford, CA: Stanford University Press, 1994).

3 Interview with Luis Moreno-Ocampo, Minneapolis, MN, September 27, 2010.

4 Interview with Patricia Valdez, Buenos Aires, Argentina, July 16, 1999.

5 Ibid.

6 Ibid.

Chapter 4: The Streams of the Justice Cascade

1 On the issue of torture and disappearances, for example, see Ann Marie Clark, *Diplomacy of Conscience: Amnesty International and Changing Human Rights Norms* (Princeton: Princeton University Press, 2001). See also Michael J. Struett, *The Politics of Constructing the International Criminal Court* (New York: Palgrave Macmillan, 2008); Naomi Roht-Arriaza, *The Pinochet Effect: Transnational Justice in the Age of Human Rights* (Philadelphia: University of Pennsylvania Press, 2005); Gary Bass, *Stay the Hand of Vengeance* (Princeton: Princeton University Press, 2000); Samantha Power, *A Problem from Hell: America and the Age of Genocide* (New York: Basic Books, 2002); and Benjamin Schiff, *Building the International Criminal Court* (Cambridge, UK: Cambridge University Press, 2008).

2 For an exception, see Ruti Teitel, "Transitional Justice Genealogy," *Harvard Human Rights Journal* 16 (2003), pp. 69–94. See also Ellen L. Lutz and Caitlin Reiger, eds., *Prosecuting Heads of States* (New York: Cambridge University Press, 2009).

3 This and the quotes that follow are from my interview with M. Cherif Bassiouni, DePaul University, Chicago, IL, March 31, 2010.

4   Interview with Nigel Rodley, Ann Arbor, MI, October 2, 2010.

5   Committee of Experts on Torture, "Committee of Experts on Torture, Syracuse, Italy, 16–17 December 1977," *Revue International de Droit Pénal* 48, nos. 3 and 4 (1977).

6   The Swedish draft included a slightly longer article on the duty to prosecute or extradite, what is now often referred to as the article on "universal jurisdiction," the language of which is almost identical to articles in three earlier conventions not directly related to human rights: The Convention for the Suppression of Unlawful Seizure of Aircraft [Highjacking Convention], which entered into force in 1971; the Convention for the Suppression of Unlawful Acts Against the Safely of Civil Aviation, which entered into force in 1973; and the Convention for the Prevention and Punishment of Crimes Against International Protected Persons, which entered into force in 1977. All three of these conventions have almost identical articles on the duty to prosecute or extradite.

7   Interview with Nigel Rodley, Ann Arbor, MI, October 2, 2010.

8   Interview with Jan Herman Burgers, The Hague, Netherlands, November 13, 1993.

9   See Jan Herman Burgers and Hans Danelius, *The United Nations Convention against Torture: A Handbook on the Convention against Torture and Other Cruel, Inhuman or Degrading Treatment or Punishment* (Dordrecht, Netherlands: Martinus Nijhoff, 1988), pp. 78–79; see also pp. 58, 62–63.

10 See Nigel Rodley and Jayne Huckerby, "Outlawing Torture: The Story of Amnesty International's Efforts to Shape the UN Convention Against Torture," in Deena Hurwitz, Margaret L. Satterthwaite, and Douglas B. Ford, eds., *Human Rights Advocacy Stories* (New York: Foundation Press: Thomson/West, 2009).

11 Burgers and Danelius, *The United Nations Convention against Torture*, p. 78.

12 Chris Ingelse, *The UN Committee against Torture: An Assessment* (The Hague: Martinus Nijhoff, 2001).

13 Interview with M. Cherif Bassiouni, Chicago, IL, March 31, 2010.

14 Veláquez Rodríguez Case, Judgment, Inter-American court of Human Rights, (Ser.C), no. 5 (1989), para. 166 (emphasis added).

15 The path from regional convention to international treaty took longer. Argentina and France, in particular, continued to push for the treaty, and the International Convention for Protection of All Persons from Enforced Disappearance was adopted by the UN in 2006, a full decade after the Inter-American Convention had entered into force.

16 Interview with Aryeh Neier, New York, NY, March 19, 1992.

17 Aryeh Neier, *Taking Liberties: Four Decades in the Struggle for Rights* (New York: Public Affairs, 2003), pp. 194–95, 224.

18 Interview with Aryeh Neier, New York, NY, March 19, 1992.

19 In some cases, he argued, international humanitarian law may even provide a stronger basis for Amnesty International's work because it was at times more specific and exacting, more countries had ratified the Geneva Conventions, and military and law enforcement officials took it more seriously. In particular, Weissbrodt wrote that Common Article III, present in each of the four Geneva Conventions, was "directly applicable to most of Amnesty's concerns," and could be an important tool for human rights organizations that hoped to apply humanitarian law to the situations

of internal conflict—David Weissbrodt, "Study of Amnesty International's Role in Situations of Armed Conflict and Internal Strife," October 23, 1984, unpublished document, AI Index: POL 03/04/84.

20 Interview with Wilder Tayler and Nigel Rodley, Ann Arbor, MI, October 2, 2010.

21 See Amnesty International, www.amnestyusa.org/war-on-terror/torture/common-article-iii-of-the-geneva-conventions/page.do?id=1351086, accessed June 28, 2010.

22 *New York Review of Books* 37, no. 1, February 1, 1990.

23 See Power, *A Problem from Hell.*

24 Interview with Richard Dicker, New Haven, CT, February 7, 2009.

25 See John Hagan, *Justice in the Balkans: Prosecuting War Crimes in the Hague Tribunal* (Chicago: University of Chicago Press, 2003).

26 Power, *A Problem from Hell*, p. 18.

27 Aryeh Neier, *War Crimes: Brutality, Genocide, Terror, and the Struggle for Justice* (New York: Times Books, 1998), pp. 120–21.

28 Bass, *Stay the Hand of Vengeance*, p. 210.

29 Power, *A Problem from Hell*, p. 326.

30 Ibid.

31 Aryeh Neier, "The Nuremberg Precedent," *New York Review of Books* 40, no. 18, November 4, 1993; www.nybooks.com/articles/archives/1993/nov/04/the-nuremberg-precedent/.

32 Bass, *Stay the Hand of Vengeance.*

33 M. Cherif Bassiouni and Peter Manikas, *The Law of the International Criminal Tribunal for the Former Yugoslavia* (Irvington-on-Hudson, NY: Transnational Publishers, 1996), pp. 210–11.

34 Richard Goldstone, *For Humanity: Reflections of a War Crimes Investigator* (New Haven: Yale University Press, 2000), p. 74.

35 Ibid., pp. 79–80.

36 Diane Orentlicher, *That Someone Guilty Be Punished: The Impact of the ICTY in Bosnia* (New York: Open Society Institute, 2010), p. 132.

37 Bass, *Stay the Hand of Vengeance*, p. 207.

38 Goldstone, *For Humanity*, p. 77.

39 David Smith, "Rwanda Genocide Conviction Quashed Leaving Monsieur Z Free," *The Guardian* (UK), November 17, 2009.

40 On evidence of the momentum in Bosnia and Herzegovina, see Lara J. Nettelfield, *Courting Democracy in Bosnia and Herzegovina: The Hague Tribunal's Impact in a Postwar State* (New York: Cambridge University Press, 2010).

41 Michael J. Struett, *The Politics of Constructing the International Criminal Court* (New York: Palgrave Macmillan, 2008), p. 71.

42 Ibid., p. 70.

43 Michael Scharf, "Getting Serious about an International Criminal Court," *Pace International Law Review* 6 (1994), p. 103.

44 Ibid., pp. 106–07.

45 See Struett, *The Politics of Constructing the International Criminal Court.*

46 Interview with Silvia Fernández de Gurmendi, Buenos Aires, Argentina, December 11, 2002.

47 Rome Statute of the International Criminal Court, UN Doc. 2187 U.N.T.S. 90, entered into force July 1, 2002.

48 William A. Schabas, *An Introduction to the International Criminal Court* (Cambridge, UK: Cambridge University Press), p. 15.

49 An *epistemic community* is a network of professionals engaged in a common policy enterprise with "recognized expertise and competence in the particular domain and an authoritative claim to policy relevant knowledge in that issue or domain." See Peter Haas, "Introduction: Epistemic Communities and International Policy Coordination," *International Organization* 46 (1992), p. 3.

50 William R. Pace and Mark Thieroff, "Participation of Non-Governmental Organizations," in Roy S. Lee, ed., *The International Criminal Court: The Making of the Rome Statute: Issues, Negotiations, Results* (The Hague: Kluwer Law International, 1999), p. 391, and Struett, *The Politics of Constructing the International Criminal Court.* Interview with Silvia Fernández, Argentine Foreign Ministry official and key participant in all phases of the ICC negotiations, Buenos Aires, Argentina, December 11, 2002.

51 Struett, *The Politics of Constructing the International Criminal Court*, p. 73.

52 Ibid., p. 75.

53 Interview with Wolfgang Kaleck, Berlin, Germany, June 6, 2010.

54 Luc Reydams, "The Rise and Fall of Universal Jurisdiction," in William Schabas and Nadia Bernaz, eds., *Routledge Handbook of International Criminal Law* (New York: Routledge, 2010).

Part III
Chapter 5: The Effects of Human Rights Prosecutions in Latin America

1 This chapter draws heavily on an article co-authored by Kathryn Sikkink and Carrie Booth Walling: "The Impact of Human Rights Trials in Latin America," *Journal of Peace Research* 44 (2007), pp. 427–45. For a related discussion, see also Kathryn Sikkink and Carrie Booth Walling, "Argentina's Contribution to Global Trends in Transitional Justice," in Naomi Roht-Arriaza and Javier Mariezcurrena, eds., *Transitional Justice in the Twenty-First Century: Beyond Truth versus Justice* (Cambridge, UK: Cambridge University Press, 2006). I thank Carrie Booth Walling for permission to use this material here.

2 Clifford Krauss, "The World; Chile Renders a Verdict on Pinochet: Let's Move On," *New York Times*, November 22, 1998, p. 6.

3 "Highest British Court Strips Pinochet of His Immunity," *New York Times*, November 26, 1998, p. A1.

4 See Ben Partridge, "Britain: Thatcher Condemns 'Kidnap' of Pinochet," *Radio Free Europe/Radio Liberty*, October 9, 1999.

5 Samuel P. Huntington, *The Third Wave: Democratization in the Late Twentieth Century* (Norman: University of Oklahoma Press, 1991), p. 228.

6 Guillermo O'Donnell and Philippe C. Schmitter, *Transitions from Authoritarian Rule: Tentative Conclusions about Uncertain Democracies* (Baltimore, MD: Johns Hopkins University Press, 1986), p. 32 (emphasis added).

7 Aryeh Neier, "What Should be Done about the Guilty?" *New York Review of Books* 37, no. 1, February 1, 1990.

8 Ellen L. Lutz, Preface, in Ellen L. Lutz and Caitlin Reiger, eds., *Prosecuting Heads of State* (New York: Cambridge University Press, 2009), p. xx.

9 Ibid., Appendix, pp. 295–304.

10 Stephen D. Krasner, "A World Court that Could Backfire," *New York Times*, January 15, 2001, p. A15, final edition.

11 Jack Goldsmith and Stephen D. Krasner, "The Limits of Idealism," *Daedalus* 132 (Winter 2003), p. 51.

12 Jack Snyder and Leslie Vinjamuri, "Trials and Errors: Principle and Pragmatism in Strategies of International Justice," *International Security* 28, no. 3 (2004). See also Leslie Vinjamuri and Jack Snyder, "Advocacy and Scholarship in the Study of International War Crime Tribunals and Transitional Justice," *Annual Review of Political Science* 7, no. 1 (2004), p. 345.

13 Snyder and Vinjamuri, "Trials and Errors," p. 353.

14 Laurel Fletcher, Harvey M. Weinstein, and Jamie Rowen, "Context, Timing, and the Dynamics of Transitional Justice: A Historical Perspective," *Human Rights Quarterly* 31 (2009).

15 Oskar Thoms, James Ron, and Roland Paris, "Does Transitional Justice Work? Perspectives from Empirical Social Science," *Social Science Research Network*, http://ssrn.com/abstract=1302084, accessed March 2, 2009.

16 Berleley-Tulane Initiative on Vulnerable Populations, "When the War Ends: A Population-Based Survey on Attitudes about Peace, Justice, and Social Reconstruction in Northern Uganda," December 2007, www.ictj.org/images/content/8/8/884.pdf.

17 See David Mendeloff, "Truth-Seeking, Truth-Telling, and Postconflict Peacebuilding: Curb the Enthusiasm?" *International Studies Review* 6, no. 3 (2004).

18 See Steven C. Poe, Sabine Carey, and Tanya Vasquez, "How Are These Pictures Different? A Quantitative Comparison of the U.S. State Department and Amnesty International Human Rights Reports, 1976–1995," *Human Rights Quarterly* 23, no. 3 (2001), pp. 650–77.

19 Prosecutions may include indictment, arrest, detention of a suspect (whether in house or in prison), or extradition that is being actively pursued, the initiation of a trial, or the continuance of a trial so long as there is active progress being made in the case, or a ruling in a trial. Civil prosecutions, the granting of reparations, apologies, or purely administrative inquiries, investigations, or punishments do not count as human rights prosecutions for our purposes.

20 See U.S. Department of Justice, Office of Justice Programs, "The World Factbook of Criminal Justice Systems," "Victims" section, Part 3, "Role of Victim in Prosecution and Sentencing" (http://bjs.usdoj.gov); M. E. I. Brienen and E. H. Hoegen, "Victims of Crime in 22 European Justice Systems: The Implementation of Recommendation (85) 11 of the Council of Europe on the Position of the Victim in the Framework of Criminal Law and Procedure," Dissertation, University of Tilburg, (Nijmegen, The Netherlands: Wolf Legal Productions, 2000).

21 See Malcolm Feeley, *The Process Is the Punishment: Handling Cases in a Lower Criminal Court* (New York: Russell Sage Foundation, 1979).

22 Clifford Krauss, "Pinochet, at Home in Chile: A Real Nowhere Man," *New York Times*, March 5, 2000.

23 For example, in Argentina in 2008, over 212 human rights lawsuits were in process, and 330 accused individuals were being held in preventive imprisonment—Centro de Estudios Legales y Sociales, www.cels.org.ar/documentos/index.php?info=detalle Doc&ids=3&lang=es&ss=&idc=663. Yet we would code Argentina as "1" for 2008, and its number of cumulative prosecution years is 20 for the entire period. In Chile, another country with a high level of country-prosecution years, in 2010 over 400 human rights–related investigations were ongoing, involving a total of almost 800 former regime agents and over 1,000 victims or survivors. See the Human Rights Observatory, Universidad Diego Portales, Santiago, Chile, Bulletin 9, August 2010; www.icso.cl/observatorio-derechos-humanos.

24 Huntington, *The Third Wave: Democratization in the Late Twentieth Century*, p. 228.

25 Ibid., p. 211.

26 Guillermo O'Donnell and Philippe C. Schmitter, *Transitions from Authoritarian Rule: Comparative Perspectives* (Baltimore, MD: Johns Hopkins University Press, 1986), p. 29.

27 José Zalaquett, "Confronting Human Rights Violations by Former Governments: Principles Applicable and Political Constraints," in Neil J. Kritz, ed., *Transitional Justice: How Emerging Democracies Reckon with Former Regimes* (Washington, DC: U.S. Institute of Peace, 1995).

28 Emilio Silva and Santiago Macias, *Las Fosas de Franco: Los Republicanos que el Dictador Dejó en las Cuentas* (Madrid: Ediciones Temas de Hoy, 2003).

29 Pablo de Greiff, "Vetting and Transitional Justice," in Alexander Mayer-Rieckh and Pablo de Greiff, eds., *Justice as Prevention: Vetting of Public Employees in Transitional Societies* (Chicago: Social Science Research Council, 2007).

30 The three transitional countries that did not have amnesties were Grenada, Guyana, and Paraguay. We want to thank Louise Mallinder for sharing with us the data on post-1979 amnesties in Latin America from her global database on amnesties.

31 The authors write, "Other mechanisms would accompany, not replace, trials to provide a comprehensive approach to accountability. We find an increased use of accountability mechanisms, as the justice cascade would suggest. Frequency alone, however, does not confirm the justice cascade. Indeed, our findings show a strong persistence of impunity into the present." See Tricia D. Olsen, Leigh A. Payne, and Andrew G. Reiter, *Transitional Justice in the Balance: Comparing Processes, Weighing Efficacy* (Washington, DC: USIP Press, 2010), p. 99.

32 I am indebted to Louise Mallinder, Leslie Vinjamuri, and Jack Snyder for helping me understand this point.

33 "Procuradoria vai denunciar militares por sequestros," *Folha de São Paulo*, January 22, 2009.

34 Snyder and Vinjamuri, "Trials and Errors," p. 6.

35 In 1990, twenty-six members of the Civil Defense Forces were sentenced to thirty years' imprisonment for the 1982 rape and murder of twenty-three peasants in San

Pedro Perulapan, Cuscatian, and an army private was convicted of the 1982 murder of U.S. citizen Michael Klein.

36 See Olsen, Payne, and Reiter, *Transitional Justice in the Balance: Comparing Processes, Weighing Efficacy.*

37 Larry Diamond, *The Spirit of Democracy: The Struggle to Build Free Societies Throughout the World* (New York: Holt Publishers, 2009), p. 376; see table 5 there.

38 Jack Snyder made this argument in his comments on the manuscript of this book.

39 See Steven C. Poe, "The Decision to Repress: An Integrative Theoretical Approach to Research on Human Rights and Repression," in Sabine C. Carey and Steven C. Poe, eds., *Understanding Human Rights Violations: New Systematic Studies* (Burlington, VT: Ashgate Publishing, 2004); and Christian Davenport, *State Repression and the Domestic Democratic Peace* (New York: Cambridge University Press, 2007).

40 M. Gibney and M. Dalton, "The Political Terror Scale," *Policy Studies and Developing Nations* 4 (1996), pp. 73–84; M. Gibney, Political Terror Scale (2004), at http://www.politicalterrorscale.org.

41 The PTS tracks the same human rights violations as those captured by our database. The Latin American transitional countries in the database include: Argentina, Bolivia, Chile, Ecuador, El Salvador, Guatemala, Haiti, Honduras, Mexico, Nicaragua, Panama, Paraguay, Peru, and Uruguay.

42 Of the ninety-nine transitional countries in the dataset, twenty-nine had prior experience with democracy. Of these, sixteen had trials, which amounts to 55.2 percent. The average across transitions was 48.4 percent, with forty-eight transitional countries holding trials. However, only eleven of twenty-nine previously democratic countries showed improvements in human rights (37.9 percent). The average for all transitions was 37.3 percent (thirty-seven out of ninety-nine). Finally, of the forty-eight transitions with trials, twenty-six showed convincing improvements in human rights measures (54.2 percent). This should be compared with the sample average of 37.3 percent. A country was considered to be a democracy if it had ever reached 5 on the PTS, and it was considered to have improvement in human rights practices if both the Amnesty International and State Department–derived Political Terror Scale data demonstrated movement in the positive direction. We are indebted to Robert Keohane for suggesting we consider this alternative explanation.

43 The full tables and analysis can be found in Sikkink and Walling, "The Impact of Human Rights Trials in Latin America."

44 Steven C. Poe, Neal Tate, and Linda Camp Keith, "Repression of the Human Right to Personal Integrity Revisited: A Global Cross-National Study Covering the Years 1976–1993," *International Studies Quarterly* 43, no. 2 (1999).

45 Olsen, Payne, and Reiter, in fact, argue based on all regions that "some evidence suggests that using transitional justice after conflict termination makes conflicts *less likely* to recur" (emphasis added). See *Transitional Justice in the Balance*, pp. 128–89.

46 According to the PRIO/Uppsala Armed Conflict Database, these seventeen countries are Argentina, Chile, Colombia, Ecuador, El Salvador, Grenada, Guatemala, Haiti, Mexico, Nicaragua, Panama, Paraguay, Peru, Suriname, Trinidad and Tobago, Uru-

guay, and Venezuela—www.prio.no/cwp/armedconflict/current/conflict_list_1946
-2003.pdf.

47 See, e.g., Fletcher, "Context, Timing, and the Dynamics of Transitional Justice: A
Historical Perspective," and Snyder and Vinjamuri, "Trials and Errors," p. 6.

48 Pilar Domingo and Rachel Sieder, eds., *Rule of Law in Latin America: The International Promotion of Judicial Reform* (London: University of London, 2001).

49 Thomas Carothers, "The Many Agendas of Rule of Law Reform in Latin America,"
in ibid., pp. 6–16.

50 Interview with Alberto Binder, Instituto de Estudios Comparados en Ciencias
Penales y Sociales, Buenos Aires, Argentina, November 21, 2006.

51 Catalina Smulovitz, "The Discovery of Law: Political Consequences in the Argentine Case," in Yves Dezalay and Bryant G. Garth, eds., *Global Prescriptions: The
Production, Exportation, and Importation of a New Legal Orthodoxy* (Ann Arbor: University of Michigan Press, 2002), pp. 249–65.

52 International Country Risk Guide measure of Law and Order. There is also a World
Bank database on rule of law, but it covers a shorter period, and is more concerned
about order than access to and impartiality of the judicial system.

53 See Brian Loveman, *For* la Patria*: Politics and the Armed Forces in Latin America*
(Wilmington, DE: Scholarly Resources, 1999), and Alfred Stepan, *Rethinking Military Politics* (Princeton: Princeton University Press, 1988).

54 This data is from the international country risk group. A high number means a low
involvement of military in politics, and a low number a threat of military takeover or
a full-scale military regime. Thus, the measure captures the issue of military subordination to civilian leaders that is of interest to us here.

55 Carlos Acuña and Catalina Smulovitz, "Adjusting the Armed Forces to Democracy:
Successes, Failures, and Ambiguities in the Southern Cone," in Elizabeth Jelin and
Eric Hersberg, eds., *Constructing Democracy: Human Rights, Citizenship, and Democ-
racy in Latin America* (Boulder, CO: Westview Press, 1996).

56 "Jobim contesta Tarso e diz que não cabe ao Executivo discutir anistia," *Estado de
São Paulo*, August 2, 2008; "Militares reagem a Tarso e criticam 'passado terrorista'
do governo Lula," *Estado de São Paulo*, August 4, 2008; "Na presence do comandante
do Leste, militares fazem ato contra Tarso," *Estado de São Paulo*, August 8, 2008;
and "Não estamos sob tutela militar," *Estado de São Paulo*, August 9, 2008. Transla-
tions by the author.

57 Observatório das Violências Policiais-SP: www.ovp-sp.org/index.htm.

58 James Holston, *Insurgent Citizenship: Disjunctions of Democracy and Modernity in
Brazil* (Princeton: Princeton University Press, 2007), p. 304.

59 Teres P. R. Caldeira, "Crime and Individual Rights: Reframing the Question of Violence
in Latin America," in Jelin and Hershberg, eds., *Constructing Democracy*, pp. 197–98.

60 See, e.g., Observatório das Violências Policiais-SP.

Chapter 6: Global Deterrence and Human Rights Prosecutions

1 Maria Piniou-Kalli, "The Big Chill: 21 April 1967—30 Years After: How Is It Possible to Forget about the Torturers?", unpublished paper, Athens, Greece.

2 Miron Varouhakis, *Shadows of Heroes: The Journey of a Doctor and a Journalist in the Lives of Ordinary People Who Became Victims of Torture* (LaVergne, TN: Xlibris Corp., 2010).

3 Maria Piniou-Kalli, "Impunity and the Tragedy Goes On," paper presented at the 6th International Symposium on Torture as a Challenge to the Medical and Other Health Professions, October 20–22, 1993, Buenos Aires, Argentina.

4 For an example of work that does evaluate justice from the point of view of victims and survivors, see Diane F. Orentlicher, *That Someone Guilty Be Punished: The Impact of the ICTY in Bosnia* (New York: Open Society Institute, 2010).

5 Jelena Subotić, *Hijacked Justice: Dealing with the Past in the Balkans* (Ithaca, NY: Cornell University Press, 2009), pp. 14–15.

6 In her conclusion, Subotić in fact recognizes that, despite her criticism, the ICTY, and transitional justice generally, had many positive effects in the Balkans. She claims that it prevented Milošević from again rising to power in Serbia; that it documented a good deal of evidence on crimes that were committed; and that it established the inappropriateness of the war crimes for the society as a whole—Ibid., pp. 190–91.

7 See Philip Tetlock and Aaron Belkin, eds., *Counterfactual Thought Experiments in World Politics: Logical, Methodological, and Psychological Perspectives* (Princeton: Princeton University Press, 1996).

8 Adam Branch, "Uganda's Civil War and the Politics of ICC Intervention," *Ethics and International Affairs* 21, no. 2 (2007), pp. 189, 192.

9 Payam Akhavan, "Are International Criminal Tribunals a Disincentive to Peace?: Reconciling Judicial Romanticism with Political Realism," *Human Rights Quarterly* 31 (2009), pp. 624–54.

10 Hunjoon Kim and Kathryn Sikkink, "Explaining the Deterrence Effect of Human Rights Prosecutions for Transitional Countries," *International Studies Quarterly* 54, no. 4 (December 2010), pp. 939–63.

11 Jack Snyder and Leslie Vinjamuri, "Trials and Errors: Principle and Pragmatism in Strategies of International Justice," *International Security* 28, no. 3 (Winter 2003–04), pp. 5–44.

12 See Abram Chayes and Antonia Handler Chayes, *The New Sovereignty* (Cambridge, MA: Harvard University Press, 1995); George W. Downs, David M. Rocke, and Peter N. Barsoom, "Is the Good News about Compliance Good News about Cooperation?" *International Organization* 50, no. 3 (1996), pp. 379–406; and Beth Simmons, "International Law and State Behavior: Commitment and Compliance in International Monetary Affairs," *American Political Science Review* 94, no. 4 (2000), pp. 819–35.

13 See, e.g., Johannes Andenaes, *Punishment and Deterrence* (Ann Arbor: University of Michigan Press, 1974); Alfred Blumstein, Jacqueline Cohen, and Daniel Nagin, eds., *Deterrence and Incapacitation: Estimating the Effects of Criminal Sanctions on Crime Rates* (Washington, DC: National Academy of Sciences, 1978); Daniel Nagin, ed., *Criminal Deterrence Research at the Outset of the Twenty-First Century* (Chicago: University of Chicago Press, 1998); Bill McCarthy, "New Economics of Sociological Criminology," *Annual Review of Sociology* 28 (2002), pp. 417–42; and Ross Mat-

sueda, David Huizinga, and Derek Kreager, "Deterring Delinquents: A Rational Choice Model of Theft and Violence," *American Sociological Review* 71 (2006), pp. 95–122.

14 The assumption that state leaders choose repression after calculating the costs and benefits is also consistent with the literature on causes of repression. See Steven C. Poe, Neal Tate, and Linda Camp Keith, "Repression of the Human Right to Personal Integrity Revisited: A Global Cross-National Study Covering the Years 1976–1993," *International Studies Quarterly* 43, no. 2 (1999); and Steven C. Poe, "The Decision to Repress: An Integrative Theoretical Approach to Research on Human Rights and Repression," in Sabine C. Carey and Steven C. Poe, eds., *Understanding Human Rights Violations: New Systematic Studies* (Burlington, VT: Ashgate Publishing, 2004).

15 Hannah Arendt, *Eichmann in Jerusalem: A Report on the Banality of Evil* (1963; New York: Penguin Books, 1994).

16 Ibid., pp. 126, 131.

17 Thomas Risse, Stephen Ropp, and Kathryn Sikkink, eds., *The Power of Human Rights: International Norms and Domestic Change* (Cambridge, UK: Cambridge University Press, 1999). Ryan Goodman and Derek Jinks, "How to Influence States: Socialization and International Human Rights Law," *Duke Law Journal* 54 (2004).

18 Risse, Ropp, and Sikkink, eds., *The Power of Human Rights*.

19 Joachim Savelsburg and Ryan King, "Law and Collective Memory," *Annual Review of Law and Social Sciences* 3 (2007), pp. 189–211.

20 Joachim Savelsburg, *Crime and Human Rights: Criminology of Genocide and Atrocities* (New York: Sage Publications, 2010).

21 See Ryan Goodman and Derek Jinks, *Socializing States: Promoting Human Rights Through International Law* (New York: Oxford University Press, forthcoming).

22 Beth Simmons, *Mobilizing for Human Rights: International Law in Domestic Politics* (New York: Cambridge University Press, 2009).

23 Samuel Huntington, *The Third Wave: Democratization in the Late Twentieth Century* (Norman: University of Oklahoma Press, 1991), p. 21.

24 To determine transition, we used the regime transition variable (Regtrans), which was derived from the yearly changing values of the Polity score. We also excluded thirty-two countries with populations less than 500,000.

25 David R. Cingranelli and David. L. Richards, *The Cingranelli-Richards (CIRI) Human Rights Database Coder Manual* (2004). We also reversed the original index into a 9-point scale where 8 indicates the highest level of repression (no respect for physical integrity rights) and zero an absence of repression (full respect).

26 M. Gibney and M. Dalton, "The Political Terror Scale," *Policy Studies and Developing Nations* 4 (1996), pp. 73–84, and M. Gibney, Political Terror Scale (2004), at http://www.politicalterrorscale.org.

27 Hunjoon Kim, "Expansion of Transitional Justice Measures: A Comparative Analysis of Its Causes," PhD dissertation, University of Minnesota, 2008.

28 These countries are Afghanistan, Algeria, Angola, Azerbaijan, Bangladesh, Bosnia and Herzegovina, Burkina Faso, Burundi, Cambodia, Central African Republic, Chad, Comoros, Republic of Congo, Côte d'Ivoire, Croatia, Djibouti, El Salvador, Ethiopia, Georgia, Ghana, Guatemala, Guinea-Bissau, Haiti, Indonesia, Iran,

Kenya, Kyrgyz Republic, Liberia, Macedonia, Mali, Mexico, Moldova, Nepal, Niger, Nigeria, Pakistan, Panama, Paraguay, Peru, Philippines, Romania, Russia, Rwanda, Senegal, Serbia and Montenegro, Sierra Leone, Spain, Tajikistan, Thailand, Turkey, Uganda, Uzbekistan, and Yemen.

29 Hunjoon Kim, "Why and When Do States Use Human Rights Trials and Truth Commissions After Transition? An Event History Analysis of 100 Countries Covering 1974–2004," unpublished manuscript, 2007.

Chapter 7: Is the United States Immune to the Justice Cascade?

1 According to the International Convention for the Protection of All Persons from Enforced Disappearance, "'enforced disappearance' is considered to be the arrest, detention, abduction or any other form of deprivation of liberty by agents of the State or by persons or groups of persons acting with the authorization, support or acquiescence of the State, followed by a refusal to acknowledge the deprivation of liberty or by concealment of the fate or whereabouts of the disappeared person, which places such a person outside the protection of the law." See UN General Assembly, 61st sess., Official Records, A/C.3/61/L.17, 2006.

2 United Nations, "Joint study on global practices in relation to secret detention in the context of countering terrorism of the Special Rapporteur on the promotion and protection of human rights and fundamental freedoms while countering terrorism, the Special Rapporteur on torture and other cruel, inhuman or degrading treatment or punishment, the Working Group on Arbitrary Detention and the Working Group on Enforced or Involuntary Disappearances," advance unedited copy, January 26, 2010, A/HRC/13/42.

3 Antonio M. Taguba, "The Taguba Report: Article, 5-6 Investigation of the 800th Military Police Brigade," Department of Defense, Washington, DC, June 2004.

4 Kathryn Sikkink, "Bush Administration Noncompliance with the Prohibition on Torture and Cruel and Degrading Treatment," in Cynthia Soohoo, Catherine Albisa, and Martha F. Davis, eds., *Bringing Human Rights Home: From Civil Rights to Human Rights*, Vol. 2 (Westport, CT: Praeger, 2008), pp. 187–208.

5 Since the initiation of the policy of "exceptional rendition" in 1995, the United States has been in violation of Article 3 of the Torture Convention, which says state parties cannot return detainees to states where there are substantial grounds to believe they will be subjected to torture. See Jane Mayer, "Outsourcing Torture," *The New Yorker*, February 14 and 21, 2005.

6 See Jane Mayer, *The Dark Side: The Inside Story of How the War on Terror Turned into a War on American Ideals* (New York: Doubleday, 2008); Jack Goldsmith, *The Terror Presidency: Law and Judgment Inside the Bush Administration* (New York: W. W. Norton & Company, 2007); and Barton Gellman, *Angler: The Cheney Vice Presidency* (New York: Penguin, 2008).

7 Quoted in Gellman, *Angler*, p. 177 (emphasis added).

8 Benedict Kingsbury, "The Concept of Compliance as a Function of Competing Conceptions of International Law," *Michigan Journal of International Law* 19, no. 2 (1998).

9 Beth Simmons, *Mobilizing for Human Rights: International Law in Domestic Politics* (New York: Cambridge University Press, 2010).

10 Oona Hathaway, "The Cost of Commitment," *Stanford Law Review* 55, no. 5 (May 2003).

11 Jan Herman Burgers and Hans Danelius, *The United Nations Convention against Torture: A Handbook on the Convention against Torture and Other Cruel, Inhuman or Degrading Treatment or Punishment* (Dordrecht, Netherlands: Martinus Nijhoff, 1988); pp. 78–79, 58, 62–63.

12 Ibid., pp. 78–79.

13 *Filártiga v. Peña-Irala*, 630 F.2d 876, 890 (2d Cir. 1980); on international law and torture, see also Andrew McEntree, "Law and Torture," in Duncan Forrest, ed., *A Glimpse of Hell: Reports on Torture Worldwide* (New York: New York University Press, 1996), pp. 1–20.

14 *Congressional Record*, U.S. Senate, October 27, 1990, p. S17491.

15 R. Jeffrey Smith, "Detainee Abuse Charges Feared," *The Washington Post*, July 28, 2006, p. A1.

16 18 U.S.C. § 2340 et seq.

17 www.state.gov/documents/organization/100296.pdf (emphasis added).

18 See Kathryn Sikkink, *Mixed Signals: U.S. Human Rights Policy and Latin America* (Ithaca, NY: Cornell University Press, 2004).

19 U.S. Congress, House, *The Status of Human Rights in Selected Countries and the United States Response; Report Prepared for the Subcommittee on International Organization of the Committee on International Relations of the United States House of Representatives by the Library of Congress*, 95th Congress, 1st sess., July 25, 1977 (Washington, DC: GPO, 1977), p. 2.

20 U.S. Department of Defense, "Memorandum for the Secretary of Defense," "Improper Material in Spanish Language Intelligence Training Manuals," March 10, 1992.

21 See "Article 15-6 Investigation of the 800th Military Police Brigade" (The Taguba Report); "Final Report of the Independent Panel to Review DOD Detention Operations" (The Schlesinger Report), August 2004; LTG Anthony R. Jones, "AR 15-6 Investigation of the Abu Ghraib Prison and 205th Military Intelligence Brigade"; MG George R. Fay, "AR 15-6 Investigation of the Abu Ghraib Detention Facility and 205th Military Intelligence Brigade"; and "Report of the International Committee of the Red Cross (ICRC) on the Treatment by the Coalition Forces of Prisoners of War and Other Protected Persons by the Geneva Conventions in Iraq During Arrest, Internment and Interrogation," February 2004. All of these reports are available in the appendices to Mark Danner, *Torture and Truth: America, Abu Ghraib, and the War on Terror*, Human Rights and Global Justice, Human Rights First, and Human Rights Watch (New York: New York Review of Books, 2004).

22 See "By the Numbers: Findings of the Detainee Abuse and Accountability Project" (2006), at http://www.chrgj.org/docs/Press%20Release%20-%20By%20The%20Numbers.pdf.

23 Neil A. Lewis, "Red Cross Finds Detainee Abuse in Guantánamo: U.S. Rejects

Accusations: Confidential Report Calls Practices Tantamount to Torture," *New York Times*, November 30, 2004, pp. A1, A14.

24 Jameel Jaffer and Amrit Singh, *Administration of Torture: A Documentary Record from Washington to Abu Ghraib and Beyond* (New York: Columbia University Press, 2007), p 29.

25 See, e.g., Mayer, *The Dark Side*, pp. 148, 224–25, 238; Scott Horton, "The Guantánamo 'Suicides': A Camp Delta sergeant blows the whistle," *Harper's* magazine, January 18, 2010; www.harpers.org/archive/2010/01/hbc-90006368.

26 Goldsmith, *The Terror Presidency*, p. 69.

27 John Sifton, "The Get Out of Jail Free Card for Torture: It's Called a Declination; Just Ask the CIA," *Slate* (March 2010).

28 Ibid.

29 Douglas Jehl and Andrea Elliot, "Cuba Base Sent Its Interrogators to Iraqi Prison," *New York Times*, May 29, 2004; www.nytimes.com/2004/05/29/world/the-reach-of-war-gi-instructors-cuba-base-sent-its-interrogators-to-iraqi-prison.html.

30 Neil A. Lewis, "Fresh Details Emerge on Harsh Methods at Guantánamo, *New York Times*, January 1, 2005; www.nytimes.com/2005/01/01/national/01gitmo .html.

31 R. Jeffrey Smith, "Detainee Abuse Charges Feared," *The Washington Post*, July 28, 2006, p. A1.

32 "Memorandum for Alberto R. Gonzales, Re: Standards of Conduct for Interrogation under 18 U.S.C. 2340-2340A," U.S. Department of Justice, Office of Legal Counsel, Office of the Assistant Attorney General, August 1, 2002.

33 I am indebted to Nigel Rodley for this particular formulation.

34 UN General Assembly, 51st sess., Convention Against Torture and Other Cruel, Inhuman or Degrading Treatment or Punishment, Article 2, A/39/51 (1984).

35 "Memorandum from Secretary of State Colin Powell to Counsel to the President, Re: Draft Decision Memorandum for the President on the Applicability of the Geneva Convention to the Conflict in Afghanistan," January 26, 2002, available at www.gwu.edu/~nsarchiv/NSAEBB/NSAEBB127/02.01.26.pdf.

36 Mayer, "Outsourcing Torture," p. 82.

37 Jane Mayer, "The Memo," *The New Yorker*, February 27, 2006.

38 "Memorandum for James B. Comey, Deputy Attorney General, Re: Legal Standards Applicable Under 18 U.S.C. 2340-2340A," U.S. Department of Justice, Office of Legal Counsel, Office of the Assistant Attorney General, December 30, 2004.

39 Gellman, *Angler*, pp. 176–80.

40 See Francis Fukuyama, *American at the Crossroads: Democracy, Power, and the Neoconservative Legacy* (New Haven: Yale University Press, 2006).

41 Department of Defense, *National Defense Strategy of the United States* (March 2005), p. 5.

42 Goldsmith, *The Terror Presidency*, p. 53.

43 Ibid., p. 58.

44 Ibid., p. 59.

45 Mayer, *The Dark Side*, p. 323.

46 Section 1004(b) of the Detainee Treatment Act of 2005 (42 U.S.C. 2000dd-1(b).

47 Interview with John Sifton, New York, NY, May 13, 2010.

48 U.S. Supreme Court, "Hamdan v. Rumsfeld," www.supremecourtus.gov/opinions /05pdf/05-184.pdf.

49 Nina Totenberg, "*Hamdan v. Rumsfeld:* Path to a Landmark Ruling," National Public Radio, June 29, 2006; www.npr.org/templates/story/story.php?storyId5751355.

50 Michael Ratner, "The Fear of Torture: Tape Destruction or Prosecution," December 14, 2007, http://michaelratner.com/blog/?p=26.

51 Mayer, "Outsourcing Torture," p. 82.

52 Statement by Brig. Gen. James Cullen, Press conference by Human Rights First and Retired Military Leaders, January 4, 2005; audio at www.humanrightsfirst.org. Transcription of remarks by the author.

53 Mayer, "Outsourcing Torture," p. 108.

54 FBI, Criminal Justice Information Services, "E-mail from REDACTED to Gary Bald, Frankie Battle, Arthur Cummings Re: FWD: Impersonating FBI Agents at GITMO," December 5, 2003; www.aclu.org/torturefoia/released/122004.html.

55 Press release, www.chrgj.org/docs/Press%20Release%20-%20By%20The%20Num bers.pdf.

56 "By the Numbers," pp. 3, 7.

57 Jan Herman Burgers and Hans Danielius, *The United Nations Convention Against Torture* (Dordrecht, Netherlands: Martinus Nijhoff, 1998), p. 41.

58 "By the Numbers," p. 7.

59 Interview with Armando Spataro, Rome, Italy, October 14, 2008. For this and more enriching detail about Spataro's background and indictments against the CIA, see Steven Hendricks, *A Kidnapping in Milan: The CIA on Trial* (New York: W. W. Norton & Company, 2010).

60 Prologue, *Nunca Más: The Report of the Argentine National Commission on the Disappeared* (New York: Farrar, Straus & Giroux, 1986), p. 1.

61 Interview with Armando Spataro, Rome, Italy, October 14, 2008.

62 Quoted in the *New York Times*, November 5, 2009.

63 Rachel Donadio, "Italy Convicts 23 Americans for CIA Renditions," *New York Times*, November 4, 2009.

64 Quoted in Hendricks, *A Kidnapping in Milan*, pp. 271–73.

65 Interview with Michael Ratner and Jeanne Sulzer by Juan Gonzalez, Information Clearing House, www.informationclearinghouse.info/article18633.html.

66 Marlise Simons, "Spanish Court Weighs Inquiry on Torture for 6 Bush-Era Officials," *New York Times*, March 28, 2009.

67 Kai Ambos, "Prosecuting Guantánamo in Europe: Can and Shall the Masterminds of the Torture Memos Be Held Criminally Responsible on the Basis of Universal Jurisdiction?" *Case Western Research Journal of International Law* 42 (2009); www .case.edu/orgs/jil/vol.42.1.2/42_Ambos.pdf.

68 Dapo Akande, "George Bush Cancels Visit to Switzerland as Human Rights Groups Call for his Arrest," *EJIL: Talk!* (blog of the *European Journal of International Law*), February 6, 2011; http://www.ejiltalk.org/george-bush-cancels-visit-to-switzerland-as-human-rights-groups-call-for-his-arrest/.

69 Quoted in the *New York Times*, October 26, 2007.

70 "Terror-War Fallout Lingers Over Bush Lawyers," *New York Times*, March 9, 2009, p. A13.

71 Quoted in R. Jeffrey Smith, "Detainee Abuse Charges Feared," *The Washington Post*, July 28, 2006, p. A1.

72 Scott Horton, interview with Jane Mayer, *Harper's* magazine, July 14, 2008, www .harpers.org/archive/2008/07/hbc-90003234.

73 "No Price to Pay for Torture," *New York Times*, June 16, 2010, p. A30.

Part IV
Chapter 8: Policy, Theory, and the Justice Cascade

 1 I'm indebted to the work of colleagues who have also charted such an approach: Michael Barnett, *Eyewitness to Genocide: The United Nations and Rwanda* (Ithaca, NY: Cornell University Press, 2002); Joseph Nye, *Nuclear Ethics* (New York: Free Press, 1986); and J. L Holzgrefe and Robert O. Keohane, eds., *Humanitarian Intervention: Ethical, Legal, and Political Dilemmas* (Cambridge, UK: Cambridge University Press, 2003).

 2 See Richard Price, ed., *Moral Limit and Possibility in World Politics* (Cambridge, UK: Cambridge University Press, 2008); and Richard Price, "Moral Limit and Possibility in World Politics," *International Organization* 62, no. 2 (2008).

 3 See Jack Snyder and Leslie Vinjamuri, "Trials and Errors: Principle and Pragmatism in Strategies of International Justice," *International Security* 28, no. 3 (Winter 2004).

 4 Quoted in Tina Rosenberg, "Overcoming the Legacies of Dictatorship," *Foreign Affairs* (May–June 1995), p. 134.

 5 See Michael Barnett and Raymond Duvall, "Power in International Politics," *International Organization* 59 (Winter 2005), p. 53. They write: "Scholars focusing on structural power conceive structure as an internal relation—that is, a direct constitution relations such that the structural position, A, exists only by virtue of its relation to structural position, B. The classic examples here are master-slave and capital-labor relations. From this perspective, the kinds of social beings that are mutually constituted are directly or internally related; that is, the social relational capacities, subjectivities, and interests of actors are directly shaped by the social positions that they occupy."

 6 Stephen D. Krasner, *Sovereignty: Organized Hypocrisy* (Princeton: Princeton University Press, 1999).

 7 Some versions of dependency theory made this argument, as did theories of "bureaucratic authoritarianism." Noam Chomsky and Edward Herman have made and continue to make this argument today.

 8 Snyder and Vinjamuri, "Trials and Errors," pp. 5–44, and Leslie Vinjamuri and Jack Snyder, "Advocacy and Scholarship in the Study of International War Crimes Tribunals and Transitional Justice," *Annual Review of Political Science* 7 (May 2004), pp. 345–62.

 9 The list of countries that have not ratified at least one of the three core treaties reads more like an inventory of small island countries with scarce state capacity than a coherent movement against the practice of individual accountability.

10 On this issue, see Judith Kelly, "Who Keeps International Commitments and Why?

The International Criminal Court and Bilateral Non-surrender Agreements," *American Political Science Review* 101, no. 3 (August 2007), pp. 573–89.

11 Interview with Silvia Fernández, Buenos Aires, Argentina, December 11, 2002.

12 On two-level games, see Robert D. Putnam, "Diplomacy and Domestic Politics: The Logic of Two-Level Games," *International Organization* 42 (Summer 1988), pp. 427–60; Lisa Martin and Kathryn Sikkink, "U.S. Policy and Human Rights in Argentina and Guatemala, 1973–1980," in Peter Evans, Harold Jacobson, and Robert Putnam, eds., *Double-Edged Diplomacy: International Bargaining and Domestic Politics* (Berkeley: University of California Press, 1993), pp. 330–62.

13 "Brazil Military Downplays Role in Condor Killings," Reuters, January 4, 2008; www.reuters.com/article/latestCrisis/idUSN04288185, accessed August 14, 2008.

14 My observation, based on interviews and field research in Brazil, August 2008.

15 See, e.g., Lisa Hilbink, *Judges Beyond Politics in Democracy and Dictatorship: Lessons from Chile* (New York: Cambridge University Press, 2007).

16 This is similar to a point that Mattli and Slaughter make about the role of individual litigants in the EU. See Walter Mattli and Anne-Marie Slaughter, "Revisiting the European Court of Justice," *International Organization* 52, no. 1 (1988), p. 186.

17 Martha Finnemore and Kathryn Sikkink, "International Norm Dynamics and Political Change," *International Organization* 52, no. 4 (1998).

18 See Peter Katzenstein, *Cultural Norms and National Security: Police and Military in Postwar Japan* (Ithaca, NY: Cornell University Press, 1996); Ann Florini, "The Evolution of International Norms," *International Studies Quarterly* 40, no. 3 (1996); David H. Lumsdaine, *Moral Vision in International Politics: The Foreign Aid Regime* (Princeton: Princeton University Press, 1993); and Finnemore and Sikkink, "International Norm Dynamics," p. 906.

19 Gary Bass, *Stay the Hand of Justice: The Politics of War Crimes Tribunals* (Princeton: Princeton University Press, 2000), p. 12.

20 Ibid., p. 14.

21 This metaphor draws on the diffusion literature on the United States, which talks about the states as "laboratories of democracy."

22 This argument is related to that of some studies of diffusion among the American states, which find that both some internal determinants and external diffusion matter for policy adoption—Dorothy Daley and James Garand, "Horizontal Diffusion, Vertical Diffusion, and Internal Pressure in State Environmental Policymaking," *American Politics Research* 33, no. 5 (2005).

23 Samuel Huntington, *The Third Wave: Democratization in the Late Twentieth Century* (Norman: University of Oklahoma Press, 1991).

24 Hunjoon Kim, "Why and When Do States Use Human Rights Trials and Truth Commissions After Transition? An Event History Analysis of 100 Countries Covering 1974–2004," unpublished manuscript, 2007.

25 This is similar to processes found in diffusion in the America states, where both determinants internal to the states and external diffusion are part of the explanation for policy change. See, e.g., Daley and Garand, "Horizontal Diffusion, Vertical Diffusion, and Internal Pressure in State Environmental Policymaking."

26 Erin Graham, Charles Shipan, and Craig Volden, "The Diffusion of Policy Diffusion

Research," unpublished manuscript, December 2008; Daley and Garand, "Horizontal Diffusion, Vertical Diffusion, and Internal Pressure in State Environmental Policymaking."

27 I am indebted to Sidney Tarrow and Andrew Karch for drawing my attention to literatures on horizontal and vertical diffusion.

28 There are, however, some important exceptions. I have learned a great deal from the work of Naomi Roht-Arriaza and Ellen Lutz, among others. See, e.g., Naomi Roht-Arriaza, *The Pinochet Effect: International Justice in the Age of Human Rights* (Philadelphia: University of Pennsylvania Press, 2005), and Ellen Lutz and Caitlin Reiger, eds., *Prosecuting Heads of State* (New York: Cambridge University Press, 2009).

29 See Emanuel Adler and Michael Barnett, eds., *Security Communities* (Cambridge, UK: Cambridge University Press, 1998), and Peter J. Katzenstein, *A World of Regions: Asia and Europe in the American Imperium*, Cornell Studies in Political Economy (Ithaca, NY: Cornell University Press, 2005).

30 Beth Simmons, *Mobilizing for Human Rights: International Law in Domestic Politics* (New York: Cambridge University Press, 2009).

31 To say the model was "appealing" worldwide does not mean that it was escaped widespread criticism. In fact, various critiques emerged and solidified around the practices of the South African Truth and Reconciliation Commission. For a comprehensive and insightful historical review of these criticisms, see Madeleine Fullard and Nicky Rousseau, "Uncertain Borders: The TRC and the (Un)making of Public Myths," *Kronos* 34 (November 2008), pp. 215–39.

32 Margaret E. Keck and Kathryn Sikkink, *Activists Beyond Borders: Advocacy Networks in International Politics* (Ithaca, NY: Cornell University Press, 1998), p. 2.

33 See Graham, Shipan, and Volden, "The Diffusion of Policy Diffusion Research."

34 In this sense, the transnational justice network also has some characteristics of what political scientists call an *epistemic community*—a network of professionals engaged in a common policy enterprise with "recognized expertise and competence in the particular domain and an authoritative claim to policy relevant knowledge in that issue or domain." But unlike what the epistemic community literature leads us to expect, states did not turn to the transnational justice network in situations of complexity and uncertainty for information to help them understand the situation and their interests—Peter Haas, "Introduction: Epistemic Communities and International Policy Coordination," *International Organization* 46 (1992), p. 3.

35 Anne-Marie Slaughter, *A New World Order* (Princeton: Princeton University Press, 2004).

36 Kim, "Why and When Do States Use Human Rights Trials and Truth Commissions after Transition?"

37 See in the Bibliography, e.g., Odell (1982), Kowert and Legro (1996), and McNamara (1998).

38 See Donald E. Brown, "Human Universals, Human Nature and Human Culture," *Daedalus* 133, no. 4 (2004).

39 Steven Pinker, "The Moral Instinct," *New York Times Magazine*, January 13, 2008.

40 David S. Weissbrodt, *The Right to a Fair Trial Under the Universal Declaration of Human Rights and the International Covenant on Civil and Political Rights: Back-*

ground, Development, and Interpretations (Cambridge, MA: Martinus Nijhoff, 2001).

41 Thomas Risse, Stephen Ropp, and Kathryn Sikkink, eds., *The Power of Human Rights: International Norms and Domestic Change* (Cambridge, UK: Cambridge University Press, 1999).

42 Kathryn Sikkink, *Mixed Signals: U.S. Human Rights Policy and Latin America* (Ithaca, NY: Cornell University Press, 2004).

43 David Mendeloff, "Truth-Seeking, Truth-Telling, and Postconflict Peacebuilding: Curb the Enthusiasm?" *International Studies Review* 6, no. 3 (2004).

44 See Laura Arriaza and Naomi Roht-Arriaza, "Social Reconstruction as a Local Process," *International Journal of Transitional Justice* 2, no. 2 (July 2008).

45 This approach is similar to what Peter Katzenstein and Rudra Sil have called "eclectic theorizing"—"Eclectic Theorizing in the Study and Practice of International Relations," in *The Oxford Handbook of International Relations* (New York: Oxford University Press, 2008).

46 "Argentianian judge petitions Spain to try civil war crimes of Franco," guardian .co.uk, October 26, 2010; www.guardian.co.uk/world/2010/oct/26/argentina-spain-general-franco-judge.

BIBLIOGRAPHY

Acuña, Carlos. "Transitional Justice in Argentina and Chile: A Never-Ending Story?" in Jon Elster, ed., *Retribution and Reparation in the Transition to Democracy*. New York: Cambridge University Press, 2006.

———, Inés González Bombal, Elizabeth Jelin, Oscar Landi, Luis Alberto Quevedo, Catalina Smulovitz, and Adriana Vacchieri. *Juicio, Castigos y Memorias: Derechos Humanos y Justicia en la Política Argentina*. Buenos Aires: Nueva Visión, 1995.

Acuña, Carlos, and Catalina Smulovitz. "Guarding the Guardians in Argentina: Some Lessons About the Risks and Benefits of Empowering the Courts," in A. James McAdams, ed., *Transitional Justice and the Rule of Law in New Democracies*. Notre Dame, IN: University of Notre Dame Press, 1997.

———. "Adjusting the Armed Forces to Democracy: Successes, Failures, and Ambiguities in the Southern Cone," in Elizabeth Jelin and Eric Hersberg, eds., *Constructing Democracy: Human Rights, Citizenship, and Democracy in Latin America*. Boulder, CO: Westview Press, 1996.

Adler, Emanuel, and Michael Barnett, eds. *Security Communities*. Cambridge, UK: Cambridge University Press, 1998.

Akande, Dapo. "George Bush Cancels Visit to Switzerland as Human Rights Groups Call for his Arrest," *EJIL: Talk!* (blog of the *European Journal of International Law*), February 6, 2011; http://www.ejiltalk.org/george-bush-cancels-visit-to-switzerland-as-human-rights-groups-call-for-his-arrest/.

Akhaven, Payam, "Are International Criminal Tribunals a Disincentive to Peace?: Reconciling Judicial Romanticism with Political Realism," *Human Rights Quarterly* 31 (2009): 624–54.

———. "Beyond Impunity: Can International Criminal Justice Prevent Future Atrocities?" *American Journal of International Law* 95, no. 1 (2001): 7–31.

Alfonsín, Raúl. *Democracia y Consenso*. Buenos Aires: Ediciones Corregidor, 1996.

———. *Inedito: Una Batalla Contra la Dictadura: 1966–1972*. Buenos Aires: Editorial Legasa, 1986.

Alivizatos, Nicos. *Les Institutions Politiques de la Grèce à Travers les Crises 1922–1974*. Paris: Librairie Générale de Droit et de Jurisprudence, 1979.

———, and P. Nikiforos Diamandouros. "Politics and the Judiciary in the Greek Transition to Democracy," in A. James McAdams, ed., *Transitional Justice and the Rule of Law in New Democracies*. Notre Dame, IN: University of Notre Dame Press, 1997.

Ambos, Kai. "Prosecuting Guantánamo in Europe: Can and Shall the Masterminds of the Torture Memos Be Held Criminally Responsible on the Basis of Universal Jurisdiction?" *Case Western Research Journal of International Law*, 42 (2009); http://www.case.edu/orgs/jil/vol.42.1.2/42_Ambos.pdf.

Amnesty International. "Torture in Greece," reprinted in *Hellenic Review* (1968): 22.

———. "Amnesty International Conference for the Abolition of Torture: Final Report." Paris, December 10–11, 1973.

———. "Publicity for Greek Report," Internal memo dated April 19, 1977.

———. *Torture in Greece: The First Torturers' Trial 1975*. London: Amnesty International, 1977.

———. "Common Article III of the Geneva Conventions," http://www.amnestyusa.org/war-on-terror/torture/common-article-iii-of-the-geneva-conventions/page.do?id=1351086. Accessed June 28, 2010.

Andenaes, Johannes. *Punishment and Deterrence*. Ann Arbor: University of Michigan Press, 1974.

Arendt, Hannah. *Eichmann in Jerusalem: A Report on the Banality of Evil* (1963). New York: Penguin, 1994.

Barahona de Brito, Alexandra, Carmen Gonzalez-Enriquez, and Paloma Aguilar, eds. *The Politics of Memory: Transitional Justice in Democratizing Societies*. Oxford: Oxford University Press, 2001.

Barnett, Michael. *Eyewitness to Genocide: The United Nations and Rwanda*. Ithaca, NY: Cornell University Press, 2002.

———, and Raymond Duvall. "Power in International Politics," *International Organization* 59, no. 1 (2005): 39–75.

Bass, Gary. *Stay the Hand of Vengeance*. Princeton: Princeton University Press, 2000.

Bassiouni, M. Cherif. *International Criminal Law: International Enforcement*. 3rd ed. Vol. 3. Dordrecht, Netherlands: Martinus Nijhoff, 2008.

———. *The Legislative History of the International Criminal Court. Vol. I: Introduction, Analysis, and Integrated Text of the Statute, Elements of Crimes and Rules of Procedure and Evidence*. Ardsley, NY: Transnational Publishers, 2005.

———, and Peter Manikas. *The Law of the International Criminal Tribunal for the Former Yugoslavia*. Irvington-on-Hudson, NY: Transnational Publishers, 1996.

Becu, Nuria. "El Filósofo y el Político: Consideraciones Morales y Políticas en el Tratamiento a los Autores de Crímenes de Lesa Humanidad Bajo la Presidencia de Raúl Alfonsín (1983–1989)," Universidad Torcuato de Tella, Departamento de Ciencias Politicas, 2004.

Beddard, Ralph. *Human Rights and Europe*. London: Sweet & Maxwell, 1980.

Blumstein, Alfred, Jacqueline Cohen, and Daniel Nagin, eds. *Deterrence and Incapacitation: Estimating the Effects of Criminal Sanctions on Crime Rates*. Panel on Research on

Deterrent and Incapacitative Effects, National Research Council. Washington, DC: National Academy of Sciences, 1978.

Bordaberry, Juan Maria. "Documentos: Para el Juicio de la Historia," end of the year speech cited in *Brecha*, October 20, 2006, p. 5, translation by the author.

Branch, Adam. "Uganda's Civil War and the Politics of ICC Intervention," *Ethics and International Affairs* 21, no. 2 (2007): 179–98.

Brienen, M. E. I., and E. H. Hoegen. "Victims of Crime in 22 European Justice Systems: The Implementation of Recommendation (85) 11 of the Council of Europe on the Position of the Victim in the Framework of Criminal Law and Procedure." Dissertation, University of Tilburg. Nijmegen, the Netherlands: Wolf Legal Productions, 2000.

Broomhall, Bruce. *International Justice and the International Criminal Court: Between Sovereignty and the Rule of Law*. Oxford: Oxford University Press, 2003.

Brown, Donald E. "Human Universals, Human Nature and Human Culture," *Daedalus* 133, no. 4 (2004): 47–54.

Brysk, Alison. *The Politics of Human Rights in Argentina: Protest, Change, and Democratization*. Stanford, CA: Stanford University Press, 1994.

Burgers, Jan Herman, and Hans Danelius, *The United Nations Convention against Torture: A Handbook on the Convention against Torture and Other Cruel, Inhuman or Degrading Treatment or Punishment*. Dordrecht, the Netherlands: Martinus Nijhoff, 1988.

"By the Numbers: Findings of the Detainee Abuse and Accountability Project," Human Rights and Global Justice, Human Rights First, and Human Rights Watch, 2006; http://www.chrgj.org/docs/Press%20Release%20-%20By%20The%20Numbers.pdf.

Caldeira, Teres P. R. "Crime and Individual Rights: Reframing the Question of Violence in Latin America," in Elizabeth Jelin and Eric Hershberg, eds., *Constructing Democracy*. Boulder, CO: Westview Press, 1996.

Call, Charles. "Is Transitional Justice Really Just?" *Brown Journal of World Affairs* 11, no. 1 (2004): 101–13.

Carothers, Thomas. "The Many Agendas of Rule of Law Reform in Latin America," in Pilar Domingo and Rachel Sieder, eds., *Rule of Law in Latin America: The International Promotion of Judicial Reform*. London: University of London, 2001.

"Carta de Wilson Ferreira Aldunate a Jorge Rafael Videla," Buenos Aires, May 24, 1976, reprinted in *Brecha*, "Documentos: Para el Juicio de la Historia," October 20, 2006, pp. 31–39. Translation by the author.

Cavallo, Gabriel. "Resolución del Juez Gabriel Cavallo," *Juzgado Federal* 4. Caso Poblete-Hlaczik, March 6, 2001.

Chayes, Abram, and Antonia Handler Chayes. *The New Sovereignty: Compliance with International Regulatory Agreements*. Cambridge, MA: Harvard University Press, 1995.

Cingranelli, David R., and David L. Richards. *The Cingranelli-Richards (CIRI) Human Rights Database Coder Manual*, 2004.

Clark, Ann Marie. *Diplomacy of Conscience: Amnesty International and Changing Human Rights Norms*. Princeton: Princeton University Press, 2001.

Clark, Ian. *Globalization and International Relations Theory*. Oxford: Oxford University Press, 1999.

Cobban, Helena. "Think Again: International Courts," *Foreign Policy* (March–April 2006).

Comisión Nacional Sobre la Desaparición de Personas (CONADEP). *Nunca Más: Informe de la Comisión Nacional Sobre la Desaparición de Personas.* Buenos Aires: Editorial Universitaria, 1984.

———. *Nunca Más: The Report of the Argentine National Commission of the Disappeared* (English edn.). New York: Farrar, Straus & Giroux, 1986.

"Como se Preparó la Acusación," *Diario del Juicio* 1, May 27, 1985.

Congressional Record, U.S. Senate, October 27, 1990, p. S17491.

Conte, Augusto. Unpublished memo to the Permanent Assembly for Human Rights, CELS Library, Buenos Aires, March 3, 1980. Translation by the author.

Costa Pinto, Antonio. "Authoritarian Legacies, Transitional Justice and State Crisis in Portugal's Democratization," *Democratization* 13, no. 2 (2006): 173–204.

———. "The Radical Right in Contemporary Portugal," in Luciano Cheles, Ronnie Ferguson, and Michalina Vaughan, eds., *Neo-Fascism in Europe.* London and New York: Longman, 1991.

Council of Europe, European Commission on Human Rights. *The Greek Case, Report of the Commission.* Strasbourg, 1970.

Crenzel, Emilio Ariel, "Génesis, Usos y Resignificaciones del *Nunca Más:* La Memoria de las Desapariciones en Argentina." PhD thesis, Faculty of Social Sciences, University of Buenos Aires, 2006.

Cullen, Brig. Gen. James. Statement at press conference by Human Rights First and Retired Military Leaders, January 4, 2005; audio at www.humanrightsfirst.org. Transcription of remarks by the author.

Daley, Dorothy, and James Garand. "Horizontal Diffusion, Vertical Diffusion, and Internal Pressure in State Environmental Policymaking," *American Politics Research* 33, no. 5 (2005): 615–44.

Danner, Mark. *Torture and Truth: America, Abu Ghraib, and the War on Terror.* New York: New York Review of Books, 2004.

Davenport, Christian. *State Repression and the Domestic Democratic Peace.* New York: Cambridge University Press, 2007.

Diamond, Larry. *The Spirit of Democracy: The Struggle to Build Free Societies Throughout the World.* New York: Holt Publishers, 2009.

Della Porta, Donatella, and Sidney Tarrow, eds. *Transnational Protest and Global Activism.* Lanham, MD: Rowman & Littlefield, 2005.

di Candia, César. "Angustias y Tensiones de Tres Políticos Uruguayos Condenados a Muerte," reprinted from "Qué Pasa," supplement of *El País*, November 13, 2004, in *Brecha*, "Documentos: Para el Juicio de la Historia," October 20, 2006, pp. 7–8. Translation by the author.

Dickenson, Laura. "Accountability for War Crimes: What Role for National, International and Hybrid Tribunals?" *American Society for International Law Proceedings* (2004).

Domingo, Pilar, and Rachel Sieder, eds. *Rule of Law in Latin America: The International Promotion of Judicial Reform.* London: University of London Press, 2001.

Downs, George W., David M. Rocke, and Peter N. Barsoom. "Is the Good News about Compliance Good News about Cooperation?" *International Organization* 50, no. 3 (1996): 379–406.

Drumbl, Mark. *Atrocity, Punishment, and International Law*. New York: Cambridge University Press, 2007.

Dykmann, Klaas. *Philanthropic Endeavors or the Exploitation of an Ideal? The Human Rights Policy of the Organization of American States in Latin America (1970–1991)*. Frankfurt: Vervuert Verlag, 2004.

Elster, Jon. *Closing the Books: Transitional Justice in Historical Perspective*. New York: Cambridge University Press, 2004.

Farer, Tom. "The Rise of the Inter-American Human Rights Regime: No Longer a Unicorn, Not Yet an Ox," *Human Rights Quarterly* 19, no. 3 (1997): 510–46.

Federal Bureau of Investigation, Criminal Justice Information Services, "E-mail from REDACTED to Gary Bald, Frankie Battle, Arthur Cummings Re: FWD: Impersonating FBI Agents at GITMO," December 5, 2003, at www.aclu.org/torturefoia/released/122004.html.

Feeley, Malcolm. *The Process Is the Punishment: Handling Cases in a Lower Criminal Court*. New York: Russell Sage Foundation, 1979.

Filártiga v. Peña-Irala, 630 F. 2d 876, 890 (2d Cir. 1980).

Filippini, Leonardo. "Truth Trials in Argentina." Unpublished manuscript, 2005.

Finnemore, Martha, and Kathryn Sikkink. "Taking Stock: The Constructivist Research Program in International Relations and Comparative Politics," *Annual Review of Political Science* 4 (2001): 391–416.

———. "International Norm Dynamics and Political Change," *International Organization* 52, no. 4 (1998): 887–917.

Fletcher, Laurel, Harvey M. Weinstein, and Jamie Rowen. "Context, Timing, and the Dynamics of Transitional Justice: A Historical Perspective," *Human Rights Quarterly* 31 (2009): 163–220.

Florini, Ann. "The Evolution of International Norms," *International Studies Quarterly* 40, no. 3 (1996): 363–89.

Fukuyama, Francis. *America at the Crossroads: Democracy, Power, and the Neoconservative Legacy*. New Haven: Yale University Press, 2006.

Fullard, Madeleine, and Nicky Rousseau. "Uncertain Borders: The TRC and the (Un)making of Public Myths," *Kronos* 34 (November 2008): 215–39.

Gellman, Barton. *Angler: The Cheney Vice Presidency*. New York: Penguin, 2008.

Georgakas, Dan. "Two Greek Commentaries," *Chicago Review* 12, no. 2 (1969): 109–14.

Gibney, Mark, and Matthew Dalton. "The Political Terror Scale," *Policy Studies and Developing Nations* 4 (1996): 73–84.

Gladwell, Malcolm. *The Tipping Point: How Little Things Can Make a Big Difference*. New York: Little, Brown, 2000.

Gleditsch, Kristian Skrede, and Michael D. Ward. "Diffusion and the International Context of Democratization," *International Organization* 60, no. 4 (2006): 911–33.

Glendon, Mary Ann. "The Forgotten Crucible: The Latin American Influence on the Universal Declaration of Human Rights Idea," *Harvard Human Rights Journal* 16 (2003): 27–39.

———. *A World Made New: Eleanor Roosevelt and the Universal Declaration of Human Rights*. New York: Random House, 1999.

Goldsmith, Jack. *The Terror Presidency: Law and Judgment Inside the Bush Administration*. New York: W. W. Norton & Company, 2007.

————, and Stephen D. Krasner. "The Limits of Idealism," *Daedalus* 132 (Winter 2003): 47–63.

Goldstone, Richard. *For Humanity: Reflections of a War Crimes Investigator.* New Haven: Yale University Press, 2000.

Goodman, Ryan, and Derek Jinks. "How to Influence States: Socialization and International Human Rights Law," *Duke Law Journal* 54 (2004): 621–703.

————. *Socializing States: Promoting Human Rights Through International Law.* New York: Oxford University Press (forthcoming).

Graham, Erin, Charles Shipan, and Craig Volden. "The Diffusion of Policy Diffusion Research." Unpublished manuscript, December 2008.

Grant, Ruth, and Robert O. Keohane. "Accountability and Abuses of Power in World Politics," *American Political Science Review* 99, no. 1 (2005): 29–43.

de Greiff, Pablo, "Vetting and Transitional Justice," in Alexander Mayer-Rieckh and Pablo de Greiff, eds., *Justice as Prevention: Vetting of Public Employees in Transitional Societies.* New York: International Center for Transitional Justice, Social Science Research Council, 2007.

"Guatemala Massacre Survivors Use Memorial Quilt to Seek Reparations," AdvocacyNet, News Bulletin 174 (January 28, 2009); http://www.advocacynet.org/resource/1228.

Guembe, María José. "Economic Reparations for Grave Human Rights Violations: The Argentinean Experience," in Pablo de Greiff, ed., *The Handbook of Reparations.* New York: Oxford University Press, 2006.

Guest, Iain. *Behind the Disappearances: Argentina's Dirty War Against Human Rights and the United Nations.* Philadelphia: University of Pennsylvania Press, 1990.

Haas, Peter M. "Introduction: Epistemic Communities and International Policy Coordination," *International Organization* 46, no. 1 (1992): 1–35.

Hagan, John. *Justice in the Balkans: Prosecuting War Crimes in the Hague Tribunal.* Chicago: University of Chicago Press, 2003.

Hammarberg, Thomas. "The Greek Case Became a Defining Lesson for Human Rights Policies in Europe." Council of Europe Commissioner for Human Rights, www.commissioner.coe.int.

Hathaway, Oona A. "The Cost of Commitment," *Stanford Law Review* 55, no. 5 (2003): 1821–62.

Hendricks, Steven. *A Kidnapping in Milan: The CIA on Trial.* New York: W. W. Norton & Company, 2010.

Hilbink, Elisabeth. *Judges Beyond Politics in Democracy and Dictatorship: Lessons from Chile.* New York: Cambridge University Press, 2007.

Holston, James. *Insurgent Citizenship: Disjunctions of Democracy and Modernity in Brazil.* Princeton: Princeton University Press, 2007.

Holzgrefe, J. L. and Robert O. Keohane, eds. *Humanitarian Intervention: Ethical, Legal, and Political Dilemmas.* Cambridge, UK: Cambridge University Press, 2003.

Horton, Scott. "The Guantánamo 'Suicides': A Camp Delta sergeant blows the whistle," *Harper's* magazine, January 18, 2010; online at www.harpers.org/archive/2010/01/hbc-90006368.

Huckerby, Jayne, and Nigel Rodley. "Outlawing Torture: The Story of Amnesty International's Efforts to Shape the UN Convention against Torture," in Deena Hurwitz,

Margaret L. Satterthwaite, and Douglas B. Ford, eds., *Human Rights Advocacy Stories*. New York: Foundation Press, Thomson/West, 2009.

Huntington, Samuel. *The Third Wave: Democratization in the Late Twentieth Century*. Norman: University of Oklahoma Press, 1991.

Ingelse, Chris. *The UN Committee against Torture: An Assessment*. The Hague: Martinus Nijhoff, 2001.

Jaffer, Jameel, and Amrit Singh. *Administration of Torture: A Documentary Record from Washington to Abu Ghraib and Beyond*. New York: Columbia University Press, 2007.

Jelin, Elizabeth. *State Repression and the Struggle for Memories*. London: Social Science Research Council, 2003.

———. "La Política de la Memoria, el Movimiento de Derechos Humanos y las Construcción Democrática en la Argentina," in Acuña et al., eds., *Juicio, Castigo y Memoria: Derechos Humanos y Justicia en la Política Argentina*.

———, and Susana G. Kaufman. "Layers of Memory: Twenty Years After in Argentina," in Dawson Graham, T. G. Dawson, and Michael Roper, eds., *The Politics of War Memory and Commemoration*. London: Routledge, 2000.

"Jobim contesta Tarso e diz que não cabe ao Executivo discutir anistia," *Estado de São Paulo*, August 2, 2008.

Kaleck, Wolfgang. "From Pinochet to Rumsfeld: Universal Jurisdiction in Europe 1998–2008," *Michigan Journal of International Law* 30 (2009): 927–80.

Katzenstein, Peter. *A World of Regions: Asia and Europe in the American Imperium*. Ithaca, NY: Cornell University Press, 2005.

———. *Cultural Norms and National Security: Police and Military in Postwar Japan*. Ithaca: Cornell University Press, 1996.

———, ed. *Civilizations in World Politics: Plural and Pluralist Perspectives*. New York: Routledge, 2010.

———, ed. *The Culture of National Security: Norms and Identity in World Politics*. New York: Columbia University Press, 1996.

———, and Rudra Sil. "Eclectic Theorizing in the Study and Practice of International Relations," in Christian Reus-Smit and Duncan Snidal, eds., *The Oxford Handbook of International Relations*. New York: Oxford University Press, 2008.

Kaye, David. "The Torture Commission We Really Need," *Foreign Policy* (March–April 2010).

Keck, Margaret E., and Kathryn Sikkink. *Activists Beyond Borders: Advocacy Networks in International Politics*. Ithaca, NY: Cornell University Press, 1998.

Kelly, Judith. "Who Keeps International Commitments and Why? The International Criminal Court and Bilateral Non-Surrender Agreements," *American Political Science Review* 101, no. 3 (August 2007): 573–89.

Keohane, Robert O., Andrew Moravcsik, and Anne-Marie Slaughter. "Legalized Dispute Resolution: Interstate and Transnational," *International Organization* 54, no. 3 (2000): 457–88.

Kim, Hunjoon. "Expansion of Transitional Justice Measures: A Comparative Analysis of Its Causes." PhD diss., University of Minnesota, 2008.

———. "Why and When Do States Use Human Rights Trials and Truth Commissions

After Transition? An Event History Analysis of 100 Countries Covering 1974–2004." Unpublished manuscript, Minneapolis, MN, 2007.

——, and Kathryn Sikkink. "Explaining the Deterrence Effect of Human Rights Prosecutions for Transitional Countries," *International Studies Quarterly* 54, no. 4 (December 2010): 939–63.

Kingsbury, Benedict. "The Concept of Compliance as a Function of Competing Conceptions of International Law," *Michigan Journal of International Law* 19, no. 2 (1998): 49–80.

Koh, Harold. "Transnational Legal Order," *Nebraska Law Review* 75 (1996): 181–207.

Kornbluh, Peter. *The Pinochet File: A Declassified Dossier on Atrocity and Accountability.* New York: New Press, 2003.

Kowert, Paul, and Jeffrey Legro. "Norms, Identity, and Their Limits: A Theoretical Reprise," in Katzenstein, ed., *The Culture of National Security.*

Krasner, Stephen D. "A World Court that Could Backfire," *New York Times*, January 15, 2001, p. A15, final edition.

——. *Sovereignty: Organized Hypocrisy.* Princeton: Princeton University Press, 1999.

Krisch, Nico, and Benedict Kingsbury. "Introduction: Global Governance and Global Administrative Law in the International Legal Order," *European Journal of International Law* 17, no. 1 (2006): 1–13.

Ku, Julian, and Jide Nzelibe. "Do International Criminal Tribunals Deter or Exacerbate Humanitarian Atrocities?" *Washington University Law Quarterly* 84, no. 4 (2006): 777–833.

Landi, Oscar, and Inés González Bombal. "Los Derechos en la Cultura Política," in Acuña et al. eds. *Juicio, Castigo y Memoria: Derechos Humanos y Justicia en la Política Argentina.*

Legro, Jeffrey. *Rethinking the World: Great Power Strategies and International Order.* Ithaca, NY: Cornell University Press, 2005.

Leonard, Eric K. *The Onset of Global Governance: International Relations Theory and the International Criminal Court.* Aldershot, UK, and Burlington, NJ: Ashgate Publishing, 2005.

"Los Testigos Claves según Strassera," *Diario del Juicio* 3, June 11, 1985.

Loveman, Brian. *For la Patria: Politics and the Armed Forces in Latin America.* Wilmington, DE: Scholarly Resources, 1999.

Lumsdaine, David Halloran. *Moral Vision in International Politics: The Foreign Aid Regime, 1949–1989.* Princeton: Princeton University Press, 1993.

Lutz, Ellen, and Kathryn Sikkink. "International Human Rights Law and Practice in Latin America," *International Organization* 54, no. 3 (2000): 633–59.

——. "The Justice Cascade: The Evolution and Impact of Foreign Human Rights Trials in Latin America," *Chicago Journal of International Law* 2, no. 1 (2001): 1–33.

Lutz, Ellen L., and Caitlin Reiger, eds. *Prosecuting Heads of State.* New York: Cambridge University Press, 2009.

Macedo, Stephen, ed. *Universal Jurisdiction: National Courts and the Prosecution of Serious Crimes Under International Law.* Philadelphia: University of Pennsylvania Press, 2004.

Mainwaring, Scott, and Aníbal Pérez-Liñán. *The Emergence and Fall of Democracies and*

Dictatorships: Latin America Since 1900. Cambridge: Cambridge University Press, forthcoming.

Manuel, Paul. *Uncertain Outcome: The Politics of the Portuguese Transition to Democracy.* New York: University Press of America, 1994.

Martin, Lisa, and Kathryn Sikkink. "U.S. Policy and Human Rights in Argentina and Guatemala, 1973–1980," in Peter Evans, Harold Jacobson, and Robert Putnam, eds., *Double-Edged Diplomacy: International Bargaining and Domestic Politics.* Berkeley: University of California Press, 1993.

Mateus, Dalila Cabrita. *A PIDE/DGS na Guerra Colonial (1962–1974).* Lisbon: Terramar, 2004.

Matsueda, Ross, David Huizinga, and Derek Kreager. "Deterring Delinquents: A Rational Choice Model of Theft and Violence," *American Sociological Review* 71 (February 2006): 95–122.

Mattli, Walter, and Anne-Marie Slaughter. "Revisiting the European Court of Justice," *International Organization* 52, no. 1 (1998): 177–209.

Mayer, Jane. *The Dark Side: The Inside Story of How the War on Terror Turned into a War on American Ideals.* New York: Doubleday, 2008.

Mayorga, Rene Antonio. "Democracy Dignified and an End to Impunity: Bolivia's Military Dictatorship on Trial," in A. James McAdams, ed., *Transitional Justice and the Rule of Law in New Democracies.* Notre Dame, IN: University of Notre Dame Press, 1997.

McAdams, A. James, ed. *Transitional Justice and the Rule of Law in New Democracies.* Notre Dame, IN: University of Notre Dame Press, 1997.

McCarthy, Bill. "New Economics of Sociological Criminology," *Annual Review of Sociology* 28 (2002): 417–42.

McCarthy, John D., and Mayer N. Zald, "The Enduring Vitality of the Resource Mobilization Theory of Social Movements," in Jonathan H. Turner, ed., *Handbook of Sociological Theory.* New York: Springer, 2001.

McEntree, Andrew. "Law and Torture," in Duncan Forrest, ed., *A Glimpse of Hell: Reports on Torture Worldwide.* New York: New York University Press, 1996.

McNamara, Kathleen. *The Currency of Ideas: Monetary Politics in the European Union.* Ithaca, NY: Cornell University Press, 1998.

"Memorandum from Secretary of State Colin Powell to Counsel to the President, Re: Draft Decision Memorandum for the President on the Applicability of the Geneva Convention to the Conflict in Afghanistan," available at www.humanrightsfirst.org/us_law/etn/gonzales/index.asp#memos.

Mendeloff, David. "Truth-Seeking, Truth-Telling, and Postconflict Peacebuilding: Curb the Enthusiasm?" *International Studies Review* 6, no. 3 (2004): 355–80.

Méndez, Juan. "In Defense of Transitional Justice," in McAdams, ed., *Transitional Justice and Rule of Law in New Democracies.*

Mignone, Emilio F. *Derechos Humanos y Sociedad: El Caso Argentino.* Buenos Aires: Centro de Estudios Legales y Sociales, 1991.

"Militares reagem a Tarso e criticam 'passado terrorista' do governo Lula," *Estado de São Paulo,* August 4, 2008.

Minotos, Marietta, ed. *The Transition to Democracy in Spain, Portugal and Greece Thirty Years After.* Athens: Karamanlis Foundation, 2006.

Moreno-Ocampo, Luis. *Cuando el Poder Perdió el Juicio: Cómo Explicar El "Proceso" a Nuestros Hijos*. Buenos Aires: Planeta, Espejo de la Argentina, 1996.

Nagin, Daniel, ed. *Criminal Deterrence Research at the Outset of the Twenty-First Century*. Vol. 23: *Crime and Justice: A Review of Research*. Chicago: University of Chicago Press, 1998.

"Não estamos sob tutela military," Estado de São Paulo, August 9, 2008.

"Na presence do comandante do Leste, militares fazem ato contra Tarso," *Estado de São Paulo*, August 8, 2008.

Neier, Aryeh. *Taking Liberties: Four Decades in the Struggle for Rights*. New York: Public Affairs, 2003.

———. *War Crimes: Brutality, Genocide, Terror, and the Struggle for Justice*. New York: Times Books, 1998.

———. "What Should Be Done About the Guilty?" *New York Review of Books* 37, no. 1, February 1, 1990.

Nettelfield, Lara J. *Courting Democracy in Bosnia and Herzegovina: The Hague Tribunal's Impact in a Postwar State*. New York: Cambridge University Press, 2010.

Nino, Carlos. "Strategy for Criminal Law Adjudication." Unpublished PhD thesis, 1977; revised Spanish translation, "Los Límites de la Responsabilidad Penal," Buenos Aires, 1980.

———. *Radical Evil on Trial*. New Haven: Yale University Press, 1996.

Novaro, Marcos, and Vicente Palermo. *La Dictadura Militar 1976–1983: Del Golpe de Estado a la Restauración Democrática*. Buenos Aires: Paidos, 2003.

Nye, Joseph. *Nuclear Ethics*. New York: Free Press, 1986.

Nzelibe, Jide, and Julian Ku. "Do International Criminal Tribunals Deter or Exacerbate Humanitarian Atrocities?" *Washington University Law Review* 84, no. 4 (2006): 777–833.

OAS, Inter-American Commission on Human Rights. *Report on the Situation of Human Rights in Argentina*. OEA/Ser.L/V/II.49 Doc. 19, corr.1, 1980.

———. *Report on the Situation of Human Rights in Haiti*. 1979.

———. *Report on the Situation of Human Rights in El Salvador*. 1978.

———. *Third Report on the Situation of Human Rights in Chile*. 1977.

Odell, John S. *U.S. International Monetary Policy: Markets, Power, and Ideas as Sources of Change*. Princeton: Princeton University Press, 1982.

O'Donnell, Guillermo, and Philippe C. Schmitter. *Transitions from Authoritarian Rule: Tentative Conclusions about Uncertain Democracies*. Baltimore, MD: Johns Hopkins University Press, 1986.

Olsen, Tricia D., Leigh A. Payne, and Andrew G. Reiter. *Transitional Justice in the Balance: Comparing Processes, Weighing Efficacy*. Washington, DC: USIP Press, 2010.

Orentlicher, Diane F. *That Someone Guilty Be Punished: The Impact of the ICTY in Bosnia*. New York: Open Society Institute, 2010.

———. "Settling Accounts: The Duty to Prosecute Human Rights Violations of a Prior Regime," *Yale Law Journal* 100 (1990): 2537–615.

Pace, William R., and Mark Thieroff. "Participation of Non-Governmental Organizations," in Roy S. Lee, ed., *The International Criminal Court: The Making of the Rome Statute: Issues, Negotiations, Results*. The Hague: Kluwer Law International, 1999.

Partridge, Ben. "Britain: Thatcher Condemns 'Kidnap' of Pinochet," *Radio Free Europe/ Radio Liberty*, October 9, 1999.

Pasik, Boris G. Letter to Sr. Don Jaime Schmirgeld, Secretary of the Permanent Assembly for Human Rights, June 3, 1979—CELS Library, Buenos Aires. Translation by the author.

Pimentel, Irene Flunser. *A História da PIDE*. Lisbon: Círculo de Leitores, 2007.

Piniou-Kalli, Maria. "The Big Chill: 21st of April 1967—30 Years After: How Is It Possible to Forget about the Torturers?" (1997).

———. "Impunity and the Tragedy Goes On." Paper presented at the 6th International Symposium on Torture as a Challenge to the Medical and Other Health Professions, Buenos Aires, October 20–22, 1993.

Pinker, Steven. "The Moral Instinct," *New York Times Magazine*, January 13, 2008; www .nytimes.com/2008/01/13/magazine/13Psychology-t.html.

Poe, Steven C. "The Decision to Repress: An Integrative Theoretical Approach to the Research on Human Rights and Repression," in Sabine C. Carey and Steven C. Poe, eds., *Understanding Human Rights Violations: New Systematic Studies*. Burlington, VT: Ashgate Publishing, 2004.

———, Sabine C. Carey, and Tanya C. Vazquez. "How Are These Pictures Different? A Quantitative Comparison of the U.S. State Department and Amnesty International Human Rights Reports, 1976–1995," *Human Rights Quarterly* 23, no. 3 (2001): 650–77.

———, and Neal C. Tate. "Repression of Human Rights to Personal Integrity in the 1980s: A Global Analysis," *American Political Science Review* 88 (1994): 853–900.

———, Neal C. Tate, and Linda Camp Keith. "Repression of the Human Right to Personal Integrity Revisited: A Global Crossnational Study Covering the Years 1976–1993," *International Studies Quarterly* 43, no. 2 (1999): 291–315.

Power, Samantha. *A Problem from Hell: America and the Age of Genocide*. New York: Basic Books, 2002.

Price, Richard, ed. *Moral Limit and Possibility in World Politics*. Cambridge, UK: Cambridge University Press, 2008.

———. "Moral Limit and Possibility in World Politics," *International Organization* 62, no. 2 (2008): 191–220.

"Procuradoria vai denunciar militares por sequestros," *Folha de São Paolo*, January 22, 2009.

Putnam, Robert D. "Diplomacy and Domestic Politics: The Logic of Two-Level Games," *International Organization* 42 (Summer 1988): 427–60.

Raimundo, Filipa Alves. "The Double Face of Heroes: Transitional Justice Towards the Political Police (PIDE/DGS) in Portugal's Democratization, 1974–1976." MA thesis, University of Lisbon, Institute of Social Sciences, 2007.

Ratner, Michael. "The Fear of Torture: Tape Destruction or Prosecution," December 14, 2007, http://michaelratner.com/blog/?p=26.

Ratner, Steven R., and Jason S. Abrams. *Accountability for Human Rights Atrocities in*

International Law: Beyond the Nuremberg Legacy. New York: Oxford University Press, 2001.

Rawls, John. *A Theory of Justice*. Cambridge, MA: Belknap Press/Harvard University Press, 1971.

Reydams, Luc. "The Rise and Fall of Universal Jurisdiction," in William Schabas and Nadia Bernaz, eds., *Routledge Handbook of International Criminal Law*. New York: Routledge, 2010.

Risse, Thomas, Stephen Ropp, and Kathryn Sikkink, eds. *The Power of Human Rights: International Norms and Domestic Change*. Cambridge, UK: Cambridge University Press, 1999.

Roberts, Steven V. "Greece Restores 1952 Constitution with Civil Rights," *New York Times*, August 2, 1972, p. 57.

———. "Greece Sees 'Z' and Gets Excited," *New York Times*, January 13, 1975, p. 6.

———. "The Caramanlis Way," *New York Times*, November 17, 1974, p. 326.

Robertson, A. H. *Human Rights in Europe*, 2nd ed. Manchester: Manchester University Press, 1977.

———, and J. G. Merrills. *Human Rights in Europe: A Study of the European Convention on Human Rights*. Manchester: Manchester University Press, 1993.

Rodley, Nigel. *The Treatment of Prisoners Under International Law*. 2nd ed. Oxford: Oxford University Press, 1999.

Rodrigo, Javier. *Los Campos de Concentración Franquistas: Entre la Historia y la Memoria*. Madrid: Siete Mares, 2003.

Roht-Arriaza, Naomi. *The Pinochet Effect: Transnational Justice in the Age of Human Rights*. Philadelphia: University of Pennsylvania Press, 2005.

———. "State Responsibility to Investigate and Punish Grave Human Rights Violations in International Law," *California Law Review* 78, no. 2 (1990): 449–513.

———, and Javier Mariezcurrena, eds. *Transitional Justice in the Twenty-First Century: Beyond Truth versus Justice*. Cambridge, UK: Cambridge University Press, 2006.

Rome Statute of the International Criminal Court. UN Doc. 2187 U.N.T.S. 90, entered into force July 1, 2002.

Ropp, Stephen, and Kathryn Sikkink. "International Norms and Domestic Politics in Chile and Guatemala," in Risse, Ropp, and Sikkink, eds., *The Power of Human Rights: International Norms and Domestic Change*.

Rosenberg, Tina. "Overcoming the Legacies of Dictatorship," *Foreign Affairs* (May–June 1995): 134–53.

Santamaria, Julian. "Spanish Transition Revisited," in Minotos, ed., *The Transition to Democracy in Spain, Portugal and Greece Thirty Years After*.

Savelsburg, Joachim. *Crime and Human Rights: Criminology of Genocide and Atrocities*. New York: Sage Publications, 2010.

———, and Ryan King. "Law and Collective Memory," *Annual Review of Law and Social Sciences* 3 (2007): 189–211.

Schabas, William A. *An Introduction to the International Criminal Court*. Cambridge, UK: Cambridge University Press, 2001.

Scharf, Michael. "Getting Serious About an International Criminal Court," *Pace International Law Review* 6 (1994): 103.

Schiff, Benjamin N. *Building the International Criminal Court*. Cambridge, UK: Cambridge University Pres, 2008.

Sen, Amartya. *The Idea of Justice*. Cambridge, MA: Belknap Press/Harvard University Press, 2009.

Shaffer, Geoffrey. "Transnational Legal Process and State Change: Opportunities and Constraints." Minnesota Legal Studies Research Paper No. 10-28 (2010), available at SSRN: http://ssrn.com/abstract=1612401.

Shklar, Judith N. *Legalism: Law, Morals, and Political Trials*. Cambridge, MA: Harvard University Press, 1986.

Sifton, John. "The Get Out of Jail Free Card for Torture: It's Called a Declination; Just Ask the CIA," *Slate* (March 2010); available at www.slate.com/id/2249126.

Sikkink, Kathryn. "Bush Administration Noncompliance with the Prohibition on Torture and Cruel and Degrading Treatment," in Cynthia Soohoo, Catherine Albisa, and Martha F. Davis, eds., *Bringing Human Rights Home: From Civil Rights to Human Rights*. Vol. 2. Westport, CT: Praeger, 2008.

———. *Mixed Signals: U.S. Human Rights Policy and Latin America*. Ithaca, NY: Cornell University Press, 2004.

———, and Carrie Booth Walling. "The Impact of Human Rights Trials in Latin America," *Journal of Peace Research* 44, no. 4 (2007): 427–45.

———, and Carrie Booth Walling. "Argentina's Contribution to Global Trends in Transitional Justice," in Roht-Arriaza and Mariezcurrena, eds., *Transitional Justice in the Twenty-First Century: Beyond Truth versus Justice*, 301–24.

Silva, Emilio, and Santiago Macias. *Las Fosas de Franco: Los Republicanos Que el Dictador Dejó en las Cuentas*. Madrid: Ediciones Temas de Hoy, 2003.

Simmons, Beth. *Mobilizing for Human Rights: International Law in Domestic Politics*. New York: Cambridge University Press, 2010.

———. "International Law and State Behavior: Commitment and Compliance in International Monetary Affairs," *American Political Science Review* 94, no. 4 (2000): 819–35.

———, and Zachary Elkins. "The Globalization of Liberalization: Policy Diffusion in the International Political Economy," *American Political Science Review* 98 (2004): 171–89.

———, Frank Dobbin, and Geoff Garrett. "The International Diffusion of Liberalism," *International Organization* 60, no. 4 (2006): 781–810.

Slaughter, Anne-Marie. *A New World Order*. Princeton: Princeton University Press, 2004.

Smith, David. "Rwanda Genocide Conviction Quashed Leaving Monsieur Z Free," *The Guardian* (UK), November 17, 2009, p. 20.

Smulovitz, Catalina. "The Discovery of Law: Political Consequences in the Argentine Case," in Yves Dezalay and Bryant G. Garth, eds., *Global Prescriptions: The Production, Exportation, and Importation of a New Legal Orthodoxy*. Ann Arbor: University of Michigan Press, 2002.

———. "Presentación en el Aniversario del Golpe." Buenos Aires, 2006.

Snyder, Jack, and Leslie Vinjamuri. "Advocacy and Scholarship in the Study of International War Crime Tribunals and Transitional Justice," *Annual Review of Political Science* 7, no. 1 (2004): 345.

————. "Trials and Errors: Principle and Pragmatism in Strategies of International Justice," *International Security* 28, no. 3 (Winter 2004): 5–44.

Stan, Lavinia. "Neither Forgiving nor Punishing? Evaluating Transitional Justice in Romania." Paper presented for the conference *Transitional Justice and Democratic Consolidation*, Oxford University, October 16–17, 2008.

Starr, Harvey, and Christina Lindborg. "Democratic Dominoes Revisited: The Hazards of Governmental Transitions, 1974–1996," *Journal of Conflict Resolution* 47, no. 4 (2003): 405–519.

Stepan, Alfred. *Rethinking Military Politics*. Princeton: Princeton University Press, 1988.

Stolle, Peer, and Tobias Singelnstein. "On the Aims and Actual Consequences of International Prosecution," in Wolfgang Kaleck et al., eds., *International Prosecution of Human Rights Crimes*. Berlin: Springer, 2007.

Struett, Michael J. *The Politics of Constructing the International Criminal Court*. New York: Palgrave Macmillan, 2008.

Subotić, Jelena. *Hijacked Justice: Dealing with the Past in the Balkans*. Ithaca, NY: Cornell University Press, 2009.

Sunstein, Cass. *Free Markets and Social Justice*. New York: Oxford University Press, 1997.

Sweeney, Joseph M. *The International Law of Sovereign Immunity: Policy Research Study*. Washington, DC: External Research Staff, Bureau of Intelligence and Research, U.S. Dept. of State, 1963.

Taguba, Antonio M. "The Taguba Report: Article 15-6 Investigation of the 800th Military Police Brigade," Department of Defense, Washington, DC, June 2004.

Tarrow, Sidney. *The New Transnational Activism*. New York: Cambridge University Press, 2005.

Teitel, Ruti. "Transitional Justice Genealogy," *Harvard Human Rights Journal* 16 (2003): 69–94.

"Testimonio del Señor Pablo A. Diaz," *Diario del Juicio* 3, June 11, 1985, p. 63.

Tetlock, Philip, and Aaron Belkin, eds. *Counterfactual Thought Experiments in World Politics: Logical, Methodological, and Psychological Perspectives*. Princeton: Princeton University Press, 1996.

Thoms, Oskar N. T., James Ron, and Roland Paris. "Does Transitional Justice Work? Perspectives from Empirical Social Science," October 19, 2008; available at SSRN: http://ssrn.com/abstract=1302084.

Torture, Committee of Experts on. "Committee of Experts on Torture, Syracuse, Italy, 16–17 December 1977," *Revue International de Droit Pénal* 48, nos. 3 and 4 (1977).

United Nations, General Assembly. 51st sess., Convention against Torture and Other Cruel, Inhuman or Degrading Treatment or Punishment, Article 2, A/39/51 (1984).

————. 61st sess. Official Records, A/C.3/61/L.17, 2006.

————. "Joint study on global practices in relation to secret detention in the context of countering terrorism of the Special Rapporteur on the promotion and protection of human rights and fundamental freedoms while countering terrorism, the Special Rapporteur on torture and other cruel, inhuman or degrading treatment or punishment, the Working Group on Arbitrary Detention and the Working Group on Enforced or Involuntary Disappearances." Advance unedited copy, January 26, 2010, A/HRC/13/42.

United States Congress, House Committee on Foreign Affairs. *The Phenomenon of Torture: Hearings and Markup Before the Committee on Foreign Affairs and Its Subcommittee on Human Rights and International Organizations.* 98th Congress, 2nd sess. on H.J. Res. 606, May 15–16; September 6, 1984. Washington, DC: GPO, 1984, p. 204.

———, House. *The Status of Human Rights in Selected Countries and the United States Response; Report Prepared for the Subcommittee on International Organization of the Committee on International Relations of the United States House of Representatives by the Library of Congress.* 95th Congress, 1st sess., July 25, 1977 (Washington, DC: GPO, 1977), p. 2.

United States Department of Defense. "Memorandum for the Secretary of Defense: Improper Material in Spanish Language Intelligence Training Manuals." March 10, 1992.

———. *National Defense Strategy of the United States* (March 2005).

———, Department of Justice, Office of Justice Programs. *The World Factbook of Criminal Justice System,* "Victims" section, Part 3, "Role of Victim in Prosecution and Sentencing"; http:// bjs.ojp.usdoj.gov.

———, Office of Legal Counsel, Office of the Assistant Attorney General. "Memorandum for James B. Comey, Deputy Attorney General, Re: Legal Standards Applicable Under 18 U.S.C. 2340-2340A," December 30, 2004.

———, Office of Legal Counsel, Office of the Assistant Attorney General. "Memorandum for Alberto R. Gonzales, Re: Standards of Conduct for Interrogation Under 18 U.S.C. 2340-2340A," August 1, 2002.

United States Supreme Court, "Hamdan *v.* Rumsfeld," www.supremecourtus.gov/opinions/05pdf/05-184.pdf.

Varouhakis, Miron. *Shadows of Heroes: The Journey of a Doctor and a Journalist in the Lives of Ordinary People Who Became Victims of Torture.* LaVergne, TN: Xlibris Corp., 2010.

Verbitsky, Horacio. *Civiles y Militares: Memoria Secreta de la Transición,* reprint. Buenos Aires: Sudamericana, 2006.

Vinjamuri, Leslie, and Jack Snyder. "Advocacy and Scholarship in the Study of International War Crimes Tribunals and Transitional Justice," *Annual Review of Political Science* 7 (2004): 345–62.

Waltz, Susan. "Universalizing Human Rights: The Role of Small States in the Construction of the Universal Declaration of Human Rights," *Human Rights Quarterly* 23 (2001): 44–72.

Weaver, Mary Anne. "Karamanlis Rules Greece with a Strong Hand," *The Washington Post,* November 23, 1976.

Weissbrodt, David. *The Right to a Fair Trial Under the Universal Declaration of Human Rights and the International Covenant on Civil and Political Rights: Articles 8, 10 and 11 of the Universal Declaration of Human Rights.* Cambridge, MA: Martinus Nijhoff, 2001.

———. "Study of Amnesty International's Role in Situations of Armed Conflict and Internal Strife. AI Index: POL 03/04/84." London: Amnesty International, 1984.

Weschler, Lawrence. *A Miracle, a Universe: Settling Accounts with Torturers.* New York: Pantheon Books, 1990.

Weyland, Kurt. "Theories of Policy Diffusion: Lessons from Latin American Pension Reform," *World Politics* 57, no. 2 (2005): 262–95.

Whitehead, Laurence. "Three International Dimensions of Democratization," in Whitehead, ed., *The International Dimensions of Democratization: Europe and the Americas.* Oxford: Oxford University Press, 1996.

Woodhouse, C. M. *The Rise and Fall of the Greek Colonels.* London: Granada Publishing, 1985.

Zalaquett, José. "Balancing Ethical Imperatives and Political Constraints: The Dilemma of New Democracies Confronting Past Human Rights Violations," *Hastings Law Journal* 43 (1992): 1425–38.

———. "Confronting Human Rights Violations by Former Governments: Principles Applicable and Political Constraints," in Neil J. Kritz, ed., *Transitional Justice: How Emerging Democracies Reckon with Former Regimes.* Washington, DC: U.S. Institute of Peace, 1995.

INDEX

Page numbers in *italics* refer to figures and tables.

Index